D0875410

08/2022
STRAND PRICE
$ 5.00

# EDITING EARLY MODERN WOMEN

This collection of new essays is a comprehensive exploration of the theoretical and practical issues surrounding the editing of texts by early modern women. The chapters consider the latest developments in the field and address a wide range of topics, including the 'ideologies' of editing, genre and gender, feminism, editing for student or general readers, print publishing, and new and possible future developments in editing early modern writing, including digital publishing. The works of writers such as Queen Elizabeth I, Mary Wroth, Anne Halkett, Katherine Philips, and Katherine Austen are examined, and the issues discussed are related to the ways editing in general has evolved in recent years. This book offers readers an original overview of the central issues in this growing field and will interest students and scholars of early modern literature and drama, textual studies, the history of editing, gender studies, and book history.

SARAH C. E. ROSS is Senior Lecturer in the English Programme at Victoria University of Wellington, New Zealand. She is the author of *Women, Poetry, and Politics in Seventeenth-Century Britain* (2015) and the editor of *Katherine Austen's 'Book M': British Library, Additional Manuscript 4454* (2011). She has written numerous articles on early modern women writers, religious writing, and manuscript culture.

PAUL SALZMAN is Emeritus Professor of English at La Trobe University, Australia. His most recent publications include *Reading Early Modern Women's Writing* (2006) and *Literature and Politics in the 1620s: 'Whisper'd Counsells'* (2014). He is the editor of four World's Classics volumes, including *Early Modern Women's Writing: An Anthology* and *Aphra Behn: Oroonoko and Other Writings*, and of an online edition of Mary Wroth's poetry, which won the Society for the Study of Early Modern Women's Digital Scholarship Award.

# EDITING EARLY MODERN WOMEN

EDITED BY

SARAH C. E. ROSS

and

PAUL SALZMAN

CAMBRIDGE
UNIVERSITY PRESS

# CAMBRIDGE
## UNIVERSITY PRESS

University Printing House, Cambridge CB2 8BS, United Kingdom

Cambridge University Press is part of the University of Cambridge.

It furthers the University's mission by disseminating knowledge in the pursuit of
education, learning and research at the highest international levels of excellence.

www.cambridge.org
Information on this title: www.cambridge.org/9781107129955

© Cambridge University Press 2016

This publication is in copyright. Subject to statutory exception
and to the provisions of relevant collective licensing agreements,
no reproduction of any part may take place without the written
permission of Cambridge University Press.

First published 2016

Printed in the United States of America by Sheridan Books, Inc.

*A catalogue record for this publication is available from the British Library*

ISBN 978-1-107-12995-5 Hardback

Cambridge University Press has no responsibility for the persistence or accuracy
of URLs for external or third-party internet websites referred to in this publication,
and does not guarantee that any content on such websites is, or will remain,
accurate or appropriate.

# Contents

# *Figures*

# Contributors

DIANA G. BARNES is a Post-doctoral Fellow at the University of Queensland with research interests in the cultural history of early modern women's letters and the politics of seventeenth-century English literature. She has recently published a book called *Epistolary Community in Print, 1580–1664* (2013), and she has written essays on Margaret Cavendish, Dorothy Osborne, and Mary Wortley Montagu.

DANIELLE CLARKE is Professor of English Renaissance Language and Literature at University College Dublin, and the author of many books, articles, and editions on early modern women writers (*'This Double Voice', The Politics of Early Modern Women's Writing, Isabella Whitney, Mary Sidney, and Aemilia Lanyer: Renaissance Women Poets*). She has also written widely on questions of sexuality and gender, language and rhetoric, and ideas of poetic form on Shakespeare, Marlowe, and Milton, among others.

ELIZABETH CLARKE is Professor of English at Warwick University, where she led the Perdita project for early modern women's manuscript writing. Her most recent book is *Politics, Religion and the Song of Songs in Seventeenth-Century England* (2011).

MARIE-LOUISE COOLAHAN is Professor of English at the National University of Ireland, Galway. She is the author of *Women, Writing, and Language in Early Modern Ireland* (2010), and she is currently Principal Investigator of 'RECIRC: The Reception and Circulation of Early Modern Women's Writing, 1550–1700', funded by the European Research Council.

SUSAN M. FELCH is Professor of English at Calvin College and director of the Calvin Center for Christian Scholarship. Among her books are *The Collected Works of Anne Vaughan Lock* (1999), *Elizabeth Tyrwhit's Morning and Evening Prayers* (2008), *Elizabeth I and Her Age* (2009), with Donald Stump, and *Teaching and Christian Imagination* (2016), with David I. Smith.

PAMELA S. HAMMONS is Professor and Chair of the English Department at the University of Miami (Coral Gables, FL). She specializes in early modern and medieval literature, manuscript culture, poetry, women's writing, and theories of gender and sexuality. Her publications include *Book M: A London Widow's Life Writings* (2013), *Gender, Sexuality and Material Objects in English Renaissance Verse* (2010), *Poetic Resistance: English Women Writers and the Early Modern Lyric* (2002), and numerous essays.

MARY ELLEN LAMB is a Professor Emerita at Southern Illinois University. Her books include *Gender and Authorship in the Sidney Circle*, *The Popular Culture of Shakespeare, Spenser, and Jonson*, and an abridged version of Mary Wroth's *Countess of Montgomery's Urania*.

LEAH S. MARCUS is Edwin Mims Professor of English at Vanderbilt University. Her books include *Childhood and Cultural Despair* (1978), *The Politics of Mirth* (1986), *Puzzling Shakespeare* (1988), and *Unediting the Renaissance* (1996). She has also published editions of *As You Like It*, *The Merchant of Venice*, *The Duchess of Malfi*, and co-edited the *Collected Works of Elizabeth I* (2000, 2003).

PATRICIA PENDER is Senior Lecturer in English and Writing at the University of Newcastle, Australia. She is the author of *Early Modern Women's Writing and the Rhetoric of Modesty* (2012) and co-editor (with Rosalind Smith) of *Material Cultures of Early Modern Women's Writing* (2014). She is sole investigator on an Australian Research Council Discovery Project, Early Modern Women and the Institutions of Authorship (2014–16).

SARAH C. E. ROSS is a Senior Lecturer in English at Victoria University of Wellington. She is the author of *Women, Poetry, and Politics in Seventeenth-Century Britain* (2015), the editor of *Katherine Austen's 'Book M': British Library, Additional Manuscript 4454* (2011), and the author of numerous articles on early modern women, religious writing, and manuscript culture.

PAUL SALZMAN is an Emeritus Professor at La Trobe University, Australia. He has published widely in the area of early modern women's writing, including two World's Classics volumes, digital editions of Mary Wroth's poetry and of *Love's Victory*, and the monograph *Reading Early Modern*

*Women's Writing* (2006). His most recent book is *Literature and Politics in the 1620s: 'Whisper'd Counsells'* (2014).

ELIZABETH SCOTT-BAUMANN is Lecturer in Early Modern English Literature at King's College London. She is the author of *Forms of Engagement: Women, Poetry, and Culture 1640–1680* (2013) and has co-edited *The Intellectual Culture of Puritan Women, 1558–1680* (2011) and *The Work of Form: Poetics and Materiality in Early Modern Culture* (2014).

ROSALIND SMITH is Associate Professor in English at the University of Newcastle, Australia. Her publications include *Material Cultures of Early Modern Women's Writing* (2014, co-edited with Patricia Pender), and *Sonnets and the English Woman Writer, 1560–1621: The Politics of Absence* (2005), as well as articles and chapters on women, genre, politics, and history in early modern England, Scotland, and France. She leads the multi-institutional, ARC-funded Material Cultures of Early Modern Women's Writing project.

SUZANNE TRILL is Senior Lecturer in English Literature at the University of Edinburgh. Her research focuses on women's writing in England and Scotland (*c.* 1550–1700), especially devotional literature. Her publications include *Lady Anne Halkett: Selected Self-Writings* (2007).

RAMONA WRAY is a Reader in English at Queen's University, Belfast. She has edited *The Tragedy of Mariam* for the Arden Early Modern Drama series, and is the co-editor of a number of books including *Shakespeare and Ireland* (1997) and *Screening Shakespeare in the Twenty-First Century* (2006), as well as numerous articles on Renaissance drama and on early modern women writers.

MARION WYNNE-DAVIES holds the Chair of English Literature in the Department of English at the University of Surrey. Her main areas of interest are Early Modern literature and women's writing. She has published two editions of primary material, *Renaissance Drama by Women: Texts and Documents* (with S. P. Cerasano) and *Women Poets of the Renaissance*, as well as several collections of essays in the same field. She has written four monographs, *Women and Arthurian Literature*, *Sidney to Milton*, *Women Writers and Familial Discourse in the English Renaissance: Relative Values*, and *Margaret Atwood*.

# Acknowledgements

Most of all, the editors would like to thank the contributors to this volume, whose scholarship in this instance and more widely has made it a pleasure and a privilege to work with them.

This volume emerges out of an Australian Research Council Discovery Project on The Material Cultures of Early Modern Women's Writing, hosted at the University of Newcastle by Rosalind Smith and Patricia Pender. Our team members, including Kate Lilley, Michelle O'Callaghan, and Susan Wiseman, have made this project inspirational, and enormously fun. *Editing Early Modern Women* also arises more specifically out of two symposia on early modern women and editing in 2012, one at La Trobe University in Melbourne and one at Massey University in Wellington. We would like to thank Susan Felch and Mary Ellen Lamb for travelling to Melbourne to work with us, and Elizabeth Scott-Baumann for making the trip to Wellington.

At Cambridge University Press, Sarah Stanton has been a keen and insightful supporter; we are grateful for her guidance, and for the assistance of Isobel Cowper-Coles, Rosemary Crawley, Sarah Starkey, and Caroline Howlett. Three anonymous readers for Cambridge University Press have made this a much better book. We would also like to thank Robyn Walton and Anna Plumridge, for their invaluable editorial assistance in Melbourne and Wellington, and the Faculty of Humanities and Social Sciences at Victoria University of Wellington for their support in the book's final stages.

# Abbreviations

| | |
|---|---|
| BL | British Library |
| *ELH* | *English Literary History* |
| *ELR* | *English Literary Renaissance* |
| *EMS* | *English Manuscript Studies* |
| *MLQ* | *Modern Language Quarterly* |
| NLS | National Library of Scotland |
| NLW | National Library of Wales |
| *NQ* | *Notes and Queries* |
| *ODNB* | *Oxford Dictionary of National Biography* |
| *OED* | *Oxford English Dictionary Online* |
| *RQ* | *Renaissance Quarterly* |
| *SEL* | *Studies in English Literature, 1500–1900* |
| *STC* | *English Short Title Catalogue* |
| *THES* | *Times Higher Education Supplement* |
| *TLS* | *Times Literary Supplement* |

# CHAPTER I

# Introduction
## Editing Early Modern Women
### Sarah C. E. Ross and Paul Salzman

Writing in 1993, when post-structuralist editorial theories were at the height of their influence, W. Speed Hill suggested provocatively that the recovery and editing of early modern women's writing was at odds with prevailing editorial trends:

> feminist scholars are actively engaged in recovering texts by and about women, scaling the very intentionalist mountain the other side of which their male confrères are descending.[1]

Hill's striking image encapsulates a number of tensions that could be seen to exist between the elision of the author and authorial intentionality that defined the mainstream editing of early modern texts, and the coterminous publication of important first modern critical editions of sole-authored female texts, such as Josephine A. Roberts's *The Poems of Lady Mary Wroth* (1983), Susanne Woods's *The Poems of Aemilia Lanyer* (1993), and Barbara Lewalski's *The Poems and Polemics of Rachel Speght* (1996). Engaging in a critical dialogue with Hill in a special issue of *Shakespeare Studies* in 1996, Roberts suggested both that editors of male-authored works were also to be found engaged in author- and attribution-centred work, and that the recovery of early modern women's texts was in fact part of a wider attempt to reconstruct a lost manuscript culture.[2] Hill's mountain, however, has continued to loom over the landscape of editing early modern women.

For much of the twentieth century, revolutionary methodological change in the editing of canonical early modern literature ran along quite different lines to the approach taken to women's texts of the same period. The editorial mainstream shifted sharply in the 1980s from the idealist model of Greg and Bowers's new bibliography, based on the quasi-scientific establishment of a conflated text, to the 'new textualism' of Jerome McGann,

---

[1] Hill, 'Editing Nondramatic Texts of the English Renaissance', p. 23.
[2] Roberts, 'Editing the Women Writers of Early Modern England', pp. 69–70.

I

D. F. McKenzie, and others, which elided the author and authorial inten-tionality, and emphasized the diplomatic or otherwise less edited text.[3] In contrast, and as Hill evokes, the approach to early modern women's writing for the most part continued to be centred on authorial identity. For the edi-torial endeavours surrounding interventions such as the Brown University Women Writers project and Ashgate's The Early Modern Englishwoman, the efficacy of the (usually) sole woman as author was taken for granted. While theorists writing from inside the literary canon, then, were seek-ing to disestablish the category of the author, the feminist recuperation of previously unknown women writers was deeply invested in that very category.

Eminent editors of early modern women, such as Roberts, have sought to apply a sociology of texts to early modern women's writing, and Ann Hollinshead Hurley and Chanita Goodblatt perceive a clear new textu-alist trajectory in the more recent editing of women's texts.[4] Hurley and Goodblatt draw on examples such as Jill Seal Millman and Gillian Wright's *Early Modern Women's Manuscript Poetry* (2005) in which authorship is 'complexly mediated' and copytexts are selected on the basis of specific manuscript contexts.[5] Certainly much has changed in the editing of early modern women since the late twentieth century; however, in our view there continue to be deep and productive tensions between the decen-tred treatment of authorship in much mainstream early modern editorial work, and the recovery of authors along with authorship that continues to be one prevailing motivation in much editorial work on early modern women writers. The unique temporalities of feminist and female-centred editing – its burgeoning at a point synchronous with historicist and tex-tualist literary-critical movements; its (arguable) maturation in the age of digital editing – have generated unique challenges as well as unique solutions and methodologies that have the potential to speak back to the editorial mainstream.

Poised at a moment some twenty-five years after that described by Hill, *Editing Early Modern Women* seeks to make explicit the conversa-tion between the editing of early modern women's texts and mainstream editing, and to address a number of questions that relate to both fields.

---

[3]  Greg, 'Rationale'; Bowers, 'Greg's Rationale of Copy-Text Revisited'; Leod [sic] (ed.), *Crisis in Editing*. For new textualist approaches to early modern literature see, for example, the collection of articles in *Shakespeare Studies*, 24 (1996); and Marcus, 'Textual Scholarship', pp. 145–9. Hurley and Goodblatt define 'new textualism' in the Preface to *Women Editing / Editing Women*, pp. xi–xviii.

[4]  Hurley and Goodblatt, 'Preface' to *Women Editing / Editing Women*, pp. xi–xviii (p. xii).

[5]  Millman and Wright (eds.), *Early Modern Women's Manuscript Poetry*, p. 2.

How do we edit texts that have no editorial history, or whose editorial histories are concerned with oddity and exemplarity rather than canonicity? How do we edit texts that do not fit easily into conventional taxonomies of 'literature', and what contexts should we present for them? How can textual editing upset conventional hierarchies of literary value, while still finding a readership? And, as the print-based editing of both male- and female-authored texts is increasingly complemented or displaced by the electronic edition, how can digital methods of editing, archiving, and amassing early modern texts facilitate multiple editorial and literary-critical aims?

Early modern women's writing has, from the very beginning, been edited in forms that emphasize a connection between 'life' and 'works', with the biographical exemplarity of the sole female author often as important as the works that substantiated these qualities. Anne Southwell's manuscripts, for example, were compiled by her husband as proof of her 'excellencye' after her death; and the 'Collections' of Elizabeth Egerton, produced in multiple copies, proved her piety for an extended familial audience.[6] Margaret Ezell has drawn attention, in her pioneering work on women's literary history, to the way that early modern women's writing was transmitted in the eighteenth century through the agency of figures like George Ballard, whose *Memoirs of Several Ladies of Great Britain* (1752) was a biographical compendium of authors.[7] Women writers were celebrated for a literary skill that went hand in hand with their virtue and their achievements of piety and education, in a model that very firmly associated women's writing with biographical exemplarity.

The anthologizing impulse exemplified in Ballard's *Memoirs of Several Ladies* predominated during the eighteenth and nineteenth centuries, and, on the whole, most of the work by early modern women that circulated was poetry. Colman and Thornton's *Poems by Eminent Ladies* (1755, 1773, 1780) anthologized poetry by women from the mid seventeenth to mid eighteenth centuries, producing the tradition of largely secular women's poetry that is familiar to us today. There were exceptions, such as the Quaker tradition of keeping Margaret Fell's religious prose alive, but much of the religious writing by women from the sixteenth and seventeenth centuries became invisible. There were some notable anthologies in the nineteenth century, especially Alexander Dyce's wide-ranging *Specimens of British Poetesses* (1825), which is a major editorial feat; and Dyce was cannibalized by Frederic Rowton for his considerably more popular compilation,

---

[6] Southwell, *The Southwell-Sibthorpe Commonplace Book*, ed. Klene; for example, Huntington Library MS EL 8376, BL MS Egerton 607.

[7] Ezell, *Writing Women's Literary History*, chap. 3.

*The Female Poets of Great Britain* (1848). These anthologies, often over-looked in discussions of the editorial histories of early modern women's writing, were important exercises in recuperation and preservation. At the same time, they provide an eighteenth- and nineteenth-century prehistory to the phenomenon to which Ramona Wray objects in her influential essay on 'Anthologizing the Early Modern Female Voice' (2000): that antholo-gies of early modern women's writing have focused on poetry and on works that fit a modern feminist agenda.[8] (In a late-twentieth-century context, 'protofeminism' could be seen to constitute a new kind of female exemplarity.)

For much of the twentieth century, and as Wray later bemoaned, the anthology, biography, and a focus on poetry continued to dominate the representation of early modern women's writing. Foundational second-wave feminist anthologies, such as Betty Travitsky's *The Paradise of Women* (1981), were vital in the processes of (re)discovery, and *Kissing the Rod* (1988), the pioneering anthology edited by Germaine Greer and associates, was instrumental in demonstrating the range of women's poetry within the seventeenth century. These groundbreaking anthologies did continue to favour certain genres and classes of author, and the bases of their engage-ment with this writing were hidden and complex, as Kate Lilley points out in her provocative essay on the 'critical erotics' of early modern women's writing.[9] Lilley's account engages a Queer politics of meta-criticism, break-ing apart the dichotomy of sameness/difference in the recovery and analysis of women's writing. She offers a Queer alternative to the oscillation between the representative and the exceptional, and endorses the turn to the mate-rial conjoined with close reading that the editorial activities we explore in this volume exemplify: 'The highly eroticized material, ideological, and rhetorical contexts of early modern women's writing as a minoritized dis-course underlines the need for readers to negotiate the unstable polarities of sex, sexuality, and desire by beginning with material questions of genre and gender, form, and textual transmission.'[10]

Lilley's critical intervention comes at what we might now consider to be a late stage in the history of approaches to and representations of early modern women's writing. As more scholarly attention has been paid to women who wrote in the sixteenth and seventeenth centuries, the scale of what was written has been revealed, perhaps to the surprise of those who thought there was nothing left to find. So too has the complexity of its contemporaneous production and transmission, the conditions of

---

[8] Wray, 'Anthologizing'.    [9] Lilley, 'Fruits of Sodom'.    [10] *Ibid.*, p. 182.

which are increasingly being understood in terms of *early modern* processes of editing and anthologizing. Throughout the seventeenth century, a number of women were themselves active as 'editors' and interpreters. The most notable of these was Mary Sidney, who presided over the edition of her brother's works and who wrote the bulk of the psalm translations that circulated widely in manuscript, so that, in Patricia Pender's terms, their authorship becomes 'a dynamic transference of debt and license'.[11] Danielle Clarke's chapter in this volume extends this model of collaborative authorship, demonstrating how the entangling and disentangling of the relationship between Philip and Mary and the psalms can stand as a paradigm for a reductive model of authorship that the editing of early modern women has at times enforced, but has increasingly challenged.

For in the sixteenth and seventeenth centuries, women writers were, if not prominent, then certainly visible, and often part of a systematic process of mediated circulation. An excellent example of this is Elizabeth Tyrwhit, as analysed in this volume by Susan Felch. In Felch's meticulous account, Tyrwhit's prayerbook, in its 1574 and 1582 versions, testifies to the way that textual transmission and the turn to a material history of the book have become vital tools in the understanding of early modern literature. As Felch argues, early modern women's writing is a special instance of this process, and one that the editors of writing by men have largely passed by. Felch offers a notion of what we might call (after Clifford Geertz) 'thick contextualization' as a necessary requirement for the kind of understanding that has to lie behind the modern editing of early modern women – and of early modern men.[12]

Later in the seventeenth century, a number of women became especially adept at circulating their work through the medium of print, while others exploited what was still a thriving manuscript culture.[13] The use of print is exemplified by Margaret Cavendish, an obsessive editor and re-editor of her own work. The complex interconnections between manuscript and print circulation are best illustrated by Katherine Philips, who one might say manipulated the aura of manuscript circulation, copying, and recopying for her own ends, and then slipped into print (perhaps inadvertently) with *Poems* (1664) and the monumentalizing folio edition of 1667. Philips, like a number of seventeenth-century women writers (the other notable

---

[11] Pender, *Early Modern Women's Writing and the Rhetoric of Modesty*, p. 100.

[12] See Geertz, *The Interpretation of Cultures.*

[13] For the importance of manuscript culture to the circulation of early modern women's writing see the pioneering work of Ezell in *The Patriarch's Wife*, followed up by work associated with the Perdita project, for example, Burke and Gibson (eds.), *Early Modern Women's Manuscript Writing.*

example being Aphra Behn), was highly visible in the first half of the eighteenth century.[14] Philips had a collected edition published in 1710 and an edition of her letters in 1705 and 1729, but then her work appeared only in anthologies until the twentieth century. Close critical work on Philips and others in recent years has drawn attention to a longer history of editing and transmission, and has revealed that the 'production' of the seventeenth-century woman poet occurred through multiple mediations of editorial collaboration and intervention, and in overlapping practices of manuscript and print publication.[15]

Early modern women's writing has, then, been the site of complex recent work on transmission, the mediation of authorship, and collaborative models of textual production and reproduction; but the fit between the editing of women and textualist and materialist literary-critical agendas has continued to be an uneasy one. Betty Travitsky's belief that the canon of women's writing has needed to be edited (implicitly in idealist, life-and-works form) before it could be deconstructed is reflective of ongoing tensions between recovery and textualist editing. So too is Pender and Smith's converse argument in their chapter in this volume that such a hierarchy of editorial processes should not hold.[16] Leah Marcus's choices in editing *Elizabeth I: Collected Works* (2001) varied markedly from some of the scholarly principles that she espoused in her influential post-structuralist analysis of the early modern literary canon, *Unediting the Renaissance* (1996). Notably, she has retrospectively described that book as targeted at literary-critical scholars rather than editors, drawing attention in doing so to the potential slippage between the two fields, at the same time as they vitally co-enable each other.[17]

A similar tension can perhaps be seen between Ramona Wray's influential essay on 'Anthologizing the Early Modern Female Voice' (2000) and her later editing of Elizabeth Cary's *The Tragedy of Mariam* for the canonical Arden series of dramatic texts. Wray argued in 2000 for a radical reshaping of the anthology in order to represent the complexity and unconventionality of early modern women's literary output, but seeks in her edition of *Mariam* (2012) to edit Cary 'as an early modern dramatist

---

[14] For an account of their contrasting fortunes see Salzman, *Reading Early Modern Women's Writing*, chap. 7.

[15] See, for example, Salzman, *Reading Early Modern Women's Writing*; and Wright, *Producing Women's Poetry*.

[16] Travitsky and Prescott, 'Studying and Editing Early Modern Englishwomen', p. 14; Pender and Smith in this volume, pp. 256–9.

[17] Marcus, 'Confessions of a Reformed Uneditor (II)', p. 1072. For 'the co-enabling role shared between editions and criticism' see Ramona Wray's chapter in this volume, p. 62.

rather than as a woman writer', and to explore the ways in which the text is implicated in 'a much broader range of contemporary dramatic activity' than the women's 'closet drama' (pp. 75, 62). The dual desirabilities of 'a new politics of selection' in editing women,[18] and of achieving visibility within mainstream student and scholarly communities continue to play out within the field, even as multiple, different editions of several women's texts are increasingly available.

Similarly, while a number of recent editions of early modern women's writing have moved away from intentionality and biographically determined readings of texts, the unshackling of 'life' from 'works' has a particular set of implications for women's texts. Susan Felch argues, in her chapter in this volume, that biographies still need to be established, not least because of what they potentially can tell us about the conditions of texts' production and reception, and because of the interpretative pitfalls from which a detailed and accurate biography can save us. Mary Ellen Lamb also argues for the value of a biographical focus in her redacted edition of Wroth's *Urania*, and Marcus et al.'s editorial work on Elizabeth I is again of interest. *Elizabeth I: Collected Works* takes a decidedly textualist postmodernist editorial approach to categories of 'author' and of 'text', even as it aims to present the corpus of speeches, letters, and poems associated with Elizabeth I. Marcus and her co-editors include multiple versions of some of Elizabeth I's most important speeches, to account for the vexed questions of authorial attribution and most reliable textual witnesses, even while they assert the value of a 'complete works' edition in bestowing canonicity on the edited texts.[19]

Precisely because the fit between defining critical and editorial scholarship and the demands of early modern women's texts has been so uneasy, the editing of early modern women has sharpened the theoretical reflections in the field in a way that offers a complementary narrative to that embraced by scholars who have edited early modern texts by men. This theoretical intervention, or potential intervention – one which we argue has until now gone unrecognized – is evident in the projects described in the chapters of this volume. The interaction between manuscript and print transmission is reflected not simply in a specialist anthology such as the Millman-Wright one, but also in the way that editions have ranged between manuscript and print sources. Similarly, the treatment of manuscript sources has not just revolutionized our sense of the range of writing by women, but also

[18] Wray, 'Anthologizing', p. 57.
[19] See Leah Marcus's chapter in this volume, esp. pp. 145–6, 151; and, for example, Marcus et al. (eds.), *Elizabeth I: Collected Works*, pp. 335–46.

brought to bear theoretical questions about the nature of genre, and the way that previously unknown or neglected material needs to be contextualized through the editing process.

Such theoretical cruces are exemplified in Suzanne Trill's replacement, in her chapter in this volume, of a narrow concentration on Anne, Lady Halkett's autobiography with a focus on her extensive manuscript 'archive' of mostly religious work. Trill's archaeological work not only shifts preconceptions about Halkett (including the nature of the so-called autobiography), but also offers a new way of dealing with the sort of material that historians may once have cannibalized as source material, but that literary scholars may now accord full textual authority and editorial intervention. Like so much of the work discussed here, this process has involved a retracing of the transmission process, and a reconceptualization of the nature of authorship and of authors' and texts' editorial prehistories. Trill's sense of the 'archive' is also one that challenges frameworks for editing early modern texts – of any kind and of any authorship – in print and online.

Where, then, does the editing of early modern women now stand in relation to the editorial mainstream? Since the 1990s, mainstream editing has moved in two distinct directions. One is back towards a recovered notion of 'major' authors, as seen in new, 'complete works' editions of writers like Jonson, Donne, and Herrick.[20] The other is further towards fragmentation, founded in the desire to 'unedit the Renaissance', and manifest in mainstream editions that present multiple versions of a text alongside each other, such as the Oxford Shakespeare, or the Norton *Doctor Faustus*.[21] This sense of textual contingency also, most strikingly, informs the growth of online editions that present all textual materials, such as the Internet Shakespeare Editions, or that foreground the sociology of the text, such as the online 'social' edition of the Devonshire Manuscript.[22]

While this dual movement in editorial practice is also broadly evident in early modern women's writing, the implications of each form of editing are, as we have shown, unique. We have now, for example, reached a moment when some women's texts are being afforded the full scholarly treatment, such as the Oxford *Works* of Lucy Hutchinson, or Janel Mueller's prize-winning edition of Katherine Parr.[23] The 'complete works' edition has

---

[20] *The Cambridge Edition of the Works of Ben Jonson*, ed. Bevington, Butler, and Donaldson (2012); *The Complete Poems of John Donne*, ed. Robbins (2010); *The Complete Poetry of Robert Herrick*, ed. Cain and Connolly (2013).

[21] *The Norton Shakespeare*, ed. Greenblatt et al.; Marlowe, *Doctor Faustus*, ed. Kastan.

[22] http://internetshakespeare.uvic.ca/; https://en.wikibooks.org/wiki/The_Devonshire_Manuscript.

[23] *The Works of Lucy Hutchinson*, gen. ed. Norbrook (2011–); *Katherine Parr: Complete Works and Correspondence*, ed. Mueller (2011).

lost none of its canonical power, and these editions represent a major – if belated – intervention in the early modern canon. We are also now at the point where there are multiple editions of some women's texts, from Mary Wroth's sonnets and her *Urania*, to Elizabeth Cary's now almost iconic *Tragedy of Mariam*, through to Katherine Austen's *Book M*. Wroth remains the writer most visible within conventional measurements of canonization, such as the *Norton Anthology of Literature* (8th edition), in which she has ten pages (though these may be contrasted to the fifty of her uncle Philip Sidney). There are authoritative editions of *Urania* and of Wroth's poetry (including Roberts's pioneering edition and Salzman's online edition), and a number of editions of *Love's Victory*. Yet none of them are truly authoritative. While the editions themselves are invaluable, there remains a sense of provisionality caused in part by them being spread across publishers and formats.

Two prolific and important writers, Aphra Behn and Margaret Cavendish, can illustrate how the process of what might be called editing from the margins has influenced the way that early modern women's writing has been transmitted in an economy which has valued authoritative editions produced by academic presses, however much that situation is now changing.[24] The most telling example is the complex editorial situation of Aphra Behn. Behn was the subject of a pioneering edition by Montague Summers in 1915; and in 1992, under the general editorship of Janet Todd, Pickering and Chatto began to publish a complete edition of Behn's works, beginning with her poetry. The edition ran to seven volumes and was completed in 1996. While an invaluable resource, this edition cannot be described as an authoritative, scholarly edition in the way that such a category is usually applied to volumes published by university presses. For example, the poetry volume is only partially collated. It is perhaps symbolic of the difference, even in the 1980s and 1990s, between the treatment of early modern women's writing and writing by men. So at virtually the same time as the Pickering Behn, Oxford University Press published *The Works of Thomas Southerne*, edited with extraordinary attention to detail by Harold Love and Robert Jordan (1987–8). Ironically, Southerne based his most popular play on Behn's *Oroonoko*. (As an individual work, though, *Oroonoko* has received sustained editorial attention, including an edition for Norton by Joanna Lipking.) So while a selection of Behn's work is available in editions especially suitable for teaching purposes, including

---

[24] It is perhaps not entirely coincidental that both Behn and Cavendish rejoice in having fully fledged societies: the Margaret Cavendish Society was founded in 1997, the Aphra Behn Society in 1996.

selections of plays and fiction for Penguin and Oxford classics, the dignity now being accorded Lucy Hutchinson by Oxford University Press's edition is not yet present for Behn.[25]

There is an even patchier history of the editing of Cavendish, a writer who presents special challenges for an editor because of her propensity to revise, not only from one impression to the next, but also by hand in individual copies of her books.[26] The editing of Cavendish has also been influenced by the – limited but growing – interest in her as an important figure in the history of science and philosophy. There have been four significant works or groups of works of Cavendish in scholarly editions, as well as the quite generous dissemination of her work through a series of anthologies, especially those published by Broadview Press, and the edition of *The Blazing World* and other writing edited by Kate Lilley for Penguin in 1994. Three of these volumes reflect the scholarly interest in Cavendish within the contexts of the history of philosophy, politics, and science. In 1997 James Fitzmaurice edited *Sociable Letters* for Garland Press. In 2001 Eileen O'Neill edited *Observations Upon Experimental Philosophy* as part of the Cambridge 'Texts in the History of Philosophy' series.

O'Neill's edition is a good example of how different disciplines fragment texts to suit their own ends. Cavendish published *Observations* and *The Blazing World* in a single volume, with significant interconnections between the two works, as scholars have begun to point out.[27] However, just as those with a literary bent have edited *The Blazing World* without *Observations*, so O'Neill's edition has *Observations* without *The Blazing World*. Cambridge has also published a volume edited by Susan James titled *Political Writings* which reproduces the Lilley text of *The Blazing World* and adds to it *Orations*. Valuable as they are, neither of the Cambridge volumes could be classified as an authoritative, scholarly edition. Only Anne Shaver's 1999 edition of six of Cavendish's plays approaches the kind of editorial information one would obtain from a full, scholarly apparatus, and even here there is only a partial or estimated collation. A complete Cavendish would be a challenging undertaking, but one that would be of great value: Cavendish's substantial body of poetry, to take one example, has a complex and fascinating textual history that asks for the extensive collation only a full scholarly edition could supply.

[25] This situation will change with the major new five-volume edition of Behn's complete works, general editor Elaine Hobby, now under contract with Cambridge University Press.
[26] On this aspect of Cavendish's revising habits see Fitzmaurice, 'Margaret Cavendish on her Own Writing'; and Salzman, *Reading Early Modern Women's Writing*, pp. 140–4.
[27] See, for example, Salzman, 'Narrative Contexts for Francis Bacon's *New Atlantis*', pp. 28–48.

Even with the Oxford *Works of Lucy Hutchinson* in production, then, and complete editions of Katherine Philips and Aphra Behn in progress,[28] women's writing has for the most part remained marginal to the resurgence in 'complete works' editing that has been one marked trend in the early modern editorial mainstream in the early twenty-first century. 'Complete works' editing has much to offer early modern women, but so too do the more experimental editorial possibilities that, while they continue to take place in the margins, speak back to more conventional editorial assumptions. Complex evaluations of the editing of women's writing in the early 2000s, notably in articles by Ramona Wray and Danielle Clarke (both contributors to the current volume), pushed at the theorization and practice of editing women writers,[29] but the relationship between the agendas and methodologies of editing women's texts and those of mainstream editing have not received a focused and comprehensive exploration. The chapters in this volume offer precisely this (re)consideration of how the tensions between editing and unediting are playing out in the field of early modern women's writing, and of how the editing of early modern women can provide invaluable insights into methodological impasses within editing and textual scholarship more broadly.

## Editorial Ideologies

The chapters in this section engage with the ideological questions of how best to contextualize the early modern woman writer that have exercised recent editors. What makes early modern women's texts readable for modern student and scholarly audiences, and how far is a unique editorial approach to women's texts required to achieve readability? Is there a tension between feminist editorial politics and editorial processes of 'making readable' and 'making familiar', as Danielle Clarke has argued?[30] These are more than just questions of how to annotate obscure references, as Alice Eardley has explored in relation to Hester Pulter;[31] they are questions of whether a whole new approach to contextualization is necessary, the kind of approach which is arguably manifest in Elaine Hobby's edition of Jane Sharp's *The Midwife's Book: Or, The Whole Art of Midwifry Discovered* (1999) and Susan Felch's edition of Elizabeth Tyrwhit's *Morning and Evening Prayers* (2008).

---

[28] Elizabeth Hageman and Andrea Sununu are editing Katherine Philips's *Works* in three volumes for Oxford University Press.

[29] Danielle Clarke, 'Nostalgia'; Wray, 'Anthologizing'.

[30] Clarke, 'Nostalgia'.     [31] Eardley, 'Hester Pulter's "Indivisibles"'.

Based on her edition of Tyrwhit's two volumes, Susan Felch offers a trenchant reappraisal of the entire process of contextual analysis and annotation required when editing early modern women, and this process if followed would be, in Felch's words, 'one gift editors may offer to scholarly discourse' (p. 39). The rigorous requirements laid out by Felch for the contextual editing of early modern women's texts becomes, in this sense, a paradigm for more general editing of texts without a history and, by extension, for a deeper understanding of the period. Danielle Clarke offers a similarly radical intervention in the relationship between editing and scholarly understanding, stressing how important the editorial work devoted to early modern women is for enhancing our appreciation of how different genre was in the Renaissance, and how the editing of male writers has to some degree blinded scholars to early modern Difference (and the intersection of that Difference with questions related to gender). Clarke's chapter and this volume as a whole testify to the need for a feminist methodology for editorial theory. In her analysis, the exemplary instance of Mary Sidney offers invaluable insights into a set of issues that, if taken seriously, impact upon early modern editing in general: 'collaborative authorship, the posthumous shaping of a poetic corpus to particular ends, indeterminacy of final intentions, lack of a printed text, versionality, structural relationships of textual dependency, restricted readership, formal experimentation' (p. 42).

Clarke's chapter is complemented by Ramona Wray's analysis of the history of modern editions of *Mariam*, given that, as Wray notes, *Mariam* is 'exemplary of the trends and problems associated with the theory and practice of textual editing as it has been employed in relation to women writers over the past twenty-five years' (p. 61). Wray offers what we may now see as a classic strategy for canonical inclusion, noting that earlier editions of *Mariam* emphasized its necessary role as a play by a woman, in a way that may have crowded out other approaches to it. So Wray's own edition of the play is an intervention to move interpretation across to something like Felch's notion of deep contextualization, and concomitantly towards a framework that sees genre and the theatre as being as important as gender.

The question of how to define and locate Cary's drama is in part related to that of how production values affect the consumption of early modern women's texts by readers. Many early modern women's texts have been published by comparatively small presses; for example, Todd's Pickering edition of Aphra Behn. This served to restrict their visibility and in some cases their scholarly respectability (in the marketplace), compared to the many authoritative texts by male writers produced by Oxford and Cambridge

University Presses. As we have already noted, this situation is changing, but the authoritative editions marked by the treatment of Wroth, Hutchinson, and Cary create a more conventional hierarchy of authors than the experimental, anarchic proliferation of texts by early modern women that smaller presses and more experimental forms of editing allowed to flourish. On the other hand, as Elizabeth Clarke illustrates, perhaps only in the kind of elaborate scholarly edition exemplified by the Oxford Hutchinson can an editor like Clarke represent the entirety of an author's work in its full religious and personal context and with the kind of exhaustive annotation that Clarke outlines as being essential to any genuine understanding of Hutchinson's 'On the Principles of the Christian Religion'.

## Editing Female Forms: Gender, Genre, and Editing

The chapters in this section take up in various ways these questions of how to read and how to package early modern women writers, and continue to consider how these issues relate to genre. Early modern women wrote prolifically in genres considered marginal to the traditional literary canon, and the interest in forms such as religious writing, autobiography, letters, diaries, and so on has been especially important in the recovery of early modern women's writing. Editing this kind of material has again raised questions about the kind of readership that this expanded body of work addressed in the sixteenth and seventeenth centuries, and the kind of readership that it addresses now. These questions are particularly acute in the case of writing by prominent women who have not previously been seen as 'writers' (Queen Elizabeth I, Katherine Parr, Mary Queen of Scots). They are, however, certainly not confined to women, and the questions of how to edit writing in 'marginal' genres have important implications for the treatment of literary-historical texts in the period more broadly.

Suzanne Trill's chapter undertakes a new archaeology of Anne, Lady Halkett's 'archive', teasing out the long editorial history of Halkett's life and works, and drawing attention to the question of 'which "lives" and which "works"' editors at any given point are 'prepared to acknowledge' (p. 97). Trill shows that Simon Couper, Halkett's eighteenth-century editor, is concerned almost exclusively with Halkett's works of exemplary piety; and Trill's exploration of Couper's practices in relation to the larger corpus of Halkett's writings draws attention to the partiality of any editorial enterprise. The example of Halkett thus foregrounds questions central to all editorial 'recoveries' of women's – and men's – writing from larger archives and repositories, and the questions of selection, inclusion and exclusion, framing and emphasis that arise. Most particularly, Trill suggests that 'Halkett's writing challenges many of the critical categories routinely deployed by editors and literary critics, including those of gender and genre' (p. 99).

Diana Barnes and Leah Marcus also demonstrate the ways in which the selection and editing of women's works from larger archives is shaped by the priorities of the popular or scholarly moment, and the ways in which these priorities change. Barnes outlines the long editorial history of women's letters for publication, revealing a focus shifting from model, paradigmatic letters, to a specific female identity manifested in letters, to a nineteenth-century notion of feminine sensibility, to modern approaches to female networks and the way that digital editing might manifest this. Leah Marcus examines not only a realignment of editorial methodologies brought about by a concerted scholarly attention to the minutiae of all Elizabeth's writing (including the neglected Armada song), but also how this re-establishment of Elizabeth's output has an impact on received views of early modern literary history. In a similarly provocative chapter, Marion Wynne-Davies discusses how the editing of plays by early modern women has shifted to reflect a movement from them being seen as token, often truncated, examples of scorned closet drama, to them being seen as performable and performed. This shift runs parallel to the way that editing plays by major dramatists like Shakespeare and Jonson has also involved a move towards performance history and performable texts, as a less rigid desire for an 'authoritative', fixed, and exemplary text has been replaced by an accommodation of the idea of a contingent, changing, and flexible textual framework that reflects the place of the theatre in history and in its contemporary social manifestation.

If dramatic texts bring their own contingencies of text and performance, one particularly common 'female form' explored in this section is the manuscript form in which very many women's texts occur. Editors face a number of issues that have been sharply defined by those who have changed our understanding of manuscript 'publication' and circulation, including those of single versus multiple manuscript proliferations, reiterations within manuscript culture, and re-readings and rewritings across time. This has given rise to complex editions of manuscript poetry that acknowledge the difficulty of processing multiple versions (such as Harold Love's edition of Rochester, or the Variorum Donne).[32] A salient instance, as analysed

---

[32] *The Works of John Wilmot Earl of Rochester*, ed. Love; *The Variorium Edition of the Poetry of John Donne*, gen. ed. Stringer.

by Marie-Louise Coolahan, is the way that the circulation of Katherine Philips's poetry in manuscript and print was in itself a practice of early modern editing that was an unusual instance of a self-created representation of Philips as a singular author, tagged as such and reproduced as such, rather than through the more usual deconstruction and dissemination within manuscript culture. Again we have an example where the complex issues raised for an editor of Philips, or raised by the editing of Philips, produce revolutionary solutions with wide-ranging implications, in this instance a way through the divide between editing on the principle of authorial final intention, and editing to reflect social authorship and circulation.

## Out of the Archives, into the Classroom

We have already discussed the feminist project of taking early modern women's writing from the archives and making it accessible, a process that in its initial phases relied heavily on anthologizing. The discussion continues in this section into the issue of student as well as scholarly access to early modern women's texts. Many scholars have pointed to the anomaly of nearly all editions of Shakespeare being modernized, while editions of most other writers are old-spelling. The direction taken by most editions of early modern women's writing is similarly old-spelling, and there has until recently been a heavy emphasis on the presentation of women's writing in diplomatic and facsimile editions. What effect does this have for a student audience, and for the teachability of early modern women's writing?

Mary Ellen Lamb is explicit in her engagement of strategies to attract a wider readership in her redacted edition of Mary Wroth's *Urania*, a text whose length and complexity otherwise renders it inaccessible to student and general readers. Lamb also describes herself as pushing back against new textualism's devaluation of the biographical in her editorial framing, suggesting that Wroth's identity as a Sidney is vital in comprehending her role in the Sidney-Herbert faction advocating Protestant causes in Europe. Lamb's argument echoes Susan Felch's in the (re)assertion of the importance of authorial identity in understanding early modern women's texts, although in the very different context of student-focused editing.

Pamela Hammons is also concerned with what is at stake in editing a text for the non-expert reader, arguing of Katherine Austen's *Book M* that the risk of losing meaning in the process of modernizing a manuscript text is offset by the benefits of rendering it accessible for a general audience. Hammons's sense of a 'still-urgent need' for modernized editions of early modern women's texts is echoed by Sarah Ross and Elizabeth

Scott-Baumann, who revisit the relationship of anthologizing to pedagogy in their chapter on editing *Women Poets of the English Civil War*. Ross and Scott-Baumann argue for the continued value of the populist poetic anthology, given the excavation of 'new' notable women poets, and the particular questions that arise around women's engagement in poetic cultures. Like Hammons and Marcus in earlier chapters, they assert the value of modernized texts to enable formalist readings of women's poetry and to effect parity in reading practices for students whose expectations have been set by modernized editions of Shakespeare.

All of the chapters in this section, then, argue for the application of mainstream editorial policies to women's writing, counter to earlier influential discussions by Wray and Danielle Clarke. All, however, do so in acknowledgement that such editions are now able to stand in a complementary relationship to old-spelling, diplomatic, or textualist approaches to the same texts. Taken together, then, these chapters reflect a stage in editorial scholarship in which a richer and more sophisticated solution can be offered to some of the problems associated with the tension between scholarly rigour and accessibility. So Mary Ellen Lamb is able to build upon the authoritative edition of Mary Wroth's *Urania* in order to produce a redacted teaching edition, and Hammons's modernized edition of Austen's *Book M* is able to refer to Ross's diplomatic one. While this may seem less than startling in the case of Wroth, a writer who has joined the canon of early modern literature (often though as the token woman), it is a sign of a ripple effect in the field that there are two editions of *Book M*, the kind of text that until this point has been one of the many virtually invisible manuscript texts by early modern women.

## Editorial Possibilities

If the editing of early modern women burgeoned at a unique point in relation to the mainstream unediting of the Renaissance, so the large-scale editorial recuperation of early modern women has been largely synchronous with the digital revolution in editorial practice. The advent of digital humanities and online editing have provided a complex set of opportunities and roadblocks, the full implications of which are still being worked through. The project of rediscovering and re-disseminating early modern women's writing has been connected to technological developments from a very early stage, notably through the Women Writers project, which began at Brown University in 1986 as a transcribed archive of texts by women writers (not only early modern ones). In its first stage, the Women Writers project was a relatively passive archive, but it developed along with advances in digital technology to encompass encoded texts, a selection of texts with introductions, published by Oxford University Press running to fifteen completed volumes, and a still developing online collection with growing resources attached to the texts.[33] The history of the Women Writers project replicates to some degree the general development of digital editing, whereby more sophisticated coding has allowed for searchable databases of texts, while such texts can also be built into pedagogical and scholarly resources with the addition of material both conventionally through annotation, and also through the richer contextual opportunities of the online environment. The Perdita collection of early modern women's manuscript writing has similarly moved into a full online environment.[34]

In a recent summing up of this situation, Margaret Ezell offers a cogent balance of the advantages and disadvantages of the digital environment for manuscript material.[35] Ezell notes that digital reproduction can be valuable when it allows us to experience what she terms the messy complicated pages of manuscripts, which are frequently the source of early modern women's writing. However, she is concerned that often these kinds of texts and their complex representation of the enormous variety of early modern women's writing may be too small, too individualized, to fit into the large digital archive projects that have seemed to be what is most funded within the digital humanities milieu. These projects might well, Ezell argues, benefit from 'a little positive feminist interrogation of editorial principles'.[36] One solution to the tension between the archive as impenetrable mass, and the individual woman's text that might fly beneath the large digital humanities radar, is the curated archive of early modern women's writing discussed by Patricia Pender and Rosalind Smith in our final chapter. There are also some significant, localized digital projects, as discussed by Pender and Smith, such as the Bess of Hardwick Project.[37]

The speculative and diverse approaches to digital editing outlined by Pender and Smith are a fitting place to end this volume, emblematic as they are of a new methodological and material plurality – or multiplicity – in the editing of early modern women's writing. Women's writing and its editing offered much to the flourishing of literary historicism in the late twentieth century, and it has provided some of the sharpest challenges to the new formalism, as Mark Rasmussen and others have articulated.[38] So, too,

---

[33] www.wwp.northeastern.edu/.    [34] www.perditamanuscripts.amdigital.co.uk.
[35] Ezell, 'Editing Early Modern Women's Manuscripts'.    [36] *Ibid.*, p. 108.
[37] www.bessofhardwick.org/; http://hri.newcastle.edu.au/emwrn/.
[38] Rasmussen (ed.), *Renaisssance Literature and Its Formal Engagements*, p. 9.

have feminist editors been quick to experiment with the possibilities offered by digital media to gather and edit the writing of early modern women. The brave new world of the digital humanities is the richer for having such women in it. Tensions remain between feminist and mainstream editorial approaches to early modern writing, but these are provocative and productive, and are being approached in ever-more complex and diverse ways. We would like to conclude by positing this volume as manifesting exactly the feminist interrogation called for by Ezell, its chapters reflecting on the long past, as well as the present and future of editing early modern women, and intervening in the current debates that cluster around the newly invigorated field of editing in all its forms.

# PART I

# Editorial Ideologies

# CHAPTER 2

# The Backward Gaze
## Editing Elizabeth Tyrwhit's Prayerbook

### Susan M. Felch

The thesis of this chapter is neither provocative nor sexy. It is not new or dramatic. It is simple: editors are, or ought to be, custodians of the backward gaze. By this, I mean that editors bring to the work of literary scholarship a certain scrupulosity – a custodianship – that disciplines our collective tendency to frame interpretive questions in terms of contemporary ideology and thereby to limit our understanding of early modern texts, and in particular texts written by early modern women. Although the strategy of the backward gaze is simple, those who study early modern women often wish to construct spaces in which female voices can be heard and understood today, thus privileging, sometimes inadvertently, the present over the past.

Editors, by virtue of their work, necessarily privilege that which chronologically precedes a text, rather than that which follows it. To be sure, as scholars we are often drawn to an archive because we see it as part of a larger and future trajectory, and we quite rightly want to interpret its significance in light of that trajectory. We cannot and should not cease and desist from speculative, synthetic scholarship. But we should recognize and be guided by the fact that authors are always responding to what has happened in the past: they cannot possibly know how their texts will be read and known in the future. As teachers, we tell our students that arguments are constructed by agreeing or disagreeing with previous writers, or by extending or modifying their claims. These four rhetorical moves (agree/disagree/extend/modify), singly or in various combinations, constitute our writing repertoire. Sixteenth-century authors are no different: their works respond to previous texts, and they were conscious of writing within, out of, and against earlier traditions.

A text, therefore, is in a certain sense always an endpoint, a conclusion, a summary statement. Perhaps better, it is always a prism that refracts light. An editor's responsibility, then, is to clarify for other readers what those streams of light are, to be a custodian of the backward gaze. Editorial work

should chasten our headlong dash into what we consider to be most important or relevant. Although this need to be sensitive to precedents may seem
so obvious as to be mundane, I have discovered over the course of working
on several critical editions that concentrating on the seemingly mundane,
the obvious, the particular, the local, and the *previous* is precisely what
illuminates a text, establishes or re-calibrates the critical terms by which it
is read, and often corrects well-intentioned but erroneous interpretations.
As editors or curators, we have the power and responsibility to establish the
critical terms by which an author is read, as Elizabeth Clarke warns in her
chapter on Lucy Hutchinson. But we also have the luxury of concentrating
our attention on the minute details of a single author or single text.

Editorial work is relentlessly and necessarily local. This localized focus
allows us to develop editorial empathy for the texts we study and also gives
us some distance from the critical imperatives that drive contemporary
scholarship. Such a focus is particularly vital when editing texts written by
women because here we work within a double bind. On the one hand, the
recovery of women's texts by editors in the twentieth century was generated
precisely by a sense that these voices had been obscured and marginalized,
which necessitated an advocacy that claimed a special position for and interpretation of their works. A contemporary feminist vocabulary was essential
in focusing serious academic attention on women's authorial agency and
establishing the language with which to talk about their texts. On the other
hand, encasing early modern women writers within the terms established
by various feminist theories can re-ghettoize and deform their particular
voices and works, doing violence to the very women we seek to honour,
as Ramona Wray argues in her analysis of the decisions made by editors of
Elizabeth Cary's *The Tragedy of Mariam*.

In this chapter, I will explore the implications of the backward gaze
and its relation to contemporary theoretical insights by way of three case
studies related to the prayerbook of Elizabeth Tyrwhit, who served in
the court of Katherine Parr and composed her devotional compilation in
the early 1550s. I will focus my comments on sixteenth-century women,
attending to Patricia Pender's astute observation that collapsing the *early*
early modern and the *late* early modern periods 'occlude[s] important
historical distinctions', the very occlusion that editors are at pains to avoid.[1]

---

[1] Pender, *Early Modern Women's Writing and the Rhetoric of Modesty*, p. 4. I take the *early* early modern
period to extend at least through the first decade of Elizabeth's reign. The particular problem faced
by scholars of early modern women is the possible distortion caused by reading the concerns and
discourses of seventeenth-century writers back onto the texts of the less numerous sixteenth-century
writers.

Similarly, although cross-confessional scholarship is essential to create a full picture of the women writers, I will limit my observations here to Protestant women.

## Case Study #1: The Introduction to Elizabeth Tyrwhit's *Morning and Evening Prayers*

There are two extant editions of Tyrwhit's sixteenth-century prayerbook: a 32mo version printed in 1574 by Henry Middleton for Christopher Barker[2] and a second version included by Thomas Bentley in the second lamp of his large 1582 compilation, *The Monument of Matrones*.[3] Here is the beginning of the 1574 version, entitled 'A briefe exhortation unto Prayer':

> LEt not to praye alway, and stand not in feare to be refourmed unto death, for the rewarde of God endureth for ever. Before thou prayest prepare thy soule, and bee not as one that tempteth God. Wee must consider therefore when wee pray, in whose presence we stand, to whom we speake, and what we desire.[4]

As we can see, this is a preface – we might call it a mini sermon – on the nature of prayer and its uses. The exhortation continues for nearly the entire first signature through A7v. A8r then picks up with 'A confession to be sayde before the morning prayer' that begins

> I Doe acknowledge and confesse unto thee O most mercifull and Heavenly father, mine often and grevous offences that I have committed against thy dyvine majestie, fro my youth hitherto, in thought, word and deede.[5]

The subsequent pages continue with morning prayers.

Here, in contrast, is the beginning of Thomas Bentley's 1582 version of Tyrwhit's prayerbook:

> I Doo acknowledge, and confesse unto thee, O most mercifull and heavenlie father, mine often and grievous offences that I have committed against thy divine Majestie, from my youth hitherto, in thought, word and deed.[6]

It is immediately obvious, even to a casual reader, that these two texts begin in quite different ways. Bentley has omitted the preface of 1574

---

[2] Lady Elizabeth Tyrwhit, *Morning and euening prayers, with diuers psalms himnes and meditations* (1574; *STC* 24477.5).

[3] Thomas Bentley, *The Monument of Matrones: conteining seuen seuerall lamps of virginitie, or distinct treatises; whereof the first fiue concerne praier and meditation: the two last, precepts and examples* (1582; *STC* 1892).

[4] All citations of Tyrwhit are from *Elizabeth Tyrwhit's Morning and Evening Prayers*, ed. Felch; here, p. 124.

[5] *Tyrwhit*, ed. Felch, p. 124.    [6] *Tyrwhit*, ed. Felch, p. 74.

from the opening pages, nor is it to be found elsewhere in the 1582 prayerbook. Furthermore, a careful perusal of the 1574 and 1582 versions reveals many other differences, including substitutions, omissions, and the rearrangement of shared materials. Critics, naturally enough, have suggested that Bentley asserted his editorial power to alter substantially the form of Tyrwhit's prayerbook, to add material of his own and to omit Tyrwhit's short sermon that instructs her readers how to pray. The decision to print the 1574 version of the prayerbook in Ashgate's Early Modern Englishwoman Facsimile Library, for instance, was predicated on the fact that it includes 'A briefe exhortation unto Prayer' and on the assumption that this exhortation displays Tyrwhit's authorial agency, the speaker standing 'in relation to [her] audience as priest to congregation by instructing it in its task'.[7] By contrast, in the 1582 *The Monument of Matrones* version, 'the editor's hand is palpable' and the text is reframed by Bentley 'as part of a corpus of texts by Protestant female worthies, rather than as a priestly guide. Tyrwhit's agency in the shaping of the individual spiritual journey is absorbed completely into official liturgical structures'.[8]

Although the assumption that Tyrwhit's authorial agency is diminished and absorbed into official structures by a male editor is understandable and fits a 'chaste, silent, and obedient' hermeneutic, it does not stand up to further scrutiny. This example of assuming that the revision of a female-authored text must be due to the manipulations of an early modern male editor is a clear example of a particular feminist agenda occluding the backward gaze. As an editor who works within woman-centred scholarship and is the beneficiary of that tradition of fine scholars, I nevertheless find myself at this point disagreeing with the fundamental assumptions that editorial work is necessarily intrusive and that early modern male editors diminish female voices. The exchange between female authors and male editors is complex and women authors, particularly religious authors, may be embedded in contexts that, while they are gender-inflected, are not gender-exclusive.[9]

---

[7]  Patricia Brace, 'Introductory Note', in Tyrwhit, *Morning and Evening Prayers*, ed. Brace, p. xii.

[8]  Brace, 'Introductory Note', p. xvi. The *Oxford Dictionary of National Biography* consolidates this reading of the prayerbooks by noting that the version in *Monument* 'differs substantially from the original . . . for Bentley changes not only structure, but also content and tone, by amalgamating some prayers, inserting others by different authors, and deleting some of Tyrwhit's altogether' (Patricia Brace, 'Tyrwhit, Elizabeth, Lady Tyrwhit (d. 1578)', *ODNB*).

[9]  'Gender-inflected' is a term that acknowledges female modes of discourse as an important context without encasing texts within a 'gender-exclusive' paradigm that reads female discourse as the only or necessarily most significant context.

To return to the Tyrwhit prayerbooks, the 1574 edition that was printed by Henry Middleton for Christopher Barker was entered in the Stationers' Register in 1569/70 and may, in fact, have been brought out that year in an edition that is now lost.[10] The previous year, in 1568, Henry Middleton had printed a prayerbook compiled by Henry Bull and published by Thomas East. In the preface to Bull's devotional text we read these words: 'Before thou pray, prepare thy selfe and be not as one that tempteth god. We must consider therfore when wee pray, in whose presence we stande, to whom we speake, and what we desire' and so forth.[11]

The implication for the two editions of Tyrwhit's prayerbook is clear. The 1574 preface was not 'original' to Tyrwhit, but rather is a somewhat generic little excerpt with minor variants – probably plucked out of the Bull preface by Middleton – that provides a brief primer on prayer. To read the two versions of the Tyrwhit prayerbook primarily through the lens of a 'silent, chaste, and obedient' hermeneutic, and thus to assume that the omission of the 'briefe exhortation' is Bentley's attempt to mitigate Tyrwhit's authorial agency, is to misread the texts. The role of the modern editor, then, as custodian of the backward gaze, is both to question contemporary critical assumptions and to pursue relentlessly the contexts that precede the publication of the target text: in other words, to develop editorial empathy and cultivate the backward gaze. Pursuing contexts, particularly in the prayerbook genre, is difficult, since sixteenth-century authors rarely bother to cite their sources or to cite them accurately. Yet tracking down sources is one of the key responsibilities of an editor. Accurate accounting of historical, cultural, generic, and other contexts deploys a certain self-correcting mechanism that can unclench tightly held ideological assumptions. As editors, we have the luxury and the responsibility of correcting errors of the sort that have distorted the Tyrwhit archive.

When I began editing Tyrwhit's prayerbook, I thought it would be a relatively straightforward project, an assumption proved wrong largely because there were so many intertwining contexts to be understood. Two, in particular, were relevant for sorting out the discrepancies between the 1574 and 1582 editions and restoring Thomas Bentley's honour as an editor: the biographical context and the generic context. Although the 'works and life' approach to women authors rightly has been called into question,

---

[10] The entry in the Stationers' Register, between 22 July 1569 and 22 July 1570, reads, 'Recevyd of CHRISTOFER BARKER for his lycense for prynting of serten prayers of my Lady TYRWETT' (Edward Arber (ed.), *A Transcript of the Registers of the Company of Stationers of London; 1554–1650*, 5 vols., vol. 1 [London and Birmingham, 1875–94], p. 183).

[11] Henry Bull, [*Christian prayers and holy meditations*], (1568; *STC* 4028), A2r–A2v.

understanding the biographical and generic contexts remains central to editorial projects that excavate authors who have not been the subject of extensive scholarly scrutiny or those whose archives have been misread, as Suzanne Trill demonstrates in her chapter on Anne, Lady Halkett. In terms of the biography of an early modern woman, an editor must often spend considerable effort simply to establish basic information about family, social situation, and life-facts; in terms of genre, there are always questions regarding the extent to which any genre is gender-inflected, gender-exclusive, or gender-enabling, that is a genre that significantly empowers women writers.

The biographical context for Elizabeth Tyrwhit is a case in point. There are at least nine recorded Elizabeth Tyrwhits in the sixteenth century, all related to one another by birth or marriage. In particular, a confusion had arisen in scholarship about two of these Elizabeths, who belonged to a Suffolk family. The elder Elizabeth was the daughter of Goddard Oxenbridge of Brede, Suffolk and Anne Fiennes. Her older half-brother, Thomas, the son of Goddard's first wife, Elizabeth Etchingham, had a daughter, Elizabeth Oxenbridge, who was younger than her aunt by about twelve years. Both Elizabeth Oxenbridges, elder and younger, went from Suffolk to London to serve various Tudor queens. At the same time, a Lincolnshire gentry family named Tyrwhit sent their children down to London to serve at Court, in this case those children being sons. The second son, Robert, served in the court of Henry VIII and married the elder Elizabeth Tyrwhit. Robert's nephew, also named Robert, the son of the eldest brother, William, came down to London as well and married Elizabeth Oxenbridge the younger. As a result, there were two Elizabeth Oxenbridge Tyrwhits, a mere dozen years apart in age, serving in the Tudor courts with their respective husbands, both named Robert. Establishing that the prayerbook author was the elder rather than the younger Elizabeth was very important, in that it located the production of this book firmly within the circle of Katherine Parr, to whom the Tyrwhits were related by marriage.[12] Given the publication dates of the two extant editions (1574 and 1582), it was crucial to consider the origins of the prayerbook within the Henrician/Edwardian context rather than as a product of Elizabeth's reign, which was the original assumption of twentieth-century scholars.

Second and more complicated than untangling the biographical context was researching the nature and context of private prayerbooks, as distinct from the liturgical Book of Common Prayer. As both Elizabeth Clarke and Suzanne Trill point out in their chapters in this volume, establishing

---

[12] Family trees may be found in *Tyrwhit*, ed. Felch, pp. 187–91.

precise theological contexts for woman-authored texts in the early modern period can be a challenging endeavour. In the case of early modern private prayerbooks, the two significant monographs on domestic devotional works, by Helen White and Charles Butterworth, were both published in the early 1950s, and they have been supplemented by only a scattering of subsequent articles and chapters.[13] No wonder Ian Green has described private prayerbooks as 'among the most neglected documents of the early modern period . . . despite their ubiquity and intrinsic value as sources'.[14] Furthermore, although White and Butterworth were excellent scholars, they asked different questions than those that interest us now, a reminder of the contingency of all our scholarly assumptions.

Crucial to editing Tyrwhit's prayerbook, then, was the need to establish a robust taxonomy of Tudor prayerbooks and to relate this emerging genre to its predecessors, the late medieval lay devotional texts, which were themselves divided into Books of Hours and devotional miscellanies. The Books of Hours revolved around the Little Hours of the Blessed Virgin Mary and other liturgical texts and were arranged into the hours of prayer used by enclosed communities: matins, lauds, prime, terce, sext, nones, vespers, and compline. Devotional miscellanies did not feature the canonical hours, but included various types of prayer.

With the advent of the Reformation, private printed (as opposed to manuscript) vernacular prayerbooks, also known as primers, branched out into five types: traditional, transitional, reformist, occasional, and authorized. Traditional prayerbooks, written in Latin and bilingually in Latin and English, were essentially printed versions of the manuscript Books of Hours. One important French printer, François Regnault, produced his last prayerbook for an English readership in October 1538 just a month before a royal proclamation banned the importation of books published abroad. It was printed in parallel columns, the English prominently displayed in the centre of each two-page opening with the Latin relegated in smaller print to the outer margin.[15] Transitional primers, such as that printed in 1535 by Robert Redman, retained a great deal of traditional material but eliminated or pruned legendary material, indulgences, and Marian prayers and added gospel accounts from Tyndale's 1534 translation.[16] Reformist prayerbooks

---

[13] Helen C. White, *The Tudor Books of Private Devotion*; and Butterworth, *The English Primers*.

[14] Ian Green, *Print and Protestantism*, p. 252.

[15] *Thys prymer in Englyshe and in Laten* ([Rouen], 1538, *STC* 16008.5).

[16] *This prymer of Salysbery vse bothe in Englyshe & in Laten, is set out a longe* (London, 1535; *STC* 15986.3); for a description of this primer, see Butterworth, *The English Primers*, pp. 87–103. For another example of a transitional primer from later in Henry's reign, see *A prymer of Salisbery vse set out a longe in Englyshe and Latyn* (1542: *STC* 16021).

followed the lead of Luther's 1522 German primer, the *Betbüchlein*. George Joye's 1530 *Ortulus Anime*, the first extant English reformist prayerbook and also the earliest printed entirely in English, presented itself as 'a garden of the soul'.[17] The occasional prayerbooks followed the precedent of the fifteenth-century manuscript prayer miscellanies by avoiding the liturgical format of the canonical hours, often selecting their material exclusively from biblical prayers or organizing the psalms into daily readings.[18] Beginning in 1545, authorized prayerbooks were issued by the crown and proposed themselves as the solution for 'the avoydyng of the dyversytie of primer bookes that are nowe abroade, wherof are almoost innumerable sortes whiche minister occasion of contentions and vaine disputations, rather then to edifye'.[19] Depending upon the monarch, these could be either more traditional or more reformist in tone.

Tyrwhit's prayerbook, despite its initial 1574 publication date, fits firmly into the milieu of the early reformist prayerbooks, inaugurated by Joye's *Ortulus*; in fact, I discovered that well over half of her material comes directly from translated Lutheran-inflected materials printed in the 1530s and 1540s. Discovering these sources was important for a number of reasons, but particularly for understanding genre. Henrician and Edwardian reformist prayerbooks follow the medieval Books of Hours by alternating prose and poetic hymns within a single set of prayers. In Matins, for instance, the traditional opening formula, 'O Lord, open Thou my lips', is followed by a psalm, the Hail Mary and Gloria Patri, a hymn, more psalms, and on through a set of prose and poetic responses. The Book of Common Prayer, however, and subsequent Elizabethan private prayerbooks contain only prose prayers and prose scripture.[20] Poetry in the Elizabethan era spun off either into sung hymns and psalms, as in *The Whole Booke of Psalmes*, which we commonly refer to as the Sternhold and Hopkins psalter, or into devotional poetry, as in Anne Lock's sonnet sequence on Psalm 51.

---

[17]  George Joye, *Ortulus anime the garden of the soule* (Argentine [i.e., Antwerp], 1530; *STC* 13828.4); see also Butterworth, *The English Primers*, pp. 28–46.

[18]  See, for instance, *The fou[n]tayne or well of lyfe out of whiche doth springe most swete co[n]solatio[n]s, right necessary for troubled co[n]sciences* (1532; *STC* 11211) and *Prayers of the Byble taken out of the olde testament and the newe* (1535?; *STC* 20200.3) for examples of collected biblical prayers. Edward Whitchurche's *Deuout psalmes and colletes, gathered and set in suche order, as may be vsed for dayly meditacions* (1547, *STC* 2999) is an example of daily readings.

[19]  *The primer, set foorth by the Kynges maiestie and his clergie, to be taught lerned, [and] read: and none other to be vsed throughout all his dominions* (1545; *STC* 16034), ***iv.

[20]  The exception is a small number of 'godly garden' prayerbooks that retain elements of Joye's *Ortulus*, for instance, two prayerbooks printed by Middleton: *A godly garden out of which most comfortable hearbes may be gathered for the health of the wounded conscience of all penitent sinners* (1574; *STC* 11555) and the slightly revised *A godlie garden out of which most comfortable hearbes may be gathered for the health of the wounded conscience of all penitent sinners* (1581; *STC* 11557).

Establishing the biographical and generic contexts – looking backward at the familial and literary sources in which Tyrwhit was anchored – was crucial to editing the Tyrwhit prayerbook and to correcting the misprision surrounding the two printed editions. Once I had established the Edwardian provenance of the non-extant manuscript, I was forced to reconsider the relationship of the 1574 and 1582 editions and to wonder if the 1574 was the 'original' that Bentley deformed in his 1582 edition or whether it was the other way around. The reason this question presented itself with such force was because the 1574 prayerbook simply does not look like an Edwardian prayerbook. Following the 'briefe exhortation unto Prayer' (noted above), the 1574 edition neatly collects the prose prayers for Morning (A8r–C8v), then the prose prayers for Evening (C8v–D8r), then a set of moral maxims 'composed by the Lady Elizabeth Tyrwhit' (E1r–E4r), and finally adds 'certaine other godly prayers' (E5r–K4r) in a section which contains first miscellaneous prose prayers and then, second and finally, the poems. The maxims and final prayers, including all the poems, are set off from the prayerbook proper by the printer's device.

On the other hand, the 1582 *Monument of Matrones* version interleaves prose and poetry throughout as was common in the medieval Books of Hours and in the Henrician and Edwardian prayerbooks – traditional, transitional, or reformist – that are based on the Books of Hours tradition. Moreover, the 1582 *Monument of Matrones* edition contains nearly one-third more material than the 1574 edition. In other words, when you look at the material form of the two prayerbooks and at the broader context of late medieval and early modern private devotional texts, it looks very much as if it is the 1574 edition that rearranges an earlier manuscript into an Elizabethan shape. To the extent that we can make a claim for an original text when we do not have an autograph, it seems best to say that the 1582 Bentley version is closer to Tyrwhit's Edwardian prayerbook than the revised, truncated 1574 edition with its added preface on 'A briefe exhortation unto Prayer'. It is not Bentley who modulates Tyrwhit's voice, but Middleton and Barker who simultaneously add to and truncate her text.[21]

It is important to note here that I began my work on Tyrwhit with the same critical assumption held by other scholars, namely that the 1574 edition represented her original text more nearly than the 1582 Bentley version. It was the backward gaze of editorial work that first confirmed the

---

[21] There are also additional printing variants that confirm Bentley's 1582 *The Monument of Matrones* edition as the more accurate text, described in *Tyrwhit*, ed. Felch, pp. 59–64.

Edwardian provenance of the missing manuscript and second led to the
conclusion that the 1574 edition was an abridgement. Armed with those
results, I became sceptical of the only new material that appears in that
1574 edition – the 'briefe exhortation unto Prayer' – and discovered the
Bull preface as I was trawling through Elizabethan prayerbooks. Finding
this preface reminded me of the five editorial principles that remain central
to my work:

> Hold all critical assumptions, especially those related to gender, lightly.
> Always look backward.
> Attend to the overlay of multiple contexts.
> Remain uneasy about initial conclusions.
> Return frequently to basic questions, such as 'Why are there two such
> different editions of Tyrwhit's prayerbook?'

## Case Study #2: Thomas Bentley, Model Editor

Research on Elizabeth Tyrwhit led me to consider more carefully what
Thomas Bentley seems to be doing in *The Monument of Matrones*. It
may be possible to see him as an editor who forces women authors into
'official liturgical structures'. For instance, the interior title page for the
second lamp may be seen to entomb women in emblematic funeral monuments and thus to reduce each female voice to that of a wraith. Funeral
monuments are a possible context for a book entitled *The Monument of
Matrones*, but another Monument would more readily come to the mind
of a sixteenth-century reader, namely Foxe's *Actes and Monuments*.[22] The
imagery of lamps, which is what Bentley uses to title the seven sections
of his compendium, pulls together the burning light of the martyrs, the
instruction of Jesus not to keep one's light under a bushel, the five wise
virgins, and the preface's argument that women writers ought to publish
their works for the greater good of the church. Since the book was a patent
appeal for Queen Elizabeth's patronage, it also seems highly unlikely that
Bentley intended, or that his readers would have read, the title page as
entombing or constricting the voices of the four queens who are featured
in the second lamp.

The main title page, however, is even more intriguing, particularly when
one looks closely at the top paired pictures (see Figure 2.1). The captions

---

[22] The prayers, letters, and other written documents of the martyrs were considered to be their
monuments and Bentley clearly intended his *Monument* to be read within this tradition. See
Wabuda, 'Henry Bull, Miles Coverdale, and the Making of Foxe's *Book of Martyrs*'.

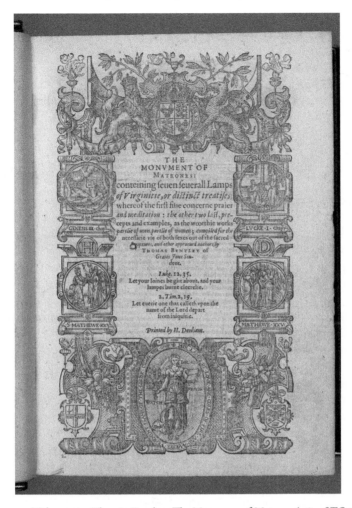

Figure 2.1 Title page to Thomas Bentley, *The Monument of Matrones* (1582; *STC* 1892).

for these pictures read 'Genesis 3' and 'Luke 1', which immediately bring to mind the centuries-old connection between Eve the sinner and Mary the holy virgin. However, when we look more closely at the Genesis picture on the left, we see that it does not illustrate Genesis 3 but rather Genesis 2, where Eve is created out of a sleeping Adam. The Geneva Bible's marginal note on this text reads: 'Signyfying that mankind was perfect, when the woman was created, which before was like an imperfect building'. That gloss, in fact, elaborates this woodcut, also included in the Bishop's Bible, which shows an emerging Eve face to face with God, without the mediation of a sleeping Adam. That viewing Eve as the crown of humanity was a standard theological interpretation is reflected in Ester Sowernam's later comment, responding to Joseph Swetnam's misogynist attacks on Eve, that 'God created the woman his last worke, as to supply and make absolute that imperfect building which was unperfected in man, *as all Divines do hold*, till the happy creation of the woman' (emphasis mine).[23]

The emblem of Eve as perfecting, rather than destroying, humanity runs parallel with Protestant rhetoric that understands women as exemplary laypeople. As women they could not – in any version of the sixteenth-century imagination – be clergy. Yet as laypeople they had both access to God without priestly mediation and the responsibility to work out their own spiritual vocations. Other visual representations of women as exemplary laypeople occur in Foxe, both on the title page and in the large woodcuts that illustrate the reign of Edward VI.[24]

Furthermore, in the preface to his *Monument*, Bentley had praised women writers who 'for the common benefit of their countrie, have not ceased ... to spend their time, their wits, their substance, and also their bodies, in the studies of noble and approved sciences, and in compiling and translating of sundrie most christian and godlie books', and he had urged all who might 'of anie singular affection for their private use conceale or deteine the woorks of anie godlie authors men or women' to bring these books forward 'for the common benefit of Christs congregation'.[25] So it is not surprising when we turn to the texts that he compiled, including but not limited to Tyrwhit's prayerbook, that we see Bentley showing all the marks of a careful antiquarian and non-intrusive editor who positioned women as exemplary laypeople, responsible for sharing their writings with the whole of the church.

### Case Study #3: The Problem of Middleton and Barker

Rehabilitating Thomas Bentley, however, raises another problem. What about Middleton and Barker and their 1574 edition of Tyrwhit's

---

[23] Ester Sowernam, *Ester hath hang'd Haman or An Ansvvere to a lewd pamphlet, entituled, The arraignment of women With the arraignment of lewd, idle, froward, and vnconstant men, and husbands* (1617, *STC* 22974), pp. 5–6.

[24] See, for instance, John Foxe, *Actes and Monuments of these latter and perilous dayes touching matters of the Church* (1563; *STC* 11222), p. 1353, as well as discussions of the exemplary layperson in Micheline White, 'Protestant Women's Writing and Congregational Psalm Singing', and Felch, 'The Exemplary Anne Vaughan Lock'.

[25] Bentley, *Monument*, B1r; B2v.

prayerbook? Have we not simply shifted the deformation of Tyrwhit's text from Bentley to her earlier publishers? The problem here, as I see it, lies in asking this question with the assumption that early modern male editors alter women's texts *because* they are female-authored. Tyrwhit's authorial agency is not necessarily undermined in Middleton and Barker's edition; her name appears, for instance, in large print on the title page. And this is a period in book history (particularly if we think in terms of the prayerbook's 1569 entry in the Stationers' Register rather than its 1574 publication) when older theological material was being reprinted not simply out of antiquarian interest, but rather to bolster the claim that the Reformation has ancient antecedents, that it could lay claim to being the true church. Examples would include not only the first edition of Foxe's *Actes and Monuments* (1563), but also John Day's traditional prayerbook, *Christian Prayers and Meditations* (1569) based on none other than Henry Bull's *Christian Praiers and holie meditations* (1568) which contributed a fragment of its preface to Tyrwhit's volume, as well as Matthew Parker's collection of Anglo-Saxon manuscripts, culminating in his publication of *De antiquitate Britannicae ecclesiae* (*c.* 1572).

Additionally, the 1574 Tyrwhit edition was bound with and possibly was printed along with Katherine Parr's *Meditations*.[26] So rather than suppressing Tyrwhit's voice, it is just as likely that Middleton and Barker were promoting the work of two acknowledged mothers of the Reformation – Parr and Tyrwhit – albeit in an 'up to date' generic form more recognizable to Elizabethan than to modern readers. That Tyrwhit remained a force in the Reformation world is suggested not only by her prominent inclusion in Bentley's *Monument*, following a trinity of royal texts, but also by a 1577 dedication to her from John Field, in which he praises her 'forwardness, fidelity and sinceritie'.[27] Perhaps the very small size and abridgement of the 1574 text may be tied to the cover in which the one extant copy is found, a lovely golden girdlebook comprised of two embossed and enamelled gold panels, the front depicting Moses and the brazen serpent and the back depicting the judgment of Solomon.[28] In sum, if we ask, what work does this 1574 edition do, rather than how did the publishers alter a female text, the answer appears to be that it takes its place amidst other contemporary

---

[26] *The Queenes Prayers, or Meditations: wherein the mynde is stirred to suffer all afflictions here* (1574; STC 4826.6).

[27] Jean de L'Espine, *An excellent treatise of Christian righteousnes, written first in the French tongue by M. I. de l'Espine, and translated into English by I. Feilde for the comforte of afflicted consciences* (1577; STC 15512), A2r–A3v.

[28] Held by the British Museum. Shelfmark: M&ME 1894, 7–29, 1.

devotional material intended both to construct a Protestant 'tradition' and
to make the more evangelical of her subjects appealing to Queen Elizabeth.

## The Promise and Peril of Empathy

As custodians of the backward gaze, editors do develop empathy for early
modern texts and a certain critical distance from contemporary scholarly
assumptions. However, it is not wrong to interrogate early modern texts
based on our own biases – in fact, it is impossible not to do so. Nor is
empathy itself either an innocent term or an unproblematic one, as Mikhail
Bakhtin has noted. In response to a question about understanding foreign,
including older, cultures, Bakhtin argued that being empathetic, viewing
'the world through the eyes of this foreign culture', is both necessary
and also one-sided. '[I]f this were the only aspect of this understanding',
he argued, 'it would merely be duplication and would not entail anything
new or enriching'. Rather than stopping with empathy, Bakhtin suggested a
'creative understanding' that 'does not renounce itself, its own place in time,
its own culture', a creative understanding which he called 'outsideness'.
The hermeneutic generativity of 'outsideness' means that we do raise new
questions that another culture cannot generate for itself, but it also means
that such questions must be 'serious and sincere' as well as dialogic; that is,
we must be willing to be read by a text as well as to be engaged in reading
it. For Bakhtin, '[s]uch a dialogic encounter of two cultures does not result
in merging or mixing. Each retains its own unity and *open* totality, but
they are mutually enriched'.[29]

What Bakhtin calls us to, as editors, is a critical but empathetic interrogation of both our own scholarly practices and the texts we are editing,
and this is particularly urgent for those of us who work within modern
woman-centred theoretical paradigms as we read earlier female authors. We
read early modern texts with critical empathy, but we also need to allow
them to read us. Good editing takes time; we must linger with a text as
well as critically interrogate it. As we linger, we realize that every contextual
boundary we draw is artificial and that, therefore, the more contextual
landscapes we can chart out, the better. Multiple contexts keep us from
fixating on reductive explanations. As Wray notes in her chapter on Cary,
'if we wish to go forward in the editing practices applied to *The Tragedy
of Mariam*, it is important to acknowledge . . . multiple points of contact.

---

[29] All quotations in this paragraph from Bakhtin, 'Response to a Question from the *Novy Mir* Editorial
Staff', in *Speech Genres*, pp. 6–7.

By moving outside the purview of gender and biography, decentring both from their pre-eminent positions as units of analysis, and accommodating equally illuminating strategies for unpacking the play, we may allow *The Tragedy of Mariam* to be responsive to a range of new contextual possibilities' (p. 67). Similarly, as the work of editing women in the sixteenth century accumulates, we are better situated to answer this question, 'What status do women have in the religious discourse of the sixteenth century?' and to contribute our own editorial empathy to the task of revising and clarifying critical assumptions.

## Charting Contexts

If we interpret the question 'What status do English women have in the religious discourse of the sixteenth century?' to mean 'What does sixteenth-century Protestant religious discourse say *about* women?', there are a variety of answers, each located within its own contextual field.

We can certainly say that women were considered to be the daughters of Eve, but as Case Study #2 revealed, daughter of Eve can refer both to the Genesis 3 Eve, the mother of sin, and to the Genesis 2 Eve, the one who perfects humanity. Even when women were coded as Genesis 3 Eves, the question was debated as to whether she was more culpable than Adam, as the one who took the fruit, or less culpable, as the one who was deceived.[30]

We can also say that women were wives and, as such, were enjoined to submit to their husbands. But here, too, the contextual landscape is complex. No less a patriarchal figure than John Knox urged his friend Anne Lock to come to Geneva during the reign of Mary Tudor with or without the blessing of her husband, suggesting that she should seek God's guidance and then inform her 'heid' what God had told her to do. In a letter written to Lock in 1557, Knox begins with a putative recognition of male headship in marriage, noting that the women should make the decision to leave only 'by the consall and discretioun of those that God hath apoyntit to your heidis (your husbandis I meane)', but then continues with this directive: 'call first for grace by Jesus to follow that whilk is acceptabill in his syght, and thairefter communicat with your faithfull husbandis' and concludes by urging Lock to trust God directly: '[T]han sall God, I dout not, conduct your futsteppis, and derect your consallis to his glorie'.[31]

---

[30] See, for instance, Kathleen M. Crowther's survey of interpretations of Eve in *Adam and Eve in the Protestant Reformation*, pp. 99–139.

[31] John Knox, *The Works of John Knox*, ed. David Laing, 6 vols., vol. IV (Edinburgh: Thomas George Stevenson, 1846–64), pp. 219, 221.

Women were also mothers but as parents they held authority with fathers over children and servants. William Tyndale's 1528 *Obedience of a Christen Man* repeatedly invokes the parity of male and female parents, expanding the biblical text 'fathers provoke not your children to wrath' to include mothers and fathers: 'Oure fathers and mothers are to vs in Gods stede . . . What we doo to oure fathers and mothers that we do to God' read two of the marginal glosses.[32] Within the framework of domestic prayer, mothers were essentially 'ministers' within home congregations, such that early Elizabethans were praised for 'instructing with all, suche as were committed to their charge in the right understanding of this godlie and absolute Catechisme, and in the comfortable singing of the Psalmes, so that in everie familie, to the comfort of all those that feared God, there was a Church or congregation erected'.[33]

Women were daughters and among the directives for their education and upbringing is a substantial concern to protect them from being merely bartered on the marriage market. As early as 1528, Tyndale argued that 'The maryage also of the childern perteyneth vnto their elders . . . Which thinge the hethen and gentyls have ever kepte and to this daye kepe / vnto the great shame & rebuke of vs christen: in as moch as the weddinges of our virgyns (shame it is to speake it) ar moare like vnto the saute [assault] of a bitche / then the marienge of a reasonable creature. Se not we daily .iij or .iiij. calengynge one woman before the Commissiary or officeall / of which not one hath the consent of her father and mother. And yet he that hath most money / hath best right and shall have her in the dispite of all her frendes and in diffiaunce of Gods ordinaunces'.[34]

Women were also exemplary laypersons, as noted above, and as such were to be studious learners and teachers of the Bible. In 1550, for instance, the Dutch émigré Walter Lynne published *A brief and compendiouse table, in a maner of a concordaunce openyng the waye to the principall histories of the whole Bible, and the moste co[m]mon articles grounded and comprehended in the newe Testament and olde, in maner as amply as doeth the great concordau[n]ce of the Bible*, dedicated to Anne Stanhope, the duchess of Somerset; the table was a translation of the concordance attached to the 1536 edition of the Swiss-German Zurich Bible, attributed to Heinrich Bullinger.[35] In

---

[32] William Tyndale, *The obedie[n]ce of a Christen man and how Christe[n] rulers ought to governe, where in also (if thou marke diligently) thou shalt fynde eyes to perceave the crafty conveyance of all iugglers* ([Antwerp, 1528]; *STC* 24446), D1r–D1v.

[33] Genevan *Form of Prayers*, 1560; *STC* 16561.a.5.     [34] Tyndale, *Obedience*, D2r–D2v.

[35] Translation of concordance from 1536 edition of Zurich Bible (Swiss-German, first edition 1534), from Euler, *Couriers of the Gospel*.

his translator's preface, Lynne situates the duchess not as a hearer of the word but rather as a serious reader and student of the scriptures. 'Youre graces chiefe and daylye study is in the holy Byble', he notes, and he suggests that a concordance is just the right 'jewel' that will most adorn her devotions, 'that your grace myghte not be destytute of so necessarye an instrumente in your godlye studie'.[36] In fact, in the first two pages alone, he mentions the word 'study' or 'studious' no less than four times. In the following generation, Anne Lock, along with the Cooke sisters, was held up as an example to Queen Elizabeth of a pious and learned woman, whom the Queen herself was encouraged to emulate: 'England hath had and hath at this day, noble Gentlewomen famous for their learning, as the right honorable my Lady Burghley [Mildred Cooke Cecil], my Lady Russell [Elizabeth Cooke Hoby Russell], my Lady Bacon [Anne Cooke Bacon], Mistress Dering [Anne Lock], with others.'[37] A few years later, John Stockwood dedicated a compendium of catechisms to Elizabeth Roydon, Lady Golding, a wealthy widow and Puritan patron, and encouraged her not only to instruct her own house 'in the true knowledge of God and principles of Christian religion' but also 'to spurre up others of your worships children, and godly kindred, and acquaintance, to treade the pathes, and walke the steppes which other the godly have gone before us'.[38]

Above all, women in England in the sixteenth century were Christians. We should be careful not to over-gender or undervalue Christian virtues such as patience and humility, particularly when the women who exhibit them are praised with a biblical, often Pauline, citation. For instance, might we modify our attitude to John Bale's editing of Anne Askew if we recognized this description 'Whan she semed most feble, than was she most stronge. And gladlye she rejoyced in that weakenesse, that Christes power myght strongelye dwell in her' as a quotation from 2 Corinthians 12:9–10 that aligns her with the Apostle Paul, as indeed Bale tells us that it is?[39]

[36] Heinrich Bullinger, *A brief and compendiouse table, in a maner of a concordaunce openyng the waye to the principall histories of the whole Bible, and the moste co[m]mon articles grounded and comprehended in the newe Testament and olde, in maner as amply as doeth the great concordau[n]ce of the Bible* (1550; STC 17117), A1r–A1v.

[37] Lodovico Guicciardini, *Houres of recreation, or afterdinners which may aptly be called The garden of pleasure* [London, 1576; STC 12465], A4r; the significance of Sanford's preface, which acknowledges the Cooke sisters and Lock as prominent and public figures, is discussed in Felch, 'Noble Gentlewomen'.

[38] Robert Cawdry, *A shorte and fruitefull treatise, of the profite and necessitie of catechising: that is, of instructing the youth, and ignorant persons in the principles and groundes of Christian religion. By Robert Cawdray, one of the ministers and preachers of the worde of God, in the countie of Rutland* (1580; STC 4882), A6r–A6v.

[39] Anne Askew, *The first examinacyon of Anne Askewe lately martyred in Smythfelde, by the Romysh popes vpholders, with the elucydacyon of Iohan Bale* ([Wesel], 1546; STC 848), *2v.

Similarly, William Cecil's praise of Katherine Parr in *The Lamentacion of a synner* as no Pharisee but a humble publican situates the queen firmly within one of the key Lollard and Reformation texts on true religion, the parable of the proud Pharisee in the Temple who upon seeing the publican, prays 'I am happy not to be like other men' while the publican himself merely cries out 'Lord be merciful to me'.[40] We should not underestimate the humble, patient, barefooted, ploughboy Christian as a powerful Protestant emblem for both men and women, particularly in the *early* early modern period.

It is easy to align these roles against one another – to say, for instance, that mothers have authority in the home but only under the direction of husbands, or that women can study and teach, but only the Bible and religious works and only at home, not in the university or church. But it is the responsibility of the editor, with her backward gaze, to recognize and articulate the complex, layered ways in which women participated in their own society, without too quickly imposing contemporary, and perhaps reductive, categories. Here, too, Pender's warning not to conflate *early* early modern with later early modern, in particular not to reduce the sixteenth century to a mere prelude of the seventeenth, is pertinent.

If we interpret the question 'What status do English women have in the religious discourse of the sixteenth century?' as asking 'What roles did Protestant women play in *shaping* religious discourse in the sixteenth century?', then again we encounter a range of answers, many of which have been rediscovered by the editorial work of women-centred scholars in the last three decades. Early modern women were translators, with all the richness and creativity this term connotes; they were poets and letter-writers; they were patrons and 'brethren', the term that Knox uses of both male and female friends and advisors; they wrote testimonies, which are essentially sermons preached without a pulpit, as can be seen in the works of Anne Askew and Anne Wheathill, the latter of whom claimed her prayerbook as 'a testimoniall to the world' applicable to friends and 'strangers' alike.[41] Of course, all these roles were further inflected by class and by the geographic location of the actors: in cities, at country houses, and in exile.

Not only are the contexts multiple, but so are the challenges of presenting them. Do we picture them as strands, layers, overlapping circles (as

---

[40] Katherine Parr, *The Lamentacion of a synner, made by the moste vertuous Lady quene Caterine, bewailyng the ignoraunce of her blind life* (1548; *STC* 4828), A6v.

[41] Anne Wheathill, *A handful of holesome (thought homelie) hearbs, gathered out of the goodlie garden of Gods most holie word; for the common benefit and comfortable exercise of all such as are devoutlie disposed* (1584; *STC* 25329), A2v. For a discussion of Wheathill's sermonic tropes, see Felch, "'Halff a Scripture Woman'".

in a Venn diagram), features of a unified landscape, or aspects of dominant, residual, and emerging cultures? Each of these organizational models takes our imagination, our questions, and therefore our answers in somewhat different directions. Are we committed to a thick description of local culture, which necessarily involves not isolating women writers into a gendered ghetto and which pushes us to describe affiliations and social circles, rather than succumbing to the alphabetized lists of names that still form our dominant biographical schema? Do we consistently use words like contradictory, paradoxical, transgressive, or disruptive to describe multiple contexts? Would the women we study recognize themselves in the descriptions we give? If we privilege some contexts over others, are we deploying a robust editorial empathy or 'creative understanding', or are we imposing our own ideological agenda on another culture?

None of these images, taxonomies, or terms is innocent. But editions necessarily pay close attention to all sorts of local detail and therefore have the potential to map a much richer contextual landscape in which to understand women writers and their texts. Editors should advocate for adductive reasoning as every bit as rigorous a mode of inquiry as deductive or inductive reasoning. Laying out multiple contexts without necessarily prioritizing them or organizing them into a hierarchy is one gift editors may offer to scholarly discourse, along with empathy and the backward gaze.

# CHAPTER 3

# Producing Gender
## Mary Sidney Herbert and Her Early Editors

### Danielle Clarke

The modes of authorship adopted by early modern women writers present multiple challenges to editors. Editing is inevitably a series of choices, set into a hierarchy of value. Often the *kinds* of materials being edited fall outside the scope and tradition of scholarly editing as it has been understood within the discipline of literature. Texts produced by women writers may be heavily mediated; they may represent an emergent rather than an established genre or form (not necessarily 'literary' in the strict sense); they may be decontextualized; they often lack a history of reception.[1] These conditions raise a series of questions about value, canonicity, context, aesthetics, and intertextuality that cannot be resolved simply by reference to the self-evident justification of the gender of the author(s). At the same time, editorial decisions about these questions serve to produce versions of female authorship.[2] Such materials challenge some of the key assumptions of scholarly editing as traditionally understood, despite increasing critical acknowledgement of the difficulties produced by a narrowly defined idea of texts and editing practices: 'elucidation is... a denial of the essential reality of obscurity'.[3]

Like many of the texts of their male counterparts (dramatists especially), it is rare that a female-authored text is purely and simply that, which inevitably troubles questions of attribution in the first instance, and literary agency in the second. With some exceptions (including the subject of this chapter), texts by women, whether manuscript and/or print, are far more likely to be represented by a single witness, and to represent something quite other than final intentions as conventionally understood: 'I was working on early modern women writers for whom in many cases only a single text, either printed or handwritten, was known', notes Margaret Ezell.[4] It is clear that the often obscure processes of textual manipulation that

---

[1] See Burke, 'Let's Get Physical', esp. p. 1668.
[2] See Clarke and Coolahan, 'Gender, Reception and Form'.     [3] Orgel, 'What is an Editor?', p. 25.
[4] Ezell, 'Editing Early Modern Women's Manuscripts', p. 103.

separate authorship from circulation were generally experienced rather differently by men and by women, by virtue of their discrete access to the public sphere. Nonetheless, a series of key issues arises: an absence of witnesses does not necessarily imply a lack of versionality, but it does compromise evidence; questions of circulation and reception are often indeterminate; attribution may be uncertain; and agency is contingent and negotiable.[5] I have suggested elsewhere that processes of editing also 'produce' or 'reproduce' women's writing and that the categories deployed in doing so tend to have a more significant critical impact than the editing of canonical male writers with an established editing history.[6]

This chapter gives an overview of changing positions in relation to the editing and textual representation of texts by early modern women, using Mary Sidney Herbert, Countess of Pembroke, as a case study. By virtue of her proximity to Sir Philip Sidney, she has been edited, anthologized, and analysed more widely than virtually any other woman writer, let alone poet. This chapter focuses on reception and circulation from the seventeenth to the late nineteenth centuries, and considers how these practices impact on the editing of Mary Sidney in the modern era. At different historical moments, Mary Sidney Herbert's gender has been more or less visible, and has been incorporated into editorial practices in a variety of ways, from being a central principle of presentation and selection through to erasure and ellipsis. Suzanne Trill has helpfully given a broad outline of these positions and notes that '[o]ur modern investment in individual ownership and authorship apparently precludes a full appreciation of what a truly collaborative project might mean'.[7] This point is significant, because it shapes fundamentally assumptions about what is to be edited, namely a text (and in this case, which text?) or an author (again, and which author?).

As Patricia Pender and others have argued, Mary Sidney's own role as editor and creator of the Sidney author-effect has been consistently over-looked and sidelined. I wish to suggest that the figure of Mary Sidney as mediated by successive editors needs to be understood not only in relation to the process of *being edited*, but in the context of her *being an editor*.[8] If, as seems to be the case, her psalm versions and revisions were undertaken alongside her extensive editorial work on Sir Philip Sidney's singly authored

---

[5] See Burke: 'Attribution is often especially fluid in manuscripts, due sometimes to error, or to the irrelevance of noting the author of a work well-known to the transcriber or audience, or simply to a greater interest in the content of the work than its originator on the part of a compiler who may be altering it further' ('Let's Get Physical', p. 1674).

[6] See Danielle Clarke, 'Nostalgia'.    [7] Trill, '"We thy Sydnean Psalmes"', p. 106.

[8] Pender, 'Ghost'.

output, we might be able to comprehend editing as a form of authorship, and authorship as a kind of editing. Or more radically, we might be able to see these activities as operating along a continuum of textual manipulation, particularly as Mary Sidney's literary output is characterized by its immersion in intertextual relationships of varying kinds. Thus, as Pender argues, 'Mary Sidney is not the "writer" of the 1598 *Arcadia*, but according to the critical insights of the history of the book, she is the material "author" of this book in print.'[9]

One of the key challenges in undertaking a diachronic analysis of the editorial strategies deployed to bring Mary Sidney's writings to a broader readership is that her body of work fails to fit any of the assumptions about early modern textuality that have historically structured ideas about how to edit Renaissance texts. As Margaret Ezell has noted, there is still no feminist cladistics, although there is now a wide range of editorial practice: much of this practice is market driven, determined by publishers, and geared to the needs of specific groups of readers, usually undergraduate students.[10] Yet many of the questions posed by Mary Sidney's corpus are also common to other early modern texts: collaborative authorship, the posthumous shaping of a poetic corpus to particular ends, indeterminacy of final intentions, lack of a printed text, versionality, structural relationships of textual dependency, restricted readership, formal experimentation, to name but a few. The conceptual underpinnings of the Countess of Pembroke's authorial strategies are clearly signalled both in the multiple paratexts that accompany her literary productions, and in her generic, modal, and stylistic choices. The oft-discussed metaphors of joining, coupling, warp, and weft all testify to the careful manipulation of the relationship between Mary and her brother: acknowledging (and appropriating) his contribution, but also asserting her own role alongside her right to present and represent Philip's work.

These metaphors testify to the *inseparability* of each writer's work, whether this is conceived as a relationship between idea or 'foreconceit', a process of working towards 'completion', or shepherding a text from manuscript circulation to print. The higher goal of realizing the Psalter as an English poetic artefact transcends singular authorial ambition, perhaps because this particular text was understood to be composite both in origin and orientation. Because of her role in bringing the Psalter to completion,

9  Pender, 'Ghost', p. 72.
10  But see the useful critical insights of Burke, 'Let's Get Physical'; Ezell, 'Editing Early Modern Women's Manuscripts'; Hageman, 'Making a Good Impression'; and Trill, 'A Feminist Critic in the Archives'.

many contemporary commentators focused on Mary as the primary producer of the text. In this regard, we might also note Mary Sidney's decision not to prepare any of the Psalms for the 1598 edition, perhaps suggesting that she did not think of them exclusively as Philip's literary 'property'.[11] Samuel Daniel, in his lengthy dedicatory poem to the Countess in 1594, mentions the precedent of Sir Philip, but in the stanza relating to the Psalter focuses exclusively on Mary's input:

> Those *Hymnes* thou doost consecrate to heaven,
> Which *Israels* Singer to his God did frame:
> Unto thy voice eternitie hath given,
> And makes thee deere to him from whence they came.[12]

Despite the repeated assertion of the authorial relationship as a collaborative one (both before and after death) and some contemporary (but less than unequivocal) acknowledgement of this (Donne, Spenser), once the texts (the Psalter in particular) move beyond the carefully controlled environment of manuscript circulation (and arguably, even then), Mary Sidney's contribution is quickly erased or overlooked.[13] As the antiquarian impulses of the post-Restoration period developed, individuals actively sought to preserve significant manuscripts, and the manuscripts of the Sidney Psalms enter a new phase of preservation and circulation. Our first 'editor' – in the sense of a mediating individual consciously producing a text for a particular readership, of the Sidney Psalter – is Samuel Woodford.[14] Woodford himself had a profound interest in the Psalter, producing a poetic paraphrase on the psalms in 1667, which presumably led him to the Sidney Psalter and enabled him to recognize what he had in front of him, having consulted the Trinity College Cambridge manuscript in the 1660s (MS G). Woodford's friendship with John Wilkins, the first president of the Royal Society, apparently secured him access to at least one of the working manuscripts of the Sidney Psalter, which he transcribed in 1694–5.[15] The erasure of the contribution of the Countess of Pembroke, already a feature of the early seventeenth-century manuscript circulation of the Sidney Psalter, is clearly articulated in Woodford's running annotations to the

---

[11] For discussion, see Clarke, 'The Psalms of Mary Sidney Herbert'.
[12] Samuel Daniel, *Delia and Rosamund Augmented* (London, 1594), H6r.
[13] See Reinstra and Kinnamon, 'Circulating the Sidney-Pembroke Psalter'.
[14] The distinction between a copyist or someone circulating a text, and an editor, is imprecise at best. But I designate Woodford the first editor because of his motivations in copying the text, namely that his orientation is towards the author rather than towards the reader.
[15] There is a set of links between the manuscripts of the Sidney Psalms and the Royal Society which may well reflect the literary and cultural interests of the Whigs.

manuscript.[16] Hannibal Hamlin asserts that the transcription was of the Countess of Pembroke's 'own autograph copy', and while this can only be speculative, the extent of the revisions indicates that the manuscript Woodford copied was one of her working copies.[17] The manuscript is significant because it provides unique evidence of the Countess's own practices of revision, as well as examples of her emendations to her brother's versions. This process of revision of 'Philip's' psalms has been a central crux both in critical accounts and in editorial practice, with some critics viewing Mary Sidney's efforts as obscuring the superior versions of Sir Philip (e.g. Ringler) or as rewriting to produce poetically less successful endings (e.g. Alexander).[18] In some editorial approaches the text is paramount, but in others, the author is pre-eminent, and where there are two potential authors, inevitably a hierarchy of aesthetic value comes into play, underpinned by an interpretation of the textual evidence. Establishing what Philip Sidney wrote is quite different from concluding that what Philip wrote constitutes the text in its final form. Clearly, the text in its final form comprises poems that are composite in their authorship, rather than singular. More recent criticism has gone to considerable lengths to confront the collaborative nature of this text fully, but as Patricia Pender has argued the inauguration of Philip as the English laureate requires a univocal point of origin, and the marginalization or erasure of the Countess of Pembroke.[19]

Woodford writes, 'The Original Copy is by mee Given me by my brother M[r] John Woodford who bought it among other broken books to putt up Coffee pouder as I rememb[r]'.[20] His authority as transcriber is underlined by questions of proximity and ownership, 'The Original Copy is *by* mee' (emphasis added). Unsurprisingly, the manuscript is incomplete, and we find: 'But from this place to the end my Copy is defective, the leaves being torn off. Ita testor Sam Woodforde who for sir Philip Sidnys sake, and to preserve such a remaine of him undertook this tiresome task of transcribing. 1694/5'.[21] Several things are striking about Woodford's exasperated comments on his labours. The first is the precision of his language:

---

[16]  Now Bodleian MS Rawlinson 25. Ringler suggests that this incomplete manuscript is derived from two of the Countess of Pembroke's working copies (*Poems of Sir Philip Sidney*, p. 503). Hannay, Kinnamon, and Brennan (eds.), *Collected Works*, argue for three (vol. II, p. 338).

[17]  Hamlin, 'Introduction', in Hamlin et al. (eds.), *The Sidney Psalter* (2009), p. xxxii.

[18]  Ringler (ed.), *Poems of Sir Philip Sidney* (1962); Alexander, *Writing After Sidney* (2006).

[19]  This process of producing an author figure is of course largely Mary Sidney's own doing.

[20]  Bodleian MS Rawlinson 25, fol. ii[r].

[21]  Woodford's annotations are quoted from Danielle Clarke (ed.), *Renaissance Women Poets*, p. 169. All subsequent references are to this text, unless otherwise noted.

using the term 'copy' to refer to his original, but pulling into play the sense of multiple witnesses, together with the word 'transcribing' (differentiated from 'copy') to mean 'to make a copy of (something) in writing; to copy out from an original; to write (a copy)' (*OED*). Woodford is one of the few early commentators to note the existence of multiple copies, although he seems unaware that these are in fact often *different* versions, suggesting that the late seventeenth century continues to understand written texts to be in some sense malleable and unstable. These senses of 'copy' are recorded in early seventeenth-century dictionaries, but gain currency in the latter part of the seventeenth century (Ia), suggesting a development in ideas about editing and the preservation of the states of different texts (*OED*). Woodford's comments on the manuscript that he is copying reveal an intention to reproduce the text as closely as possible, as he notates each addition and deletion. His comment on Psalm 49, for example,

> This third staffe is so blotted and often mended, that it is hardly perceptible what should and what should not stand. At first it stood thus . . . The second verse is also thus mended . . . expunged. The fifth also has *The wise and foole*, expunged. The sixth has *And others*, which is expungd, then *And who then spends*, expunged: Then the word *others* instead of *strangers* is left to stand as the last correction.[22]

Several things stand out. First, this is not a mere 'transcript' as Woodford subsequently claims, nor is it an attempt to arrive at a clean, 'final' version, rather it is a somewhat unsystematic snapshot of what Woodford saw on the page in front of him, with a speculative account of the sequencing of the additions, deletions, and alterations. He notes of Psalm 82: 'So it was at first corrected and the other expungd but this being after expung'd, *stet* is putt to the other.'[23] His term 'expunged' is used throughout the transcription, a relatively rare and rather erudite term; the *OED* defines it as 'to strike out, blot out, erase, omit (a name or word from a list, a phrase or passage from a book or record)', citing Fulbecke and Fuller. The manuscript itself uses strike-outs to indicate an altered or amended word, line, or passage, with a range of methods for writing in alterations (inter-lineation, superscript, marginalia). Woodford develops his own system of notation, gamely attempting to track the chronology of alterations, using the nomenclature of temporality. Once again in relation to Psalm 49 (one of the most fully recorded of the Psalms, perhaps because it occurs relatively early in the manuscript), we find 'Expunged, as also *Lord* in the fifth verse

[22] Clarke (ed.), *Renaissance Women Poets*, p. 58, n. 9.     [23] *Ibid.*, p. 108, n. 2.

after the correction putt for, *prince*'.[24] Woodford does not only take note of lexical changes, but also records alterations in verse length and pattern. For this purpose he distinguishes between 'verse' and 'staffe', where the latter almost always indicates a stanza and the former a line. So in relation to the final stanza of Psalm 49, Woodford notes:

> instead of the three first verses of this staffe there stood at first five thus, for which (possibly because therby the staffe was too long) the whole Psalm was crossd and mended.[25]

The evidence of the manuscript proves contradictory and perplexing to Woodford, who notes of Psalm 55 that a phrase has been deleted and then 'the verse in the Staffe enterlin'd in another hand'.[26] Yet this other hand does not lead Woodford to conclude anything other than that the annotations are authorial; indeed, the degree of alteration and revision strongly suggests to him the 'original' status of the text:

> The very manner of this Psalms being crossd and alterd almost in every line and in many words twice makes me beleive this was an originall book, that is that the book before me was so for none but an author could or would so amend any Copy.[27]

The glossing the use of the term 'originall' is intriguing when juxtaposed with the proper noun 'Copy' which presumably refers to the written text without any evaluative hierarchy in play. The insistence that the corrections are authorial persists throughout: 'all expunged as appears and correted [sic] by the Authors own hand'.[28] At no point does Woodford consider the possibility of more than one author, although he registers that not all corrections are in the same hand. Like many subsequent readers and critics, Woodford finds it difficult to conceive of anything other than a singular model of authorship. It is significant that this manuscript is the most important document for editors seeking to bifurcate the entangled collaboration of brother and sister so powerfully articulated in the dedicatory poems, and subsequently by Samuel Daniel and John Donne, given its assumption that text and revisions derive from a single point of origin.[29] Over the course of the seventeenth century, the reception of the Sidney Psalter registers a shift from a collaborative, doubled model of authorship incorporating male and female perspectives, to a singular model that all but ignores Mary Sidney's contribution. Woodford ultimately misinterprets the fragmentary manuscript evidence he has in front of him in the light of what he already

---

[24] *Ibid.*, p. 59, n. 14.   [25] *Ibid.*, p. 59, n. 16.   [26] *Ibid.*, p. 67, n. 1.
[27] *Ibid.*, p. 57, n. 1.   [28] *Ibid.*, p. 69, n. 6.   [29] See Trill, '"We thy Sydnean Psalmes"'.

knows (or thinks he knows) about the Sidney Psalter. After Mary Sidney's death in 1621, her contribution is frequently erased, unlike the 1618 van de Passe portrait, where the Countess is represented holding 'Davids Psalmes', though the medallion allies her with her husband, and not her brother. Because of the nature of coterie authorship and publication, those who were part of her circle knew what her role had been. Once the texts passed out of that circle, Mary Sidney's authorship was subject to erasure and loss, a pattern that endured, by and large, until the nineteenth century. Woodford assumes that his 'Author' is male: 'Before the Correction (by the Author under *his* own hand)', 'Written as I judg by the Author *himself* and added'; and subsequently identifies 'him' as Philip. Woodford's transcription is an attempt at preservation, and to transmit a 'remaine' of Sir Philip Sidney.[30] The identification of the 'author' as male, and the reluctance to consider the possibility of a more complex model of authorship, is of a piece with the development of the 'author function' in English culture and publication in the latter half of the seventeenth century, perhaps nowhere more boldly stated than in the redaction of the complexity of dramatic authorship into 'Shakespeare's' First Folio.

The reception history of the Sidney Psalms (and the designation is productive, I think, for its evasion of both the possessive and the pronoun) shows a consistent pattern of tension around authorship. One of the rare examples of the reception of the Psalms in the eighteenth century appears in the short-lived *Guardian*, edited by Richard Steele and Joseph Addison, first published in March–June of 1713. Citing it as a rarity, they include a version of Psalm 137, which has variants consistent with manuscript E, but others that derive from no obvious source, and which may merely be transcription errors.[31] The Psalm, one of the most popular within the English poetic tradition,[32] is introduced thus:

> Sir Philip Sidney was a noble example of courage and devotion. I am particularly pleased to find that he hath translated the whole book of Psalms into English verse. A friend of mine informs me, that he hath the manuscript by him, which is said in the title to have been done 'By the most noble and virtuous Gent. Sir Philip Sidney, Knight.' They having been never printed, I shall present the public with one of them, which my correspondent assures me he hath faithfully transcribed, and where I have taken the liberty only to alter one word.[33]

---

[30] Clarke (ed.), *Renaissance Women Poets*, p. 99, n. 1; *ibid.*, p. 165, n. 1.

[31] l. 14, the rain Q, E] their A; l. 15 no voice] nor voice A; l. 17 far I be I] farre I ly A; l. 26 plaines of Edom] paines of Edom A; l. 32 and a waste] all platt pais A; l. 38 make thee see I, E] cause thee see A.

[32] Hamlin, 'Psalm Culture in the English Renaissance'.      [33] *Guardian*, 18 (1 April 1713), 109.

This issue of the periodical is attributed to 'Steele', but the account of the provenance of the text uncannily echoes earlier rhetorics of modesty and privacy that structure manuscript circulation. The 'friend' is the witness; his access to the manuscript is authorized by proximity (if not ownership); he has 'faithfully transcribed' what he sees in the text, and Steele himself has only altered 'one word' – according to the text from Steele copied into MS L (Huntington Library), 'Nigh' for 'High' in the first line.[34] Yet the presentation of the text merely confirms and underlines the emergent notion of the Sidney Psalter as a 'private' text – in ways that are not unequivocally true of its contemporary circulation, where, in Hannay's words, it might be better understood in terms of restricted circulation.[35] Steele's quoted title suggests a manuscript from the sigma group, which all incorporate 'most noble and virtuous gentleman', but the most likely candidate for Steele's source, based on contextual evidence, is MS D (Wadham College, Oxford).[36] The manuscripts from this group assert Philip's authorship and do not mention the role of the Countess of Pembroke. The editors of the *Collected Works* note that the 'old title' written in probably comes from Steele's essay, where the phrase '"Translation of the Book of Psalms" may be particularly significant because no other title in the extant manuscripts describes the metrical Psalter in just that way'.[37]

In a later collection of the *Guardian*, Philip's authorship is questioned by the addition of a footnote which reads '[h]as not Mr Wharton settled it that only a part of the book of psalms was translated, and that by sir Philip's sister?'[38] This must refer to Thomas Warton, author of the four-volume *History of Poetry*, which includes a substantial and informative chapter on the translation and reception of the Psalter in the sixteenth century. Yet, this work nowhere refers specifically to a Sidney translation of the Psalms, despite Warton's abiding interest in Sir Philip. Warton does refer, however, to Hall's *Epistles*, quoting the following passage:

> Many great wits have undertaken this task.—Among the rest, were those two rare spirits of the Sidnyes [sic]; to whom poesie was as naturall as it is affected of others.[39]

Warton's *History and Antiquities of Kiddington* discussing Gervase Babington, the chaplain at Wilton, notes that Babington was 'an assistance to Mary Sidney, Countess of Pembroke, in her translation of the Psalms'.[40]

---

[34] Hannay et al. (eds.), *Collected Works*, vol. II, p. 332.
[35] Hannay, 'The Countess of Pembroke's Agency in Print and Scribal Culture', p. 35.
[36] Hannay et al. (eds.), *Collected Works*, vol. II, pp. 327–34.    [37] *Ibid.*, vol. II, pp. 324–5, n. 37.
[38] *Guardian*, ed. J. Johnson (1806).    [39] *History of Poetry*, vol. IV (London, 1774), p. 53.
[40] Warton, *History and Antiquities of Kiddington*, 3rd edn (London, 1815), p. 46.

Cumulatively, these examples suggest that Mary Sidney's contribution to the Psalter, whilst unquantified and not studied, was known throughout the seventeenth and eighteenth centuries, even if the texts of the Psalms themselves were not. The editing and reprinting of the *Guardian* by figures like Alexander Chalmers did keep the texts in circulation, despite the critical narrative which suggests that they largely disappeared from view.[41] Equally, the *idea* of Mary Sidney's authorship and interest in poetry was kept alive by a series of texts related to the emergent notion of biography, starting with Aubrey's *Lives*. Aubrey mentions the Psalter kept at Wilton, but merely quotes the partial title of the manuscript, 'all the *Psalmes of David* translated by Sir Philip Sydney, curiously bound in crimson velvet',[42] truncating the contribution of Mary Sidney: '& finished by the R: honnorable the Countesse of *Pembroke*, his Sister, & by her dirrection & appointment'.[43] Ballard, nearly a century later, continues a tradition of lauding exceptional and exemplary women in his *Memoirs of Several Ladies of Great Britain*, with his account of Mary Sidney 'Sister of the matchless Sir Philip Sydney'. He writes:

> She had an excellent natural Genius: And having the advantages of a polite education, when according to the custom of that age, literature was reckoned a considerable part of politeness, she made an illustrious appearance among the literati of that time, who have given ample testimony of her great merit . . . As her genius inclined her to poetry, so she spent much of her time in that way. She translated many of the Psalms into English verse, which are bound in velvet, and as I told, still preserved in the library at Wilton.[44]

This derives from Aubrey, but is reframed in terms of the eighteenth-century expectations and sensibilities ('polite education', 'Genius') that came to define the transmission of early modern women's writing (see the Introduction to this volume, pp. 3–4).

Equally, representations of the *idea* of Mary Sidney as poet and author are found in various texts, including Lanyer's *Salve Deus Rex Judaeorum* (1611), Bathsua Makin's *Essay to Revive the Antient Education of Gentlewomen* (London, 1673), and John Heywood's *Guneikeion* (1624), where she is compared to Vittoria Colonna:

> with whom (though not in that Funerall Elegaicke straine) I may ranke (if in the comparison I underprise not) the beautifull and learned ladie *Mary*,

---

[41] See *The Psalms of Sir Philip Sidney and the Countess of Pembroke*, ed. Rathmell, p. xxx.
[42] Oliver Lawson Dick (ed.), *Aubrey's Brief Lives* (London: Penguin, 1949), p. 220.
[43] Title page of MS A, facsimile reproduced in Rathmell (ed.), *The Psalms*, p. xxxiii.
[44] Ballard, *Memoirs of Several Ladies of Great Britain* (Oxford, 1752), pp. 259–60.

Countesse of Penbrooke, the worthie sister to her unmatchable brother Sir *Philip Sydney*. But not to dwell too long on her prayse (whom I never can commend sufficiently) I will onely bestow upon her Muse that Character which *Horace* bequeathed to *Sapho*.[45]

There are close links between many of these texts, so that Chalmers' *General Biographical Dictionary* (1795) cites the publication of Psalms in Harington's *Nugae Antiquae*, as well as composing the following entry:

HERBERT (Mary), countess of Pembroke, and a very illustrious female... She was not only a great encourager of letters; but a careful cultivator of them herself... She is supposed to have made an exact translation of 'David's Psalms' into English metre.[46]

Even though Chalmers knew of Mary Sidney's translation, he clearly had not seen the manuscript itself, and possibly refers to the van de Passe portrait.

Almost all of the printed witnesses to the Sidney Psalter in the later seventeenth and eighteenth centuries rely on a single manuscript witness (or sometimes an intermediary printed text) and they mostly appear to be unaware of the multiple manuscripts, or that the versions they reproduce only have contingent authority. Woodford, for example, notes the existence of another manuscript in the context of the missing psalms in MS B:

But here all the leaves are torn off, to the 23 verse of the CII. Psalme, to be supplyed if possible from some other Copy, of w$^{ch}$ there is a fayre one in Trinity Colledg library in Cambridg, & of w$^{ch}$ many years since I had ye sight when I first began my Paraphrase.[47]

Woodford's own *Paraphrase upon the Psalms of David* was printed in 1667, so he must have seen the Trinity manuscript in the 1660s. Despite his attempts to convey the complexities of revision in MS B, Woodford does not speculate on the possible relationship between the two texts he has witnessed, admittedly thirty years apart. The various printed texts of a small selection of Psalms also give some clues to circulation and reception, although, once again, they almost all rely on a single manuscript, and seem to have no knowledge of the various manuscripts in existence at this time. I have already outlined the evidence for the text in the *Guardian* being the manuscript now kept at Wadham College, Oxford, but the texts of Psalms 51, 104, 137, 69, 112, 117, and 128 (the last three added in 1779)

---

[45] John Heywood, *Guneikeion* (1624), p. 398.
[46] Alexander Chalmers, *General Biographical Dictionary* (1795), p. 186.
[47] Bodleian MS Rawlinson 25, fol. 82$^{v}$.

printed in *Nugae Antiquae* (1775) by Henry Harington are taken from BL MS Additional 12047, which 'probably descends from a Harington source'.[48] This assumption is strengthened by the fact that versions of Psalms 51, 104, and 137 were sent by John Harington to Lucy, Countess of Bedford, in a letter dated 29 December 1600, described as follows:

> I have sent yow heere the devine, and trulie devine translation of three of Davids psalmes, donne by that Excellent Countesse, and in Poesie the mirroir of our Age.[49]

There is no sense in these versions that there might be more than one text, nor that revision might be a central element in textual production, nor that authorship might be collaborative. The Harington 'tradition' of transmission and circulation preserves the Countess of Pembroke's authorship, perhaps because of Harington's close knowledge of her working practices; other traditions, removed from the original circle, make the default assumption that the work must be Philip's.

In Thomas Zouch's *Memoirs of the Life and Writings of Sir Philip Sidney* (1808), the Psalms are included in the list of Philip Sidney's works, even as Zouch argues for the Countess of Pembroke's authorship, which is symptomatic of a tendency for assumptions about the gendering of authorship to frame evidence that unsettles these alliances. His commentary is heavily influenced by both Aubrey and Ballard, revealing how interpretation of these texts is frequently influenced by a small number of commentators, not all of them reliable or authoritative:

> A copy of this version, curiously bound in crimson velvet, is said to be in the library at Wilton; which Mr Ballard in his memoirs of several ladies of Great Britain, &c. attributes to the Countess of Pembroke. It seems very probable, and may I think, be easily inferred from Dr. Donne's poems on the translation of the Psalms by Sir Philip Sidney and his sister, that it was the joint work of them both.[50]

It is surprising that Donne's poem has not been taken more seriously as evidence of contemporary understanding of the nature of collaborative authorship in the case of the Sidney Psalter, rather it has tended to be used as a way to prove circulation and reception, as well as a kind of celebrity poetic endorsement of a very particular kind of aesthetic project.[51] Zouch, unusually, takes the poem as evidence, reading it through the lens of

---

[48]  Hannay et al. (eds.), *Collected Works*, vol. II, p. 318.
[49]  Inner Temple Library, MS Petyt 538/43, fol. 303[v].
[50]  Ballard, *Memoirs of Several Ladies*, 2nd edn (York, 1809), p. 366.
[51]  Trill, '"We thy Sydnean Psalmes"'.

authorship. Zouch reproduces two Psalms, 93 and 137 (the latter appearing in the *Guardian* and in *Nugae Antiquae*) in his Appendices, using the fair copy in Trinity College, Cambridge – a highly influential manuscript in terms of circulation, presumably because it was relatively accessible in a way that other manuscripts were not.

The next phase in the reception and editing of the Sidney Psalter is spearheaded by the work of Henry Cotton, whose discovery of the Psalms ushers in the first complete edition of the modern era, and opens up the prospect of the need for serious editorial work on the manuscripts of the Psalms. Cotton's initial interventions are found in an essay 'On Psalmody' printed in volume 3 of the *Christian Remembrancer* in June 1821. His response to the Sidney Psalter is primarily aesthetic:

> passages of considerable beauty: and notwithstanding the stiffness character-
> istic of the poetry of that day, there is often peculiar happiness of expression,
> a nerve and energy, a poetic spirit that might have disarmed, even if it could
> not extort praise from, the fastidious Warton himself.[52]

For Cotton, the key to the Sidney Psalter's neglect and lack of reputation is the fact that it has not been printed – Cotton was sub-librarian of the Bodleian library until his resignation in 1822, so he probably encountered the text in the course of his work (including Rawlinson B and C, the former being Woodford's transcript). He writes

> a translation of them little known amongst us, because it has never yet
> been communicated to the world through the medium of the press. The
> version to which I allude, is that by Sir Philip Sidney, or as Ballard and some
> others maintain, the joint production of him and his accomplished sister
> the Countess of Pembroke.[53]

For Cotton the question of authorship is ultimately less important than the neglect of the text itself, and his arguments mark a further phase in the circulation of the Psalter – one that interprets the text primarily through the mediation of print; at least until the sustained scholarly attentions of editors such as Ringler and Rathmell in the 1960s brought the subtleties and complexities of manuscript circulation into play – a focus that has formed a crucial part of the critical interpretation of the Sidney Psalter subsequently. Cotton alludes to the restricted circulation of the text up until this point, and sees its continuing obscurity as a form of adherence to tradition, a tradition that he thinks should be broken:

---

[52]   Henry Cotton, 'On Psalmody', *Christian Remembrancer*, 3 (June 1821), p. 330.
[53]   Cotton, 'On Psalmody', p. 330. Note the echo of Zouch's 'joint'.

Will it be thought an answer, to say, that all this was done by gentlemen, by amateurs, by collectors? who laid down to themselves a narrow path, that of giving *again* to the world what it had once possessed, before, and that from this they were unwilling to depart? What had been once edited, might be *edited again*: but as this work of Sir Philip Sidney had never been *printed*, it was clear that no *print* of it could be made.[54]

One might notice here the elision of the Countess of Pembroke from the previous conditional invocation of her authorship ('as Ballard and some others maintain'), a move that is replicated in Ruskin's *Rock Honeycomb*, where he seems to have no awareness of the Countess's role in the production of the Psalter. Cotton, like many others before him, reproduces Psalm 137, because it has already been printed, but also, more radically, because this opens the way to a fuller understanding of the complexities of transmission:

> This very circumstance . . . has added to my reasons for producing it here, in order that other variations between the manuscripts from which it was before printed, and my own, may be perceived: and that should hereafter any person feel disposed to put the whole version in print, he may be aware that a collation of several manuscripts will be desirable, if not absolutely necessary, for his work.[55]

Cotton's work is of primary importance, first because of his editorial insight (only fully developed in the editorial work of Feuillerat and Ringler), and second because of his endorsement of the aesthetic value of the Psalter. This is said to have resulted in the production of the first printed edition of the Sidney Psalms – the text produced by the Chiswick Press in 1823, an edition which represents a significant development, both in the acknowledgement of collaborative authorship and in tackling the textual complexity of the Psalter.

These developments can be calibrated by the subtle, but highly significant shifts in the use of the word 'version' from Zouch (where it seems to allude to the Psalter as a whole), to Cotton (where it seems to suggest an acknowledgement of the plurality of the text), to Samuel Weller Singer, who confronts the issues of transmission, originals, and authorship directly without arriving at any kind of resolution.[56] The title page of the Chiswick Press edition uses the titular format of the manuscript now known as A: 'The Psalmes of David, translated into Divers and Sundry Kindes of

---

[54] *Ibid.*     [55] Cotton, 'On Psalmody', p. 331.

[56] I am indebted to Sarah Ross for this point. Singer was a prolific editor of English poetry and drama: see Sidney Lee, rev. P. J. Connell, 'Singer, Samuel Weller (1783–1858)', *ODNB*.

Verse', and notes that the Psalter was started by Sir Philip and 'finished' by the Countess of Pembroke. The verso of the title page uses the van de Passe portrait of the Countess of Pembroke holding a (manuscript) copy of 'David's Psalmes', thus reinforcing her authorial position in relation to the resulting text. Singer makes the point that the edition

> was undertaken at the suggestion of James Boswell, Esq. who purposed writing an Introduction, in which the different Versions were intended to have been compared.[57]

The text, taken from the copy made by John Davies of Hereford (the Penshurst MS), has been, it is claimed, collated with at least two other manuscripts, the one owned by Cotton, and another owned by the prolific collector Richard Heber, which Henry Woudhuysen, following Peter Beal's research, identifies as MS H.[58] Singer writes, 'this has been carefully collated with a MS copy in his [Cotton's] collection, and some errors of transcription amended', and his preface goes on to note Woodford's transcription in the Bodleian Library, with an overt focus on the question of the division of authorial labour, as well as a recognition of the wide divergence between different manuscripts, a divergence that quickly resolves into a question of authorship.[59] At this point, it is clear that the goal of an authoritative, authorial manuscript has been set up as the high-water mark, but that the possibility of further manuscripts has not been ruled out:[60]

> it is possible that the original Autograph MS. of Sir Philip Sidney may still exist in the library at Wilton. It would have been desirable to have ascertained this, as it might prove which were versified by him, and which by his sister. This I have not been able to accomplish.[61]

What is striking about this edition is the way in which it marks a clear transition into a much more systematic textual criticism, and the extent to which it considers the question of authorship to be largely quantitative, namely the division of a collaborative undertaking into two discrete parts, notwithstanding Singer's listing of Donne's poem as one of the texts in which the Sidney Psalter 'has been incidentally mentioned'.[62] The edition,

57  Samuel Weller Singer (ed.), *The Psalmes of David* (London: Chiswick Press, 1823), p. v.
58  Woudhuysen, *Sir Philip Sidney and the Circulation of Manuscripts*, p. 399, n. 8.
59  Singer (ed.), *The Psalmes of David*, p. vi. The citations from Woodford's transcription (discussed above) Singer took from the notes published by Bulkeley Bandinel, Bodley's Librarian from 1813 to 1860. They use Woodford's comments to suggest that the first part was written by Sir Philip, and the rest by the Countess of Pembroke (Singer (ed.), *The Psalmes of David*, p. vii). See Mary Clapinson, 'Bulkeley, Bandinel (1781–1861)', *ODNB*.
60  'There is no doubt that other copies are to be found on a diligent search in the public libraries' (Singer (ed.), *The Psalmes of David*, p. x).
61  *Ibid.*, p. vi.    62  *Ibid.*

following Bandinel's lead (in turn based upon his interpretation of the title of the manuscript, which may or may not be contemporary), assumes that Philip and Mary are each authors in their own right, and that the relationship between the two 'parts' of the manuscript is sequential and temporally defined:

> the first portion was written by Sir Philip, and the latter by the Countess, and not certain Psalms, or various parts, by either of them.[63]

What is suggested here is a model of dual authorship, or a completion scenario, rather than the process of rewriting and revision that later editors, with access to a fuller range of manuscripts, have identified, viewing this either as a positive (*Collected Works*; Hamlin; Rathmell) or as a negative influence requiring correction (Ringler).

This evidence, along with the work produced by the essayist Nathan Drake, suggests that Ruskin's excision of the Countess of Pembroke's authorship in *Rock Honeycomb* is in fact anomalous in the context of a broader history of reception, rather than typical, as various commentators have assumed. In *Mornings in Spring, or Retrospections, Biographical, Critical and Historical*, Drake devotes three chapters to the literary production and lives of the Sidneys, and reproduces excerpts from several of Mary Sidney's Psalm versions, alongside other biographical and contextual materials. Drake highlights Mary Sidney's authorship to a greater extent than any of his predecessors, while depending largely on the same source materials, as mediated through Singer's edition, characterizing the Psalter as 'one of the strongest proofs of their piety and reciprocal attachment'.[64] He notes the Countess of Pembroke's role as editor of the *Arcadia*, 'subsequently revised and corrected by her pen', arguing that it is effectively a joint production.[65] Drake's conceptualization of authorship is more obviously collaborative than those of his predecessors, seeing its genesis in shared origins, education, temperament, and talent: 'they appear almost uniformly to have trodden the same paths and to have studied the same writers'.[66] This model then erases gender in an entirely different way – by seeing it as entirely invisible and/or irrelevant:

> There is, in truth, something inexpressibly pleasing and interesting in picturing to ourselves this accomplished brother and sister, the beautiful, the brave, thus conjointly employed in the service of their God, thus emulously endeavouring to do justice to the imperishable strains of divine inspiration.[67]

---

[63] *Ibid.*, p. vii.
[64] Nathan Drake, *Mornings in Spring*, vol. 1 (London: John Murray, 1828), p. 114.
[65] *Ibid.*, pp. 133, 158.  [66] *Ibid.*, p. 164.  [67] *Ibid.*, p. 208.

While detailing the Countess's literary output, Drake concludes 'it is . . . on her version of the Psalms, written in conjunction with her brother, that her poetical fame must be built'.[68] Repeatedly, Drake insists on the aesthetic quality of the Psalter *and* on Mary Sidney's joint role in its production: 'much the greater part of this joint version came from the pen of the Countess of Pembroke'.[69] It is as if the precedent and example of Sir Philip enables Mary to achieve poetic brilliance, even as she outdoes him (as both of them are seen to surpass previous versions): 'I cannot but think that she has on this occasion, struck the lyre with a fuller and deeper inspiration than her brother.'[70] Significantly, perhaps, this evaluation focuses on 'inspiration' rather than intellect or poetic skill as such.

Ruskin's *Rock Honeycomb* (1877), subtitled 'Broken Pieces of Sir Philip Sidney's Psalter', attempts to domesticate the Psalter, as part of Ruskin's project for education and enlightenment, St George's Guild, and this intended purpose and audience frames his interpretation of the text. Ruskin is throughout concerned with a specifically English poetic and devotional ideal, embodied for him by the figure of Sir Philip Sidney, but also with the domestication and dissemination of the Psalter for both moral and aesthetic reasons. That this is a masculine ideal is repeatedly underlined by Ruskin's continual scepticism about attribution and his consistent marginalization of the figure of Mary Sidney. Later critics have assumed that Ruskin was simply unaware of the role played by the Countess of Pembroke, but the evidence I have analysed suggests that this was unlikely to have been the case; not least because the edition upon which Ruskin relied was Singer's, and most of his preface is taken up with precisely this question. At no point does Ruskin specifically rule out her authorship, and he repeatedly raises the possibility that the text is not solely attributable to Philip. This statement might be seen as fairly representative:

> I have chosen this body of paraphrases of the Psalter, attributed *in part* to Sir Philip Sidney, and *whether his or not*, better written than any other rhymed version of the Psalms . . . of peculiar value as a classic model of the English language at the time of its culminating perfection.[71]

Here the doubt over authorship is raised ('attributed in part', 'whether his or not') but not developed, even to the point of speculating on the contribution of other hands. For Ruskin, the apparent impossibility of separating out Sir Philip's work is indicative of the editorial and textual

---

[68] *Ibid.*, p. 170.     [69] *Ibid.*, p. 178.     [70] *Ibid.*, p. 183.
[71] John Ruskin (ed.), *Bibliotheca Pastorum*, vol. II (London, 1877), pp. x–xi. Emphasis added.

deficiencies of Singer's text, rather than being an intrinsic feature of the manuscript upon which Singer relied:

> I had with me the little Chiswick press edition... expecting to find it tolerably correct, and not doubting but that I should be able, with little difficulty, if any part of it were really Sidney's, to distinguish his work from that of any other writer concerned in the book, and arrange it for publication in a separate form... I perceived it to require complete revision, the punctuation being all set at random; and the text full of easily corrigible misreadings.[72]

Thwarted by textual evidence, Ruskin turns to different criteria for selection: 'I omit the pieces which, either by accident or *by inferior authorship*, fall greatly below the general standard.'[73] Ruskin does not go so far as to equate 'inferior authorship' with non (Philip) Sidney authorship, although the implication is clear. Yet by p. xvii, these authorship issues have been redacted into a single figure:

> Sir Philip will use any cowboy's or tinker's words, if only they help him to say precisely in English what David said in Hebrew.[74]

At almost every point where Ruskin identifies a stylistic infelicity, he resorts to a formulation that implies a distance between the text as he has it and the figure of Sir Philip Sidney. In the commentary on Psalm 44, for example, Ruskin observes, 'This writer (Sidney, or whoever it may be) is apt to be strangely careless in his last lines.'[75] This equation between singular masculine authorship and aesthetic triumph leads to a significant degree of irony in the light of subsequent (and previous) scholarship:

> This entirely beautiful psalm [55] has been made the subject by Sidney of his best art of verse; and the paraphrase is one of the notablest pieces of rhythmic English in existence.[76]

Stylistic similarity to Sidney's other work is occasionally enlisted to clinch the (singular) authorship question, as in the case of Psalm 69, where Ruskin comments:

> The measure of it is so good, and this quaintness so like Sidney, that I should now hold it quite characteristically his, *if reading without prejudice*.[77]

Quite what 'reading without prejudice' means in this context is not clear, but presumably Ruskin means the (to him) unsubstantiated claims that the

---

[72] *Ibid.*, p. xi.   [73] *Ibid.*, p. xiii, my emphasis.   [74] *Ibid.*, p. xvii.
[75] *Ibid.*, p. 155.   [76] *Ibid.*, p. 174.   [77] *Ibid.*, p. 191, emphasis added.

Countess of Pembroke wrote or completed Psalms 44–150. Even Woodford's transcript of the partial working copy is unable to distinguish between
Sidney and his sister; it is based on the assumption that all corrections,
re-workings, and amendments are authorial, and that that author is Sidney,
not Mary.

The early editorial and textual history (which is also a reception history)
of the Sidney Psalter points to several key strands that inform and underpin
subsequent scholarship; what is striking is that the same kinds of arguments
have been played out in relation to the sophisticated scholarly work that has
been done on the Sidney Psalter, with slightly different emphases in virtually
every case. The first and most dominant topic has been that of attribution:
who wrote what, in what order, and which Psalms can be said to 'belong' to
which writer. Singer's edition (like that of Rathmell in 1963 and latterly that
of Hamlin in 2009) treats the Psalter as an autonomous text, the product
of collaborative authorship, with the focus squarely on the production
and establishment of an authoritative *text*. For some editors, aiming at the
establishment of a text with authority, informed by the concept of final
intentions, the role of Mary Sidney has proved problematic (many of these
editors are relatively uninterested in Mary Sidney as a poet in her own right)
because of her role as reviser, editor, and producer of her brother's work, a
role that for her involves processes more active than simply attempting to
preserve or reproduce exactly what her brother wrote.[78] Ringler's edition of
the works of Sir Philip Sidney specifically sets out to remove the revisions
made by the Countess of Pembroke and to restore 'Philip's' texts; here
the question of authorship is elevated above the integrity of the text as a
whole, and individual psalms are prioritized above the Psalter, suggesting
their alliance with poetry rather than with devotion.[79] Equally, but with a
different critical agenda in place, the authoritative two-volume Clarendon
Press edition of the works of the Countess of Pembroke similarly attempts
to establish the text(s) of what Mary Sidney *wrote* (its textual conclusions
are for the most part very similar to those of Ringler), without wider
reference to the purpose and functions of the Psalter as a whole, namely
that no contemporary (or later reader for that matter) would have thought
to divide a text so powerfully indebted to an inherited model into two
truncated parts, an action that disrupts the internal patterning of the
Psalter as a formal entity, as well as elevating a category (authorship) that is
at best marginal to the production of a divine text. It is notable that the very
earliest presentation of the Sidney Psalter, the presentation copy prepared

---

[78]  See Pender, 'Ghost'.        [79]  See Greene, 'Sir Philip Sidney's Psalms'.

for the proposed royal visit to Wilton in 1599, engages with the question of attribution, the prefatory poems by Mary Sidney asserting simultaneously that it is 'this coupled work', produced by 'their Senders', but also suggestive of the sequential model of authorship that informs most critical accounts, 'hee did warpe, I weav'd this webb to end'.[80] Nonetheless, the final text is the undifferentiated work of brother and sister: 'And I the Cloth in *both our names* present', and this assertion of the collaborative nature of the text's production needs to be taken seriously as a key interpretive and critical principle.[81]

[80] 'To the Angell Spirit', line 2; 'Even Now that Care', lines 20–1, 27.
[81] 'Even Now that Care', line 33.

# CHAPTER 4

# Editing the Feminist Agenda
## The Power of the Textual Critic and Elizabeth Cary's
## The Tragedy of Mariam

### Ramona Wray

Elizabeth Cary's *The Tragedy of Mariam* – the first original drama to be authored by a woman – was composed between *c.* 1603 and *c.* 1606, entered in the Register of the Stationers' Company on 17 December 1612, and printed by Thomas Creede for Richard Hawkins in 1613.[1] While there is only one early edition of *The Tragedy of Mariam*, it is possible that the play circulated in manuscript form for several years before publication.[2] That Cary was recognized in her time as a translator, poet, and dramatist is clear both in the evidence of Cary's surviving work and in the light of contemporary reference. In addition to Richard Bellings's 1624 preface to a continuation of the Countess of Pembroke's *Arcadia*, in which he thanks Cary, his '*patronesse*', for her '*many favours*', there is the 1633 edition of the dramatic works of Marston addressed to her, which confirms Cary's attachment to metropolitan theatrical culture.[3] Given that the corpus of plays of which *The Tragedy of Mariam* is a part (that is, the broad corpus of Renaissance drama) has been edited more than any other dramatic

---

My thanks to Sarah Ross, Paul Salzman, and two anonymous readers for their very helpful feedback on an earlier version of this chapter.

[1] Unless otherwise stated, all quotations from *The Tragedy of Mariam* are taken from the Arden Early Modern Drama edition, ed. Wray, and appear in the text.

[2] The printing survives in twenty-one extant copies. The one major variant resides with leaf A1 (the dedicatory poem and *dramatis personae*): this is missing from all but two copies.

[3] Richard Bellings, *A Sixth Booke to the Countesse of Pembrokes Arcadia* (1624), sig. A2ʳ; John Marston, *The Workes* (1633), A4ʳ. Cary's own extant work includes a manuscript translation from the French of *L'Epitome du Théâtre du Monde d'Abraham Ortelius* (1588/1590), a history of Edward II written in 1626 and published in two versions in 1680, and a 1630 translation of Jacques Davy du Perron's *Reply* dedicated to Queen Henrietta Maria. Cary's surviving letters are edited by Heather Wolfe (*Elizabeth Cary, Lady Falkland: Life and Letters* (Cambridge: RTM, 2001)). Missing, but mentioned in the *Life*, which is reprinted in the Wolfe volume, are translations of Seneca's epistles (p. 106), a religious treatise (p. 214), a 'life of Tamberlaine in verse' (p. 110), 'verses...on...our Blesed Lady' (p. 135), a letter of advice (p. 114), a translation of the writings of Louis de Blois (p. 106), and other assorted literary materials. Most intriguing, perhaps, is John Davies's reference, in a 1612 dedication, to a play by Cary, her first, set in Syracuse on the island of Sicily (John Davies, *The Muses Sacrifice* (1612), sig. *3ᵛ).

grouping at any point in history, one might expect *The Tragedy of Mariam* to have a long editorial tradition. Editions of Shakespeare, as critics such as Andrew Murphy have demonstrated, are an industry in and of themselves. Similarly, in part because of his critical standing and influence, editions of Shakespeare's contemporaries, such as Marlowe and Middleton, have been produced over a long period stretching from the seventeenth century to the present.[4] However, in contradistinction to many early modern plays, *The Tragedy of Mariam* was not edited until 1914, three hundred years after it first appeared in print. Presented in facsimile by A. C. Dunstan and W. W. Greg as part of Oxford University Press's Malone Society Reprints Series, the edition's major contribution was in identifying Cary as the play's author (previously, the initials, E. C., had meant that the play had not been definitively attributed).[5]

Despite the clarification of the play's authorship, after 1914 editorial silence descended once again. It seemed as if Elizabeth Cary was to fit what Margaret Anne Doody has described as the typical profile of the 'Also Ran', a woman artist who is 'admired... during her own time... published... widely discussed and known – and then vanishes'.[6] But then, in 1994, and like buses, two fine scholarly editions came along at once.[7] And more editions were to follow. In fact, in the latter years of the twentieth and the early years of the twenty-first centuries, the play was edited many times as part of the great flowering of interest in women's writing. *The Tragedy of Mariam* was edited in conjunction with Cary's other writing, alongside writing by other women writers and, most recently, as single editions.[8] As one of a handful of early modern texts by a woman that has been multiply edited, Cary's *The Tragedy of Mariam* stands as exemplary of the trends and problems associated with the theory and practice of textual editing as it has been employed in relation to women writers over the past twenty-five years.[9] A history of editing Cary is, in many ways, a

---

[4] See Murphy, *Shakespeare in Print*; Lopez, *Constructing the Canon*.

[5] The Dunstan and Greg edition was reprinted in 1992 with a new introduction by Marta Straznicky and Richard Rowland.

[6] Doody, 'Response', p. 127.

[7] These were Purkiss (ed.), *Renaissance Women* (1994); '*The Tragedy of Mariam, The Fair Queen of Jewry' with 'The Lady Falkland: Her Life',* by One of Her Daughters, ed. Weller and Ferguson (1994).

[8] *The Tragedy of Mariam*, ed. Britland (2010); *The Tragedy of Mariam*, ed. Hodgson-Wright (2000); Cerasano and Wynne-Davies (eds.), *Renaissance Drama by Women* (1996); *The Tragedy of Mariam*, ed. [Hodgson-]Wright (1996); Purkiss (ed.), *Renaissance Women* (1994); '*The Tragedy of Mariam*', ed. Weller and Ferguson (1994).

[9] The possibility of multiple editions of female-authored texts is still relatively rare – for other singular examples, see the chapters in the present volume by Mary Ellen Lamb on Mary Wroth, Danielle Clarke on Mary Sidney, Marie-Louise Coolahan on Katherine Phillips, Suzanne Trill on Anne Halkett, and Pamela Hammons on Katherine Austen.

history of feminist editorial practice; hence, her example serves to illustrate how thinking about the production and reproduction of women's texts has shaped an important field.

The first section of this chapter will look at the main trends that editions of the play reveal. As I argue, these late twentieth- and early twenty-first century editions of *The Tragedy of Mariam* are immensely valuable in terms of their scholarship, while their contribution to bringing women writers into greater visibility cannot be over-stated. But, as with all influential texts, editions of *The Tragedy of Mariam* bring unforeseen interpretive consequences. Throughout this chapter, I want to stress the co-enabling role shared between editions and criticism, at all times remembering Leah S. Marcus's warning about the 'subtle, pervasive rhetorical power exerted by the editions we use'.[10] In particular, I argue in the first section of this chapter that editions of *The Tragedy of Mariam* have had a narrowing effect, positioning the play as only 'women's writing' or 'biographical adjunct' and downplaying the significances of a text that is actually implicated in a much broader range of contemporary dramatic activity. In consequence, and despite the fact that the play merits exploration as a mediation of biblical history, a reflection upon non-English geographies, a study of Jewish practice, and a unique form of theatrical entertainment, *The Tragedy of Mariam* has remained something of a 'fringe' work in Renaissance studies – a state of affairs that has as much to do with its editorial backstory as with any set of related critical factors. The second section develops an alternative methodology that I began to pursue when editing the play for the Arden Early Modern Drama series. As I argue, the play gains in resonance and import when addressed in terms of its relations to other early modern plays in a variety of genres. Intimately connected to the play's editorial history is the extent to which *The Tragedy of Mariam* has suffered as a result of its association with 'closet drama'.[11] The third section argues for the unhelpfulness of the label and for an editorial strategy that foregrounds performance history. By engaging with alternative ways in which the play matters, editions, I suggest, can play a key role in reconfiguring how drama by women might continue to be accessed, studied, and debated. Germane here is the word 'continue'. As Isobel Grundy argues, academic editing practices are 'time-bound like everything else . . . shaped by a particular concept of the canon of English Literature, by the needs of a particular education system

---

[10]  Marcus, *Unediting*, p. 3.
[11]  Marta Straznicky defines a closet drama as 'a play that was either never intended for performance or never performed' (Straznicky, 'Closet Drama', p. 416).

and by the goals of a class of intelligentsia which is changing too'.[12] Any edition of *The Tragedy of Mariam* is bound to recognize what has come before even as it also tries to build on the example of previous editors: crucially, it is only because of work already undertaken that we can move forward in fresh editorial directions.

## Editing *Mariam* as Women's Writing

Editors have tended to present *The Tragedy of Mariam* in tandem with related texts, either those authored by Elizabeth Cary herself and/or those produced by other women writers of the period.[13] A biographical approach is both facilitated and encouraged by Barry Weller and Margaret W. Ferguson's 1994 edition of the text, which editorially situates next to each other *The Tragedy of Mariam* and Cary's daughter's biographical account – *The Lady Falkland: Her Life*. Written in 1645 at Cambrai, the *Life* is the main source of information about Cary.[14] Although in the organization of the volume the play appears first and the *Life* second, it is clear that they are to be appreciated together as companion pieces. For example, the accompanying commentary often discusses the two works in the same breath, as in the remark: 'we have wanted to make the play accessible to . . . those who may encounter the tragedy and/or biography in a course in history or women's studies'.[15] Similarly, a later observation runs: 'we believe that *The Lady Falkland: Her Life* . . . for most readers . . . will be an ancillary text to *Mariam*'.[16] In such formulations is suggested a doubled approach that reads the play through the life and vice versa, making the two texts critically co-dependent.

In line with Weller and Ferguson's editorial juxtaposition, scholarship over the past two decades has consistently probed the play in terms of its personal resonances. Emphasis on the biography means that attention is invariably directed to the extent to which *The Tragedy of Mariam* recasts Cary's own material experience. To cite Elaine V. Beilin, writing in 1987, the 'play may be seen as a psychomachia, one that Elizabeth Cary resolved by extending the limits of her personal conflict'.[17] A particularly popular approach maintains that *The Tragedy of Mariam* ventilates the tribulations of an unhappy marriage, yet, as Stephanie Hodgson-Wright notes in her

---

[12] Grundy, 'Editing Lady Mary Wortley Montagu', p. 72.
[13] The single exception to this rule is the one modern-spelling play-only edition of *The Tragedy of Mariam* edited by Stephanie J. Wright (see note 8).
[14] See note 7 above.    [15] '*Tragedy*', ed. Weller and Ferguson, p. 48.
[16] '*Tragedy*', ed. Weller and Ferguson, p. 50.    [17] Beilin, *Redeeming Eve*, p. 164.

edition, the play's date of composition militates against this argument; 'it is likely that Henry [Cary's husband] and Elizabeth spent most of the first six years of their marriage apart', she writes.[18] A second identification between Mariam and Cary is found in the representation of the protagonist as a religious dissenter. Yet, although there are hints in the *Life* that Cary 'grew into . . . doubt of her religion' at a young age, the actual conversion to Catholicism did not occur until much later: the parallel between life and work is once again temporally out of kilter.[19] In both cases, *The Tragedy of Mariam* can only be said to be directly related to Cary's domestic circumstances if one reads it either retrospectively or as miraculously proleptic. More broadly, and as Suzanne Trill argues in her chapter on Anne Halkett in this volume, equating a literary text and a life has increasingly been seen as a problematic enterprise.[20] Any biographical reading is inflected by surviving representations and, as critics have noted, Cary's *Life* is no exception. A highly crafted and self-justifying production with a discrete mission, the *Life* is of necessity to be accessed guardedly. As Heather Wolfe states, 'the story of a woman who suffered for her faith, *Life* is . . . engaged in "discrimination", "interpretation", and "omission"'.[21] An early edition, then, has encouraged and reinforced the drawing of some reductive elisions between life and text. And, while not as prevalent as it has been, the influence is still felt. So, in Karen Raber's 2009 volume of reprinted essays for the *Ashgate Critical Essays on Women Writers in England, 1550–1700* series, the first four essays are devoted to 'The Life And/In the Work', suggesting that biography continues to assume a privileged position in some critical encounters.

The argument that the play recasts Cary's material experience as a woman writer has often sat comfortably in the company of the second main editorial trend – to concentrate on *The Tragedy of Mariam* as an example of women's writing that bears fruitful comparison with other women's texts. In such criticism, questions about gender and female-authored work move to the forefront because *The Tragedy of Mariam* appears within a larger female-writing context. In Diane Purkiss's 1994 edition, for instance, the play is placed next to *The History of the Life, Reign, and Death of*

---

[18] *Tragedy*, ed. Hodgson-Wright, p. 12. Marion Wynne-Davies is even more definitive, stating that 'during the period of the play's composition [Cary's] husband was a prisoner', a hostage of the Spanish allies of the Italian army ('The Theatre', p. 189).

[19] *Life*, ed. Wolfe, p. 110.

[20] See Liz Stanley's argument that 'biography . . . lay[s] claim to facticity, yet' is 'by nature an artful enterprise which selects, shapes, and produces a very unnatural product' (*The Auto/Biographical I*, pp. 3–4).

[21] *Life*, ed. Wolfe, p. 66.

*Edward II*, also by Cary, and Aemilia Lanyer's extended poetic reflection, *Salve Deus Rex Judaeorum*.[22] In the case of Purkiss, the context insisted upon is a genre-free assessment, which unfolds inside the field of Renaissance women's writing in general. Hence, the emphasis of the edition, as its title indicates, is on women as writers, speakers, thinkers, and agents in the Renaissance period. Certainly, such an orientation is writ large in the edition's editorial apparatus and introduction, Purkiss attending to such matters as the obligations placed on women to be 'absent, silent, other'.[23] These are the lenses, then, through which the pairing of Cary and Lanyer is to be interpreted. Like the biographical approach, this gendered selection approach has been influential, and it has shaped, in turn, a second major critical trend – that is, to explore *The Tragedy of Mariam*'s gendered representations (its construction of female roles and relationships, its elaboration of gender-inflected ideologies, and, above all, its ideas around female speech). A wave of articles, chapters, and books throughout the 1980s and 1990s testifies to the impact of this gender-centred approach, and it is one that retains considerable authority in current interventions.[24]

The continuing trend to present *The Tragedy of Mariam* in tandem with other writing by women took a more selective turn with the 1996 publication of S. P. Cerasano and Marion Wynne-Davies's collection, *Renaissance Drama by Women*. This textbook pursues the same path as the Purkiss edition by featuring *The Tragedy of Mariam* in the company of other women writers, but here the sample selected is wholly dramatic. On the one hand, the strategy is highly enabling in drawing attention to the range of dramatic production by women in a variety of performance venues, and the edition also makes a vital contribution by including a plethora of documents by and about women touching on the business and practice of theatre. On the other hand, *The Tragedy of Mariam*, it might be argued, is robbed of its historical specificity by being linked to plays of very different dates (the sample moves from the late sixteenth century to the mid seventeenth century). At the same time, *The Tragedy of Mariam*, by virtue of the selection, remains firmly stamped as the work of a woman writer (albeit a female dramatist), with many of the attendant critical manoeuvres. Hence, while the illuminating introduction stresses what is to be gained by considering

---

[22] Purkiss (ed.), *Renaissance Women*. Similarly Margaret Ferguson's 1996 facsimile edition for Scolar Press's 'The Early Modern Englishwoman' collection (Aldershot, England) follows Purkiss's lead in reprinting *The Tragedy of Mariam* alongside *The History of the Life, Reign, and Death of Edward II* and a third work sometimes attributed to Cary, *The History of the Most Unfortunate Prince*.

[23] Purkiss (ed.), *Renaissance Women*, pp. vii.

[24] See, for instance, the arguments in Green, '"Ears Prejudicate"'; Luckyj, 'A Moving Rhetoricke'; Walker, *Women Writers*.

the play as part of the 'development of Renaissance tragedy', it also circles
back to some traditional shibboleths, as suggested by such observations
as '*The Tragedy of Mariam*... needs to be read... as addressing concerns
particular to women and to Cary herself.'[25] *Renaissance Drama by Women*
is typical of editions that, ensnared within a specific interpretive design
(a prioritizing of biography, gender, or a mixture of the two), push the
reader towards particular contexts for reading Cary's play. A concern here
is not that these kinds of readings are invalid – clearly, they possess a wealth
of invention and insight – but that they have negated other, more relational avenues of investigation. Such editorial approaches remove the play
from conversations with its early modern comparators and endow it with
a uniqueness and singularity. As Susan Felch notes in her chapter for this
volume, we might benefit more from a mode of 'editorial empathy' that
demonstrates the importance of locating women's texts in precise historical
contexts rather than within the broad generalization of 'women's writing'
(pp. 34–5).

## Editing *Mariam* as Early Modern Drama

As something of an antidote, more recent editorial approaches have begun
the process of recognizing some of the ways in which *The Tragedy of Mariam*
is tied to (male-authored) early modern drama. Perhaps most daring in its
positing of inter-connections is Clare Carroll's edition, which puts *The
Tragedy of Mariam* and *Othello* side by side in one volume.[26] The pairing
decision has its origin in the work of critics such as Maureen Quilligan who
highlight the plays' shared concerns with jealousy and possessiveness.[27]
Carroll hedges her bets in terms of the plays' dates, but if we accept
E. A. J. Honigmann's argument in his Arden 3 edition that *Othello* dates to
1601–02, it might certainly be suggested that *The Tragedy of Mariam* looks
back to this earlier Shakespearean example – Herod resembles Othello
not least in his conviction that his erring wife must be killed and in
his subsequent grief and self-condemnation.[28] *The Tragedy of Mariam* and
*Othello*, then, are marshalled to be in conversation with each other but
also belong to a similar order of dramatic achievement, for implicitly

[25]  Cerasano and Wynne-Davies (eds.), *Renaissance*, p. 47.
[26]  Carroll (ed.), *William Shakespeare's 'The Tragedy of Othello, the Moor of Venice' and Elizabeth Cary's
       'The Tragedy of Mariam'* (2003).
[27]  Quilligan, 'Staging Gender'.
[28]  'Shakespeare may have read Cary's work. Alternatively, she may have read or heard his', she writes
       (Carroll (ed.), *William... Elizabeth*, p. xvii).

the edition is constructed in such a way as to permit Cary to share in Shakespeare's lustre. The integration of Cary's name and work within an established constellation of Renaissance plays is presumably also a goal of recent editors of anthologies. For example, in *English Renaissance Drama: A Norton Anthology*, *The Tragedy of Mariam* is sandwiched between plays by Jonson and Marston, the effect of which is to allow Cary to occupy the same terrain as canonical dramatists.[29] A similar point might be made about the edition of *The Tragedy of Mariam* edited by Karen Britland; because this appears in the New Mermaids imprint, the play takes on some of the characteristics of other dramatists, such as Dekker, Kyd, Peele, and Webster, who are also represented in the series.[30] By association if not design, these editions locate Cary's play in a comparative environment.

Yet, these affirmative editorial initiatives notwithstanding, familiar critical procedures remain in place, namely the focus on biography and women's themes. David Bevington, in his edition of the play for the *English Renaissance Drama* anthology, for instance, cannot resist referring back to Cary's biography, and not entirely helpfully, as when he states: 'A woman's right to initiate divorce is something that Cary must have pondered a great deal.'[31] The play's ideas, in other words, are looped back to a woman's imagined personal experience. By the same token, in Clare Carroll's edition, while very helpful contextual extracts are provided, those devoted to *Othello* are more varied and take up a greater amount of space, while those centred on *The Tragedy of Mariam* tend to be shorter and more gender-centred (concerning marriage and idealized female behaviour). Moreover, the contextual section of the edition concludes with extracts from the *Life*, the suggestion being that this is the inevitable biographical point to which critical understandings of *The Tragedy of Mariam* are destined. The gravitational pull of the edition is towards Cary as the point of origin and meaning as opposed to an alternative trajectory that might steer the play towards other points of comparison and sites of interaction. Yet, if we wish to go forward in the editing practices applied to *The Tragedy of Mariam*, it is important to acknowledge precisely these multiple points of contact. By moving outside the purview of gender and biography, decentring both from their pre-eminent positions as units of analysis, and accommodating equally illuminating strategies for unpacking the play, we may allow *The Tragedy of Mariam* to be responsive to a range of new contextual possibilities.

[29] Bevington et al. (eds.), *English Renaissance Drama: A Norton Anthology*.
[30] See the listing at note 8 above.
[31] Bevington et al. (eds.), *English Renaissance Drama: A Norton Anthology*, p. 619.

There is, for instance, a revealing interface between *The Tragedy of Mariam* and male-authored drama. Given the fact that Cary composed two plays, both of which were known to, and celebrated by, contemporaries, it is more than likely that she was generally cognizant of theatrical genres rather than indebted to a much smaller set of examples.[32] The popularity of Marlovian drama (much of which predates *The Tragedy of Mariam*) in the late sixteenth and early seventeenth centuries may be refracted in Cary's play; certainly, *The Tragedy of Mariam*'s preoccupation with social status is paralleled in *Edward II*, while the protagonist's rejection of a fantasy in which the world is ruled by women (3.3.57–9) would seem to invert equivalent male-dominated passages in *Tamburlaine the Great*. At two points (4.1.18, 4.8.21–8), Cary's phrasing appears to recall *Doctor Faustus* and, in particular, the address to Helen of Troy.[33] Nor is *Othello* is the only Shakespeare text which echoes in *The Tragedy of Mariam*. Other resonant examples include *Hamlet*, a version of which existed before 1602–3. Crucially, the representation of a grieving Mariam attired in black matches the appearance of a similarly discontented Hamlet. No less striking are comparable statements of mental anguish: 'I suit my garment to my mind, / And there no cheerful colours can I find' (*Mariam*, 4.3.5–6) and, from *Hamlet*, 'But I have within that which passes show, / These but the trappings and the suits of woe'.[34] *Antony and Cleopatra* is also part of *The Tragedy of Mariam*'s frame of reference. Here, temporal proximity (*Antony and Cleopatra* is dated 1606–7) again suggests two possible relations, with *The Tragedy of Mariam* either anticipating Shakespeare's play or reflecting upon it. The most obvious continuities reside in the references to Cleopatra/ Mariam and the chariot (*Mariam*, 1.2.117–19), comparisons between the beauty of the two, and the phrase 'Egyptian blowse' (*Mariam*, 5.1.195), which appears to approximate Shakespeare's 'Egyptian dish'.[35]

Of course, there is always the possibility that Cary was recalling other narratives about Antony and Cleopatra (such as Sir Thomas North's *Plutarch*) rather than Shakespeare's play (although the verbal parallels noted seem too specific to admit of other candidates). But it is clear that *The Tragedy of Mariam* is interested in, and absorbed by, circulating narratives about historical figures. Critics have readily positioned *The Tragedy of Mariam*

---

[32] In the dedication to the play, 'To Diana's Earthly Deputess', there is reference to plays set in Palestine (line 15), this being *The Tragedy of Mariam*, and Syracuse, Italy (line 14), this being a lost work.

[33] See *Doctor Faustus* (1604), 5.1.90–1 and *Tamburlaine the Great, Part One*, 1.2.91–2, 209; 2.7.62 in Bevington and Rasmussen (eds.), '*Faustus*' and Other Plays.

[34] '*Hamlet*': The Texts of 1603 and 1623, ed. Thompson and Taylor, 1.2.85–6.

[35] See *Antony and Cleopatra*, ed. Wilders, 4.12.35–6, 2.6.128.

as a contemporary writing of its source text, Josephus's popular *Antiquities of the Jews* (in its 1602 Thomas Lodge translation), yet less mentioned is how this appropriative practice powerfully links Cary to other playwrights drawn to the work for dramatic material. Thus, for his play *The Duke of Milan*, which was first performed in 1621–2 and is similarly based on the Herod and Mariam narrative, Philip Massinger 'probably used Thomas Lodge's translation of Josephus, translated in 1602', following consciously or unconsciously Cary's example.[36] Josephus-inspired Herodian dramas are also part of the intertextual constellation, including the continental examples highlighted in Maurice Jacques Valency's study, which includes Hans Sachs's *Tragedia . . . der Wütrich König Herodes* (1552) and Alexandre Hardy's *Mariamne* (1600). Ludovico Dolce's *Marianna* (*c.* 1565) offers the most obvious parallels with *The Tragedy of Mariam* in its focus on an inward-looking heroine, a moralizing chorus, and a Herod who suffers from mental instability.[37] Most importantly here, all these plays evidence a cultural fascination with the Herod and Mariam narrative and indicate that Cary's play belonged with established traditions of adaptation and reinvention.

A further set of relations between Cary's drama and that of her contemporaries is opened up by the interpretive opportunities embodied in the play's geographies. The idea that place is central to Cary's drama is specified in the dedication where *The Tragedy of Mariam* is identified in terms of its connection with 'the now-obscured Palestine' (line 15), implying that setting and meaning are inextricably associated. Similarly, when John Davies honoured Cary's achievements as a dramatist in 1612, it was her 'Scenes of . . . Palestine' that he singled out for attention.[38] Yet, in the gender-conscious criticism of the play, the drama's Jerusalem setting barely receives mention. Interestingly, Cary's awareness of the city had been signalled at a much earlier stage for, as a child, she translated the commentaries to the maps accompanying *L'Epitome du Théâtre du Monde d'Abraham Ortelius* (1588/1590), one of which concerns 'The HOLY LAND' and, in particular, the 'heavenly . . . magnificent towne of HIERUSALEM the name of which is

---

[36] *The Selected Plays of Philip Massinger*, ed. Gibson, p. 3. Although Cary's immediate sources were Thomas Lodge's translations of Josephus's *Antiquities of the Jews* and *The Jewish War*, both published in the 1602 edition of *The Famous and Memorable Works of Josephus*, she may also have used Joseph Ben Gorion's *A Compendious and Most Marveilous History of the Latter Tymes of the Jewes Commune Weale*, first published in 1558 (see Callaghan, 'Re-reading Elizabeth Cary's *The Tragedie of Mariam, Faire Queene of Jewry*', p. 332, n. 29).

[37] Maurice Jacques Valency, *The Tragedies of Herod & Mariamne* (New York: Columbia University Press, 1940).

[38] Davies, *Muses*, sig. *3ᵛ.

divulged about all the worlde'.[39] The pre-eminence accorded Jerusalem is replicated in *The Tragedy of Mariam*. Here, the city is explicitly invoked, the mode of direct address signalling a sense of Jerusalem as a construction vital to characters' self-definitions. At 2.3.8, the returning Doris's greeting to the 'fair city' invites an audience to read Jerusalem in aesthetic terms, while the detail of 'Nine times' (2.3.5) or years since Doris 'did behold' (2.3.8) Jerusalem suggests a felt separation or loss. Paralleling Doris's return is Herod's address, 'Hail, happy city! Happy in thy store, / And happy that thy buildings such we see!' (4.1.1–2). Associated, like Mariam herself, with beauty, and discovered through reproductive metaphors (the reference to Jerusalem's 'store' [4.1.1] looks forward to the designation of Judaea as 'fertile ground' [4.7.20]), Jerusalem comes to stand in as a female type. Constabarus' leave-taking – 'farewell, fair city! Nevermore / Shall I behold your beauty shining bright' (4.6.29–30) – makes the process explicit. The repetition of 'behold' reinforces for Jerusalem a restorative power premised on visual apprehension and finds an echo in contemporary travel literature. As Andrew Hadfield notes, there had been considerable contact between Europe and the Eastern Mediterranean from the middle ages onwards – Jerusalem, and similar sites, were places of pilgrimage.[40] The primacy of the eye is a key component in relevant descriptions. Fynes Moryson notes in 1617 that 'I thought no place more worthy to be viewed in the whole world, then this City', while William Lithgow's comment in 1632 suggests why: 'wee beheld . . . *Ierusalem* . . . rauished with a kinde of vnwonted reioycing, the teares gushed from my eyes for too much ioy'.[41] Common to accounts is the incomparability of Jerusalem; to behold the city, it is implied, is to participate in a charged and intense inner experience.

All scenes of greeting and leave-taking in *The Tragedy of Mariam* imply external settings. Both Herod and Doris acknowledge the 'buildings' (2.3.1; 4.1.2) of Jerusalem, suggesting that these particular speeches are delivered in relation to the architecture of their environs. The singling out of the 'temple where w'adore' (4.1.1–3) in Herod's paean belongs with a more general tendency in the travel literature to designate Jerusalem through this building (albeit in its subsequent incarnations).[42] And the arrival of Ananell in haste in 3.2 is due to his having recently completed his 'temple'

39 *'The Mirror of the Worlde'*, ed. Peterson, p. 216.
40 Hadfield (ed.), *Amazons, Savages, and Machiavels*, p. 117.
41 Fynes Moryson, *An Itinerary* (1617), fol. 217; William Lithgow, *The Totall Discourse, of the Rare Adventures, of Long Nineteene Yeares Travayles* (1632), fol. 234.
42 Visiting Jerusalem in 1632, for instance, William Lithgow describes the temple, a place of the 'greatest beauty and glory' (*Totall*, fol. 251), as the high point of his first day's sojourn.

(3.2.6) duties, the play informs us, reminding an audience of the central role of the building in daily life. Constabarus' reference to 'the stately carved edifice / That on Mount Zion makes so fair a show' (1.6.9–10) reveals the power of the temple as a point of emotional reference, since he swears by it in a protestation of love. Related parts of the play conjure Jerusalem's other renowned sites and monuments. Sohemus' fraught recollection that he 'yielded up at [Mariam's] command / The strength of all the city, David's Tower' (3.3.77–8), one of Herod's chief fortifications, recalls that Jerusalem was characterized by a history of conquest and defence. (In this formulation, Sohemus is as vulnerable as the city whose safety he has jeopardized). And, on a later occasion, Herod contemplates opening 'David's sepulchre' (4.3.19): the reference operates to invoke an ancient past even as it underscores Herodian sacrilege. Jerusalem, then, figures in *The Tragedy of Mariam* as a litany of landmarks with individual stories to tell and the potential to function in meaningful dramatic applications. Via its invocations, the play's 'Holy City' setting is reinforced and the pre-Christian sphere of its action is highlighted. Writing on early modern maps of Jerusalem, Rehav Rubin notes their 'implementation of [a] diachronic concept of time': buildings and monuments are a-historically juxtaposed so as to emphasize issues of accretion and tradition.[43] *The Tragedy of Mariam* might be seen to function in similar fashion; the play invests not so much in historical authenticity but, rather, in the ideas and values that multiple locations, within the Jerusalem setting, communicate.

As a Jerusalem-set drama with scriptural underpinnings, *The Tragedy of Mariam* may be profitably compared with a number of late sixteenth- and early seventeenth-century plays devoted to Old Testament biblical stories. While George Peele's *David and Bethsabe*, set in Rabba, and Thomas Lodge and Robert Greene's *A Looking Glass for London and England*, set in Nineveh, have survived, the majority of these plays are now lost. Accounting for the increased number of biblical plays performed between *c.* 1590 and *c.* 1602 (records indicate that at least thirteen biblical plays were commissioned, written, or performed for a public theatre audience during this period), Annaliese Connolly suggests that it was part of the companies' commercial strategy 'to complement and prolong the stage life of existing plays in the repertory', such as *Tamburlaine the Great* and *The Jew of Malta*, through a focus on soldier kings and prophets whose campaigns are figured inside ancient and distant locales.[44] By choosing Jerusalem as an informing

43    Rubin, 'Sacred Space and Mythic Time in the Early Printed Maps of Jerusalem', p. 128.
44    Connolly, 'Peele's *David and Bethsabe*', para 20.

presence, Cary was following a number of contemporary dramatic works that used the city as setting and revealing herself as attuned to the theatrical trends of her moment.

To reflect on setting – and the play's Jerusalem emphases – is to open up opportunities to investigate the drama's imaginative investments in debates around Jewish identity, lineage, and race.[45] Invocations of Judaic culture and mores in the play are mediated through language which underscores a sense of Jerusalem's rich history. For example, Constabarus' reference to 'mildest Moses' and his 'wonders in the land of Ham' (1.6.71–2) brings Jerusalem powerfully to mind, since, according to Josephus, the city gained much of its fame from accommodating the 'Arke and Tabernacle that *Moses* had before time made'.[46] *The Tragedy of Mariam* works to position its characters against an immersive Old Testament backdrop. 'Methinks our parting was in David's days' (4.1.14), states Herod: the allusion to David, who established Jerusalem as a capital city, locates the speaker in relation to a long line of royal incumbents. Less obvious conjurations of Jerusalem, such as Constabarus' reference to the 'holy lamb' (1.6.74) – Passover – or Doris's brief description of 'the feast that takes the fruit from ground' (2.3.7) – Sukkot – underline the city's material and symbolic importance to Judaism. By threading these opportunities for interpretation through the edition itself, as reflected in the textual notes, there is room to shift thinking and reorient assumptions.

## Editing *Mariam* as a Performance Text

In returning *The Tragedy of Mariam* to a multiplicity of early modern dramatic contexts, attending to the dramatic and theatrical qualities the play embodies is crucial. Most editors ignore the staging elements of *The Tragedy of Mariam* on the grounds that, as closet drama, the play would never have received a public performance; until recently, the consensus of opinion was that the play was read aloud by Cary's domestic circle rather than staged as part of an aristocratic entertainment. However, a recent critical trajectory which is slowly gaining support holds that we cannot deduce from the fact of the play's non-performance in the seventeenth century a lack of theatrical responsiveness or ambition on Cary's part. As Alison Findlay, Stephanie Hodgson-Wright, and Gweno Williams observe, 'It is mistaken to assume that plays for which we have no production history

---

[45] I am thinking here of Dympna Callaghan's influential reading of Jewishness and racial hybridity. See note 36 above. See also Macdonald, *Women and Race*, pp. 60–4.

[46] Flavius Josephus, *The Famous and Memorable Workes* (1602), fol. 197.

are unperformable and not even intended for performance.'[47] Liz Schafer goes further when reflecting on her exciting venture to stage passages from the play in Burford's St John the Baptist Church, where Cary married, as part of the '*Mariam* Project'; 'some aspects of *Mariam* do not make sense unless the play was performed', she states, instancing 'long entrances', the presence on stage of attendants, and clothing decisions.[48]

Posing this argument, Schafer goes further than any edition or editor in constructing *The Tragedy of Mariam* as a performative statement. This is not to suggest that the play's potential on the stage has always been neglected in editorial practice. In Cerasano and Wynne-Davies's anthology *Renaissance Drama by Women*, for example, the editors both retain original staging directions and augment them, marking additions in square brackets. As an example from *The Tragedy of Mariam*, one can cite the opening of Act One: '*Enter* CHORUS' and '*enter centre stage . . .* MARIAM' indicates a specific and spatially purposeful staging procedure.[49] More directive still is David Bevington in his edition; he includes precise indications of action on four occasions (he adds a '[*She weeps.*]' at one point), making him a particularly interventionist editor.[50] In this, he arguably follows a Norton template, which is to make accessible the drama of the past via the provision of gestural aids to meaning and understanding. My own edition incorporated some of these decisions, not least because, in keeping at the forefront a range of staging opportunities (which might extend to the Chorus remaining on stage throughout and entering and exiting at different points), I wished to encourage future productions. In the same spirit, I used the commentary to note several representational options, including the use of curtains and a balcony and the possibility that different lines of the Chorus were delivered by its different constituent members.

In addition to producing a text in which performance possibilities are always/already inscribed, my edition was the first to situate editorial decisions inside a comprehensive production history of the play, looking at those productions of *The Tragedy of Mariam* that have emphasized the play's theatrical potential. Notably, as Marion Wynne-Davies argues in her chapter in this volume, most women's drama from the early modern period has not had an equivalent professional production; hence, by default, in discussing the stage history of *The Tragedy of Mariam*, it is generally amateur performances, independent productions, and staged readings on which we

---

[47] Findlay et al., *Women and Dramatic Production*, p. 3.
[48] Liz Schafer, 'An Early Modern Feminist', *THES*, 6 June (2013), www.timeshighereducation.co.uk.
[49] Cerasano and Wynne-Davies (eds.), *Renaissance*, Act 1, s.d.
[50] Bevington et al. (eds.), *English Renaissance Drama: A Norton Anthology*, 1.1.67.

focus. To consider staged readings in an Arden edition, as I did, is perhaps unconventional, yet still, I would argue, necessary to a reorientation of a feminist editorial initiative. Of great interest, then, was Catherine Schuler and Sharon Ammen's performance script comprised of literary and musical extracts from the period (their strategy of juxtaposing male voices and female voices in the reading made for a dynamic experience, argument and counter-argument combining in dialogic fashion).[51] Exciting, too, was the Primavera theatre company's staged reading in 2007 at the King's Head Theatre, London, distinctive for emphasizing the play's political themes rather than its representation of female experience.[52] These two readings and others like them allowed for new explorations of the text, thereby confirming that the play, like any of Shakespeare's plays, could be appropriated in inventive ways.

All manner of productions can inflect an editorial focus – hence the premium my edition placed on the pioneering work of the 'Women and Dramatic Production 1570–1670' project.[53] Directing the Tinderbox Theatre Company at the Bradford Alhambra Studio in 1994, Stephanie Hodgson-Wright utilised an imaginatively conceived set that combined a satirical poster of Herod, seen as a 'petty dictator'; busts of Octavius Caesar, Mark Antony, and Julius Caesar; and a graveyard populated by the victims of a corrupt regime.[54] The choruses were delivered by a sculptor and a gravedigger, and these figures jostled with each other in musical renderings of Cary's moralizing that played up a competition for 'supremacy'.[55] It was a bold move, and one that acoustically drew attention to the play's mixture of voices and perspectives.[56] Independent productions such as that staged by Tinderbox compare productively with student performances that, as academics/editors, we are sometimes in a fortunate position to be able to influence if not direct. This was the case with the 1995 production directed by Liz Schafer at Royal Holloway, University of London, in which

[51] The performance script was delivered at the Attending to Women in Early Modern England symposium sponsored by the Centre for Renaissance and Baroque Studies at the University of Maryland, College Park, in 1990.

[52] Actors and actresses from the National Museum of Women in the Arts and the Washington Shakespeare Company staged a further reading of *The Tragedy of Mariam* on 4 May 2009 in Washington, DC.

[53] Via this initiative, four early modern plays by women – Elizabeth Cary's *The Tragedy of Mariam*, Jane Cavendish and Elizabeth Brackley's *The Concealed Fancies*, Margaret Cavendish's *The Convent of Pleasure*, and Jane Lumley's *Iphigenia at Aulis* – were professionally produced.

[54] Findlay, Williams, and Hodgson-Wright, '"The Play is Ready to be Acted"', p. 133.

[55] *Ibid.*, p. 135.

[56] Extracts from all four of the plays performed, with commentaries, are found on a teaching video, *Women Dramatists 1550–1670: Plays in Performance*, which was produced in 1999 by Lancaster University Television Unit.

the all-female cast provided a counterpoint to early modern male play-ing conventions. Particularly striking was the casting of Elizabeth Cary (Ruth Aldridge) herself as the Chorus: her struggles with ideology were hinted at in her reading from a book, while her authority was registered in her unveiling of a scroll showing the Hasmonean family tree. All the members of the cast were introduced in black burkas; when one of the figures stripped off her headscarf to reveal herself as Mariam, a powerful impression of a resistance to custom was implied. Throughout, indeed, the production underscored a relationship between word and appearance that insisted upon the audience's critical engagement. And, most importantly, it showcased the ways in which performance decisions had their origins in textual clues, which editors have tended to bypass, and implied stage busi-ness. Highly attuned to performance suggestion, these productions confirm that *The Tragedy of Mariam* is eminently actable. They illustrate the fact that seeing a play such as *The Tragedy of Mariam* in a theatrical guise adds to our sense of Cary's achievement, allowing the work a social and cultural hinterland that a concentration on the solitary writer precludes. Certainly, the play takes on new associations and shades of meaning when reimagined according to a spectrum of performance options.

An awareness of the play's production history is integral to the gen-eration of new performance possibilities. Liz Shafer's ongoing 'Mariam Project', for instance, is excitingly staging the play, or parts of it, in differ-ent performance venues around the country. Thus far, the play has been staged as a pop-up event and as an installation, with a gallery and a church serving as the performance space, the effect being that the capacity of *The Tragedy of Mariam* to function in a highly theatrical register has been further confirmed.[57] As editors, we have a continuing role to play in *The Tragedy of Mariam*'s theatrical rehabilitation. What, for instance, would an edition of the play look like if it included the script of a modern adaptation or other (cut) versions designed for site-specific performance? Exposing *The Tragedy of Mariam* to dramaturgy creates opportunities for the play to speak to a much greater range of interests and constituencies.

*The Tragedy of Mariam* which emerges from the most recent editorial process is a differently marked dramatic creation, more generous in its frame of reference and more sensitive to its own potential. Editing Cary as an early modern dramatist rather than as a woman writer challenges separatism and permits the play to move inside a looser and less straitjacketed interpretive terrain. It facilitates fresh types of identification and designation and it

---

[57] See the description at www.burfordfestival.org/Events_Daily/Mariam.html.

allows for a greater integration of the play into ongoing conversations. The virtues of a plural editorial approach are that points of connection can be highlighted and the play's involvement in a larger dramatic world is illuminated. Imagined dialogically, *The Tragedy of Mariam* comes into a visibility that is not wholly dependent on either gender or author. And, in the process, the play presents itself as open to cross-fertilization, receptive to comparison, and, above all, capable of being revitalized by the ever-evolving editorial initiative.

# CHAPTER 5

# Contextualizing the Woman Writer
## Editing Lucy Hutchinson's Religious Prose

### Elizabeth Clarke

Oxford University Press is currently publishing its first 'complete works' of an early modern woman writer: a four-volume edition of Lucy Hutchinson, under the general editorship of David Norbrook. This is tantamount to enrolling Lucy Hutchinson in the canon, presenting the works of a woman writer who has increased greatly in prominence in recent times in the form afforded to 'great' writers. I am editing a theological treatise for *Volume II: Religious Prose*; this treatise is untitled in manuscript, and it was first published in 1817 along with Hutchinson's translation of Book I of John Owen's *Theologumena*.[1] We have followed the 1817 edition in assigning the title *On the Principles of the Christian Religion*, partly because of Hutchinson's frequent use of the word 'principles' and also because she described her husband likewise as having started from basic principles when trying to work out theological problems, such as whether to baptise their children as infants.[2] This title, however, helps to give the impression that this is a theological treatise in a conventional sense, when it is anything but.[3] Rather, this manuscript document with no title begins with a personal letter to Hutchinson's eldest daughter Barbara, who was born in about 1645, and we think it was written to her when she married Andrew Orgil in August 1668. This piece of writing, then, does not as it was written announce itself as a theological treatise.

*The Works of Lucy Hutchinson* bestows canonicity on the author and provides the opportunity to edit her works in a fuller and deeper context than is usually available for an early modern woman, but in editing this treatise, a number of questions arise that are particular to the editing of

---

[1] *On the Principles of the Christian Religion Addressed to her Daughter; and on Theology*, by Mrs Lucy Hutchinson (London: Longman, Hurst, Rees, Orme & Brown, 1817). Page references are to this edition.

[2] Hutchinson, *Memoirs of the Life of Colonel Hutchinson*, ed. Keeble, pp. 210–11.

[3] See Suzanne Trill's discussion of similar issues in the critical categorization of Anne, Lady Halkett's texts, in this volume, pp. 97–9.

women's texts. How do we categorize a work that does not fit conventional models of literary and non-literary writings? It is very important in the *Works* that Hutchinson's theological writings are not treated as context for the literary writings which will appear in the last two volumes, in particular the *Memoirs of the Life of Colonel Hutchinson* and *Order and Disorder*. To treat the theological texts in this way would reinforce the hierarchies of genre that early modern women's writing has done much to overturn, and so we have tried to treat the religious works in the same way as the more straightforwardly 'literary' works, looking for sources and the reading that has informed them. There are, however, numerous challenges in treating Hutchinson's treatise in this way. In particular, how do we annotate and supply context in a way that does not 'obscure the differences between texts by men and those by women', a risk identified by Alice Eardley in the annotation of early modern women's texts?[4] And what kind of context is the most appropriate for the editor to supply in order best to facilitate the reading and interpretation of this woman's document? These are versions of the questions also raised by Susan Felch in her discussion of approaching Elizabeth Tyrwhit's *Morning and Evening Prayers* with 'editorial empathy', and in Ramona Wray's exploration of the variant contexts provided by different editions of Elizabeth Cary's *Mariam*; although in the case of Hutchinson's treatise, the challenges are even greater.

Certainly a male-authored seventeenth-century theological treatise would be edited in the context of other public, printed theological works. One of the sources for Lucy Hutchinson's treatise is Thomas Shepard's *First Principles of the Oracles of God* (1655) and another is the Westminster Confession. *Principles* (as it will be called from now on), however, is not a controversial document: rather than agreeing or disagreeing with Shepard or the Westminster Confession, it is claimed in the initial letter to be 'a little summary' of these theological works (p. 1). This reticence, which will be exemplified later, is typical of the authorial stance in much women's manuscript writing. It is important to Lucy Hutchinson not to claim to be a theologian, although this chapter will argue that while the treatise starts as an orthodox summary, it becomes a very interesting and original piece of theological thinking. Given the religious context of 1668 – the recent ejection of Nonconformists like the Hutchinsons from the State Church in 1662, and the death of Lucy's husband John in 1664 (in prison for alleged involvement in a Republican plot against the king), let alone the role of the Hutchinsons in the Interregnum – the establishment of what she felt

---

4 Eardley, 'Hester Pulter's "Indivisibles"', p. 119.

strongly enough in 1668 to pass on to her daughter is fascinating. However, the fact that *Principles* is formed as a long and 'private' letter to Barbara from her mother means that there are issues for the editor to consider that are not present for male-authored, printed discourse: the context of the writing would of course be known to Barbara, and a modern editor needs to work harder to supply it. In addition, editing the 'first' piece of writing to be found so far in a particular genre, which one is often doing when editing women's writing, is very difficult, and the editor carries the responsibility of adding annotation and supplying a contextual framework which may become established as authoritative.

Annotating phrases such as the cliché about Antinomianism which Lucy Hutchinson uses twice, 'turning the grace of God into wantonnesse', is easy (p. 22). After all, the same basic language that all seventeenth-century readers know is being used, and a resort to the 'advanced search' function of *Early English Books Online* will show how often and in whose work this particular phrase appears. It is also difficult to see how men and women would have different meanings for words that are commonplace. However, there are words which can mean different things depending on the context they are used in, like the word 'fanatic', used by Lucy Hutchinson in the sense that Calvin used it. Calvin devotes Chapter 9 of Book 1 of the *Institutes* to this: the title is 'All the principles of piety subverted by fanatics, who substitute revelations for Scripture'.[5] Lucy Hutchinson herself was called 'fanatic' in a different sense, a way that reflects the politics of the 1660s: sense 2a of the *OED*, 'A fanatic person; a visionary; an unreasoning enthusiast. Applied in the latter half of the 17th c. to Nonconformists as a hostile epithet'. Choosing a context for a text which is by a religious Independent, a persecuted religious and political grouping, in the theologically fraught year of 1668 is difficult, let alone when that member is a woman, and this chapter traces two contexts within which *Principles* looks very different. One is a context within English dissenting writing of 1668, which is mostly by men, and one is specifically a female context of mid-seventeenth-century America.

Of course, very few women have published their writing by 1668, particularly not theological writing.[6] Hutchinson states that she does not intend to publish this work, but she does imply at the start that others are to read this treatise. 'I intend to communicate it, that what hath fixt me may fix others' (p. 6), she announces, a confidence echoed by the authoritative

---

[5] Calvin, *Institutes*, trans. Thomas Norton (1578), p. 24.
[6] For 'cultural disincentives to the production of women's theological writings' see Elizabeth Clarke, 'The Legacy of Mothers'.

attitude to theology, and the familiarity with many doctrinal concepts, expressed in the rest of the work. If it were read outside of her immediate family, however, Hutchinson's manuscript treatise must have been copied by hand, and no copy is known to have survived. This document is nothing like a spiritual journal, of which many by women like Mary Rich, Elizabeth Jekyll, and Anne Halkett survive from this period, although they are often not extant in modern editions, partly perhaps because of our unfamiliarity with the spiritual journal genre.[7] Hutchinson may have bequeathed a journal to the Earl of Anglesey on her death, in 1681 at the height of the Exclusion Crisis, which would be characteristic of an instinct to use every piece of writing in the most effective way.[8] He was still a member of the privy council and likely to give credence to the spiritual diary of a friend. She does promise her daughter at the end of this treatise a 'book of experiences', which according to Isaac Ambrose is a way of recording spiritual experiences in writing to learn what God intends from letting them happen.[9] Sadly it has not survived.

One genre that had achieved popularity in theological writing by women by 1668 was the 'mother's legacy', a form that, like Lucy Hutchinson's text, is conceived of as private in its original – from mother to child. Both Dorothy Leigh and Elizabeth Jocelin had written documents of this kind which were published throughout the century. Leigh's volume went into twenty-three editions between 1616 and 1674 – there were editions in 1663 and 1667, close to when we believe *Principles* was written. The long title of her volume in 1616, *The Mothers Blessing. Or the Godly Counsaile of a Gentle-woman not long since Deceased, Left Behind her for her Children: containing Many Good Exhortations, and Godly Admonitions, Profitable for All Parents to Leave as a Legacy to Their Children, but Especially For Those, who by Reason of their Young Yeeres Stand Most in Need of Instruction*, makes clear the nature and point of the publication: it is a mother's instructions to her children in the event of her death, commonly in childbirth. Leigh had three young sons, to whom she communicated her most precious beliefs.[10] In her case, and in others', this rationale for writing led to

---

[7] For example, Centre for Kent Studies, MS U1015 F 27, 'Elizabeth Turner's journal'; Beinecke Library Osborn MS b. 221, 'Elizabeth Jekyll's spiritual journal'; and see Elizabeth Clarke, 'Beyond Microhistory', pp. 216–25. See Suzanne Trill's chapter in this volume (pp. 97–120) for an extended discussion of editing Anne Halkett's archive.

[8] Norbrook, 'Lucy Hutchinson's "Elegies"', p. 485; Arthur Annesley, Earl of Anglesey, Diary 1675–84, BL Additional MS 18730, fol. 100v, 8 October 1682, cited in Hutchinson, *Works*, vol. i, p. cxix.

[9] Hutchinson, *Principles*, p. 153. For an example of how to record 'Experiences' see Isaac Ambrose, *Media* (1650), pp. 166–71.

[10] Jocelyn Catty, 'Leigh, Dorothy (d. in or before 1616)', *ODNB*.

something like systematic theological reflection – and must have formed seventeenth-century expectations of what women's religious writing should be like.[11]

Lucy Hutchinson's initial letter to Barbara presents her manuscript text as a mother's advice to her daughter, in employing a certain rhetoric that emphasizes the sense of a change in relationship with her daughter. She calls her writing 'my last exhortation', even though she is not imminently dying, like many of the authors of mothers' legacies in the seventeenth century, in manuscript or in print.[12] The rhetoric of ultimate instruction is referring to her changing relationship with her daughter. She is writing at a critical stage, when Barbara is marrying Orgil, a merchant who will often go to the West Indies, thus removing Barbara from her mother's immediate influence, and as Hutchinson insists, transferring spiritual responsibility for her from her mother to her husband: 'you are now under another's authoritie' (p. 90). In emphasizing the finality of her endeavour Hutchinson invokes the rhetoric of the mother's legacy, making a self-consciously feminine choice of genre and indicating that she was thinking about writing as a woman. Sylvia Brown's modern edition of three mothers' legacies shows the form of the writing being established, with the theological work prefaced by a personal letter from the mother; she argues that the men who oversaw publication often used these volumes to reinforce their own particular religious position.[13] Lucy Hutchinson's work is not 'authorized' in this way by a man, but the occasion of the treatise, the 'last' directions to a daughter on her marriage, reflect an awareness of the mother's legacy form, and a deliberate use of its rhetoric.

Although several mothers' legacies are printed, they all claim an origin in a very private if posthumous communication between (dead) mother and (living) child. Hutchinson may well have wanted to keep this treatise private between herself and Barbara even though she as mother was still alive; however, the use of this well-known female rhetoric of privacy is in itself significant. Wendy Wall has shown how the strategy of posthumous publication annexes the authority of 'last words' while

[11] This volume was one of the most popular publications in the seventeenth century; see Green, *Print and Protestantism*, p. 637. For the possibility that the mother's legacy could be used to express oppositional views see Gray, 'Feeding on the Seed of the Woman'. Kristen Poole notes that the female author of a 1627 text actually cited Leigh and Jocelin as her authorization to write; see Poole, '"The Fittest Closet"', p. 83.

[12] Hutchinson, *Principles*, p. 2. See the document by Katherine Austen in *Katherine Austen's 'Book M'*, ed. Ross, pp. 142–4. For the probably political use of Elizabeth Richardson's *A Ladies Legacie* see Brown, *Mothers' Legacies*, p. 150.

[13] See Brown, 'The Approbation of Elizabeth Jocelin'.

negating the accusation, very common for women writers, that they are self-publicists:

> The very power of this position rests in its doubleness: in the anticipated movement towards death, in the sanctity of the final departure. It is a strangely performative and self-constituting gesture dependant on the erasure of the subject. Many women writers' works gained power and authority through the articulation of their final legacy, a framework that allowed them to . . . place themselves in the public eye.[14]

Hutchinson is very aware of the perils of writing as a woman. She acknowledges in the opening letter the perceived inferiority of her sex:

> The Apostle reproaches the weaknesse of our sex more than the other, when speaking of the prevalency of seducers, he says they lead about silly weomen, who are ever learning and never able to come to the knowledge of the truth; therefore every wise and holy woman ought to watch strictly over herselfe, that she become not one of these; but as our sex, through ignorance and weakenesse of iudgement (which in the most knowing weomen is inferior to the masculine understanding of men). (pp. 5–6)

Hutchinson states that she does not intend to publish this work, as it is a personal communication, using the common female apology that (a) her own ideas would not be worth publishing and (b) publication would be equivalent to advertising: 'I write not for the presse, to boast my owne weaknesses to the world but to imprint on your hart the characters I have receivd of God' (p. 91). She may well be alluding to Dorothy Leigh, who says at the start of her mother's legacy: 'setting aside all fear, I have adventured to shew my imperfections to the view of the World'.[15] Both authors seem aware of the particular problems for women of publishing: it is viewed as self-advertisement, and given the inferior nature of women's brains, what is being advertised may not be worth reading – though as Hutchinson says, 'I intend to communicate it, that what hath fixt me may fix others' (p. 6), a confidence echoed by the authoritative attitude to theology expressed in the rest of the work.

So the answer to the first and all-important question when editing this piece is answered – it is in genre a mother's legacy, a genre very familiar to seventeenth-century readers, and indeed expected of women writers. Yet, as we shall see, the treatise to her daughter deals authoritatively with matters of importance that are relevant to the religious controversies of mid-century England – but which controversies? What follows is an account of two

---

[14] Wall, *The Imprint of Gender*, p. 286.
[15] Leigh, *The Mothers Blessing* (1616), sig. A7v; Brown, *Mothers' Legacies*, pp. 17–18.

different arguments that Lucy Hutchinson may or may not be alluding to. In editing a printed work clues to the context of the writing may well be gleaned from the introduction to the book, or from extra-textual material such as the dedications. Because much women's writing at this period in the middle of the seventeenth century is in manuscript, the problem of determining a context, which is often established from aspects of printed publication, affects women's writing more than men's.

One of the interesting elements of Lucy Hutchinson's biography that might affect the editing of *Principles* is her close relationship with John Owen, Vice-Chancellor of Oxford University during the Interregnum and a leading Nonconformist in the Restoration.[16] Owen merged his own congregation with the larger group of the recently deceased Joseph Caryl in 1673, and Hutchinson's religious notebook indicates that she attended his sermons in that year.[17] Hutchinson, then, was attending Owen's meetings in the 1670s, difficult times for dissenters, and being a dissenter herself this is clearly an important context for the *Principles*. She is also associated with the Scottish divine Robert Ferguson, who had run an academy in Islington whose pupils included a son of the republican Slingsby Bethel, as well as Lucy Hutchinson's son Lucius.[18] Ferguson had already allied himself with Owen in the pamphlet war against Bishop Samuel Parker before Owen appointed him as a personal assistant in 1674.[19] Moreover, Ferguson was deeply involved in the production and dissemination of pamphlet material, as the discovery of a printing press at his house in the early 1680s proved.

The printed publications of a pamphlet controversy between Nonconformists and some Anglicans are a compelling context for the *Principles*. John Owen had written, in *Truth and Innocence Vindicated in a survey of a discourse concerning ecclesiastical polity, and the authority of the civil magistrate over the consciences of subjects in matters of religion* (1669), a response to Samuel Parker's *Discourse of Ecclesiastical Polity* (1670), which explicitly attacked dissenters. Owen indignantly refuted what he saw as an accusation that some of the most precious doctrines held by dissenters were simply metaphorical expressions of Scripture:

> What if the principal Doctrines of the Gospel about the grace of God, the Mediation of Christ, of Faith, Justification, Gospel-obedience, Communion with God, and Union with Christ, are esteemed and stigmatized by some as

[16] Richard L. Greaves, 'Owen, John (1616–1683)', *ODNB*.    [17] Nottingham Archives, DD/ HU3.

[18] Zook, *Radical Whigs and Conspiratorial Politics*, pp. 93–114; David Norbrook, 'Hutchinson, Lucy (1620–1681)', *ODNB*.

[19] Dzelzainis, 'Robert Ferguson and Andrew Marvell'.

*swelling Mysteries of Fanaticism;* and the whole work of our Redemption by the blood of Christ as expressed in the Scripture, be deemed *Metaphorical?*[20]

In particular Owen and Parker seemed to be opposed on the nature of the believer's relationship with God – as Owen says, Parker seems to be talking about civil obedience rather than a relationship with a Christian Saviour:

> the *Scheme* he hath given us of Religion, or Religious duties, wherein there is mention neither of . . . a Redeemer, without which no man can entertain any one true notion of *Christian Religion*, would rather bespeak him a Philosopher, than a Christian.[21]

This treatise set the tone for several of the publications of the 1670s. William Sherlock started a pamphlet war with *A Discourse concerning the Knowledge of Jesus Christ and our Union and Communion with Him* (1674), which began with a controversial statement:

> some men, where-ever they meet with the word *Christ* in Scripture, always understand by it the Person of Christ, . . . And first *Christ* is originally the name of an Office.[22]

To see Christ as a Person rather than an Office was fundamental to Reformed Christianity. 'Union and communion' were words used to describe the relationship between God and the believer from the works of Richard Sibbes in the 1630s through to the dissenters of the 1660s. In his 1654 treatise *The Doctrine of the Saints Perseverance, explained and confirmed*, Owen carefully explains what his concept of the union with Christ is: it is not a personal union, which he sees as doing violence both to the personality of Christ and the personality of the individual, but a spiritual union, achieved by the indwelling of the Holy Spirit. Such a union is not to be despised, because it is the same union as the man Christ had with God.[23]

The most frequent illustration of this union in Scripture is earthly marriage: 'What the Apostle had spoken of the one, he would have understood of the other'.[24] Owen selects the phrase 'one flesh', used of the married couple in Genesis 2:24, and used by the Apostle Paul in I Corinthians 6, and finds a metaphorical equivalent to describe the union between Christ and the soul: 'one spirit'.[25] In Owen's *Of Communion with God* (1657) the

---

[20] John Owen, *Truth and Innocence Vindicated* (1669), p. 20.    [21] *Ibid.*, p. 10.
[22] William Sherlock, *A Discourse concerning the Knowledge of Jesus Christ and our Union and Communion with Him* (1674), p. 4.
[23] Owen, *The Doctrine of the Saints Perseverance*, pp. 193–5.    [24] *Ibid.*, p. 349.    [25] *Ibid.*, p. 196.

relationship offered with the Divine, based on this union, is represented as truly intimate: 'he presseth her hard to a closer union with him in the conjugall bond'.[26] The result of such union is ecstatic love to a Christ who is described in the rapturous terms of a human lover. At stake is the believer's personal relationship with Christ, emphasized in Reformed thought and more experiential Protestantism in England since the Reformation.

In her *Principles*, Lucy Hutchinson spells out a threefold 'union with Christ', insisting on the Reformed version of Christianity:

> This union, though it be most reall, is very misticall, and hard to be conceived any way, but by the experimentall feeling of it, which every true Christian hath in some measure, and finds unspeakable benefitts and consolations thereby; The Scripture describes it to us by divers simillitudes, that of the head and body, of the husband and wife, of the vine and branches, the olive and grafts, the foundation and building. (pp. 61–2)

The description of the relationship with Christ as an 'experimentall feeling' and the scriptural comparison with a marriage is fundamental to English Christianity before the rise of Arminianism and characteristic of Nonconformist Christianity.[27] Sherlock and Parker, in comparison, seemed to be advocating a political morality of obedience to human superiors. It is tempting, given her relationship with Owen, to see Hutchinson's treatise as part of this Restoration debate on the nature of Christianity. Editing the treatise in this framework would lead the editor to emphasize the relationship of the opinions expressed in *Principles* to the explicit controversy of the 1670s between royalist Anglicans who stressed civil obedience and Reformed Christians.

So – do the contents of *Principles* need to be read in this particular religious and political context in order to make sense? It is certainly true, as we have seen, that Hutchinson assumes throughout that a personal relationship with God is the basis of Christianity. This 'union' of the divine and human was mainstream before the Civil War, although in the Restoration Anglicans tried to redefine it.[28] Moreover she is insistent that the three persons of the Trinity are all persons, with personal characteristics (pp. 17–18). She also stresses throughout that what she is putting forward is mainstream Christianity: 'the truths are not weake but the powerfull word and precepts of the Lord, and the duties commanded are allow'd by all Christians

---

[26] Owen, *Of Communion with God*, p. 61.
[27] Clarke, *Politics, Religion and the Song of Songs*, pp. 65–6.     [28] Winship, *Seers of God*, p. 33.

without dispute' (p. 137). However, there is no sense in her treatise that this is the version of Christianity that was to be attacked by Sherlock and Parker. They held that this strong belief in the individual's relationship with God was threatening to the corporate obedience to the monarch that they saw as vital to English politics and which was intrinsic to the 1662 Act of Uniformity. There is, in Hutchinson's treatise, a section on obedience; however, it is not the political obedience of Parker, but an 'inward Obedience of the hidden man of the heart' taken from William Perkins's *The Whole Treatise of the Cases of Conscience* (1606) and elaborated.[29] There is even, in the last part, an investigation into how the relationship with God works: using the writing of Catholic writer St François de Sales she develops a new vocabulary for the way the human being and the Holy Spirit interact. If the primary intended audience is indeed the daughter who is going abroad with her new husband, this non-Anglocentric context makes sense. There is very little in this theological treatise that is specifically designed for a political interpretation; it is a very personal theology.

So if this pamphlet controversy of the 1670s, or even the Anglican/ Nonconformist split of the 1660s, is not the context within which Hutchinson's treatise should be edited, what is? The only references to external movements are to opposite extremes – 'Antinomians' and 'Arminians' – and these references would seem to be to earlier controversy.[30] 'Arminians' were of course the main opponents to Puritans in the 1630s: Owen had written in disgust *A Display of Arminianisme*, with the ominous subtitle *Being a discovery of the old Pelagian idol free-will, with the new goddesse contingency* (1643). Lucy's famous *Memoirs of the Life of Colonel Hutchinson* shows hostility to Arminianism.[31] Arminian theology was a modification of the Calvinism which had been dominant in England since the start of the century: for instance, 'depravity' was not total but modified, and 'predestination' was based on God's foresight, not his choice. 'Antinomians' were sects which held an extreme form of Calvinism: for example, they thought that, once saved, Christians could not sin, and thus Lucy Hutchinson notes derogatorily 'no unsanctified person is actually iustified, whatever the Antinomians assert to the contrary' (p. 81). The most famous heretics were 'the Seekers, Anabaptists, Antinomians' as Thomas Edwards put it in 1646.[32]

---

[29] Hutchinson, *Principles*, p. 135 onwards; Perkins, *The Whole Treatise*, p. 259.
[30] Hutchinson, *Principles*, pp. 94, 128, 23.
[31] Hutchinson, *Memoirs of the Life of Colonel Hutchinson*, p. 42.
[32] Thomas Edwards, *Gangraena, or, A catalogue and discovery of many of the errours, heresies, blasphemies and pernicious practices of the sectaries of this time* (1646), A3v.

Here we move from the actual words of the text to an assumed context, and from now on I sketch it out. By the 1640s, and even into the 1660s, it was often attested to in publications that the most famous Antinomian scandal took place in Boston, New England, in the late 1630s, and involved a woman called Anne Hutchinson.[33] Not only did Lucy share the same surname, Anne Hutchinson came from the same area of England and had the right to bear the same coat of arms. In *Early English Books Online*, Anne's name is second only in number of mentions of 'Hutchinson' to Lucy's husband John. I wonder whether Lucy and her daughter would be more aware of this context, a trans-Atlantic one in the physical direction of which Barbara Orgil was about to move, than the English one of the 1670s pamphlet wars surrounding Sherlock. Tempting as it is to involve Lucy Hutchinson in what is clearly an up-to-date and politically significant pamphlet controversy of the 1670s, she has chosen to present her theology in a feminized, unthreatening, domestic context.

The kinds of publications that discuss the New England heresy trials are popular and – by 1668 – fairly old pamphlets, of a kind that may have been more likely to be known by women. John Winthrop's 'official' version of the scandal in Boston, *A Short Story of the rise, reign, and ruine of the antinomians, familists & libertines, that infected the churches of New-England*, was reprinted often in 1644, and Edward Johnson's *A History of New England* was printed in 1653. In these pamphlets the Antinomian scandal is often represented as initiated primarily by Anne Hutchinson, who is still associated with the Antinomian heresy in Boston into the 1660s.[34] Deborah Schneider argues that the real target of the 1637 trials was John Cotton: nonetheless Anne Hutchinson, the 'American Jezebel' as John Winthrop called her, was the main name associated with the crisis.[35]

John Wheelwright, who was married to Anne Hutchinson's sister Mary and represented as one of Anne Hutchinson's main supporters, was still suffering from his involvement with the Antinomian controversy in 1658. By this time he was back in England and had achieved what Michael Winship calls a 'tepid' acknowledgement of his innocence in the Hutchinson affair from the general court in New England.[36] He still, however, felt inclined to publish a defence of his views in 1658, *A Brief, and Plain Apology written by John Wheelwright: wherein he doth vindicate himself, from al* [sic] *those*

---

[33] Michael P. Winship, 'Hutchinson, Anne (*bap.* 1591, *d.* 1643)', *ODNB*.
[34] Richard Baxter, *The Reasons of the Christian Religion* (1667), p. 355; John Spencer, *A Discourse concerning Prodigies* (1663), p. 90; John Trapp, *A Commentary or Exposition* (1660), pp. 94, 426.
[35] Schneider, 'Anne Hutchinson'; Winthrop, *A Short Story* (1644), p. 66.
[36] Michael P. Winship, 'Wheelwright, John (1592?–1679)', *ODNB*.

*errors, heresies, and flagitious crimes, layed to his charge by Mr. Thomas Weld,
in his short story, and further fastened upon him, by Mr. Samuel Rutherford
in his survey of antinomianisme.* Not only does this publication refer back
to the original 1644 pamphlet, *A Short Story*, indicating that the contents
were well known in 1658, it also is written in answer to the Presbyte-
rian Samuel Rutherford's attack on Antinomianism in 1648, *A Survey of
the Spirituall Antichrist opening the secrets of familisme and antinomianisme
in the antichristian doctrine of John Saltmarsh and Will. Del, the present
preachers of the army now in England.* Although the title of this publication
mentions the Antinomians in England, Saltmarsh and Dell, Chapter 16
describes the New England scandal, with John Wheelwright mentioned in
the same breath as Anne Hutchinson. By contrast, in his own pamphlet
Wheelwright does not mention his sister-in-law Anne Hutchinson – she
had been dead for fifteen years, killed, as her opponents never tired of
pointing out, in providential glee, by the Indians she refused to fear. He
was probably trying to avoid the sensationalism associated with her name:
most publications talk about the 'monsters' to which she is supposed to
have given birth.

Wheelwright does, however, spell out four 'theses' that he believes might
have led to him being labelled an Antinomian. Taken together, these four
statements certainly represent the stressing of grace over works – in particular, an emphasis on the internal witness of the Holy Spirit for assurance
of salvation rather than on good works as the first fruits of salvation.[37] As
Lucy Hutchinson points out in her discussion of preparatory grace in *Principles*, the adjective used to describe those who disagree with Antinomians
is 'legal': relying on obedience to commandments, the opposite of relying on grace.[38] In her somewhat conflicted account of 'preparatory grace',
Hutchinson shows that she is torn between the sense that conversion is
down to the supernatural intervention of God's grace, and the idea that
common-sense human factors (in this case, human emotions) are involved.
In the end she comes down on the side of preachers like Thomas Shepard,
calling them 'sound':

> There are many devines who also absolutely denie this preparatory worke
> and call them legall preachers that presse it: but I find it the generall roade
> of the most sound preachers first to convince men they are sinners, and to
> humble them for their sins, and then to propound Christ as a Redeemer.
> (*Principles*, p. 63)

---

[37] Wheelwright, *A Brief, and Plain Apology* (1658), passim.
[38] See Hutchinson, *Principles*: 'There are many devines who . . . call them legall preachers' (p. 63).

She also discusses in the same context 'the first act of life' which she sees as faith – Wheelwright in his four statements of faith which he admits are controversial talks twice about the 'first evidence' which he sees as the witness of the Holy Spirit. On this issue both are on the same side against Arminians, who see 'good works' as the first evidence. Wheelwright quotes Calvin in his defence, who, he says, denied that the 'good works' of sanctification were the first evidence of justification.[39]

Lucy Hutchinson's *Principles* seems preoccupied with the issues that were at the heart of the Boston trials. For instance, the order of the Christian processes of sanctification and justification is crucial: Antinomians are believed to see the two processes as occurring simultaneously, so that on becoming a Christian the believer was instantly holy. In his *Antapologia* (1644) Thomas Edwards, the Presbyterians' great heresiographer, mentions Anne Hutchinson and John Wheelwright as believing that sanctification was the proof of justification: 'in the business of M. *Wheelwright*, and Mistris *Hutchinson*, and some of those opinions about Sanctification evidencing Justification'.[40] As Lucy Hutchinson says in *Principles*: 'Concerning the order of these graces of iustification, and sanctification, which precedes the other there is great dispute' (p. 81). She is very careful to spell out the exact biblical order of justification and sanctification, which she says in her religious commonplace book she is taking from Romans 7 and 8.[41] 'In the end' sin will be overcome, and the believer will be sanctified, but it does not happen 'in this life':

> This grace of sanctification is, throughout, in the whole man, through the vertue of Christs death and resurrection, by his word and spirit, dwelling in the saints; the dominion of the whole body of sinne is destroyd, and the lusts thereof dayly more and more mortified, and graces increased: but the body is not fully redeemd from all bondage in this life, but there is a perpetuall combate betweene the flesh and the spirit, yet though remaining corruption sometimes prevaile through the continuall supplie of grace from Christ by his spirit. (p. 93)

Lucy Hutchinson is making clear that there is quite a long time-lag between justification and sanctification, and this is a conscious argument against Antinomianism.

Moreover, Lucy Hutchinson talks a great deal about good works, which she calls 'duties'. She is very keen to stress the importance of duties, like Thomas Shepherd, who was both Anne Hutchinson's main opponent in

---

[39] John Wheelwright, *A Brief, and Plain Apology* (1658), p. 3.
[40] Edwards, *Antapologia*, p. 40.    [41] Nottingham Archives, DD/HU3.

the Boston trials and one of Lucy Hutchinson's main sources in *Principles*. 'Duties' is a word Shepard uses quite often, despite the fact that in his writing William Sherlock represents all Nonconformists as being anti 'duties'.[42] At the beginning of *The Parable of the Ten Virgins* Shepard explains what he means by it, against the Antinomians, whom he calls 'they': 'Justification by Faith is too narrow a path, unless they may be justified before and without Faith, it is not free enough; they complain of it as if it laid them under a Covenant of works'.[43] In *Principles* Lucy Hutchinson explains to Barbara what she sees as the orthodox position on 'duties' which is that the Christian is enabled to do these 'duties of love' by faith:

> he forbidds not the morall duties of the law, but contrarily presses and urges them as duties of love, whereby faith worketh in every true believer, but not as workes whereby wee are iustified before God, which is a benefitt that wee only receive from his free grace in Christ, in whom all the righteous law of God is confirmd, and by whom it was fullfilld for us, yet not so that wee are freed from all dutie, but made free to dutie. (p. 56)

She does not use the unpleasant word 'works', which the Antinomians use; she is talking in the context of Paul's Epistle to the Galatians, which is often read as pro-grace, anti-works.[44] Hutchinson's point is that Christian Liberty does not mean that the individual does not have to do duties, but that he is able to do them. Number 5 of her ten points on 'Christian Liberty' is that Christians are delivered 'from the spiritt of bondage and feare in duties' (*Principles*, p. 80).

Particularly interesting is what Lucy Hutchinson says about 'duties' in *Principles*. Unlike Shepard, she never implies that 'duties' are what Antinomians call 'works' – concrete examples of obedience to God's Law, like keeping the Sabbath. When she says 'I thinke it will not be impertinent to my purpose to treat those duties more particularly', she identifies these 'duties' as love, admiration, reverence, and adoration – states of mind rather than actions.[45] The 'duties' involved in loving God she specifies as:

> 1 Joy & delight in God alone, when all creature streames either are wholly dried up, or come in with a full flood.

[42] Sherlock, *Discourse*, p. 12.    [43] Thomas Shepard, *The Parable of the Ten Virgins* (1660), p. A2v.

[44] See the introduction to Galatians in the Westminster Assembly's *Annotations upon all the Books of the Old and New Testaments* (1657).

[45] *Ibid.*, p. 107.

2<sup>dly</sup> Feare of God alone according to Christ's precept: – Feare not them that can kill the body, but feare Him who is able to kill both soule and body, and cast both into hell

3<sup>dly</sup> Desire of enioying him only, which is called in Scripture hungring and thirsting after God . . .

4<sup>thly</sup> Hope and Confidence in God alone. (pp. 94–5)

These are certainly not what Antinomians would refer to as 'works' – they are aspects of the believer's relationship with God, resembling what look like 'emotions' rather than 'duties'. This final section of *Principles* is, however, devoted to 'inward worship'. Hutchinson is very clear that 'inward worship' must accompany all 'outward worship' (p. 137).

It seems that Lucy Hutchinson is redefining 'duties' not as what Antinomians call 'works' but as something else – emotions, or what would be called 'motions' in the seventeenth century – holy impulses produced by the Holy Spirit (something that Antinomians would recognize). Lucy Hutchinson does not seem to be interested in the external details one might expect from 'duties', such as alms-giving – she relegates these to another book, which has not survived if it existed. Clearly the 'inward virtues' are pre-eminent:

> These inward virtues are requisite in the true inward worship of God, without which the outward worship is but a false shew, a painted sepulcher, and hath no acceptance with the Lord; but concerning the duties and cerimonies of outward worship, I shall send you my experiences in another booke. (p. 137)

As an editor I would be fascinated to know precisely what she is talking about. It is tempting to think she is referencing the Arminian Anglican church of 1668 and indeed one could add a note to that effect, but the responsibility of the first editor of the manuscript is great – for the subsequent careful reader of the edition, the notes become part of the text, and the editor may be wrong.

Throughout *Principles* Lucy Hutchinson insists that she is orthodox and that what she is telling her daughter is true Christianity. As she says at the end:

> I beg of you make conscience of all these things which I have weakely, according to my ability, sett before you; but the truths are not weake, but the powerfull word and precepts of the Lord, and the duties commanded are allowd by all Christians without dispute. (p. 137)

This fits well with the opening letter, in which she seems to be warning against sects.

> if some one opinion draw men into a sect, for that they espouse all the erronious practises and opinions of that sect, and reiect the benefitt they might have by spirituall converse with Christians of other iudgements, at least receive nothing from them without it passe the verdict of that sect they encline to . . . Sects are a great sinne. (p. 4)

A modern reader is influenced by the modern usage of the word to substitute one of the many mid-century sects like Diggers or Ranters, but John Owen does not use the word like that, and neither does Richard Baxter.

Hutchinson does not make it clear what sect she is referring to, and it may be that she is influenced by the rise in heresiography in the mid-1640s led by Thomas Edwards and his volumes of *Gangraena* which Ann Hughes identifies consisting of works like Robert Baillie's *A Dissuasive from the Errours of the Time wherein the tenets of the principall sects, especially of the Independents, are drawn together* (1645) and Ephraim Pagitt's 1645 *Heresiography*, reprinted several times up to 1662.[46] Both publications mention Anne Hutchinson, and Robert Baillie spends most of his time treating the Independents. William Prynne, in his *The Sword of Christian Magistracy Supported, or, A vindication of the Christian magistrates authority under the Gospell* (1653), praises the Independents, who are clearly seen by him as having a toleration of heresy, for finding against Anne Hutchinson:

> The Independents in *New-England* it selfe, as Master *Cotton*, Master *Hooker*, and others, are of the same judgment, and *de facto* banished Master *Williams*, Mistris *Hutchinson*, and other Hereticks and Schismaticks, out of their Plantation.[47]

*Principles* does not contain any of the detailed descriptions of erroneous practices and beliefs we would expect from seventeenth-century heresiography, despite the preoccupation of the initial letter with 'sects'; it offers an account of what Lucy Hutchinson feels is orthodox, not a condemnation of any particular sect. Perhaps it is an attempt to find an answer to the problem of 'good works', the problem which had been at the centre of the Boston Antinomian trials. It was a huge point of difference between Arminians and Antinomians and was still very much an issue in England,

---

[46] Hughes, *Gangraena and the Struggle for the English Revolution*, pp. 55–229.
[47] Prynne, *The Sword of Christian Magistry*, p. 152.

as the expanded definition of 'sanctification' in the Savoy Confession in 1658 made clear.[48]

In any case, this text is a useful illustration of how helpful or otherwise the choosing of a context in editing a new text can be. It is important to decide what knowledge is being assumed in a seventeenth-century reader: the author may or may not make his or her assumptions explicit, especially when the designated reader is as intimately connected to the author as a daughter. With a theological treatise like this piece of writing, the choice of a consciously feminized genre I think indicates that a female context is valid for this particular text: the choice of the Anne Hutchinson scandal as the context makes *Principles* more about the issue of what the first fruits of salvation for a reader should be. I believe it also draws more attention to what could be seen as the most original aspect of *Principles*. Most of the last part of the treatise seems to be dedicated to how it feels to be a Christian: how the human believer discerns the presence of a Divine Spirit dwelling in her and how she facilitates its operations. The 'duties' Lucy Hutchinson talks about, which are the way a human believer relates to the divine presence, are the most original aspect of this theological treatise, and their very difference from the way 'works' are understood in the Arminian-Antinomian quarrel helps to illuminate the freshness of the theological thinking that is going on here.

It is not always easy to identify a context for the women's writing one is editing, especially if, as is often the case, it is in manuscript. Seventeenth-century women like Lucy Hutchinson are very aware that the orthodoxies of gender ideology which they are keen to observe prohibit not only the printing of their writing, but in the wider sense their participation in a shared field of public discourse. Thus, as with *Principles*, the approved genres for women to write in are those which are aimed at their families: in the case of a mother's legacy, the writing woman fulfils the role prescribed for her in conduct books of teaching her family.[49] Such a writing situation must be to some extent private, as the writing refers to a common female family reading experience. This means that early modern women's writing, and their manuscript writing in particular, is likely to reference a very

---

[48] *A declaration of the faith and order owned and practised in the Congregational Churches in England agreed upon and consented unto by their elders and messengers in their meeting at the Savoy, October 12. 1658*, p. 26. There is a tabular comparison of the Westminster Confession, the Baptist Confession, and the Savoy Confession at www.proginosko.com/docs/wcf_sdfo_lbcf.html. In *Memoirs*, Lucy Hutchinson made it clear that her husband never suffered from the 'carelessness of life' for which Calvinists were often criticized (p. 54).

[49] See Richard Brathwaite, *The English Gentlewoman* (1631): 'Onely for *vertues* honour, is shee become a Teacher; that the *Younger* may be instructed by those that are *Elder*' (p. 9).

different context from men's writing, and to reference it in different ways partly because the readership is assumed to be different. This chapter has discussed one woman's theological writing, which is perhaps a particularly fraught area in the seventeenth century, as male theological writers are likely to be university educated, and have an unproblematic relationship to public discourse: the choice of a contemporary academic frame of reference would seem to be a legitimate strategy for the editor of male-authored theological writing. The question for an editor of a woman's theological treatise is, how do we identify and supply the context for such writing? We have decided in editing this work not to be too dogmatic but to give various options, and to allow this writing to take its place among future research on what Lucy Hutchinson believed.

# PART II

# Editing Female Forms
## Gender, Genre, and Editing

CHAPTER 6

# Critical Categories
## Toward an Archaeology of Anne, Lady Halkett's Archive

### Suzanne Trill

While it is generally true that 'editing early modern women writers for whom there was very little biographical data' is a task that is 'particularly challenging, given that the standard format of "works and life" is problematical from the start', tracing the archaeology of Anne, Lady Halkett's archive leads me to suggest that the critical treatment of her 'life and works' reveals an important exception to this rule which requires us to address this issue from another perspective.[1] For in Halkett's case, the editorial history and critical reception of her life and works suggest that only a very small part of them is of interest; thus, the question becomes which 'lives' and which 'works' are we (as feminist editors) prepared to acknowledge? Ironically, Halkett's first editor, Simon Couper, positioned her precisely within the classic 'life and works' paradigm when he published *The Life of the Lady Halket* (1701), followed by four volumes of her 'Meditations' (1701–2).[2] Couper's biography draws heavily on her writings and concludes with a six-page listing of the contents of 'Books written by' her. Yet, with only a few exceptions, modern feminist critics have focused their energies on one text which Couper did *not* include in his list: that is, 'A True Accountt of My Life', more frequently referred to as her 'Autobiography' or 'Memoirs'. It seems likely that Couper self-consciously suppressed the existence of the 'True Accountt' to suit his own political ends; for him, Halkett was predominantly a writer of sacred texts (or 'Select Meditations'). By the twentieth century, both Couper's prior work and Halkett's other volumes had become marginalized: until very recently, the most cited modern edition of Halkett's writing was Loftis's *The Memoirs of*

I would like to thank the University of Edinburgh's School of Literatures, Languages and Cultures for their financial assistance in permission to reproduce images from the National Library of Scotland.

[1] Hurley and Goodblatt, 'Preface' to *Women Editing/Editing Women*, pp. xi–xviii (p. xi).
[2] *The Life of the Lady Halket* (1701), *Meditations and Prayers, upon the First Week* (1701), *Meditations on the Twentieth and fifth Psalm* (1701), *Meditations upon the Seven Gifts of the Holy Spirit* (1702), and *Instructions for Youth* (1702).

*Anne, Lady Halkett and Anne, Lady Fanshawe* (1979) in which Couper is
identified only by the initials 'S. C.' and Halkett's other writings are barely
alluded to. Impressive as Loftis's edition undoubtedly is, it established the
critical framework within which Halkett's writing continues to be understood: that is, as an individual, isolated text by an English female, royalist,
Civil War memoirist.[3] Consequently, there is so much interest in Halkett's
'life and work' between the years 1648 and 1656 that the rest of her life
and works are sidelined. Fascinating as this period of her life undoubtedly
was, Halkett lived for seventy-nine years and wrote at least twenty-two
manuscript books; thus, to understand her 'life and works' more fully –
including the 'True Accountt' – we need to extend *what* we study and
reassess *how* we have studied it.

Here I aim to trace an archaeology of Anne, Lady Halkett's archive
in order to uncover why there is such a fundamental difference between
Couper's 'Halkett' and our own. Much critical ink from a wide range of
disciplines has been spent on attempting to define the archive and, in part,
this chapter seeks to establish of what exactly Halkett's archive consists.[4]
Where are her texts located and how did they come to be there? Which
of these materials have been edited and read since her death in 1699?
And what do the answers to these questions reveal about the impact of
feminist editorial practices on the field of early modern women's writing?
Texts in Halkett's own hand are currently dispersed across a number of
institutionally recognized archives (the British Library, the National Library
of Scotland, the National Registers of Scotland, the National Archives, at
Kew, and Dunfermline Public Library). Partly because of Couper's editorial
interventions, Halkett's 'archive' also extends well beyond the materials
listed by him. A surprising number of copies of Couper's posthumously
published *Life* and *Meditations* can still be found in libraries across the world
(including Australia, Canada, Ireland, and the USA).[5] Thus it would seem
that Halkett was a figure of international interest even before her 'True
Accountt' was re-discovered. Drawing on the insights of new textualism

---

[3] Important exceptions to this rule are Ezell, 'Posthumous Publication'; and Ezell, 'Ann Halkett's
   Morning Devotions'; Murphy, '"A Stranger"'; Eales, 'Anne Halkett'; and Wiseman, '"Most Consid-
   erable"'; and Wiseman, *Conspiracy and Virtue*.
[4] The concept of the archive has been widely debated across and within disciplines. See Manoff,
   'Theories', and Voss and Werner, 'Toward a Poetics'. My work here aims to complement that of
   Ezell, 'Posthumous Publication'; and Wiseman, '"Most Considerable"'. Patricia Pender and Rosalind
   Smith extend the concept of the archive in the final chapter in this volume.
[5] According to the *STC*, fourteen copies of Couper's biography remain extant. (This list does not
   include the copy currently held in Dunfermline Public Library.) The *STC* also lists between fifteen
   and twenty extant copies in libraries worldwide of each of the other volumes of Halkett's writing
   edited by Couper.

and paying careful attention to the processes by which this particular volume has come to occupy centre stage for modern-day feminist critics, I will demonstrate how its material peculiarities require us to revise our understanding of both its own meaning and its position within the rest of Halkett's writing. Ultimately, I argue that Halkett's writing challenges many of the critical categories routinely deployed by editors and literary critics, including those of gender and genre. A case in point is the title of her 'autobiography' or 'memoirs'. In accordance with Halkett's own practice I will be referring to this volume as her 'True Accountt' throughout; for, especially in the context of this present volume, it is ironic that the other terms (which are not coterminous) are the result of the choices made by her two previous (male) editors, John Gough Nichols (1875) and John Loftis (1979). The title of a text is a powerful determinant of how readers will respond to it and the apparently simple task of classification simultaneously categorizes it within a critical field which imposes certain critical constraints – a consideration that also affects the nomenclature of Lucy Hutchinson's 'On the Principles of the Christian Religion', as Elizabeth Clarke explores in this volume.[6] Below I explore what influence such categorization has had within the historical transmission and editing of Halkett's texts, and what effects this has had upon our conceptualization of her 'life and works'.

## Halkett in the Eighteenth Century: Simon Couper and Halkett's 'Books'

In an entry dated 'Satturday 19th of February 1697/8', Halkett explains how she finally reached the decision to entrust Couper (and two other ministers, James Graeme and Mr Marshall) with all of her 'Bookes' with the instruction that they might publish them posthumously 'if they thought fit then to make them knowne'.[7] Initially, she offers 'to send the Trunke to him with as many of them as itt would hold', along with a 'Sealed Paper' in which she had recorded the contents of each volume. However, acceding to Couper's request, Halkett actually sent him her volumes one at a time.[8] Significantly, she specifies that the first volume she delivered was 'The

---

[6] For an outline of the traditional divisions of 'memoir' and 'autobiography', see Weintraub, 'Autobiography and Historical Consciousness'. For a discussion of recent developments, see Dowd and Eckerle, *Genre*. Seelig looks specifically at early modern women's autobiography in *Autobiography and Gender*. Shelvin, '"To Reconcile Book and Title"', explores the historical contract performed by titles. For Halkett's definition of this book as 'A True Accountt of my Life', see *Lady Anne Halkett*, ed. Trill, pp. xxxvi–vii.

[7] *Halkett*, ed. Trill, p. 188.     [8] *Ibid.*, p. 189.

Parchment booke with Pincke & Ashe riban where the most considerable of my troubles are registred'. Despite its omission from his list of her books, it seems likely that the first volume Halkett sent to Couper was her 'True Accountt'. Furthermore, Halkett states that her ministers had known of that volume's existence for some time, as she 'had formerly aquainted them with the Account of my Life'.[9] While we may have cause to question Couper's apparent suppression of this volume, it is important to recognize that Halkett specifically chose to position him as her literary executor. Her 'desorder' and 'disquiett' after handing over her first book signals both the magnitude of this decision and the high degree of the trust in which she held him; thus, rather than dismissing his biography as 'hagiographical', I suggest we should pay far more attention to his role as Halkett's editor than has so far been the case.[10]

Most obviously, Couper's involvement speaks to the immediate context of Halkett's textual production: that is, the bitter and frequently bloody disputes over the organization of the Church/Kirk in post-Restoration Scotland. While the Episcopalians had experienced a brief period of ascendancy during the early years of the Restoration, the turbulent years of James VII/II's and William and Mary's reigns had seen greater moves toward religious tolerance and resulted in the reassertion of Presbyterianism as the founding principle of the Scottish Kirk.[11] Couper and Graeme were Halkett's favourite ministers in Dunfermline; like her, they supported Episcopalianism even though this worked to their personal detriment. Couper was officially deprived of his ministry in 1694, while Graeme managed to hold onto his office until 1701, this giving him the dubious honour of being the last Episcopalian minister of Dunfermline.[12] Neither gave in easily to the pressure from the General Assembly and Halkett charts their clashes with this body throughout the 1680s and 1690s. Although Couper's biography downplays Halkett's youthful relationships, focusing instead on her activities during her twenty-nine years of widowhood, this representation accords with Halkett's own frequently reiterated desire to conduct herself 'as a Widow Indeed'; indeed, the *Life* closely paraphrases – or quotes wholesale – from what remains of the 'True Accountt'.[13] However, the

[9]  *Ibid.*, p. 188.
[10] Walker, "'Divine Chymistry'", p. 134. See also *Halkett*, ed. Trill, p. xxxiii; and Wiseman, "'Most Considerable'", p. 29.
[11] For a detailed discussion of Scottish ecclesiastical and political history, see Buckroyd, *Church and State*, and Jackson, *Restoration Scotland*.
[12] Couper and Graeme's cases are discussed by Raffe, *Culture of Controversy*, pp. 83–4, 114.
[13] Couper's access to Halkett's 'True Accountt' is clearly indicated by his extended citation of the conversation Halkett has with Colonel Overton at the dining table at Fyvie (1650). See his *Life* (1701), pp. 24–5 and *Halkett*, ed. Trill, pp. 110–12.

'exemplary' nature of the *Life* is suited to Couper's immediate political purposes, as he utilizes Halkett's *Life* as part of an attempt to prove the extent of Episcopalian piety. This political intention is further evidenced by Couper's publication of a series of treatises on the 'true' order of the Church during the same period as he published Halkett's texts.[14]

## Catalogues and Categories: The Missing Volumes

By the late seventeenth century it was relatively commonplace for exemplary biographies of early modern women to include references to and extracts from their daily devotional writings.[15] To my knowledge, however, Halkett's is unique insofar as it concludes with 'a Catalogue of some Books writ by her, the bare Contents of which will shew, how well she was imployed, and how Conversant in Spiritual Things' intended 'as a Confirmation of the preceeding Account and Character' (p. 58); for Couper, Halkett's 'Books' validate both her life and his *Life*. As well as an outline of their contents, this chronological catalogue provides a brief bibliographical description of each of the twenty-one 'Books' Halkett wrote between 1644 and 1699, which records the size and length of each volume, whether or not it was bound, and its dates of composition (see Figures 6.1 and 6.2). However, Couper himself acknowledges that his list is incomplete when he signs off stating '[t]here are besides the forementioned, about thirty stitched Books, some in *Folio*, some in *4to*. most of them of 10 or 12 sheets, all containing occasional Meditations'.[16] Although not always fully acknowledged, Couper's list has formed the basis upon which our understanding of Anne, Lady Halkett's textual production is founded. Ballard used his material for his entry on Halkett in *Memoirs of Several Ladies* (1752); Nichols drew on it for his *Autobiography of Anne, Lady Halkett* (1875); Loftis cites the *Life* in his introduction; and it was studying the extant volumes at the NLS that stimulated my selection for the Ashgate edition. But what might Couper's list reveal about both his editorial decisions and the nature of Halkett's archive?

For practical purposes, I include here a condensed version of it (below). As a general principle, Couper divides Halkett's volumes into 'Select' and

---

[14] Couper's texts were published both singly and collectively between 1704 and 1705, all four being printed together as *Four Essays Concerning Church Government* (Edinburgh, 1705). For a discussion of the politics of printing in Scotland, see Ezell, 'Ann Halkett's Morning Devotions', pp. 226–8 and Mann, *Scottish Book Trade*, pp. 139–48.

[15] See, for example, Anthony Walker's funeral sermon and biography of Mary Rich, Countess of Warwick, *Eureka, Eureka* (1678) 'to which are Annexed some of her Ladyships Pious and Useful Meditations'.

[16] Couper, *Life*, p. 64.

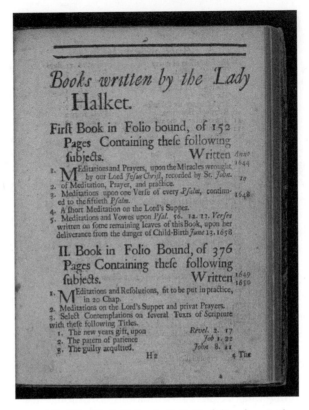

Figure 6.1 *The Life of Lady Halket*, by S. C. Croft (London, 1701), p. 59.

'Occasional' Meditations. Wherever possible, my abbreviated title is based
on that of the first entry within each volume (where that first entry is
simply given as 'Meditations', I also provide an indication, in brackets,
of a text which is unique to that volume). Volumes in this list whose
titles are italicized are no longer extant. Those which are also underlined
identify the volumes upon which Couper based some of his editions (1701–
2). Volumes with dates in bold are those which Couper acknowledges to
contain 'Occasional Meditations'.

1. *Meditations and Prayers, upon the Miracles (1644–8, plus Childbirth in
   1658)*
2. *Meditations on the Lord's Supper (1649–50)*
3. *Meditations on the 25 Psalm (1651)*
4. *Meditations on Death (1652)*

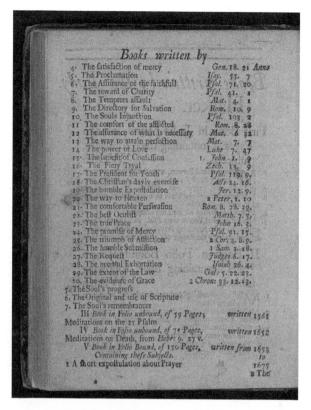

Figure 6.2 *The Life of Lady Halket,* by S. C. Croft (London, 1701), p. 60.

5. An Expostulation about Prayer (1653, inc. The Mothers Will (1675))
6. Select and occasional Meditations intermixed (**1657–60**)
7. Meditations and Prayers on the Festival Days observed in the Church of England (**1661–2**)
8. *Meditations and Prayers upon the first Week (**1663–5**)*
9. Meditations (**1666–70**, inc. Instructions to her Son)
10. The Widows Mite (**1673–4**)
11. *The True Balm (1675–6)*
12. The Arte of Divine Chymistry (1677–8)
13. Joseph's Tryall & Triumph (1678–9)
14. *Meditations on the Fruits of the Spirit (**1682–3**)*
15. Meditations on the Book of Jonah (1684–5/6)
16. Meditations on the Passion of our Lord (**1687–8**)
17. Meditations on Moses and Samuel (1689)

18.  Meditations on the Book of Nehemiah (**1690–2**)
19.  Upon Watchfulness (**1693–5**)
20.  Meditations (**1696–7**, inc. Esther)
21.  Meditations on the Articles of the Creed (**1698–9**)

While much has been written about the missing pages in Halkett's 'True Accountt', very little has so far been said about the seven volumes of her writing that have been unaccounted for since at least 1875. Why have some of these volumes survived and not the others? One possibility for at least two of these volumes (3 and 8) is that they were retained by Couper for editing purposes. Indeed, the inside flyleaf of the *Life* carries an advertisement for the forthcoming publication of Halkett's *Meditations on the 25th Psalm* which also appeared in 1701. Also that year, he published the 'Select Meditations' section of volume 8 in his list, under the title *Meditations and Prayers, upon the First Week*. However, Couper's final edition of Halkett's 'Books', *Meditations upon the Seven Gifts of the Holy Spirit* (1702), raises another question about the accuracy of his listing. Given the closeness of their titles, I had originally assumed that the first part of this volume was based on the 'Select Meditations' section of volume 14; however, Couper includes Halkett's date of completion at the text's conclusion, which states it was 'written at Edinburgh, in the month of Ianuary 1679/80' (p. 22). Thus, Couper's last and longest edition appears to include material from an *unlisted* manuscript. In addition to these inconsistencies, Couper's published editions include further evidence that his catalogue was incomplete: for also missing are *Instructions for Youth* (1701) and *Meditations upon Jabez His Request, 1 Chron iv. 10* (1702), which the title page proclaims was 'Written by the Lady Halket. Begun 24 Oct: ended 30 Nov: 1686'.[17] While two of the volumes which have long been missing may have become separated from the others because Couper retained them for editorial purposes, it would seem that there were others in his possession which did not even make it into his list. Thus, although twenty-one volumes of manuscript writing is an unusually large output for an early modern woman writer, these discrepancies suggest that Halkett's original corpus was even more extensive. Ironically, Couper's faithful reproduction of Halkett's own dating system reveals incongruities between her own sense of her texts and his presentation of them. Despite his task being made 'much easier' as it was 'Halkett's practice . . . to include a "Table of Contents" for her

---

[17]  The volume includes a separate title page for the *Meditations upon Jabez*: 22. The contents of *Instructions for Youth* are not the same as her 'Instructions to her Son' (NLS MS 6492) nor do they correlate with 'The Mother's Will' (NLS MS 6489).

volumes',[18] the surviving evidence also suggests there are some significant differences between Couper's and Halkett's categorizations of her texts. Examining where their systems coincide and conflict not only assists in the excavation of the archaeological organization of Halkett's archive but also calls modern classifications of her texts into question.

## Contents and Classification: Missing Genres

Couper is so intent on representing Halkett as a figure of exemplary piety that his publications consist almost entirely of what he refers to as 'Select Meditations'. Despite referencing 'Occasional Meditations' in his catalogue, only his final volume includes any such materials; even then, these materials take up only a total of eighteen pages. According to the concluding sentence of that volume, these were 'collected out of the Originals, mentioned in the last three Lines of the Catalogue of the Lady Halket's Manuscripts, subjoin'd to her *Life*'.[19] The title page of the final volume clearly highlights Couper's priorities, which relegate this material to the end of the volume and position it as an afterthought (via the final conjunction).[20] Even so, this material is almost subsumed into the 'Sacramental Meditations' and the generic classification of 'Occasional Meditation' does not appear. In many ways, then, Couper's presentation of this material renders it almost indistinguishable from what he defines as Halkett's 'Select' Meditations. Indeed, he also entitles them so that they appear more theological than personal. For example, the first section, designated as 'Prayers upon Several Occasions' (pp. 68–75), contains two items entitled 'A Prayer for the Publick, February 7th 1678/9' and 'A Prayer in a long Continued Storm of Frost and Snow. January 24. 1684'; yet, in the extant volumes, Halkett never uses the title 'Prayer' for any entry she defines as an 'occasional meditation', which suggests this designation reflects Couper's classificatory system.

Strictly speaking, according to Couper, Halkett did not write any 'occasional' meditations at all until 1657: he defines the first five volumes' contents as meditations and resolutions, select contemplations, meditations and vows, meditations and prayers, and an expostulation (about prayer), but finds no 'occasional' meditations. If we take Couper's word, it would

---

[18] Ezell, 'Ann Halkett's Morning Devotions', p. 219.

[19] Halkett, *Meditations upon the Seven Gifts* (1702), p. 86.

[20] The full title of this text is: *meditations upon the Seven Gifts of the Holy Spirit, Mentioned in Isaiah XI. 2, 3. As also meditations upon Jabez his Request, I. Chron. IV. 10. Together with Sacramental Meditations on the lord's supper; and Prayers, Pious Reflections and Observations.*

seem that, having started writing such materials in 1657, Halkett continues to do so until 1674 when she takes a complete break from this form of writing for the next seven years; after this, her practice appears rather disjointed until the final years of her life, during which she returns to writing such materials regularly (see list, above). While the five extant volumes confirm Couper's list of their contents, given the amount of such materials Halkett writes, the amount of time she spends doing it, and how habitual it is, it seems strange that there should be such gaps: even if we allow it to be the case that Halkett didn't start writing such materials until her marriage, this doesn't explain their later fragmentation. And, even if every one of the 'stitched books' contained occasional meditations, Couper's assessment of their length and number means their contents are unlikely to cover all the gaps identified above.

Couper's lack of interest in Halkett's 'Occasional Meditations' is reinforced by the minimal references to them in his catalogue. Typically, he simply identifies them under this broad-brush generic classification, without further comment. Importantly, this is in complete contrast to the attention with which Halkett herself records them. One particular volume, number 6, stands out in this regard, which Couper describes as follows:

> *VI Book in Octavo Bound,*                                   *written from 1657*
> *Containing 35 Select and occasional Meditations intermixed*               *to*
>                                                                        *1660*

> The select Meditations are,

> 1.  On Hypocrisy,
> 2.  Upon the Sacrament,
> 3.  Upon Riches,
> 4.  Upon 2 *Chron: 28. 10 v.*
> 5.  Upon Beauty,
> 6.  Upon Poverty,
> 7.  Upon Imagination,
> 8.  Upon the Power of Faith, from *Mark 16 Chap:17. 18.v.*
> 9.  Upon Covetousness,
> 10. Upon the Failings of great Professors.

> The Occasional Meditations are upon several publick and privat Occurences; whereof the two last are upon the late Change of Publick Affairs, and upon the Return of the King, *May 1660.*

First, although the extant volume (NLS MS 6490) is entitled by Halkett herself specifically as *Occasional Meditations*, Couper redefines its contents to include some 'Select' meditations according to some unacknowledged principles of his own. In the process, he rearranges them into his own order, for they do not follow Halkett's numerical system (see Appendix 1 at the end of this chapter). While Couper generally retains Halkett's own titles, for example 'Upon Riches', he eliminates Halkett's sense of 'Conviction' with reference to 2 Chron 28:10 and standardizes her biblical references as well. More importantly, Couper's list eradicates the entries we might see as more personal; for example, he does not include those entries which deal with family illness or household disputes. With the exception of 'Vpon the peace made betwixt France & Spaine', the rest of the entries would not strike a modern audience as directly relating to 'publick' affairs. Thus, Couper's list might also tell us something about the emerging distinction between the 'public' and the 'private' at the turn of the eighteenth century.

While this book is unusual among Halkett's extant volumes, it provides a particularly marked example of the discrepancies between Halkett's practice and Couper's editorial interventions. To date, the genre of the 'Occasional Meditation' has received little critical attention; however, according to Halkett's own 'Tables of Contents', such meditations make up a significant section of her surviving autograph texts.[21] Although Halkett does paste or copy things into her books, in the other extant volumes she characteristically 'casts off blanks';[22] that is, she leaves several pages blank in order to create distinct sections, and by this signifies her intention of dividing her books into 'select' and 'occasional' meditations. Ezell has argued that Halkett's use of paratextual materials (such as titles and tables of contents) indicates that she 'already viewed her writings as texts, requiring those assistances to the reader found in printed volumes' and that, further, such practices suggest that Halkett 'clearly had anticipated the possibility of an unknown reader perusing her books'.[23] My own research reaffirms these speculations; indeed, Halkett specifically considers this prospect:

> I haue for some days intermitted writing my morning thoughts. And haue beene imploying that time I vsed for that, in looking ouer some books that I formerly haue writ. And hauing put papers vpon every one of them to know the date when euery one of them was written & resoluing to transcribe the contents of euery one to Lye by them, that if I Liue I may the sooner find out any Subiect I haue a desire to read: And if I dy itt may bee the more vsefull to such as the Lord shall thinke <fitt> to make them knowne to.[24]

---

[21] For specific discussions of the 'Occasional Meditation' as a genre, see Coolahan, 'Redeeming', and Anselment, 'Feminine Self-Reflection'. Anselment's editions of the life writings of Mary Rich, Countess of Warwick and Alice Thornton also shed light on the complexity of this genre.

[22] Gibson, 'Casting Off Blanks'. Gibson focuses on cases in which writers leave such spaces for copying other texts into manuscript form; Halkett uses the practice primarily to divide her volumes into 'occasional' and 'select' meditations.

[23] Ezell, 'Ann Halkett's Morning Devotions', pp. 219, 222.    [24] NLS MS 6500, p. 146.

Dated 26 February 1694/5, this clearly demonstrates a conscious decision to make her texts accessible to others. This, coupled with that dated 19 February 1697/8 (cited above), indicates that her concern for other readers affects her most in the 1690s, the final decade of her life. Her worries about her son's and her own mortality seemingly encourage her to get her papers in order, and it is the untimely death of an unnamed gentleman that finally persuades Halkett to hand the volumes over to Couper and her other ministers.[25] One might argue that Halkett became slightly obsessive about this issue: not only are there lists of contents on the flyleaves of most of her extant volumes but both entries indicate that she also provided her ministers with a separate list of her volumes' contents. Furthermore, the NLS volumes which remain in their original binding also have labels attached to their spines with an indication of their contents and dates of writing. Thus, Halkett was actively entitling her own books and constructing her own classification system for a library of her own works. Fascinatingly, this was an ongoing process. As Halkett revisits her earlier writings, telling differences emerge between the titles she gave her writings as she produced them and how she positions them after re-reading them. Halkett's archive embodies an enchanting example of how an early modern 'subject-in-process' changes her attitude toward her own writing over time.

Even in this Halkett's practice is not uniform. However, only one volume can be discussed in detail here (NLS 6493, *The Widows Mite*, 1674-5) and I will focus on the major differences in recording the 'Occasional Meditations'. For Couper these are subsumed within the summary '2d part, 32 occasional Meditations on publick and private occur'. Here, as elsewhere, Couper marginalizes these texts by quantifying them collectively rather than providing any information that might identify them individually. For Halkett things are a little more complicated. In contrast to NLS MS 6490, in which Halkett self-consciously writes in the form of the 'occasional meditation' (giving each entry a title beginning with 'upon'), in this later volume she identifies her entries first and foremost by their date of composition, which makes these appear to conform to our expectations of a diary entry. Or, at least, she does so at the time of writing. However, by the point of recording them, she apparently views them differently; for, instead of recording them by date, she predominantly lists them by what

---

[25] Couper claims that it was the sudden deaths of 'several persons' that prompted Halkett to reveal her Books to him (*Life*, p. 58), which is partially confirmed by Halkett's account (*Halkett*, ed. Trill, pp. 188–9). Halkett's only surviving biological child, Robert (or Robin), died in Holland in 1692; her stepson, Sir Charles Halkett (whom she consistently refers to as her 'Son' throughout her writing), died in 1697.

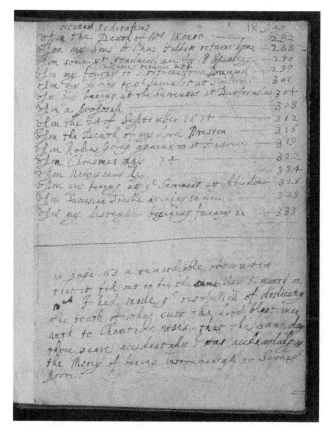

Figure 6.3 National Library of Scotland, MS 6493, Folio IX.

she sees as their main subject and provides an 'occasional' title. For example, whereas the penultimate entry is originally dated 'Tuesday the 12 of Ianuary 1674/5', in Halkett's list it is entitled 'Vpon Successiue Trouble ariuing to mee' (see Figure 6.3).[26] In this, and in many other ways, Halkett's 'Books' reveal themselves very much to be used – and useful – objects whose form and content are not static.[27]

Halkett's 'occasional meditations' are generally less formulaic and more idiosyncratic than those of her contemporaries. Nevertheless, Couper manages to de-personalize even the few he does select for publication, under the

[26] In this particular volume, even the number of meditations is disputable: Couper lists thirty-two; Halkett records twenty-nine; and by my reckoning there are thirty-seven.

[27] Sherman, *Used Books*; Knight, '"Furnished" for Action'.

subtitle 'Pious Reflections and Observations, collected out of the Lady H's Occasional Meditations'. The last two entries, although given the titles 'Of Emulation and Contention' and 'The Safety of the Godly', record Halkett's reflections on the activities of sparrows, merlins, and larks.[28] Couper's marginalization of these materials may be partially explained by his aware-ness of the contemporary low esteem in which such materials had come to be held: indeed, in the very year that Couper began publishing Halkett's texts, one of her favourite writers within this genre, Sir Robert Boyle, found his work satirized when Swift published 'Upon a Broom-stick' (1701).[29] In this instance, Couper might be argued to be saving Halkett from her-self. However, for the most part, Couper's publication of Halkett's texts (1701–2) forms part of his own agenda of religious and political propaganda surrounding the lead-up to 'The Act of Union' (1707). Ironically, although Couper's publication of Halkett's texts was politically motivated, his needs ultimately occlude Halkett's own politics.[30]

While Couper may not be an entirely unreliable witness, the discrep-ancies described above cast doubt upon how compendious his 'Catalogue' actually is. We know that Halkett intended to give Couper all of her 'Books', and we know from the *Life* that he had certainly read her 'True Accountt', yet his list excludes that volume (along with some other materi-als which he thought 'fitt' to publish) and yet includes 'the bare Contents' of a number of 'Books' which went missing sometime before 1875. Not all of the missing material can be accounted for within the '30 or so stitched books' which have also disappeared. Thus it seems logical to suggest that Halkett's corpus was once even more extensive than Couper has led us to believe. Bearing this in mind it may be significant that, when Halkett eventually decides to give her books to Couper, she initially offers 'to send the Trunke to him with as many of them as itt would hold'.[31] Halkett's extant volumes are mostly in quarto and even twenty-two of them, along with a selection of stitched books and a few folios, would not take up very much space. Although, of course, trunks came in varying sizes, there is evidence to suggest that even one would take far more than twenty-one books to fill it.[32]

Whatever the size of the trunk, the fact that seven of the volumes Couper does list – three of which relate to Halkett's life prior to 1653 – are

---

28  Halkett, *Meditations upon the Seven Gifts*, pp. 85–6.      29  See Coolahan, 'Redeeming', p. 136.
30  *Halkett*, ed. Trill, pp. xxv–xxxiv.      31  *Ibid.*, p. 189.
32  There are two examples of late seventeenth-century trunks in the Victoria and Albert Museum's col-lection: http://collections.vam.ac.uk/item/O372181/trunk/ and http://collections.vam.ac.uk/item/O158511/trunk-unknown/

missing, makes me suspicious: one could be a mistake; two, carelessness; but three strikes me as deliberate (especially as this becomes four if one includes the 'True Accountt' which we know Couper had had in his possession). Of course, these volumes relate most directly to the period in which Halkett was involved with Bampfield, about which there has been so much speculation. Yet, if – as I suggest below – Couper had more than one motive to suppress this material, it is perhaps curious that he provides so much detail about the second volume which, by his own account, was written at the height of Halkett's complicated relationship with Bampfield. While the short titles Couper provides imply a narrative moving from guilt through to redemption, a close look at the biblical references is suggestive of a specific concern with female sexuality: 'the guilty acquitted' refers to the story of the woman caught in the act of adultery and 'the power of love' to the tale of the female 'sinner' who washed Christ's feet. Several other passages refer to the wrongdoings of men. Thus, here we have an (admittedly unusual) disclosure of Halkett's gender consciousness. While this reading involves some speculation, how much more might it have done so for a seventeenth- or eighteenth-century reader so much better versed in biblical allusions? While one might ask why Couper provided so much information, perhaps what he writes provides potential reasons for the disappearance of some of these volumes. As I explain below, exploring this matter may also partially explain why Halkett spent so much narrative space on the stories concerning Mr Nicholls, the chaplain at Naworth Castle, in her 'True Accountt', which has been dismissed 'as a storm in a tea cup'.[33]

## Halkett in the Nineteenth Century: The Re-Emergence of 'A True Accountt'

Ironically, had it not been for the re-emergence of at least part of it in the nineteenth century, we would probably never have known that the 'True Accountt' was 'missing'. For me, the most intriguing question is how the extant version of this manuscript became separated from the rest of Halkett's 'books' and therefore survived, even in its incomplete form. While not a unique occurrence, it is curious for one text to get separated in this way. Why did this happen to this particular manuscript? And what

---

[33] Delany, *British Autobiography*, p. 163. I made some reference to Nicholls in *Halkett* (ed. Trill), p. xxi; however, usually his story is marginalized. The only minister listed in the *Fasti Ecclesiae Anglicanae 1541–1857* whose dates match those given by Halkett is William Nicholls (1644–57).

might this tell us about that text's status both in its own right and its relationship to the rest of Halkett's writing?

According to the British Library's manuscript catalogue, Halkett's 'auto-biography' was presented in 1884 by one William Johnston Stuart, after it had been edited for the Camden Society by John Gough Nichols in 1875. The catalogue entry says nothing more of Stuart, merely designating him as 'unspecified'. Quite how he acquired the manuscript – and, indeed, his exact identity – is currently unknown, although there is one promising lead.[34] By 1872, however, the manuscript was with the Camden society as in that year John Gough Nichols wrote to Sir Peter Halkett informing him that 'an original manuscript of the personal memoirs of Anne, Lady Halkett' had 'been offered to the Camden Society' and the council had 'deemed it to be of sufficient historical interest to be printed as one of their works'.[35] Nichols does not specify how or by whom the manuscript was delivered, but there is nothing in the correspondence to suggest that it originated with the Halkett family. Nichols is not seeking Halkett's permission to publish the 'autobiography'. Rather, the remaining correspondence implies that he had already borrowed the rest of Halkett's manuscripts that remained in the family's private collection. Indeed, there is a slightly anxious letter from Sir Peter to Nichols which enquires about the potential return of the volumes 'as such things are too apt to be forgotten & lost and they are of much value to my family'.[36] In his reply, Nichols not only reassures Sir Peter that he has the volumes safe and is putting them to good use but, having checked those he has received against Couper's list, also notes the absence of the seven volumes discussed above.[37] Although Sir Peter expresses his desire to 'supply' any 'missing' material, the remaining correspondence is silent on this matter.[38]

However, an inserted note at the front of NLS 6489, the earliest of Halkett's surviving volumes, reveals that Nichols was not the first person to borrow Halkett's books from the Pitfirrane library. The note, dated c. 1843, records that 'this box' (which itself no longer exists) had contained Halkett's volumes which had been 'brought away by the Reverend Dunbar Halkett' who, 'not having the leisure to proceed with any steps which he

[34] The BL MS catalogue also records a William Johnston Stuart, in its 'India Office Records and Private Papers, IOR/L/MIL/9/389/149–54 (1841–1843)'. A 'William Johnston Stuart' of 'Glouces-ter Terrace, London' (x) was a subscriber to the *Supplemental Descriptive Catalogue of Ancient Scottish Seals* by Henry Laing (Electric Scotland), and Ancestry.com confirms that a W. J. Stu-art lived at 97 Gloucester Terrace in 1887 and 1889, was born in December 1818, and died in August 1900. The 1881 census confirms that he was an ex-soldier (http://search.ancestry.com/cgi-bin/sse.dll?indiv=try&db=uki1881&h=13095511).

[35] NLS MS 6412, fol. 206.    [36] *Ibid.*, fol. 217.    [37] *Ibid.*, fol. 210.    [38] *Ibid.*, fol. 219.

might then have had in view regarding them' returned them to Pitfirrane.[39] In addition, Halkett's work attracted the attention of another man of the cloth, the Scottish Episcopal Bishop of Moray, Alexander Jolly; although, as his notes relate only to her *Meditations on the Days of Creation* (specifically Thursday), it is possible he read this in Couper's edition rather than an original.[40] Prior to their arrival at the British Library and the National Library of Scotland, Halkett's manuscripts had passed through the hands of several male readers, most of whom were involved in the Episcopalian church. With the exception of J. G. Nichols, they therefore – individually or collectively – had reason not to draw attention to the existence of the 'True Accountt'.

More significantly, in her introduction to another of her volumes, *The Art of Deuine Chimistry*, Halkett intimates that she was prompted to write this narrative because she had once again found herself the object of suspicion in a potential sexual scandal that involved a minister who was engaged to another woman.[41] That the 'True Accountt' serves a self-justificatory purpose is apparent not only in its title but in the suggestion that she was prompted to write because of the 'Seueare Censare' of others. Writing in June 1676, Halkett states that she began this book because she is resolved 'by the Deuine assistance to extract Good outt of all the Crose occurrences I haue mett withall of Late'.[42] Intent on performing a kind of divine alchemy, Halkett provides more details about the specific crosses she has met with. These she lists as 'The failings of A Good Man / A proffesed friend / A faithfull Saruantt / And y^e vnkindnese of many / in a time when I expected / (And had need of) Consolation / beeing destemperede with paine & sickenese' (6494, 2). Elaborating on these points, Halkett reveals that she has, once again, inadvertently become the subject of sexual slander. While the details are hazy, Halkett's phraseology suggests a direct connection between this incident and both the Bampfield and the Nicholls episodes described in her 'True Accountt':

> Oh that my Sins had been Confined only to my youth then I might haue pleaded ignorance (I Tim/1.13) as St Paul did ... Butt now in my old Age affter fiuety yeares experience of the infinitt mercy of God ... Oh why was

[39] According to the version of the 1851 England Census available at ancestry.com, one 'Dambas Stewart Halkett' was Rector at Little Bookham at this time.

[40] Rowan Strong, 'Jolly, Alexander (1756–1838)', in *ODNB*. Jolly's notes on Halkett's *Meditations* are held at the National Registers of Scotland, CH12/15/96.

[41] I would like to thank Frances Harris of the British Library for drawing this comment to my attention.

[42] NLS MS 6494, p. 1. I follow here Halkett's own pagination, which differs at times from that of the cataloguer.

I nott then more Watchfull to restraine my thoughts and words & actions from beeing too much placed vpon any earthly Sattisfaction.

I Confese I thought my designes so inocentt and allowable that I gaue way to intertaine my Selfe with y^e aduantages that I might haue, by the Conuerse of a Pious Man from whom I expected more of his Care & Conduct in what I left behind mee when I died then while I Liued. & I had nott the feare of hauing any Suspect mee Guilty of my breach of resolution (I dare nott Call itt Vow) of holy widowhood because all that saw or knew my Conuerse with him beleeued as I did that his affections were placed vpon another[,] & euen in that I had a Sattisfaction because I had a kindenese for her & therfore did from both expect there care of my Deare Child if they Surviued mee.[43]

While this might be taken as another indication that 'romance' is the key motivation of Halkett's life writing, I would suggest that it further bolsters Wiseman's argument that one of her main concerns is to defend her virtue.[44] Concluding her preamble to this volume, Halkett desires 'that the remainder of my days may bee Wholy Spent in the Study of this Art of Deuine Chimestry so shall I extract such Cordialls as may bee vsefull to my Selfe or others if when I am dead My Lord thinkes fitt to make them Visible'.[45] As with the 'True Accountt' Halkett alludes to the possibility of posthumous publication. While she is, understandably, concerned about the harm this might do to her own reputation, if my conjectures about the possible identity of the 'Pious Man' are correct, this would also constitute a powerful motive for Couper, Jolly, and Dunbar Halkett to ensure that her narrative did not survive intact.

Tempting as it might be to point the finger at Couper himself, he didn't take up the charge at Dunfermline until 1681, by which time he had been married to Elizabeth Meldrum for three years. Of the incumbent ministers, the two main possibilities are John Balneves/Balnevis or Alexander Monro. Halkett was close enough to Monro, who was the minister at Dunfermline from 1673 to 1676, to write an extended meditation on the death of his first wife in 1674.[46] Like the 'Pious Man' Halkett mentions above, Monro would have been engaged at the time to which she refers, as he married Marion Collace in 1676. While Monro was simply a minister at this time, he became Professor of Divinity at St Andrews, Principal of Edinburgh University and, ultimately, Bishop of Argyll. A well-respected, staunch Episcopalian, Monro died in England in 1698.[47] Given Couper's political allegiances, it

---

[43] NLS MS 6494, pp. 3–4.    [44] Wiseman, *Conspiracy and Virtue*, pp. 319–33.
[45] NLS MS 6494, p. 6.    [46] *Halkett*, ed. Trill, pp. 45–8.
[47] Tristram Clarke, 'Monro, Alexander (*d.* 1698)', in *ODNB*.

would hardly have been in his interests to besmirch the reputation of a figure like Monro, but it would provide the motivation to suppress any parts of Halkett's narrative that might have done so. Most readers have concentrated on Halkett's doomed relationship with Bampfield, so little attention has been paid to the amount of narrative space she devoted to her analysis of the difficulties caused by her relationship with Mr Nichols, the chaplain at Naworth Castle. Yet, roughly one-fifth of the extant narrative relates to how his machinations caused divisions between Halkett and her best friend, Lady Anne Howard. Sarcastically described as a 'Tutelar Angell',[48] Nichols's perceived piety is undermined by both his betrayal of Halkett and his dubious behaviour toward other young women in the household. To most modern readers, Halkett's concern with this clergyman's morals are a diversion from the main narrative (i.e., Halkett and her 'lovers'); however, given the context in which Halkett was writing her 'True Accountt', it may be that we have misidentified the main narrative. For the material cited above indicates that Halkett's immediate motivation for writing was prompted by her disappointment in discovering – once again – that an apparently godly man could pose a threat to her reputation. In this context, the amount of time spent on the story of Mr Nicholls suggests it is more than a diversion and perhaps points to a different way of reading the 'True Accountt'.

In addition to this there are two features of this volume's material properties which suggest that perhaps Halkett herself saw her 'True Accountt' as a rather different kind of 'Book' to the rest of her collection. She specifically draws attention to its being a 'Parchment Book': parchment was, of course, more expensive than paper and was often used for presentation manuscripts or for texts intended to survive for longer periods. However, the extant BL manuscript is neither written on parchment nor in its original binding. The surviving fragment has many hallmarks associated with a working copy rather than a fair copy, which tantalizingly suggests that there is yet another missing volume among Halkett's archive: the full version of her 'True Accountt'. It is also worth noting that BL MS Add. 32, 376 is a folio volume. One aspect of Couper's list which is entirely consistent with the surviving 'Books' is his description of each volume's size. Of those twenty-one volumes, only the first five (written from 1644 to 1651) are defined as Folios; thus, by the time of writing the 'True Accountt', Halkett had not used a folio volume for over twenty-five years. In many ways then, this text is peculiar: originally written on parchment, in folio format, omitted

---

[48] *Halkett*, ed. Trill, p. 79.

from Couper's list, wrongly categorized as 'memoir' or 'autobiography', and somehow separated from the rest of her writings.

## Halkett in the Twentieth and Twenty-First Centuries: Editorial Practice and Potential

The 'True Accountt's peculiarity could, perhaps, provide a justification for its being discussed in isolation. Yet, although Halkett seems to have viewed it as special, she presented it to Couper and Graeme as the first in a series, not as a single object. Furthermore, the results of such separation have been detrimental to our understanding of the full significance of both that text and Halkett's extensive archive. In 1875, Nichols intended to provide some context from the 'Meditations' and some entries were appended to his (posthumous) edition.[49] It is also clear that Nichols was aware of Simon Couper's identity; however, this information did not make it into Loftis's edition with the result that, in the twentieth century, he became 'mysterious' and his powerful influence over Halkett's reputation has been overlooked. While his propagandist aims partially account for Couper's erasure of particular aspects of Halkett's politics, modern critics have unfortunately continued this depoliticization in other ways. Specifically, the focus on Halkett's 'autobiographical memoirs' has erased its Scottish contexts. Not only do two-thirds of the events narrated in the 'True Accountt' take place in Scotland, but Halkett wrote it (and the majority of the rest of her extant texts) while living at either Pitfirrane or Abbott House, Dunfermline. Many of the extant texts are comprised of extensive analysis of Scottish parish politics and its connections to the broader political and ecclesiastical issues affecting the 'three kingdoms'. In this, she appears to be an ideal figure of study for those interested in 'British' history. Indeed, in an entry recording her husband's death, written in 1670 – after twenty years of living in Scotland – Halkett defined herself as 'a Stranger, born and bred in another Country'.[50]

As an Englishwoman who has now lived in Edinburgh for nearly eighteen years, I am in a not dissimilar position which is, at least in part, why I am interested in Halkett's writing. However, I am also fascinated by the ways in which Halkett's work resolutely refuses to be contained within our current critical categories: is her work 'literary', 'historical', or 'theological'? And, whatever the answer to that question, should she be studied

---

[49]  Nichols, *Autobiography*, pp. 109–16.
[50]  *Halkett*, ed. Trill, p. 30; see also Trill, 'Beyond Romance'.

within Scottish or English (or 'British'?) traditions or paradigms? It is perhaps precisely because she traverses traditional disciplinary boundaries and challenges received nationalistic identifications that Halkett's achievements have not yet been fully understood. Few researchers of English literature see the need to visit the National Library of Scotland and, to date, the study of Scottish history has been less inclined to incorporate gender as a category of analysis.[51] My geographical location provides me with the access necessary to redress such imbalances and, I hope, my literary-historical interests will help to further our understanding of the significance of Halkett's archive. My attempt to relocate Halkett's 'True Accountt' within the broader corpus of her writings has been read as an invitation to reject romance and replace the spirited Anne Murray with the exemplary Anne, Lady Halkett.[52] That was certainly not my intention; rather, I hope that my editorial work will enable us to examine in more detail how, as Lamb has recently observed, for Halkett 'religion constituted a form of desire, fully compatible with sexuality'.[53] This, I believe, is reflected precisely in the tension between Halkett's self-conception as *both* a 'romantic heroine' *and* 'A widow indeed'. Indeed the continual intersection of religious beliefs and sexuality is apparent in the material discussed in the previous section, but, given the extent of Halkett's corpus, to represent its diversity fully in a traditional printed format is problematic.

This difficulty is nicely illustrated by the fact that, although there is some resistance to recontextualizing Halkett's 'True Accountt' within her other writings, Seelig regretted my omission of 'the biblical meditations' and points out that this arguably 'perpetuates the somewhat partial understanding' of Halkett's work that I was 'attempting to rectify'.[54] While I hope to include some such materials in my forthcoming edition for The Other Voice series, their prior exclusion was primarily based on the desire to illustrate that Halkett's writing goes beyond what one might expect from materials which remain defined in the NLS catalogue as 'Religious Meditations'; or, as John Gough Nichols put it, they 'afford a higher proportion of Intrigues of historical & biographical importance than . . . expected'.[55]

[51] Barclay et al., 'The State of Scottish History' and Ewan, 'A New Trumpet?'.

[52] Eckerle, *Romancing the Self*, p. 126; Ellen Moody, '"A Hole in the Manuscript Big Enough to put your Finger Through": The Misframing of Anne Murray Halkett's Autobiography', paper delivered at the American Society for Eighteenth Century Studies Conference, www.jimandellen.org/halkett/AHole.html, fn. 17.

[53] Lamb, 'Merging the Secular and the Spiritual', p. 94.

[54] Carol, Seelig, '*Lady Anne Halkett: Selected Self-Writings*, and: *Witchcraft, Exorcism and the Politics of Possession in a Seventeenth-Century Convent: "How Sister Ursula was Once Bewiched and Sister Margaret Twice"* (review)', *RQ*, 61.2 (2008), 680–2 (p. 681).

[55] NLS MS 6412, fol. 209.

While it is true that even the most strictly exegetical volumes, such as *Joseph's Trialls & Triumph*, contain personal comments which reveal parallels with contemporary political events, such observations are brief compared to the size of the volumes concerned. For, like the rest of Halkett's volumes, these 'Books' usually cover around 350 pages, which would make a rather expensive set of *Works* if published in print form. Ultimately, for the full extent and complexity of Halkett's writing to be appreciated, these volumes ideally require online editing.

For now, though, this means that – in contrast to Couper's selection – my selection of Halkett's writing focuses on the materials she defined as 'occasional meditations'. So far, this genre and its conventions have received little critical attention, but the materials Halkett designates in this manner are surprisingly diverse. Given the importance of the labels we ascribe to texts, and my desire to remain true to Halkett's own 'intentions' in her writing, I hesitate to emulate Couper and redefine them; however, in modern terms, her writing frequently exhibits signs of what we would call either 'diaries' or 'essays'. Some of Halkett's earliest meditations – upon Beauty, Riches, and Imagination – have much in common with Bacon's *Essays*. Would the latter's work be so widely read if they were called 'Occasional Meditations'? Would Pepys's diary be so popular if every entry began and ended with a reference to God? In Bacon's case, in particular, this question is highly ironic insofar as the first edition of his work was entitled *Essaies. Religious Meditations. Places of Perswasion and disswasion* (1597). Here it seems to me that the generic categories we use for writers of different sexes intersect in ways which work to Halkett's disadvantage.

Halkett's writing does not only trouble our generic classifications but also our conceptions of gender and writing in the early modern period. While Halkett was female, her work rarely exhibits a primary concern with questions of gender,[56] and historically at least, it seems that Halkett's works have also been more appreciated by a male audience: her works have been transmitted mostly by and between men, most of whom – as men of the cloth – are primarily interested in her theological writings. Indeed, I suspect that Halkett would have liked a (contemporary) male audience for her writing. While it is perhaps unsurprising that the books she records reading are all by men, she obviously sees her own work as in a similar vein: in a concluding note on the final page of one volume Halkett wrote

---

[56] Potential exceptions might include the mother's legacy materials (see note 17 above) and Halkett's discussion of female biblical figures in NLS MS 6499.

'Since I ended the Meditations vpon the festiualls of the Church I haue seen another booke vpon the same subject w$^{ch}$ yett I haue nott had time to Looke ouer'[57] and, although she continues by disclaiming any desire for publication, she clearly sees her work as comparable to that which is in print.

If in this Halkett challenges categories of gender, I hope the above has also begun to draw attention to the way in which the materiality of her texts also disrupts the perceived boundaries between print and manuscript. Both Halkett and Couper refer to her volumes as 'Books'. In the *Life* Couper also distinguishes between the 'Books by the Lady Halket', which he lists in full, and the 'stitched Books', which he summarizes in three lines. What, then, counts as a book in this period? How interchangeable are print and manuscript? Halkett and Couper's nomenclature suggests that Halkett's writing is neither entirely public nor entirely private; here, as elsewhere, Halkett seems to be on the cusp of our categories and perhaps invites us to revise our thinking. Halkett's work, it seems, resolutely refuses to be contained within our current critical categories. It traverses traditional disciplinary boundaries and does not fit easily into our modern predilection for binary opposites: to understand Halkett's 'lives' and 'works' more fully we need to move beyond 'either/or' toward 'both/and'. While it was obviously very special to her, and we are fortunate part of it survived, the 'True Accountt' is but 'a node within a network' of Halkett's extensive archive.[58]

## Appendix 1

Contents of NLS MS. 6490; those in bold are specifically identified in Couper's catalogue.

1. **Vpon my Miscarying of 2 children March 2 1658/9**
2. Vpon hipocrisy
3. Vpon seeing one in a very great discontent good Friday night 59.
4. Vpon beeing in a Coale pitt.
5. **Vpon the violent sicknese of my Son henry Aprill 1657**
6. Vpon variety of troubles suceeding one another.
7. Vpon Mr D$^{ck}$ sending to Sue mee vpon an vniust pretence.
8. Vpon the report of new troubles like to begin
9. Vpon the peace made betwixt France & Spaine
10. Vpon an vnhapy child beeing a Crose to his mother

---

[57] NLS MS 6491, p. 326.    [58] Foucault, *Archaeology*, p. 23.

11. Vpon a fall Sr james had off a Mare may [xx]
12. Vpon the recouery of a very extenuated child that was brought to mee (Gil[e/s] child att Gilandestone.
13. Vpon the sacrament.
14. Vpon seeing one tormented with the toothach
15. Vpon an inward dispute aboutt keeping the hows.
16. Vpon discention amongst the Saruants.
17. Vpon riches.
18. Vpon one dying sudainly affter taking a falce oath.
19. Vpon a great an vnusuall storme august 1 1659.
20. The Conuiction vpon the 10th verse of the 28of the 2d f Chron.
21. vpon the report of two ministers beeing murderd
22. vpon Beauty.
23. Vpon pouerty
24. vpon imagination.
25. Vpon the sicknese of my children
26. The power of faith, vpon marke 16, verses 17 & 18.
27. vpon the feare of death
28. vpon a new expectation of discontent from an old cause.
29. vpon fire.
30. vpon couettuounese.
31. vpon the birth of my son Robert on the first of febr 1659/60 beeing vpon Wednesday betwixt 2 & 3 affternoon & other pasages in my childbed.
32. vpon sad afflictions succeeding one another to a very good woman.
33. vpon the failing of some that are great proffesors.
34. vpon the late change of puplicke affaires
35. vpon the return of his Mast afftir his long banishment and variety of other troubles.

# CHAPTER 7

# Editing Early Modern Women's Letters for Print Publication

## Diana G. Barnes

Literate early modern women were far more likely to write a letter than any other literary or non-literary genre. The early moderns viewed the letter as a quotidian form dignified by classical precedent and scholarly tradition. Although it is true that only a small number of women letter-writers self-consciously claimed this heritage, and most wrote for prosaic reasons, nevertheless in writing letters women engaged a respected rhetorical and cultural discourse to conduct conversations unbound by time and space, participate in all facets of public life, intervene in established political, intellectual, familial, and religious networks, and establish new terms of engagement.[1] As James Daybell has shown, women's letters were collated, emended, adapted, copied, and circulated in manuscript.[2] Recent work on women's manuscript letters has raised a range of issues about authorship and attribution, as Leah Marcus discusses in her chapter on the editing of Elizabeth I's letters in this volume. In print, however, women's letters had an even broader circulation, a topic neglected in scholarly discussions of early modern letters. The editing of women's letters for print publication has a surprisingly long history dating back to the sixteenth century. Early modern editors of women's letters established the place of women's letters in print culture and, at the same time, disseminated the radical idea that the virtuoso woman writer could emerge from quotidian beginnings. Whereas some editors highlight the identity of the individual woman letter-writer, others present her as a type. Focusing largely upon the paratexts in which editors set forth their rationale, this chapter will sketch the long history of editing early modern women's letters in English from sixteenth-century epistolary manuals to seventeenth-century political pamphlets; eighteenth-century posthumous collections of the literati; nineteenth-century family-produced and antiquarian volumes; twentieth-century

---

[1] As established by Daybell (ed.), *Early Modern Women's Letter Writing*; Couchman and Crabb (eds.), *Women's Letters Across Europe*; and Campbell, Larsen, and Eschrich (eds.), *Crossing Borders*.

[2] Daybell, 'Women, Politics and Domesticity'.

scholarly editions and feminist recovery; and the databases of the twenty-first century.

The earliest women's letters edited for print appeared in Elizabethan letter-writing manuals. These popular volumes are important to understanding early modern women's writing as they constructed the idea of the woman letter-writer. Women's letters feature in two of the most frequently reprinted epistolary manuals: William Fulwood's *The Enemy of Idleness* (1568–1621) and Angel Day's *The English Secretary* (1586–1635). They are not prominent in either, however. Fulwood includes 5 alongside approximately 106 male-authored letters, and Day includes 4 to 96 in the expanded 1595 edition. Although the letters were probably composed to fit the manuals, and may not reflect 'real' letter-writing practice,[3] through a combination of rhetorical exegesis and sample letters these volumes described women as writers, modelled an epistolary practice suited to different kinds of women, and established a template for editing women's letters.

Letter-writing manuals are closely related to civility manuals, and as such they model conservative social values. Following medieval dictaminal precepts they define letter-writing according to the standing of the writer and recipient, the nature of their relationship, and the purpose of the letter. Fulwood and Day's women letter-writers are social types, that is, mothers, daughters, wives, sisters, kinswomen, or mistresses. In this regard women's letter-writing is treated no differently from men's. Day makes some rhetorical specifications, for example, the subscription: 'Your Ladyship's loving and obedient Daughter'.[4] Day and Fulwood represent women's writing in two epistolary species, familiar and love letters, and not in formal modes, such as letters of petition.[5] Their familiar letters rehearse women's compliance to social expectations. Day's example of a 'remuneratorie' letter is typical. Only too aware of her debt, the gentlewoman writer dutifully pledges to 'acknowledge [her kinsman's] great goodness, beyond any merit of [her] owne' evermore.[6] Sometimes the letter and reply format provides a means of reminding women of their proper position. In Fulwood's 'The Wife writeth unto hir Husband', the wife expresses concern for her husband's 'health and welfare rather than [her] owne' but turns quickly to complaint. She speculates that 'some great affairs of the Court' are distracting him, and regrets that 'no care of [herself and their children]

---

[3]  On manual precepts see Daybell, *Women Letter-Writers*, pp. 22–3.

[4]  Angel Day, *The English Secretary* (1595), p. 15.

[5]  Although early modern women did employ these subgenres: see Magnusson, 'A Rhetoric of Requests'; and Broomhall, '"Burdened with Small Children"'.

[6]  Day, *The English Secretary* (1595), p. 64.

doeth prick [him] forward' to write regularly as he promised.[7] In reply the husband chides his 'Loving Wife' for her 'verie lamentable Letters' and reminds her of the virtue, chastity, and honesty of a good wife.[8] Fulwood provides no direct exegesis of this pair (or any other in this chapter), but the exchange appears in a chapter on 'the maner and forme how to write by aunswer', and his editorial agenda is implied in the husband's reply. A mixed rhetorical template, such as the 'gratulatory' letter, provides a more subtle tool by which to negotiate social relations. Day gives an example of a wife who writes to express sympathetic pleasure in her husband's success, then urges him to come home 'the sooner the better' but ultimately leaves the matter to his discretion.[9] Nonetheless, the letter models her accommodation to social ideals.

Whereas the familiar letters attributed to women in Fulwood and Day's manuals model social compliancy, the love letters model independent judgment. This is demonstrated through examples; only Day theorizes the form and his commentary is directed solely at male writers. Interestingly, when women write love letters they rearticulate forcefully the values and ideals of the manual, effectively policing epistolary practice. In Fulwood's manual a woman writes that she 'cannot marvell inough to imagine what cause moved [her suitor], & gave [him] such presumptuous boldnesse'.[10] Both volumes give editorial weight to women's judgment, and have women write love letters to temper their suitors' high poetic raptures in favour of everyday language and mores.[11] This is driven by *ars rhetorica* rather than social inclusiveness. Ovid's *Heroides* was important to the rhetorical and pedagogical traditions that spawned the manuals.[12] Although Fulwood and Day's women writers have been neither cruelly abandoned nor imprisoned, as Ovid's pen-wielding heroines were, the precedent gives their prosaic love letters literary and rhetorical authority. Over the seventeenth and eighteenth centuries manuals continued to include women's letters, and some were developed specifically for women, for example, Henry Care's *The Female Secretary* (1671).[13]

The title of *The Secretary of Ladies*, Jerome Hainhofer's 1638 translation of a French work by Jacques de Bosc, acknowledges the importance of

---

[7] Fulwood, *The Enemy of Idleness* (1568), pp. 110–11.

[8] Fulwood, *The Enemy of Idleness* (1568), pp. 111–111 verso.

[9] Day, *The English Secretary* (1595), part II, p. 67.

[10] Fulwood, *The Enemy of Idleness* (1568), p. 134 verso.

[11] On Day's love letters, see my *Epistolary Community in Print*, pp. 32–46; and Newbold, 'Letter Writing and Vernacular Literacy', pp. 134–6.

[12] See Clarke, '"Form'd into Words by your Divided Lips"'; Bate, *Shakespeare and Ovid*.

[13] See Bannet, *Empire of Letters*; Tanskanen, '"Proper to their Sex"'.

Day's manual to establishing a template for women's letters in print. This allusion is somewhat misleading, however, as *The Secretary of Ladies* is not a manual directed modestly at 'any learner'. It is a collection of paired female-friendship letters exchanged between two ladies who argue *pro et contra* on matters of civility and religion in courtly style. The writers are identified simply as 'Madam', but this is not manual-style generic stereotyping. Rather the editorial emphasis is upon presenting women's letters as a remarkable adaptation of a masculine discourse. Hainhofer hints that du Bosc composed the letters himself, implying that the collection's value lies in the feminization of the form. This is supported by du Bosc's promise to 'vindicate the honour of dames, to make it appear that Letters are not the peculiar heritage of one sexe' (sig. A5). In the original French this idealization of women's letter-writing expresses the devout humanism of the *précieuses*. By dedicating the translation to Mary Sackville, Countess of Dorset, a courtier with known Roman Catholic sympathies, the editors of the English edition connect women's letter-writing to the community of English women converting to Roman Catholicism at court under the French Queen consort, Henrietta Maria.

The breakdown of royalist censorship during the English Civil War caused a radical revision of print conventions, and, in turn, the editing of women's letters for publication. The identity of certain individual women letter-writers gained currency in political pamphlets. The best example of this is the inclusion of Henrietta Maria's letters in *The King's Cabinet Opened* (1645), a collection of royal papers seized at battle and then published by Parliament. At first glance Henrietta Maria's letters seem insignificant: they are not mentioned on the title page; they get a passing reference in the editors' preface; they represent only 7 of the 39 letters (26 are Charles I's); and they appear late in the sequence (Letters 27 to 33). Careful editing, however, ensured that her letters stood at the centre of the political scandal stimulated by the publication. The editors open with a promise to reveal 'a Prince seduced out of his proper sphear',[14] thereby invoking the multiple meanings of cabinet as a box in which correspondence is stored, a room in which a secretary writes letters (as Day described), *and* a private chamber in which a husband and wife could be intimate. For Parliament's propagandistic purposes it was important that readers accepted the pamphlet as an unmediated transcription of the royal correspondence.[15] To this end the editors promised to 'affirm nothing necessary to be believed, but

---

[14]  *The King's Cabinet* (1645), Preface, p. A3.
[15]  The original missives were displayed in Westminster; see Maddison, '"The King's Cabinet Opened"'. See also Dolan, *Whores of Babylon*, pp. 126–8; Jagodzinski, *Privacy and Print*, pp. 78–86.

what the printed papers will themselves utter in their own language',[16] and followed each letter with the assurance that '*This is a true Copie examined by*' Edmund Prideaux, Miles Corbet, or Zouche Tate, a member of the Parliamentary editorial team.

The editors of *The King's Cabinet Opened* needed to establish an argument about Henrietta Maria's authorship without appearing to alter her text (although, as Laura Knoppers establishes, the published versions were translations of French originals).[17] Sequencing and italics were useful tools. The collection opens with ten of Charles I's letters to Henrietta Maria. Italics emphasize his unmanly deference to his wife, which the editors view as particularly unseemly in a king. In Letter 3, for example, he writes regarding the award of offices '*I intend (if thou like it) to bestow Percies place on the M. of Newcastle*' and in Letter 11 he asks her to chide their son, the future Charles II, for appointing a master of the bedchamber without permission.[18] The queen's letters are arranged to support this portrait of her influence. In Letter 27 (her first) she moves quickly from their customary conjugal greeting – 'My deare heart' – to issuing commands on political matters. Italicized sections in Letters 28, 29, 30, and 31 underscore her antipathy to Parliament and the peace process. For example, a section of Letter 29 reads:

> My Lord *Dillon* told me, *not directly from you, though he says you approve it; that it was fit I should write a Letter to the Commissioners of Ireland to this effect, That they ought to desist from those things for the present, which they had put in their Paper, and to assure them, that when you shall be in another condition then you are now, that you will give them contentment.*

Thus the editors sought to stress that Henrietta Maria's letter-writing cemented an alliance between the crown and Roman Catholic Ireland. They heighten a stridency that is not consistent throughout the letter, however. She continues tremulously: 'I dare not doe it without your command', begging Charles to clarify his wishes (pp. 29–30). After Letters 27 to 31, which are chronologically arranged (30 March 1644 to 27 January 1644/5), the sequence diverts to two earlier letters, Letters 32 and 33 (dated 13 March 1644 and 17 June 1643 respectively). This pair reveals the emotional tenor of the royal marriage, providing no further evidence of her political involvement. In Letter 32 she frets over maintaining his trust, giving a picture of a marriage under considerable strain, and in Letter 33, joking about her role in the ongoing war, she gives herself the mock heroic title of 'her

---

[16]   *The King's Cabinet* (1645), Preface, p. A4.
[17]   Knoppers, *Politicizing Domesticity*, pp. 51–2.   [18]   *Ibid.*, pp. 3, 10–11.

she Majestie Generalissima' in charge of the baggage train.[19] These purely familiar letters support the editors' insinuation that the queen has seduced the king – via intimate manipulation, palpable in her epistolary rhetoric – thereby blinding him to the loyalty of Parliament and drawing him into a Roman Catholic alliance. If placed earlier, in chronological sequence, Letters 32 and 33 may well have incited readers' sympathy.

Margaret Cavendish, Duchess of Newcastle, was a 'shrewd' and interventionist self-editor of her many published works.[20] When she prepared her *Sociable Letters* (1664) and *Philosophical Letters* (1664) for publication after the Restoration of monarchy (1660), she sought to distance her letters from scandalous political publications such as *The King's Cabinet*. To this end she blended the generic rhetorical manual mode with the new emphasis upon individual authorship. Her frontispieces and paratexts assert the specific and singular socio-political credentials that underpin her ethos as a published writer describing her as 'the Thrice Noble, Illustrious, and Excellent Princess the Lady Marchioness of Newcastle'. The two volumes' paratexts follow a similar format in spite of different conditions of publication: *Sociable Letters* was published commercially by William Wilson, whereas *Philosophical Letters* was privately published. Each opens with a poem by her husband, William Cavendish, Duke of Newcastle, on Cavendish's wit and accomplishment designed to signal his complicity in her endeavour, and link it to his own royalist statesmanship and writing.[21] This is followed by a series of authorial dedications: the first to acknowledge William Cavendish's support, the second to the scholarly community – Cambridge University (*Philosophical Letters*) and 'all the Professors of Learning' (*Sociable Letters*) – addressing women's exclusion from learning, and then a preface to the reader. *Sociable Letters* includes further poems on 'Her Excellency the Authoress' and 'To the Censorious Reader'. Cavendish draws attention to her sex by opening her dedication to William Cavendish: 'MY LORD, It may be said to me, as one said to a Lady, *Work Lady, Work, let writing Books alone, For Surely Wiser Women ne'r writ one*; But your Lordship never bid me to Work, nor leave Writing'. She cites Edward Denny, Baron of Waltham's well-known vitriolic poem on *The Countess of Montgomeries Urania* (1621) in which he describes, Mary Wroth, as a 'Hermaphrodite in show, in deed a monster'. By identifying with Wroth, Cavendish tags her letters as women's writing and locates them within a

---

[19]  *The King's Cabinet* (1645), p. 33.
[20]  Scott-Baumann, *Forms of Engagement*, p. 80. See also Fitzmaurice, 'Margaret Cavendish on Her Own Writing' and 'Problems with Editing Margaret Cavendish'; and Masten, 'Material Cavendish'.
[21]  See Raber, '"Our Wits Joined"'; Lilley, 'Contracting Readers'.

fiery debate about the proprieties of publication.[22] Although Cavendish invokes her authorial identity to position the volumes in the print market-place, with a couple of exceptions, the letters within are generic. In *Sociable Letters* Cavendish explains that she has 'Endeavoured under the Cover of Letters to Express the Humors of Mankind, and the Actions of a Man's Life by the Correspondence of two Ladies'.[23] This ambitious project is realized through letters addressed to 'Dear Madam' and subscribed 'Madam, Your Faithful Friend and Servant'. They are organized to cover civility in *Socia-ble Letters*, and contemporary philosophy in *Philosophical Letters*. Together the volumes situate women's writing in the republic of letters, and thereby validate the active role Cavendish's contemporaries, including Elisabeth of Bohemia, and Katherine Jones, Lady Ranelagh, were playing in intellectual epistolary networks across Europe, as Carol Pal and others describe.[24]

From the late seventeenth century through the eighteenth century, women's letters appeared in an increasing variety of print formats, from society periodicals, such as the *Tatler*, to epistolary novels, such as Aphra Behn's *Love-Letters between a Nobleman and his Sister* (1684), and collec-tions, such as Elizabeth Singer Rowe's *Friendship in Death: Letters from the Dead to the Living* (1728) and *Letters Moral and Entertaining*, 3 volumes (1729–32).[25] Although women letter-writers were rarely named, they were not entirely anonymous either. Mary Astell's authorial identity is invoked, albeit veiled, for example, in *Letters Concerning the Love of God, Between the Author of the Proposal to the Ladies and Mr John Norris* (1695).[26] Across the channel, women letter-writers were named; this practice survived English translation effecting a distinction between otherwise similar publications. For example, whereas Madame de Sévigné was identified as the author of the 1727 English translation of her letters, Lady Mary Wortley Montagu's letters appeared under the title *LETTERS Of the Right Honourable Lady M—y W—y M———e: Written, during her Travels in EUROPE, ASIA and AFRICA, To Persons of Distinction* (1763).[27] Montagu was already a famed writer, traveller, and intellectual and her letters had been circulating in

---

[22] Edward Denny, 'To Pamphilia from the father-in-law of Seralias' (1621), in *The Poems of Lady Mary Wroth*, ed. Josephine A. Roberts (Baton Rouge: Louisiana State University Press, 1983), pp. 31–5; see Paul Salzman, 'Hermaphrodite: An Introduction', in *Mary Wroth's Poetry: An Electronic Edition*.

[23] Margaret Cavendish, *Sociable Letters*, ed. Fitzmaurice, p. 8.

[24] Pal, *The Republic of Women*. See also Broad, *Women Philosophers*, and Atherton (ed.), *Women Philosophers*.

[25] Brant, *Eighteenth-Century Letters*.

[26] See Ezell, 'Mask of the Feminine'; Mary Astell and John Norris, *Letters*, ed. Taylor and New.

[27] France had a long tradition of publishing the letters of named women authors; see Altman, 'The Letter Book'.

manuscript since the 1720s.[28] The faux veiling of her identity was designed
to remind readers of the letters' prior circulation in an elite coterie. As more
women's letters were published over the eighteenth century, a key concern
for editors was how to register class in the field of print.

Montagu is an interesting case in editorial history as her letters went
through numerous print editions between the eighteenth and twentieth
centuries. The first editor was Montagu herself. She prepared the collection
for manuscript circulation from sent letters, her journal, and notes, ordering
them as a chronological record of her travels from Europe to the East,
and matching each decorously to the addressee. Sometimes this involved
adapting and readdressing sent letters.[29] In the spirit of the enlightenment,
she aimed to unsettle readers' assumptions. The most famous example is
Letter 27 (To Lady —', Adrianople, 1717) in which she recounts 'receiv[ing]'
her at the bathhouse. She describes the Turkish 'Ladies of Quality' as
fulfilling Western ideals: they receive her with 'obliging civility', they are
'as exactly proportioned as ever any goddess was drawn by the pencil of
Guido or Titian, and most of their skins shiningly white'. The ladies sat
with their slaves behind them, she writes, 'but without any distinction of
rank by their dress, all being in the state of nature, that is, in plain English,
stark naked'. She counterpoises her perception of their liberty with their
perception that she herself is trapped in her corsetry.[30] The collection was
not edited to emphasize the twenty-two Turkish letters over the other
thirty-six letters. Rather at every turn Montagu models the principle that
all knowledge derives from experience, presenting her journey to the East
as an intellectual return to the classical origins of Western culture, and
her travels through Catholic Europe as justification for her repudiation
of religious superstition.[31] Voltaire praised her for this attitude in his own
published letters.[32]

The version published in 1763 was a palimpsest. Prior to circulation
the manuscript edition that Montagu prepared was layered over with the
editorial agenda of her friend Mary Astell. In a polemical preface Astell
stressed Montagu's class and sex as follows:

> I was going, like common editors, to advertise the reader of the beauties and
> excellencies of the work . . . But if the reader after perusing *one* letter only, has

[28] Halsband, 'Introduction', to Mary Wortley Montagu, *Complete Letters*, vol. I, p. xvii; Grundy, *Lady Mary Wortley Montagu*, pp. 625–6; and Grundy, 'Editing Lady Mary Wortley Montagu', pp. 61–5.

[29] Halsband, 'Introduction', pp. xiv–xv.    [30] Heffernan, 'Feminism'.

[31] In a letter to Pope she describes visiting Hebrus. This, she observes, is 'the same river in which the musical head of Orpheus repeated verses so many ages since', and then cites Virgil's *Georgics* and praises Pope's translation of Homer (1 April 1717, *Letters*, vol. II (1763), p. 38).

[32] Voltaire, *Lettres Ecrites de Londres sur Les Anglois* (1734; first English transl. 1778).

not discernment to distinguish that natural elegance, that delicacy of sen-
timent and observation, that easy gracefulness, and lovely simplicity . . . let
him lay the book down, and leave it to those who have. (pp. v–vi)

Such discerning readers will also note 'to how much better purpose the
LADIES travel than their LORDS' (pp. vii–viii). Doubtless anxious about
Montagu's Whiggish attitudes, her son-in-law, John Stuart, Earl of Bute,
then Tory Prime Minister of England, tried in vain to prevent the posthumous publication. In the second Preface appended to the printed edition
and placed prior to Astell's preface, another editor, who introduces himself as a friend of the 'ingenious and elegant author', claims that it was
'the manifest intention of the late Lady M—y W——y M———e, that
this SELECT COLLECTION of her Letters should be communicated to the
public' (sig. A4). It 'will be an immortal monument to [the] memory' of
'the sprightliness of her wit, the solidity of her judgment, the extent of her
knowledge, the elegance of her taste and the excellence of her *real* character' (sig. A4). Evidently anxious that Astell's polemic might alienate print
readers, the anonymous editor of the 1763 edition footnotes: 'This fair
and elegant prefacer has resolved, that *Malice* should be of the Masculine
Gender: I believe it is both *Masculine* and *Feminine*, and I heartily wish it
were *Neuter*' (sig. A3).

Montagu's *Turkish Embassy Letters* was regularly reprinted over the following century, much to her family's discomfort. In an attempt to take editorial control, her descendants authorized two new editions of her works.
The first, *The Works of the Right Honourable Lady Mary Wortley Montagu: Including her Correspondence, Poems and Essays* (1803) in five volumes,
introduced new letters into the public domain. Like Montagu, the editor,
James Dallaway, had travelled to Turkey, and he testified to 'the accuracy
of her local descriptions', specifically of 'the interior of the Harém'. The
fact '[t]hat access has since been denied to the Seraglio at Constantinople
[he insisted] is no proof that Lady Mary did not obtain an unrestrained
admission'.[33] This motivated the next generation of Montagu's heirs to
prepare *The Letters and Works of Lady Mary Wortley Montagu* (1837) in
three volumes. In the Preface to this collaboratively edited collection her
great-grandson, James Archibald Stuart-Mackenzie, Lord Wharncliffe – to
whom the editing was credited, in the belief that his pedigree would ensure

---

[33] James Dallaway, 'Memoir of Lady Mary Wortley Montagu', [1803] repr. in Mary Wortley Montagu,
*The Letters and Works*, ed. James Archibald Stuart-Mackenzie, Lord Wharncliffe, vol. 1 (London:
Bentley, 1837), pp. xvi, xviii.

the volume's success[34] – promised to 'remed[y]' the 'defects' of the 1803 *Works* and 'giv[e] the Reader a more complete view of the character of Lady Mary' by supplying omitted letters and passages, remedying editorial interpolation and blending of letters, and supplying 'suppressed' names.[35] On some matters Wharncliffe directs readers to Dallaway, whose *Memoir* is reprinted after the Preface with liberal editorial annotation. A note underneath Dallaway's discussion of Montagu's visit to the seraglio (cited above) reads: 'There is not the least reason to believe that Lady Mary ever was admitted to the interior of the Harem, either at Constantinople or Adrianople, as Mr Dallaway supposes. Vide Introductory Anecdotes, p. 45'.[36] The unattributed 'Biographical Anecdotes', written by Montagu's granddaughter, Lady Louisa Stuart, promises truths 'received directly from' her mother, Mary Wortley Montagu Stuart, Lady Bute, or 'documents formerly seen in Lady Mary Wortley's own hand-writing'.[37] One such document is Montagu's journal, destroyed by her daughter, which Stuart claims 'proved that the story so generally prevalent, of Lady Mary's having had admittance into the Seraglio, was totally false and groundless'.[38]

Montagu's indiscrete prose and behaviour worried her editors. Wharncliffe acknowledges that her letters to her sister, Lady Mar, 'are written with a freedom of expression which would not be tolerated in the present day; and those parts may perhaps be deemed sometimes to trespass beyond the bounds of strict delicacy'. He explains 'that these letters were written as confidential communications... at a period when the feeling upon such subjects was by no means so nice as it now is'. He adds that 'it would have been difficult to alter or curtail them without injury to their spirit'.[39] In any case these letters were already in print. Stuart admitted privately that refuting rumours of Montagu's promiscuity 'would indeed be drawing the attention of the public more closely to them and thus giving them a greater force'. The editors felt no compunction in rewriting lesser-known manuscript letters, and excising sections, in order to present Montagu's separation from her husband as amicable.[40] Although Stuart advised Corbett to watch that the publisher, Richard Bentley, did not lower the tone of the collection, warning that his 'Literary adviser is likely enough to think even Lady Mary's own letters would be the better for a little polishing and

---

34  Louisa Stuart wrote to her niece, Louisa Bromley, 'I had a mind to say to Corbett that *he* might as well be the ostensible editor of a work by which he would get a little money, & I would revise it & supply him with anecdotes & notes: but *a Lord's* name will do better still'; cited in Rubenstein, 'Women's Biography', p. 5.

35  *Letters*, ed. Wharncliffe, vol. 1 (1837), p. ii.      36  *Ibid.*, vol. 1, p. xviii.

37  *Ibid.*, vol. 1, p. 3.      38  *Ibid.*, vol. 1, p. 44.      39  *Ibid.*, p. iii.

40  Stuart to Wharncliffe, 10 December 1836, cited in Rubenstein, 'Women's Biography', p. 8.

re-touching, not to speak of what we have furnished'.[41] While on the Continent the English poet, Lord Byron, secured a group of love letters exchanged between Montagu and the Italian intellectual Francesco Algarotti, which he loaned to Bentley for publication.[42] Wharncliffe decided against their inclusion in the second edition, doubtless with Stuart's support.[43] The editors sought to enhance the impression of Montagu's gentility at all costs.

Over the nineteenth century, the age of the novel put a premium upon moving accounts of feminine sensibility. This is how the letters Dorothy Osborne wrote to her fiancé, Sir William Temple, between 1652 and 1654, were marketed from the outset; a selection was published in a supplement to *Memoirs of the Life, Works and Correspondence of Sir William Temple* (1836), a biography of her husband written by Thomas Peregrine Courtenay, a retired Tory politician. Courtenay distinguished his biography of Temple from others in print on the grounds that Osborne's hitherto-unpublished letters gave emotional depth. In an otherwise critical review in the *Edinburgh Review* (1838), Thomas Macaulay praised Osborne's letters for their natural charm. This spiked the interest of the judge and writer, Edward Abbott Parry, who sought the family's permission to prepare an edition. Sarah Rose Longe, a descendant, readily handed over the collection along with her editorial transcriptions, dating, and annotations requesting that her name be suppressed. Although the first publisher Parry approached rejected the manuscript on commercial grounds, Longe managed to interest Griffith, Farran, Okeden & Welsh in the project. Farran agreed but excluded seven letters he believed would not interest readers. The collection was a great success. Pirated editions entitled *Love Letters of Dorothy Osborne to Sir William Temple 1652–54* were published in Toronto in 1901 and London in 1903. Parry's complete edition of Osborne's letters was published in 1903. A few years later, the letters of Martha Giffard, Osborne's sister-in-law, was published as a novelistic sequel: *Martha, Lady Giffard, her Life and Correspondence, 1664–1722; A Sequel to Osborne's Letters*, edited by Julia Georgina Longe (1911).

Professional and amateur antiquarianism motivated further editions of early modern women's letters. From the late eighteenth century, there

[41] Stuart to Corbett, 2 January 1836, cited in Rubenstein, 'Women's Biography', p. 9.
[42] Hegele, 'Lord Byron, Literary Detective'.
[43] Halsband describes Montagu's extant letters to Algarotti as 'unique for her in their extravagant passion and rhetoric'. In 1938 the Bodleian Library purchased a collection of Montagu-Algarotti letters that circulated in Venice over the nineteenth century (Introduction, *Collected Letters*, vol. II, pp. x–xi).

was a push to make accessible unedited archival documents that told the story of Britain's past. Letters were an important subspecies. Six Royal Commissions, known as the 'Record Commission', were held between 1800 and 1836; the result was a series of publications and the establishment of the Public Record Office. In spite of the success of *Original Letters, Illustrative of English History*, edited by Sir Henry Ellis, British Museum librarian and chief (from 1827), and published in three series and twelve volumes between 1827 and 1846, London publishers viewed volumes of records as financially risky. This was owing to the commercial failure of Samuel Bentley's *Excerpta Historica: or, Illustrations of English History* (1831) and the Record Commission collections. The government suspended the Record Commission project. In its wake, printing societies, such as the Camden Society, were established to publish historical documents, establish a readership, and pressure the government to resume the calendaring and publication of documents.[44] Between 1838 and 1872, the Camden Society published various editions of early modern women's letters (Camden Old Series). John Bruce, one of the founders, edited the letters of Elizabeth I and Mary Queen of Scots for publication, and Cecil Monro edited the letters of Queen Margaret of Anjou.[45] Women's letters were included in miscellanies and family archives published by the Camden Society.[46] *Letters of the Lady Brilliana Harley, Wife of Sir Robert Harley, of Brampton Bryan, Knight of the Bath*, volume 58 in the Camden Old Series, for example, was edited by Thomas Taylor Lewis, a local vicar who gained access to the family archive. The letters document Harley's valiant defence of Brampton Bryan, during the English Civil War, and protection of local Puritans. In the biographical introduction, however, Lewis sandwiches her story between lengthy accounts of the achievements of her husband and son, both actors in the English Civil War and conscientious Puritans. Thus he implies that the collection is important primarily owing to Harley's connection to great men. Lewis provides notes identifying people, places, and other contemporary references, and presents the letters marking indecipherable passages with asterisks and occasionally commenting upon the condition of the manuscript or the hand.

[44]  Levy, 'The Founding of the Camden Society'.
[45]  Volume 46: *Letters of Queen Elizabeth and King James VI of Scotland*, ed. John Bruce (1849); volume 63: *Letters of King Charles the First to Queen Henrietta Maria*, ed. John Bruce (1856); volume 86: *Letters of Queen Margaret of Anjou and Bishop Beckington and others, written in the reigns of Henry V and Henry VI*, ed. Cecil Monro (1863); volume 93: *Accounts and Papers relating to Mary, Queen of Scots*, ed. Allan J. Crosby and John Bruce (1867).
[46]  For example, volume 87: *Miscellany*, vol. v (1864), includes an 'Inquiry into the genuineness of a letter dated February 3, 1613 and signed "Mary Magdaline Davers"'.

Nineteenth-century antiquarianism stimulated both amateur and professional editing of early modern women's letters. Mary Anne Everett Green, a historian with an interest in early women's biography was employed on the government calendaring project from 1855.[47] The two editions of early modern women's letters she edited, *Letters of Royal and Illustrious Ladies*, 2 vols. (Henry Colburn, 1849) and *Life and Letters of Henrietta Maria* (Bentley, 1857), established standards for future editors. The latter was possibly stimulated by the Camden Society's 1856 publication of *Letters of King Charles the First to Queen Henrietta Maria*, edited by John Bruce, which left Henrietta Maria's story untold. As Green explains in her preface, this was a difficult task as Henrietta Maria's letters were dispersed across English and French archives, some were in French, her hand was difficult to read, and she employed four different ciphers during the English Civil War. Some of Henrietta Maria's letters in English collections were already calendared but badly transcribed by someone ignorant of French, who struggled to read her hand (confusing similarly formed letters, such as v's and r's), failed to decode the cipher in her Civil War letters, and inadvertently blended letters 'without the slightest regard to date, or place, or even to the unity of the letters' (pp. vi–vii). Green painstakingly compiled keys to the ciphers.[48] Green asserts that she did not set out to illustrate the 'changeful personal history' of 'one of [the] most talented and unfortunate English Queens', but her edition did effectively highlight the key role played by an early modern woman letter-writer in English Civil War history.

Other scholarly editions of early modern women's letters followed, expanding the representation of the kinds of women who wrote letters. In America A. J. F. van Laer, an archivist at the New York State archives in Albany, translated and edited a number of collections of seventeenth-century Dutch letters, including the letters of the Dutch colonist Maria van Rensselaer published in 1935. This collection introduces into the public domain the letters of a literate woman of the merchant class, thereby redressing the bias towards royal and elite women's letters. Interestingly where two drafts of a letter survive, van Laer includes both, thereby revealing the labour van Rensselaer invested in letter-writing, an activity that evidently did not come easily.[49]

---

[47] Christine L. Krueger, 'Green, Mary Anne Everett (1818–1895)', *ODNB*.
[48] Green, *Life and Letters of Henrietta Maria* (1857), p. vii.
[49] Maria van Rensselaer to Rygart van Rensselaer, [January? 1683], *Correspondence of Maria van Rensselaer 1669–1689*, pp. 84–8.

Twentieth-century scholarly editions of early modern women's letters continued to be selective. For example, Robert Halsband presents Montagu's letters without the extant replies of her correspondents in his *Complete Letters of Lady Mary Wortley Montagu* published by Oxford University Press in three volumes between 1965 and 1967. By contrast George Sherburn's five-volume Clarendon edition of the correspondence of her contemporary and associate, Alexander Pope, published in 1956, includes correspondents' replies. Marjorie Hope Nicolson's *The Conway Letters: The Correspondence of Anne, Viscountess Conway, Henry More, and their Friends 1642–1684* (Oxford University Press, 1930), provides a more nuanced picture of Conway's place within an epistolary network. Nicolson distinguished between familiar letters and 'philosophical treatises' which she excluded, however.[50] Although she applied this rule to letters written by both Conway and Cambridge Platonist Henry More, it obscured Conway's motivation for writing to More, and the scope of her intellectual participation in the republic of letters.[51] Whereas More's contribution to seventeenth-century philosophy was established by his many published works, Conway's lay in relative obscurity until Nicolson's edition. Letters were often women's only means of participating in intellectual discussion.

From the late twentieth century the scope of women's letters edited for publication was radically expanded as a result of feminist publishing initiatives including Virago; Women Writers in English 1350–1850 published by Oxford University Press between 1995 and 1999; the ongoing Ashgate series The Early Modern Englishwoman 1500–1750: Contemporary Editions; and The Other Voice in Early Modern Europe published by University of Chicago Press and ITER, Centre for Reformation and Renaissance Studies, Toronto. The second book published in the Women Writers in English 1350–1850 series was Sara Jayne Steen's edition of *The Letters of Lady Arbella Stuart* (1995). Steen's introduction has become a touchstone for editors of early modern women's letters. Like other feminist editors of the period, Steen viewed her role as primarily biographical.[52] As she explained in a later essay, she viewed it as her 'responsibility' to provide the cues necessary to make the voice of the woman writer readily accessible to modern

---

[50] This omission was corrected in the revised edition of Nicolson's *The Conway Letters*, ed. Sarah Hutton (1992).

[51] On the distinction between letters and dialectics see Lynette Hunter, 'Introduction', in *The Letters of Dorothy Moore, 1612–64*, ed. Hunter, pp. xv–liv. On Conway see Broad, *Women Philosophers*, pp. 65–89; Hutton, *Anne Conway*; Pal, *Republic of Women*, pp. 262–3.

[52] Doody, 'Response', p. 129.

readers. To that end, she provided a 100-page biography of Stuart, and just five pages of textual notes.[53] She presented the letters with a minimum of information about original manuscripts, as she feared that this would clutter the volume, and possibly overwhelm readers. Steen included variant drafts when extant, as this gave access to 'Stuart's mind as she shaped her prose'.[54]

Quick to note the importance of the collection, Barbara Lewalski commended Steen's nuanced categorization of the correspondence into 'loosely structured, associational, and often angry complaints and recriminations; informal, affectionate, often bantering letters to her favorite uncle, Gilbert Talbot, and her aunt Mary; and formal, carefully structured, conventionally humble and submissive court letters'.[55] Lynn Magnusson commended its introduction of women's letters of petition into the public domain.[56] Although editors continue to favour personal letters over official correspondence, or 'corporate' authored missives, there are practical reasons for this, as Marcus explains in her discussion of editing *Elizabeth I: Collected Works*, in this volume.[57] The Other Voice in Early Modern Europe sought to make early modern women's writing in European languages other than English more widely available through English translation and scholarly editing. Nineteen of the 127 titles (published and forthcoming) in the Toronto series are early modern women's courtly, philosophical, mercantile, religious, and familial letters. The series both reissues early modern publications, such as Arcangela Tarabotti (Toronto) and Madeleine de Scudéry's letters (Chicago), and makes available archival collections, such as the intellectual letters of Anne-Marie-Louise d'Orléans, Duchess de Montpensier (Chicago), or Mesdames des Roches, and the mercantile letters of the merchant wife Margherita Datini (Toronto).[58] The theme of the series, resistance to the 'three-thousand year history of the derogation of women', motivated the publication of a great variety of epistolary

---

[53] Steen, 'Behind the Arras'; and Steen, Introduction and Textual Introduction, in *The Letters of Lady Arbella Stuart*, ed. Steen, pp. 1–105, 107–11.

[54] Steen, Textual Introduction, *ibid.*, p. 110.     [55] Lewalski, *Writing Women*, p. 67.

[56] Magnusson, 'A Rhetoric of Requests', pp. 51–66.

[57] See Marcus, 'Confessions of a Reformed Uneditor (II)', p. 1073.

[58] Arcangela Tarabotti, *Letters Familiar and Formal*, ed. and trans. Ray and Westwater; Madeleine de Scudéry, *Selected Letters, Orations and Rhetorical Dialogues*, ed. and trans. Donawerth and Strongson; Anne Marie-Louise d'Orléans, Duchesse de Montpensier, *Against Marriage: The Correspondence of La Grande Mademoiselle*, ed. and trans. De Jean; and Margherita Datini, *Letters to Francesco Datini*, trans. James and Pagliaro.

collections, although, as this chapter shows, women's letter-writing has long been respected and edited with care.[59]

The most dramatic recent development in the editing of early modern women's letters is the advent of the database in the 1990s.[60] In 2013 *Bess of Hardwick's Letters: The Complete Correspondence, c. 1550–1608*, a collection of all extant letters written and received by Bess of Hardwick, was published online. The wider significance of this for online representations of women's writing is discussed further by Patricia Pender and Rosalind Smith in their chapter at the conclusion of this volume. *Hardwick's Letters* makes available an extensive corpus of familiar and formal letters written over a forty-year period. Very aware that 'editions are narratives' produced by 'recast[ing]' letters 'to fit' an editorial agenda, Alison Wiggins, the project director, distinguishes *Bess of Hardwick's Letters* from the 'author-focused model' Steen employed in editing Arbella Stuart's letters. Steen advocated 'retaining valuable textual signifiers of voice and eliminating aspects of the document that interfere with that voice for modern readers'. By contrast, *Bess of Hardwick's Letters* stresses the collaborative nature of early modern letter-writing (scribes and carriers, for example, contribute to the communicative act), and situates Bess of Hardwick's letters amid networks of exchange, early modern epistolary discourse, and the materiality of epistolary culture.[61] Letters appear in diplomatic (that is, direct transcription of the text including abbreviations and other marks and signs), normalized (that is, with contractions expanded and signs, such as the thorn, rendered into words), and digitized forms. Users are offered pedagogical guidance in the form of a paleography tutorial designed by Wiggins and Graham Williams, and introductory essays on early modern letter-writing. The database is variously searchable by the author's biography, correspondents, carriers, or material features such as letter folding, seal, floss, and so on. In order that 'Bess,' as she is familiarly called throughout, is not lost in the detail users can bring 'Bess herself. . . to the forefront as required'.[62] The edition strives to satisfy the material turn in editing, without abandoning the older biographical mode.

*Bess of Hardwick's Letters* was edited collaboratively. The editorial team transcribed individual letters, contributed supplementary essays, and

---

[59]  From Margaret L. King and Albert Rabil, Jr, 'The Other Voice in Early Modern Europe: Introduction to the Series' a preface appended to each volume in the series.

[60]  On epistolary databases see Dalbello, 'Digitality, Epistolarity and Reconstituted Letter Archives'.

[61]  Alison Wiggins, 'Ontology', in *Bess of Hardwick's Letters*, www.bessofhardwick.org.

[62]  Wiggins, 'Locating the Letters', in *Bess of Hardwick's Letters*.

dramatized biographical podcasts created for *Unsealed: The Letters of Bess of Hardwick*, a National Trust exhibition. The database documents relevant activities of other members of the project during its active life, including papers given by editors, research associates, and project doctoral students. It also provides links to other scholarly communities, such as the *Centre for Editing Lives and Letters*, and digitized archives, such as the University of Helsinki's *Corpus of Early English Correspondence*, and finding aids such as *Early Modern Letters Online* (Oxford University and the Bodleian Library), and its sister project *Women's Early Modern Letters Online*. *Bess of Hardwick* embeds Hardwick's letters within early modern epistolary culture, a correspondence network, a community of editors, web developers, researchers, students, *and* a multilayered editorial practice.

Over the past four hundred years the editing of early modern women's letters in English has been influenced by changing attitudes to women's authorship, and to letter-writing as a species of writing. Initially, editors followed epistolary rhetorical tenets widely disseminated over the sixteenth, seventeenth, and eighteenth centuries, and defined women's letters according to generic stereotypes. A mother would write one kind of letter to her daughter, a wife another to her husband, and so on. By the mid seventeenth century, as the political press developed during the Civil War period, the individual identity of women letter-writers gained currency, most spectacularly in the case of Henrietta Maria. Nevertheless, over the following century or so most women's authorship was veiled, although editors gave clues to ensure easy identification. Letter-writing is a quotidian mode of writing, and yet one enhanced by classical and humanist precedents. Although the manuals that first published women's letters were involved in the popular dissemination of classical learning, their focus was on everyday vernacular commonsense discourse. Manuals continued to be published over the following centuries but writers with literary aspirations, such as Margaret Cavendish, began to publish their letters to proclaim their literary and cultural authority. Nineteenth-century editorial practice was dominated by an antiquarian interest in letters as biographical and historical documents. Family members who edited their foremothers' letters for publication, such as Wharncliff et al., however, worried over how to shape the writer's life for a public readership. Over the twentieth century antiquarianism gave way to the establishment of scholarly principles for editing, upheld in the Oxford editions of Conway and Montagu, for example. The mid twentieth century saw the development of feminist editorial principles institutionalized in feminist publishing series. At least initially, their focus was upon the woman writer's voice.

The advent of the database has enabled an increased focus upon locating women's letters within epistolary networks and illuminating the material culture of letter-writing. As this chapter has shown, the principles guiding the editing of early modern women's letters are dynamic and constantly evolving.

# CHAPTER 8

# Editing Queen Elizabeth I

## Leah S. Marcus

We begin with an anonymous broadside ballad of which the earliest sur-viving copies date from the 1650s, according to the British Library Online Catalogue: 'A sweet Sonnet, wherein the Lover exclaimeth against Fortune for the loss of his Ladies Favour, almost past hope to get it again, and in the end receives a comfortable answer, and attains his desire, as may here appear', to be sung to the tune 'Fortune my Foe'.[1] The ballad consists of two columns, each containing the same number of lines and stanzas, the left titled 'The Lovers Complaint for the loss of his Love' and the right headed 'The Ladies Comfortable and pleasant Answer'. Peter Beal spec-ulates that the first copy of this ballad may have been published in 1590, though probably with significant variation from the versions we have, and many intervening copies may well have been lost.[2]

The tune to which this 'Sweet Sonnet' was attached put it in rather mixed company: other ballads of the period sung to 'Fortune my Foe' include 'The complaint and lamentation of Mistresse Arden of Feversham' (*STC* 732), 'The godly end . . . of one Iohn Stevens . . . hang'd, drawne, and quartered for high-treason' (*STC* 23260), 'Saint Bernards vision. Or, A briefe discourse (dialogue-wise) betweene the soule and the body' (*STC* 1910), 'The lamentation of Edward Bruton, and James Riley . . . for the bloody murder . . . of Henry Howell, and his wife' (*STC* 3945.7), 'A godly song, entituled, A farewell to the world' (*STC* 4241), and 'A cruell murther committed lately upon the body of Abraham Gearsy' (*STC* 5418), among others. Who would imagine, given the miscellaneous company it kept

---

[1] *Early English Books Online* lists the ballad as 'Anon' and dates its text even later – *c.* 1685.

[2] See Beal's *Catalogue of English Literary Manuscripts 1450–1700 (CELM)*, Elizabeth I item E!Q 35 and Ralegh item RaW 133–5 www.celm-ms.org.uk/authors/; see also *Poems of Sir Walter Ralegh*, ed. Rudick, 15A–D and pp. xxxix–xli; and *Elizabeth I: Collected Works*, ed. Marcus, Mueller, and Rose, pp. 307–9. For known copies of the ballad, see *EEBO* under 'Sweet Sonnet', which lists five copies from the British Library and one from the National Library of Scotland. According to *EEBO*, two of the copies are also catalogued as Roxburghe Ballads: Rox.III.192–3, and one copy made it into the Wing catalogue (2nd edn), S6249A.

during the late sixteenth and seventeenth centuries, that the 'Sweet Sonnet' of the 1650s originated in a verse exchange between Sir Walter Ralegh and Queen Elizabeth I from the late 1580s? In the printed versions from the 1650s, both poems are amplified so that they are exactly the same length and the stanzas of the Lover's complaint on the left match up horizontally with the Lady's comfortable responses on the right. Ingeniously, they can therefore be read either column-wise, so that the full complaint of the lover is heard before the lady's response, or left to right by stanza, so the exchange is more intensely dialogic. The identifying language that would reveal the ballad's Elizabethan courtly origin is, of course, missing in the broadside version: 'Princess' becomes 'mistress' in Ralegh's poem; and the first two lines of Elizabeth's answer, which identify Ralegh through her pet names for him – 'Ah, silly Pug, wert thou so sore afraid? / Mourn not, my Wat, nor be thou so dismayed' – appear more anonymously in the broadside as 'Ah silly soul, art thou so sore afraid? / Mourn not my dear nor be not so dismaid'.

The fact that this verse exchange could migrate so readily from the courtly circles in which it circulated in manuscript – and from George Puttenham's *Arte of English Poesie* (1589), where small segments of both poems were cited, discussed, and attributed to Ralegh and Elizabeth I respectively[3] – suggests that the writings of a queen carried no special aura during the period. As we shall see later on, Elizabeth was celebrated for her verbal eloquence in her own day, but that veneration did not, for the most part, translate into any particular veneration of her written records. Elizabeth I's formal political pronouncements and official letters were generally credited to her when they were copied, circulated, and printed because they were of inherent political importance as the utterances of a monarch, but her other writings could be stolen, appropriated, freely revised, and published without attribution. Scholars of the rise of literary authorship during the sixteenth and seventeenth centuries in Britain have sometimes connected it to the rise of royal absolutism, suggesting that an author's control over the publication and dissemination of his or her work developed along with the monarch's assertion of control over the kingdom. That was certainly not the case with Elizabeth I: she is said to have remarked that 'We princes are set as it were upon stages in the sight and view of all the world' and contemporaries sometimes celebrated her as 'queen' among writers as well as queen of England, but her writings often circulated anonymously. Attribution to the queen was typically a

---

3  Puttenham, *Arte of English Poesie*, sigs. Z2$^r$, Aa3$^r$, and Ddr$^r$.

question of political and religious strategy rather than of authorship in the Foucaultian sense of the term.[4]

*Elizabeth I: Collected Works*, edited by Leah S. Marcus, Janel Mueller, and Mary Beth Rose (Chicago, 2000; revised paperback edition, 2002), originated in a conversation as Mary Beth Rose, Judith Kegan Gardiner, and I were walking south from the Newberry Library in Chicago to a Japanese café for lunch. It was the late 1980s, during the heyday of second-wave feminism, and we were eager to teach women writers of the early modern period in our surveys of Renaissance literature. We lamented the fact that Elizabeth's writings were not available in a convenient form for classroom and scholarly use, and I suggested that we create an edition ourselves. Judy Gardiner immediately (and wisely) bowed out of the project, but Mary Beth Rose and I soldiered on, adding Janel Mueller to the editorial team when the birth of a new child made it evident that I would be unable to make extended visits to the archives for several years. Janel Mueller has a genius for interpreting difficult hands, especially Elizabeth's, and I had a useful range of archival skills, so we made a good team, with Mary Beth Rose on hand to arbitrate disputes. There were plenty of those because at every level we found difficulties, beginning with the question, much discussed in the present volume of essays, of whether to use original or modern spelling.

The use or abandonment of original spelling was a more fraught issue for Elizabeth's writings, which use highly creative spellings even for a period when spelling was still very erratic, than it would be for women's writings of, say, the late seventeenth century, by which time spelling had become much more standardized and original spelling editions would therefore be comprehensible to a wide range of modern readers. I argued for modernized spelling on the grounds that we wanted the volume to be accessible to general readers as well as scholars: to have used original spelling for Elizabeth's works would have rendered them effectively unusable by the average undergraduate student and the general reader not blessed with world enough and time to decipher the originals. We compromised by creating a 'trade' volume of *Collected Works* (hereafter identified as *CW*) that modernized spellings, and augmenting it with a second volume, *Elizabeth I: Autograph Compositions and Foreign Language Originals*, ed. Janel Mueller and Leah S. Marcus (Chicago, 2003; hereafter identified as *ACFLO*), that supplemented the modern-spelling versions of all documents we had

---

[4] See Foucault, 'What is an Author?', pp. 141–60.

transcribed from Elizabeth's own hand as well as untranslated originals of her foreign-language compositions recorded in other hands.

*ACFLO* gave me, in particular, endless headaches since it fell to me to determine the precise form of the texts on the page. The difficulty was not so much Elizabeth's spellings but her use of capitalization, especially in the middle of words or sentences. In her mature, running mixed italic style, miniscules and majuscules of many letters are distinguishable only by size; moreover, she frequently used the unusual size of a word in manuscript to indicate special emphasis. This is particularly true in her correspondence, where she occasionally wrote a word larger than the rest of the sentence to indicate vehemence, much as we might now use capital letters or underlining. How to distinguish the use of majuscules for emphasis from the use of majuscules as part of her ordinary practice as a writer? That proved to be almost impossible in some cases. We used majuscules in our transcriptions everywhere that we thought her contemporaries would have detected majuscules, which made for a strange-looking text from our modern point of view. We also tried to reproduce the differential size of her script in words of particular emphasis. Moreover, the queen was extremely economical in her use of punctuation, particularly between sentences, a trait we wanted to preserve. Here is a brief sample from our original-spelling version of a letter to James VI of Scotland, dated 4 October 1586:

> Wisching alL meanes that may maintaine your faithful trust in me that neuer wyL seake aught but the incr^e^ase of^your^ honor and safty I Was in mynd to haue sent you suche accidentz as this late monethe broght furthe but the sufficientie of mastar ArchebaL made me retaine him and do rendar you many loVing thankes for the Ioy you toke of my narroW escape from the Chawes of Deth to Wiche I might easely haue fallen but that the hand of the hiest saued me from that snare and for that the Curse of that desaing rose vp from the wicked sucgestion of the Iesuites Wiche make hit an axceptable Sacrifice to God and meritorious to themselves that a kinge not of ther profession shuld be murthered therfor I could kipe my pen no longar from discharging my care of your person that you suffer not suche Vipars to inhabite your lande.[5]

As it turned out, our choice of modern spelling for *CW* proved decisive: the University of Chicago Press chose to publish our edition in preference to a proposed edition in original spelling by another highly reputed researcher, and *CW* went on to become one of the press's best sellers for the year 2000, when it finally appeared in hardcover. The reader of both proposals was the

---

[5] *ACFLO*, ed. Mueller and Marcus, p. 65.

noted Shakespearean scholar and editor David Bevington, who had been publishing Shakespeare in modern spelling for decades and was therefore receptive to the idea that Elizabeth I should receive the same treatment. Whether appropriately or not, the modern-spelling Shakespeares have set a standard for other authors of the period. Modern spelling, or at least the availability of modern-spelling editions, makes an author appear more like Shakespeare, which is to say more canonical, while the use of original spelling makes an author appear more quaint and embedded in his or her own original period. Authors who are not routinely offered in modern-spelling editions may suffer in consequence, even though there are also obvious advantages in terms of subtlety and multiplicity of meaning to preserving original spellings. We may wonder how Edmund Spenser would fare in the eyes of our students if *The Faerie Queene* were routinely taught in modern spelling as opposed to regularized original-spelling editions. Our edition offered Elizabeth I both ways: in a modern-spelling edition that included notes alerting readers to possible ambiguities in her spelling of words that had been ironed out by our modernizations, but also in an original spelling version that complemented the *CW* and made it possible to delve into the complexities of the original texts. I am still convinced that our decision was the right one. We were extremely lucky that the University of Chicago Press was willing to publish both versions.

But the issue of spelling was undoubtedly easier to deal with than the frequently vexed matter of authorial attribution, already referred to above. The problem is particularly acute in determining the text for Elizabeth I's memorable and justly celebrated speeches, beginning with the 'speech to her secretary [then Sir William Cecil] and other her lords before her coronation' in 1558 and ending with her final speech before Parliament, 19 December 1601. Particularly in the final decades of her reign, Elizabeth's speeches were often printed in official versions, which would, one might suppose, make the editor's task easy: all we would need to do would be to edit and reproduce the printed texts. But as we quickly realized in working with the early materials, the printed text of a speech was often a pale reflection of the speech as it survived from other sources, particularly in informal manuscript copies that were made by auditors who took down Elizabeth's words as she uttered them or (more likely) as quickly as possible after the conclusion of the speech, while her language was still fresh in their minds.

We might assume that such a fluid origin would guarantee inaccuracy, but educated people of the period were trained to remember much longer texts, especially sermons, as they heard them delivered and to write them down afterward from memory. For that reason, important sermons of the period often exist in multiple forms: the form in which a preacher planned to deliver it, possibly from a mere list of notes or biblical citations; the form in which he delivered it (always unavailable to us because there were no recording devices as yet); the form in which it was taken down by contemporary listeners; and the form in which it might finally reach publication. The published version could be a revised version of the preacher's own copy, a memorial text reproduced by an auditor, or a combination of both.

The composition of parliamentary speeches offers a closer analogy to the situation of Elizabeth, many of whose speeches were in fact delivered before Parliament. Some parliamentary speakers may have read out their orations from a full text or delivered the full from memory, but others operated differently. The Ellesmere Collection at the Huntington Library includes a set of notes from Sir Thomas Egerton, Lord Ellesmere, that records his practice as a speaker. First he wrote copious notes on each of the points he wished to emphasize during his speech, then he gradually boiled them down over a series of drafts from a written text approaching the length of the speech as he would eventually deliver it, into a list of brief points that he could carry with him as an aide-memoire during the actual performance of the speech. When he spoke in Parliament, his oration would appear spontaneous, but it would be the result of careful preparation: he would expand more or less extemporaneously from the pre-digested points to a discourse approximately the same length as his original notes.

In the instance of Queen Elizabeth I, the process was different, but similarly adapted to the needs of oral delivery. Elizabeth's speeches were typically short and pithy, unlike the long oratorical performances common in Parliament. As we finally came to realize in working with the documentary material, none of the manuscripts recording Elizabeth's speeches was written by her in advance of the speech itself; rather, her habitual practice was to gather the main points she planned to discuss in her memory, then speak extemporaneously. Any manuscripts associated with the speech are therefore after the fact and some may be highly unsatisfactory as records of what the queen actually said.[6]

Royal speeches were relatively rare and Elizabeth's best speeches were events of high contemporary interest. As in the case of the 'Golden Speech', the government might scramble to produce a printed version of such a notable event, but the printed form of the speech was short and abstract, lacking the verve, eloquence, and emotional vibrancy of the speech as we

---

[6] For more detail on this process, see my 'From Oral Delivery to Print'.

find it preserved in contemporary manuscripts, some of which explicitly state that the text they offer was taken down from memory and represents the closest approximation of the queen's actual words possible under the circumstances. How were we to edit the speeches, given such an array of conflicting versions? We made the decision to offer more than one text of the most important speeches that existed in multiple manuscript and printed forms. In the case of the 'Golden Speech' we reproduced three versions, two authoritative manuscripts of the queen's words that differed significantly but offered the same basic points and much language in common, and the 'official' printed version, which compared to the other two appears more like a summary than a full report. Ironically, the printed version, the version that is shorter and less vivid than the others, claims the most authority for its text: '*The same being taken verbatim in writing by A. B., as near as he could possibly set it down*' (*CW*, p. 343).

There are, of course, problems with presenting any edited text in multiple versions. We clearly indicated in our notes to *CW* that some versions of Elizabeth's speeches were more authoritative than others. In fact, in the case of Elizabeth's first oration before Parliament, 10 February 1559, we deliberately juxtaposed a reliable contemporary report of the speech with William Camden's much later made-up version, so readers could see how unreliable Camden's alleged report was.[7] But our tactic backfired in this instance, in that some scholars have failed to heed our caveats in the note and cited the speech from our volume in Camden's fictitious version rather than in the version with more textual authority! Camden's was the version they were accustomed to since it referred to Elizabeth's marriage to her kingdom, an idea that she broached not in that speech, so far as we are able to determine, but in her conversations with the Scottish ambassador William Maitland in 1561.[8] Subtlety of editorial intervention, alas, has its costs. But I still believe that subtlety is preferable to a false aura of editorial certainty in cases of multiple versions with an equal claim to textual authority. In editing the speeches, since an authoritative text of verbal utterance was unattainable, we strove for editorial openness, offering readers an array of texts that demonstrate the fluidity of Elizabeth's language as it cycled through manuscript transcriptions and recopyings and into print versions that may have claimed to be authoritative but often were not.

Editing Elizabeth's letters was a much more straightforward matter than the speeches, though here too the question of attribution looms large.

---

[7] *CW*, ed. Marcus, Mueller, and Rose, p. 58, n. 1.     [8] *CW*, ed. Marcus, Mueller, and Rose, p. 65.

No reliable inventory of Elizabeth's letters has ever been created. Since the queen's signature has had significant value for nineteenth- and early twentieth-century collectors, many letters signed by her have drifted into private collections and out of scholarly view, where they remain unless the collection is later acquired by a major library, as in the case of Elizabeth's 1548 'love letter' to Thomas Seymour now in the Pierpont Morgan Library as part of a collection of autographs.[9] A whole volume of state papers containing key – and often highly dramatic – correspondence between Elizabeth I and Mary Queen of Scots has disappeared from the Public Record Office, as I discovered when I went back to triple-check all our transcriptions of the letters. They appear somehow to have been spirited out of the library and sacrificed, we can speculate, to the voracity of collectors.

Elizabeth reputedly had the ability to dictate several letters at once to copyists, but it is likely in many such cases that the content of such letters as sent was a blend of Elizabeth's own style and that of her assistants: as in modern corporations, official letters and other written material had their own 'company style', somewhat standardized formats, and language. In the British Library Additional Manuscripts collections and elsewhere, we can find hundreds of routine diplomatic letters, especially to foreign Protestant allies, sent over Elizabeth's signature but unlikely even to have been dictated by her. Should they be regarded as Elizabeth's compositions? We judged not, and included in our edition only one of these because of its particular interest: a letter from Elizabeth to the Ottoman Sultan Mahumet Cham of 20 January 1601.[10] As a general rule, Elizabeth wrote in her own hand only to sitting monarchs like James VI, Mary Queen of Scots, or Henry IV of France. For a favourite to receive a letter in the queen's hand was a sign of special regard, such as the love letters she wrote to the Duke of Anjou/Alençon during their courtship in the 1570s and 1580s. But her correspondents were not necessarily happy with the task of deciphering her hasty italic scrawl. She apologized more than once to James VI for the illegibility of her hand. In a letter of March 1593, for example, she goes on at vehement length about James's inability to contain attempts at 'hideousest treason' against him, then at the very end of a long letter acknowledges belatedly, 'Now do I remember your cumber to read such scribbled lines'.[11] Even my quotation above from the same letter – 'hideousest treason' – may be transcribed incorrectly because of the difficulty of her

9   See *ACFLO*, ed. Marcus and Mueller, p. 19; and my discussion of the letter in 'Elizabeth on Elizabeth' – the letter is reproduced on p. 215.
10  *CW*, ed. Marcus, Mueller, and Rose, pp. 400–2.
11  *CW*, ed. Marcus, Mueller, and Rose, pp. 368–9.

hand. The word in manuscript appears to be 'hideust', which could be transcribed as 'hideous', 'hideousest', or even, if the *u* is actually an *n*, 'hiddennest', meaning most secret. At least some of Elizabeth's letters to Monsieur were sent to him in transcription rather than in the queen's own hand because, however much he may have professed love for her, he could not read her writing.

These difficulties aside, in cases where we have Elizabeth's original letter bearing remnants of a seal and a notation of its delivery, we can usually be confident about what she wrote. For example, a 1593–4 letter exchange between Elizabeth and James that we reproduced for our edition shows the two responding in precise and amusing detail to elements of the most recent letter from the other.[12] Once we depart from letters in Elizabeth's hand and enter the realm of transcriptions, however, we are on shifting sands. Even official transcriptions of letters identified as having been Elizabeth's could take the form of 'minutes', which could range from mere summaries to full copies of the letter as sent. More often, Elizabeth's letters in the archives are letters in the hands of official secretaries that might or might not contain elements of Elizabeth's own prose. In such cases secure attribution becomes much more doubtful. Even when Elizabeth added a personal note at the top of a missive in her hand to give her own intimate touch to an important communication that was otherwise in the hand of a secretary, the text of the letter often contrasts markedly in style from her note, suggesting that the bulk of the missive was composed by someone other than the queen. As we shall see, a major difference between the queen's own writing and that of many of her assistants even given the homogenization implied by the idea of a 'company style' was that her ministers and secretaries tended to be wedded to an ornate, humanist Ciceronianism that the queen herself avoided.

In our edition, we strove to exclude letters that lacked early and reliable documentation, which meant that we were forced to exclude some of Elizabeth's most famous letters, such as her well-known ultimatum to the Bishop of Ely. We couldn't find this letter in any early manuscript copies, and it sounds suspiciously like a later artefact modelled on her genuine letters of scolding and admonition:

Proud prelate,

You know what you were before I made you what you are now. If you do not immediately comply with my request, I will unfrock you, by God.

*Elizabeth*[13]

---

[12] *CW*, ed. Marcus, Mueller, and Rose, pp. 372–84.
[13] Discussed *CW*, ed. Marcus, Mueller, and Rose, p. xiv.

For most women of the period, we can assume that letters allow us fairly unmediated access to the writer's actual words, if not to the intent behind the words. That is not true for Elizabeth, except perhaps in the case of some of her early letters written when she was a young girl living on the fringes of national political culture. The fact that even the queen's letters to Alençon were routinely shared with secretaries shows how collective and politically inflected Elizabeth's correspondence was: even the so-called love letters to Monsieur were understood to be documents of state. Unlike most other women of the period, Elizabeth I did not attain (and probably did not seek) epistolary privacy even in matters that she protested were matters of the heart. Then too, unlike most other women writers of the period, Elizabeth continued to be a celebrated public person even after her death. Her genuine writings were augmented for decades and centuries after 1603 by politicians who wished to enlist her authority or well-meaning fans who misattributed writings to her or even, as in the case of Camden, manufactured texts that they attributed to her. As Diana Barnes discusses in the previous chapter, nineteenth-century editors were engaged in a substantial re-representation of key early modern women's letters, with Elizabeth's, 'real' or constructed, prominent along with those of other notable royals, Mary Queen of Scots and Henrietta Maria.

We might suppose that the poetry of such an illustrious individual would be cherished both by her contemporaries and by more recent historians of her rule, but such has not been the case. 'The Doubt of Future Foes' was understood to be a poem of political importance and was therefore widely copied and attributed to Elizabeth. But other poems that look to us to have political import seem to have fallen quickly into obscurity. Elizabeth's 'Song on the Armada Victory, December 1588', for example, is a fascinating composition credibly attributed to the queen in the one known extant manuscript, a transcription by the antiquarian Henry Spelman, who headed his copy '*A song made by her majesty and sung before her at her coming from Whitehall to Paul's through Fleet Street in Anno Domini 1588*'.[14] We know that this celebratory procession took place, but we do not know from other sources that a song of Elizabeth's own composition was performed as part of the event. Since the manuscript is located in the library of the National Maritime Museum, Greenwich, it is out of the way of most literary scholars, categorized more in terms of its nautical occasion than in terms of its status as a poem by the queen. Here is the text of the poem as we offered it in *CW*:

---

[14] *CW*, ed. Marcus, Mueller, and Rose, p. 410.

Look and bow down Thine ear, O Lord.
From Thy bright sphere behold and see
Thy handmaid and Thy handiwork,
Amongst Thy priests, offering to Thee
Zeal for incense, reaching the skies;
Myself and scepter, sacrifice.

My soul, ascend His holy place.
Ascribe Him strength and sing Him praise,
For He refraineth princes' sprites
And hath done wonders in my days.
He made the winds and waters rise
To scatter all mine enemies—

This Joseph's Lord and Israel's God,
The fiery Pillar and day's Cloud,
That saved his saints from wicked men
And drenched the honor of the proud;
And hath preserved in tender love
The spirit of his turtle dove.[15]

As it happens, this is quite an interesting poem, offering an extended comparison between England's successful defeat of the Spanish Armada and the Children of Israel's deliverance from Egypt, protected by the Red Sea flood that scattered the pursuing chariots of the Pharaoh, the cloud by day and fiery pillar by night that accompanied the House of Israel in its journeys as a sign of divine presence and protection. In the poem's first stanza, Elizabeth offers herself as a sacrifice in thanksgiving for the Armada victory. As I have argued elsewhere, this strange proposed self-immolation at the moment of the nation's triumph suggests that Elizabeth viewed the death of her favourite, Robert Dudley, Earl of Leicester earlier in 1588, as the sacrifice exacted from her by God to ensure the Armada victory. Contemporaries reported that while the nation exulted over England's great triumph over Spain, Elizabeth mourned Leicester's death in solitude.[16]

This interesting and important poem was in private hands when the cataloguers of the *Historical Manuscripts Commission* made their rounds and recorded its existence. However, they reproduced only the poem's first two lines. If it had been a royal speech or letter, they would almost certainly have transcribed it in full as a significant document of the reign, as they habitually did in other cases. Elizabeth's 'Armada Speech' gained instant celebrity in her own time and has retained that celebrity over the

---

[15] *CW*, ed. Marcus, Mueller, and Rose, pp. 410–11.
[16] See my 'Elizabeth on Elizabeth', pp. 224–32; and my further elaborations in 'Elizabeth on Ireland'.

centuries because of the importance of its occasion, but her Armada poem has been nearly forgotten. For nineteenth- and twentieth-century archivists and literary scholars, it would appear, because Elizabeth was categorized as a monarch, she could not simultaneously be considered as a poet, and her literary reputation has suffered accordingly.

Elizabeth's poetry was above all occasional: often couplets or short epigrams written in answer to verses addressed to her, of which several instances are reproduced in *CW*. Aside from 'The Doubt of Future Foes', few substantial poems are regularly attributed to her in manuscript. The graceful lyrics 'When I Was Fair and Young' and 'Now Leave and Let Me Rest' are frequently named as hers but they also circulated anonymously. Male editors of the early to mid twentieth century considered them too good to be Elizabeth's, attributing them instead to the Earl of Oxford, among other contenders. Elizabeth I therefore shares with Shakespeare (as debunked by Oxfordians) the dubious honour of being considered too unaccomplished to have created the works attributed to her, though in Elizabeth's case, unlike Shakespeare's, there actually are a few manuscript attributions of her poems to the Earl of Oxford from the period.[17] For early modern women writers who were neglected until recently, we can attribute much of the inattention to gender bias; but in Elizabeth's case, oddly, her status as monarch also disabled her from being counted as a poet in the eyes of traditionally minded modern editors.

Elizabeth's poetry has also suffered in modern times by being labelled 'drab' as opposed to 'golden', to reinvoke C. S. Lewis's remarkably unhelpful categories in the sixteenth-century volume of the *Oxford History of English Literature* (Oxford, 1954). There is no question that she wrote the 'drab' poem 'The Doubt of Future Foes', and therefore, the argument goes, she could not have written the 'golden' lyrics attributed to her later reign – as though a writer could not alter her style appreciably over three decades along with prevailing literary fashion. There are many things wrong with the characterization of Elizabeth as a 'drab' poet. First of all, 'The Doubt of Future Foes' was not considered a turgid and lacklustre poem in its time but was admired for its gnomic wit and indirection, as analysed in Jennifer Summit's discussion of the queen's 'poetics of covertness'.[18] Second, there is not as much difference between Elizabeth's early lyrics and her later 'golden' verses as has been claimed. The topic of love tends to bring out the latent Petrarchism in any sixteenth-century poet, and Elizabeth was no exception, as is evident from her poem of lament 'On Monsieur's Departure', which

---

[17]  *CW*, ed. Marcus, Mueller, and Rose, pp. 303–6.      [18]  See Summit, '"The Arte of a Ladies Penne"'.

is routinely attributed to her in manuscripts, though the best legible copies we have derive from an early seventeenth-century copy, Bodleian, MS Ashmole 781*, which is now illegible because of water damage.[19]

The other love lyrics attributed to Elizabeth from the 1580s share a similar style and ethos in that they too repudiate love while simultaneously giving it a wistful backward glance. Were they attributed to her because they matched the public perception of her situation as a queen condemned never to wed, or would that perception of her situation have disincentivized attribution to her as disrespectful? We can seldom be certain in attributing poems to Queen Elizabeth I, but this is also the case with other courtier poets of the period such as Sir Walter Ralegh, whose canon has until recently appeared to be stable only because of the deceptive certainties induced by traditional 'standard' editions (for a corrective, see Rudick, *The Poems of Sir Walter Ralegh*). It may well be that all the poems attributed to Elizabeth I in manuscripts circulated as hers during her lifetime were in fact written by her; it may also be the case that we have failed to attribute other genuine poems to her because they circulated only anonymously.

The case of Elizabeth I suggests that the experience of editing women authors has forced a reconceptualization of the practice of editing itself. As discussed elsewhere in this collection, not only does the editing of women writers cast a fresh light on the uncertainty of manuscript attribution in general, but it also prompts a reinvestigation of other features of the standard edition, such as the dating of poems, defining what counts as a literary text, and determining how to treat any work that is suspected of collective authorship. For the rest of this chapter, I would like to discuss another effect of the editing of women writers on literary studies more broadly: the frequent rewriting it imposes on literary history. We used to know that Ben Jonson wrote the first English country house poem in 'To Penshurst'. We are now likely to accord Aemilia Lanyer the honour of having inaugurated the genre because her 'Description of Cookham' almost certainly preceded 'To Penshurst'. In the case of Elizabeth I what is at stake is not a single poetic form, but a broad stylistic shift that is visible in poetry and in prose but discussed traditionally in terms of prose.

Putting a wide array of Elizabeth I's writings together in a single volume allows us to recognize her as an early English anti-Ciceronian, and in fact, as the single most influential purveyor of what has been characterized as a Senecan or 'Attic' style attributed to Francis Bacon and others in the

---

[19] Various stages of our thinking in attributing the poem to Elizabeth are reflected in Marcus, 'Elizabeth I as Public and Private Poet', pp. 135–53; and the introductory note to the poem *CW*, ed. Marcus, Mueller, and Rose, p. 302, n. 1.

early seventeenth century. Already in Richard Flecknoe's 'Discourse of Languages' (1653), which notes that English literary style varies 'according to the severall Inclinations and Dispositions of *Princes* and of *Times*', the prevailing Ciceronianism under Elizabeth I is associated with her mode of dress, as if to suggest an intrinsic connection between the two: the style of 'our *Ancestors*' was 'plain and simple' but 'That of Queen *Elizabeths* dayes, *flaunting* and *puffed* like her *Apparell*'.[20] In this formulation, Elizabeth is inseparable from the florid Ciceronianism that dominated serious prose during her reign. Here is J. Max Patrick summarizing the received view as promulgated in essays by Morris W. Croll:

> The precepts governing 'Ciceronianism', the dominant academic prose style of sixteenth-century Europe, were prescriptive and proscriptive. Indeed, although this widely established mode of writing was based on exclusive imitation of Cicero, it lacked the flexibility and adaptability which that master of rhetoric himself exhibited in varied styles, particularly in his epistles. In the minds of its proponents and practitioners, this orthodox style and the rhetoric behind it were identified with law, order, propriety, decency, and, like themselves, with what today is called 'the establishment'. To depart from this style – for example, to lecture to students on Tacitus urging that imitation of his prose might be more rewarding and more relevant to the realities of the period after about 1575 – was to threaten the social order, to undermine all virtue, and to corrupt the young, or so it seemed to the supporters of Ciceronianism. Nevertheless, opposition to this stylistic stranglehold developed into a movement which was anticipated by Montaigne, fomented by Muret, programmed by Lipsius, advanced by Bacon, and carried to extremes by Gracián, to mention only a few of its practitioners.[21]

The preeminent English Senecan, according to Croll, was Francis Bacon, later Lord Verulam. Bacon was brought up in the court of Elizabeth I. His father was Sir Nicholas Bacon, the queen's Lord Keeper, whose sons were active in their father's political career and in the culture surrounding the queen. Francis's brother Anthony collected copies of Elizabeth's speeches, and so did Nicholas Bacon himself. The innovative, Tacitean style credited by literary historians to Francis Bacon should instead be credited to the much earlier Elizabeth I, who was specifically praised for her interest in

---

[20]  Richard Flecknoe, *Miscellania, or Poems of all sorts, with divers other Pieces* (1653), p. 77.

[21]  Patrick, Evans, and Wallace (eds.), *'Attic' and Baroque Prose Style*, p. 3. Williamson's *The Senecan Amble* manages to avoid Patrick's association of Senecanism with subversion; Williamson discusses the beginnings of English anti-Ciceronianism in figures around Elizabeth, including Sir Henry Savile, but never makes the leap to conceptualizing the queen herself as an agent in the gradual turn to a more terse, Tacitean style.

Tacitus by Sir Henry Savile in his important translation of Tacitus dedicated 'To Her Most Sacred Maiestie' and urging the queen to make public her own original writings and translations in the same vein.[22] It was, of course, quite standard for authors to flatter their patrons, yet accolades of Elizabeth's pithy style are too frequent in the period to be mere flattery. Though she was much admired for her verbal eloquence, as I have indicated earlier, actual copies of her writing were difficult to come by and not necessarily treated with any particular respect. Savile's desire for a collection of Elizabeth's own writings shows that already in the late sixteenth century, in elite circles at least, was a desire for more publication of Elizabeth's compositions. Unlike scholars of the nineteenth and twentieth centuries, the queen's subjects who admired her writing did not consider writing and queenship incompatible.

In his *Arte of English Poesie*, Puttenham claims that the queen's 'learned, delicate, noble Muse easily surmounteth all the rest that haue written before her time or sence' and reproduces 'The Doubt of Future Foes' to illustrate the rhetorical trope of the 'gorgeous', which Puttenham defines as a figure notable for its 'ability to cloak and to reveal at the same time'.[23] The 'covert and dark terms' in which Elizabeth hid, yet revealed, her policy in poems like 'The Doubt of Future Foes' and in many of her speeches were what made her style particularly like that of Tacitus and therefore particularly admired. She was surrounded by practitioners of orotund Ciceronianism – a style that was prominent in the writings of her chief minister, Sir Robert Cecil, later Lord Burghley, and in treatises like Robert Hooker's *Laws of Ecclesiastical Polity* (the first five books of which were published between 1594 and 1597). She was taught to worship Ciceronianism by some of her schoolmasters, but she resisted it all her life, preferring a more terse, freeform style that strove for an effect that '*imitated the thinking mind*' in that it appeared to develop ideas freely and flexibly,[24] as opposed to the more formal, intricately parallel structures that Elizabethans so admired in Ciceronian oratory.

To illustrate the difference between the standard orotund Ciceronianism of the era and Elizabeth's more terse and asymmetrical Senecan or Tacitean style, I offer two contrasting passages: a highly formal and abstract

---

[22] Cited from the dedicatory epistle to Henry Savile (trans.), *The Ende of Nero and Beginning of Galba. Fower Bookes of The Histories of Cornelivs Tacitus* (1591). The second edition of 1598 contains the same dedication.

[23] Summit, "'The Arte of a Ladies Penne'", p. 88; Puttenham, *The Arte of English Poesie*, sigs I2[r] and Ee2[r].

[24] Morris W. Croll, in Patrick, Evans, and Wallace, *'Attic' and Baroque Prose Style*, p. 6.

argument urging Elizabeth to marry and declare a succession from 'The Commons' Petition to the Queen at Whitehall, January 28, 1563', delivered both orally and in writing by Thomas Williams, speaker of the House; and the queen's much pithier response to the request of the Commons. I should add that in modernizing the Commons' petition in *CW*, we split up single sentences as much as possible in the interest of intelligibility for modern readers, thus diluting some of the accumulated effect of its formal, periodic prose.

Commons' Petition:

> And forasmuch as your said subjects see nothing in this whole estate of so great importance to your majesty and the whole realm, nor so necessary at this time to be reduced into a certainty, as the sure continuance of the governance and th'imperial crown thereof in your majesty's person and the most honorable issue of your body, which almighty God send us to our highest comfort, and for want thereof, in some certain limitation to guide the obedience of our posterity; and where almighty God to our great terror and dreadful warning lately touched your highness with some danger of your most noble person by sickness, from which so soon as your grace was by God's favor and mercy to us recovered, your highness sent out your writs of Parliament, by force whereof your subjects are at this present assembled; your said subjects are, both by the necessity and importance of the matter and by the convenience of the time (calling them immediately upon the recovery), enforced together. And confess your majesty, of your most gracious and motherly care for them and their posterity, have summoned this Parliament principally for stablishing some certain limitation of th'imperial crown of your realm, for the preservation of your subjects from certain and utter destruction if the same should not be provided for in your life, which God long continue.[25]

Elizabeth's response:

> There needs no boding of my bane. I know now as well as I did before that I am mortal. I know also that I must seek to discharge myself of that great burden that God hath laid upon me; for of them to whom much is committed, much is required. Think not that I, that in other matters have had convenient care of you all, will in this matter touching the safety of myself and you all be careless. For I know that this matter toucheth me much nearer than it doth you all, who if the worst happen can lose but your bodies. But if I take not that convenient care that behoveth me to have therein, I hazard to lose both body and soul.[26]

As is visible in this example, Elizabeth's speeches are often concrete and earthy, flowing and natural in that they resemble the rhythms of ordinary

---

[25] *CW*, ed. Marcus, Mueller, and Rose, p. 73.   [26] *CW*, ed. Marcus, Mueller, and Rose, p. 71.

speech; she was particularly admired for her ability to create an aura of intimacy and directness with her subjects, even though her speeches, letters, and verses are often terse and epigrammatic. But through all the variation of her writing from one genre and occasion to another, in everything she spoke and wrote she represented a break from the stylistic 'law, order, and propriety' associated with sixteenth-century Ciceronianism.

The history of early modern prose style obviously needs to be rewritten: Croll's terms as interpreted by Patrick – particularly in so far as they quaintly associate Ciceronianism with establishment orthodoxy and a nascent Senecanism in its various guises with rebellion against pre-existing order – are seriously out of date, with a curious whiff of the Cold War era about them. Yet more recent studies of the decline of Ciceronianism have continued to omit Elizabeth. Twenty-five years later, in a 1992 book revisiting of Elizabethan and Jacobean models of eloquence, Neil Rhodes was still arguing that it was in the early seventeenth century that 'orotund patterns of Ciceronean eloquence, of which Hooker's *Laws* is the most striking example, were superceded by much terser styles modelled on Seneca and Tacitus. Conciseness was preferred to amplification, and concrete to abstract language'. Rhodes goes on to cite the usual suspects, especially Bacon, whose disparagement of the typical Ciceronian paradigms of humanist rhetoric appeared in *The Advancement of Learning* in 1605.[27] Like Croll and Williamson, Rhodes omits Elizabeth.

The queen herself was first among the early anti-Ciceronians in terms of power and influence, and in future rewritings of the history of the rise of Senecan or 'Attic' style, we can hope that her name will feature prominently as an innovator who modelled and disseminated the new mode of writing in England. For that to happen, of course, historians of literary style will have to accept the possibility that stylistic influence could be wielded by women writers. It is, perhaps, because of the lack of a serious, comprehensive literary edition of the writings of Elizabeth I that such an omission was still possible during the 1990s. The editing of women writers is important for its own sake, but also for what it can contribute to the critique and revision of received literary history.

[27] Rhodes, *The Power of Eloquence*, pp. 60–1.

# CHAPTER 9

# Editing Early Modern Women's Dramatic Writing for Performance

*Marion Wynne-Davies*

## Introduction

If you exit Russell Square Tube station in London and turn left, just two doors down you will encounter an old Italian café, unchanged for over twenty years. At first sight it is hardly inviting: the old-fashioned bare tables and the rickety wooden chairs cannot compete with the gleam of glass and faux red leather proffered by its neighbour, one of a chain of international coffee shops. But if you were to venture inside the doorway, the dark aroma of freshly ground coffee and the sight of pastries dusted with thick sugar and bursting with sweetened fruits, might well incline you to stay. Moreover, if you wanted to have a scholarly discussion with your companion, one which might take longer than an hour, then I'd advise you to sit over on the right, where a brief nod to the waiter will serve to replenish both cup and plate. It was here, on a dank cold morning in 1994, that Susan Cerasano and I devised the idea of editing a collection of plays written by early modern Englishwomen, which was published as *Renaissance Drama by Women: Texts and Documents* (1996). At that meeting, our primary intention was to expand the canon, but we also wanted to make the drama accessible to students, practitioners, and the general reader alike. The editorial choices consequent upon our ideas led us towards modernizing and away from sustaining the authenticity of the original manuscripts or printed texts, a decision which, in hindsight, I still agree with. Yet, for all our pioneering intent, it would be wrong to assume that we were initiators. While the editing of early modern women's writing is often discussed in terms of a lack of editorial histories, it is essential to perceive our contribution as just one small example of how the plays written by early modern Englishwomen have been edited for more than 150 years.

In order to understand the history of this perhaps unexpectedly long-standing editorial practice in relation to early modern women's dramatic texts, it is necessary to excavate the earnest scholarship of the nineteenth century, the feminist anthologizing of the 1970s and 1980s, as well as the versatility of today's publications, while at the same time engaging with the battle between modernization and authenticity, the debate about performability, and the thorny question of whether Renaissance women dramatists have been treated differently from their male counterparts. In order to explore these issues and in line with the overarching aims of this collection, this chapter re-evaluates the theory and practice of editing plays by early modern women dramatists by considering a range of editorial practice, from early versions, through anthologies and single-text editions, to a consideration of how text transfers to performance.[1] Yet, this history is not only surprisingly long-standing and embedded in controversy, it is also illuminated by a range of quite unexpected characters, claims, and institutions: an Oxford don who fought for the integrity of original texts against the mercenary 'dumbing-down' materialism of an international publisher; plays that have been harnessed to challenge 'insidious sex oppression' and regarded as 'hot property' in the gossip-laden environment of the Jacobean court; as well as works that have been seen as the exclusive property of a 200-year-old society of forty bibliophiles. Whatever editing plays by early modern Englishwomen is, it is neither predictable nor boring.

## 1853–1964: Recovering Texts

It is important to recognize that the history of editing plays by early modern Englishwomen did not begin in the 1990s; rather those late-twentieth-century incursions into the editorial process were founded upon earlier scholarship that was intent, not upon recovering lost female authors, but upon accruing a range of scholarly editions that encompassed all early modern dramatic production. As such, these editions do not represent the theoretically informed incursions that are practised by present-day editors. Nonetheless, the scholarship of their editors should not be underestimated, since they often provided detailed textual analysis, in particular with regard to translation, as well as an often impeccable attention to historical detail. More intriguingly, however, there are two recurrent features that deserve mention because they persist, in some form, throughout over 150 years of subsequent editorial practice. First, none of these early editors considers the plays to be performable, often castigating the dramatic quality of

---

[1] This chapter deals with pre-Restoration dramatists; the situation is different for Aphra Behn, as discussed in the Introduction (see p. 9) and on p. 161, below.

the works, yet second, they are simultaneously driven to an oppositional judgment, worriedly acknowledging that staging might be a possibility. Before undertaking a more detailed analysis of this contradiction, however, it is useful to provide a list of the first editions of plays written by early modern Englishwomen. The six most well known are: the excerpts from Mary Wroth's *Love's Victory* presented in James O. Halliwell's *A Brief Description of the Ancient and Modern Manuscripts Preserved in the Public Library Plymouth* (1853); Alice Luce's edition of Mary Sidney Herbert's *The Tragedie of Antonie* (1897); Harold H. Child's 1909 edition of Lumley's *Iphigenia* for the Malone Society; W. W Greg and A. C. Dunstan's 1914 edition of Elizabeth Cary's *The Tragedy of Mariam* also issued by the Malone Society; the 1931 edition of Jane Cavendish and Elizabeth Brackley's *The Concealed Fancies* by Nathan Comfort Starr for the *PMLA*; and finally, Geoffrey Bullough's 1964 edition of Mary Sidney Herbert's *The Tragedie of Antonie* in his *Narrative and Dramatic Sources of Shakespeare*.[2]

The first known editor of a play written by an early modern Englishwoman was James Orchard Halliwell, who established the dominant critical approach that would be adopted by other early editors; that is, a condemnation of the play's quality, particularly in terms of dramatic possibility. Halliwell did not find *Love's Victory* 'to be of sufficient interest for publication [as a whole text]'.[3] Similarly, Luce concluded of *The Tragedie of Antonie* that,

> Today these plays [closet dramas] interest the historian of literature less from their literary merit, than because they indicate, by their very failure, the dramatic strength and artistic soundness of the native growth which they attempt to displace.[4]

Of Lumley's *Iphigenia*, Child suggests that the translation was 'in all probability... [an] exercise... of childhood', while Greg and Dunstan assume that Cary's play was intended to be read, not acted, and was circulated 'in manuscript copies among Lady Cary's friends'.[5] Of all condemnations, Starr's is the most emphatic: 'as a literary production, *The Concealed*

---

[2] James O. Halliwell (ed.), *A Brief Description of the Ancient and Modern Manuscripts Preserved in the Public Library Plymouth* (London: C. and J. Adlard, 1853), pp. 212–36; Mary Sidney Herbert, *The Tragedie of Antonie: Done Into English*, ed. Alice Luce (Weimar: Verlag Von Emil Felber, 1897); Jane Lumley, *Iphigenia at Aulis Translated by Lady Lumley*, ed. Harold H. Child (London: The Malone Society, 1909); *The Tragedy of Mariam*, ed. Dunstan and Greg; Cavendish and Brackley, 'Concealed Fancies', ed. Starr; Bullough (ed.), *Narrative and Dramatic Sources*, pp. 215–53. A further edition, of Wroth's *Love's Victory*, was undertaken by C. H. J. Maxwell in 1933 as a PhD thesis; I have not been able to obtain a copy of this at the time of writing.

[3] Halliwell (ed.), *Brief Description*, p. 212.      [4] *Tragedie*, ed. Luce, p. 50.

[5] *Iphigenia*, ed. Child, p. vi; *Mariam*, ed. Dunstan and Greg, p. ix.

*Fansyes* is practically without value . . . The chief interest of the work lies in the artless revelation of the activities of seventeenth century ladies of fashion, living in the country'.[6] Finally, Bullough makes little commentary upon Sidney Herbert's play in itself, since the primary purpose is to make a comparison with Shakespeare; however, he classifies it as part of the 'courtly Senecan movement'.[7] In his terms this is in effect code for closet drama and hence means that the drama was to be read aloud and not performed.

At the same time, however, each editor evinces an open or tacit acknowledgement of the possibility of staging. Halliwell and Greg include basic stage directions. Luce, while she does not add stage directions, demonstrates anxiety because the text itself suggests performance, indicating that the Senecan convention of placing violent action offstage appears to be 'violated in the death of Cleopatra, which it would seem takes place on stage'.[8] Greg and Dunstan reproduce the original printed text with all stage directions given, as evidenced from their argument about original manuscript versions, by Cary herself; and, for all Starr's rejection of dramatic sensibility, he dutifully includes a wide range of stage directions, from the basic '*Enter Corpolant and Courtley*', through the more specific reference to costume, '*Enter Courtley in the Habbit of one his Mris Servants*', to the explicit and detailed necessity for stage machinery, '*A Songe/ Sunge by. 2. Gods comeing downe out of the Skye to the Nunns*'.[9] Bullough, like Luce, displays concern about the conclusion of Sidney Herbert's play, since it demands that Cleopatra 'Dies of grief' onstage, an action that was not commensurate with the classical rules that all such violent acts should occur offstage.[10] In terms of early modern Englishwomen's dramatic texts, therefore, the editorial practice of the nineteenth and early to mid twentieth centuries left behind it a conundrum: the plays were seen as either unperformable or never intended for performance, and yet each editor in some way acknowledged the texts' propensity towards dramatic production.

### 1977–88: Anthologizing Excerpts and Feminist Enterprise

A significant change in editing plays by early modern Englishwomen occurred in the 1970s and 1980s, when the advent of feminist theory, alongside feminist political activism, set out to transform the canon of English literature. In this era the primary purpose of reproducing the works was to

---

[6] *Concealed Fansyes*, ed. Starr, p. 837.  [7] Bullough (ed.), *Narrative and Dramatic Sources*, p. 229.
[8] *Tragedie*, ed. Luce, p. 81.  [9] *Concealed Fansyes*, ed. Starr, pp. 812, 813, 830.
[10] Bullough (ed.), *Narrative and Dramatic Sources*, p. 223.

make them known and, in consequence, little formal editorial work was undertaken.

The first anthology to include a play written by a Renaissance woman was *The Female Spectator: English Women Writers Before 1800* (1977), edited by Mary R. Mahl and Helene Koon.[11] It was a wide-ranging collection intended primarily to prove that women living before 1800 had written and published texts, and it included excerpts from Elizabeth Cary's *The Tragedy of Mariam, Fair Queen of Jewry*. While their enterprise is clearly feminist, Mahl and Koon reproduce the contradictions of the earlier editors, claiming that 'the blank verse of Marlowe and Shakespeare held no charms for the Viscountess',[12] while at the same time including stage directions. A second anthology was published shortly afterwards by Betty Travitsky, *The Paradise of Women: Writings by Englishwomen of the Renaissance* (1981), which included, like Mahl and Koon's earlier anthology, a considerable range of short extracts by early modern women writers.[13] Like the earlier anthology, the only example of drama is Cary's *Mariam*, and an even more damning critique as to its performability was added, '*Mariam* was almost certainly intended for reading, rather than for acting, in the tradition of the dramas of the Pembroke group. And it is not actable.'[14]

The third major anthology to be published in the late twentieth century was Katharina M. Wilson's *Women Writers of the Renaissance and Reformation* (1987), in which individual scholars edited key works.[15] Here Coburn Freer contributed the text of Sidney Herbert's *Antonie* in which he followed the original printing closely and, as such, added no stage directions. At the same time, he offered a trenchant defence of Sidney Herbert's work and condemned those scholars who belittle closet drama, although he hardly accepted that performance was possible, remarking that: 'No doubt the Countess would have been appalled at any effort by the vulgar entrepreneurs on the Bankside to stage her play.'[16] Finally, parts of a less well-known work, Elizabeth Brackley and Jane Cavendish's masque 'A Pastorall' were included in Germaine Greer's *Kissing the Rod: An Anthology of Seventeenth-Century Women's Verse* (1988), an anthology with the overall rousingly feminist purpose of challenging 'the peculiarly insidious and destructive nature of sex oppression'.[17]

Overall, there are three trends to note from these first anthologies: first, the collections have a self-conscious feminist agenda; second, as such, no

---

[11]  Mahl and Koon (eds.), *Female Spectator*, pp. 99–114.     [12]  *Ibid.*, p. 102.
[13]  Travitsky (ed.), *Paradise*, pp. 220–33.     [14]  *Ibid.*, p. 215.
[15]  Wilson (ed.), *Women Writers*, pp. 481–521.     [16]  *Ibid.*, p. 485.
[17]  Greer (ed.), *Kissing the Rod*, pp. 106–18 and p. xvi.

full plays needed to be included since the primary purpose was to highlight the existence of women writers, rather than to induce study, reading, or acting of a full play text; and third, critical commentary remained enmeshed within earlier editorial discourses. By the end of the 1980s, therefore, the canon of early modern English literature had shifted to include plays written by women writers, although little had changed with regard to the evaluation of their status. In terms of genre they had to be acknowledged as drama, but at the same time, with regard to quality, they were considered to be unperformable.

This situation for pre-Restoration writers can be contrasted with the case of Aphra Behn. Following the successful 1986 Royal Shakespeare Company production of *The Rover*, directed and adapted by John Barton, Behn, at least with this particular play, became seen not merely as performable, but as a reliable addition to the repertoire, with a number of more authentic productions of *The Rover* following in fairly rapid succession.[18] As noted in the Introduction, Behn is about to receive a new complete edition from Cambridge University Press, which will, again in a unique situation for an early modern woman writer, be the third, following the 1915 Montague Summers edition and the 1992–6 Janet Todd edition. The success of *The Rover* on the modern stage is reflected in recent editions for Methuen Drama, New Mermaids, and for Oxford Student Editions, all of which provide clear performance texts.[19] The key, though, is that Behn was a dramatist who flourished on the Restoration stage, in contrast to the earlier dramatists analysed at length here who conceived of less public and certainly not commercial performances for their plays.

## 1988–2000: The Complete Text

While excerpts from plays by pre-Restoration early modern Englishwomen have continued to be anthologized, the 1990s saw the development of a different editorial policy: the production of whole plays, alongside other drama or further material by Renaissance women writers. The most significant change occurred in the mid-1990s with two collections devoted entirely to drama written by women, as well as three single editions of Cary's *Mariam* and two of Mary Wroth's *Love's Victory*. But let's step back a little, because before this self-conscious foregrounding of women's

---

[18] See Owens and Goodman (eds.), *Shakespeare, Aphra Behn and the Canon*, Chap. 5.
[19] Behn, *The Rover*, ed. Naismith (2006); Behn, *The Rover*, ed. Bolam (2014); Behn, *The Rover*, ed. Croft and Maybank (2014).

dramatic writing occurred, Michael Brennan produced in 1988 an authoritative edition of the Penshurst manuscript of Mary Wroth's *Love's Victory*,
thereby providing scholars with the first complete version of that play.[20]
Intriguingly, the work was undertaken for the Roxburghe Club, a society that was founded in 1812, is dedicated to the printing of unpublished
documents or reprinting rare printed texts, and has a limited membership
of forty, each of whom is 'expected to produce a book at his or her own
expense for presentation to the other members'. *Lady Mary Wroth's Love's
Victory* was the 253rd book to be so 'presented', in this case by William
Philip Sidney, Viscount de L'Isle, who was a member of the club from 1961
to 1991 and president for the last three years of that period.[21]

Given the antiquarian aims of the Roxburghe Club, one might have
expected Brennan to have followed the practices and assumptions of
the early editors described in this chapter, but instead, his meticulous textual editing is matched by a path-breaking commentary. Brennan was the
first editor of a play by an early modern Englishwoman to include a thorough and well-researched performance history; in other words, he was the
first editor to take performance seriously. The commentary began by
demonstrating that Wroth had sufficient 'significant' experience of 'dramatic entertainments' to enable her to compose a drama that would have
been intended for performance, before acknowledging that, because 'there
are only a few stage directions, the most common being the exiting of characters from stage (indicated by *ex:*) . . . the play would have been best suited
to an amateur performance by some of the author's friends'.[22] Nevertheless,
rather than allowing this deduction to stand as a damning dismissal of, in
Starr's earlier phrase, 'the activities of seventeenth century ladies of fashion,
living in the country', Brennan explores the possibility of a performance
by Sir Edward Dering, who once owned the Plymouth manuscript, from
which excerpts were printed by Halliwell, as described above.[23] Without
Brennan's edition, subsequent studies of Wroth's play would have been
impossible, but more than that, by taking performance seriously, he initiated a subtle alteration in the way dramatic works by early modern women
would in future be edited.

By the mid-1990s, therefore, editorial practice shifted again, this time
towards an acknowledgement of dramatic use, both past and present, which

---

[20] *Lady Mary Wroth's Love's Victory*, ed. Brennan. There are two manuscript versions of *Love's Victory*:
the complete Penshurst version and the incomplete Huntington (MS HM600); a detailed analysis
of the correspondence between these as well as the 'lost' Plymouth manuscript (now considered to
be the Huntington) may be found in Brennan's introduction, pp. 16–20.
[21] See www.roxburgheclub.org.uk.        [22] *Love's Victory*, ed. Brennan, pp. 11, 13.        [23] *Ibid.*, p. 14.

would in future result in the production of full texts, a serious consideration of modernization, and the self-conscious inclusion of stage directions. Seven key publications emerged that, by employing these editorial incursions, changed the ways in which the plays written by early modern Englishwomen were read and performed. In effect, the works ceased to be the preserve of the researcher and began to be studied in the classroom and by the practitioner. It was the desire to teach the works, comparable to the motivations of the student-focused editorial projects discussed by Lamb, Hammons, and Ross and Scott-Baumann in later chapters of this book, that led to the meeting between Susan Cerasano and myself described at the start of this chapter. Our discussion led to the production of the first anthology of full-text plays by early modern Englishwomen, *Renaissance Drama by Women* (1996); it included Mary Sidney Herbert's *The Tragedy of Antonie*, Elizabeth Cary's *The Tragedy of Mariam*, Mary Wroth's *Love's Victory*, Elizabeth Brackley and Jane Cavendish's *The Concealed Fancies*, as well as a series of contemporaneous documentary evidence about early modern Englishwomen's engagement with dramatic production. This range of texts was expanded and complemented in 1998 by the second anthology, Diane Purkiss's *Three Tragedies by Renaissance Women*, which covered Jane Lumley's *Iphigenia*, Sidney Herbert's *The Tragedie of Antonie*, and Cary's *The Tragedy of Mariam* (the latter play following Purkiss's 1994 *Renaissance Women: The Plays of Elizabeth Cary, The Poems of Aemilia Lanyer*).[24] In addition to these two collections, five further publications provided three separate editions of the first original tragedy to be written by an Englishwoman, Cary's *Mariam*, and two of the first original comedy, Wroth's *Love's Victory*. Cary's play occurred in: the reprint of the 1914 Malone Society edition of *Mariam* with a supplementary introduction by Marta Straznicky and Richard Rowland (1992); Barry Weller and Margaret Ferguson's *Elizabeth Cary, Lady Falkland. The Tragedy of Mariam The Fair Queen of Jewry with The Lady Falkland: Her Life* (1994); and Stephanie Hodgson-Wright's edition of Cary's *Mariam* (1996).[25] In parallel, Wroth's comedy appeared in extensive extracts included in Randall Martin's and Paul Salzman's respective collections, *Renaissance Women Writers in England* (1997) and *Early Modern Women's Writing: An Anthology, 1560–1700* (2000).[26]

---

[24] Purkiss (ed.), *Three Tragedies*, and Purkiss (ed.), *Renaissance Women*.

[25] Straznicky and Rowland, 'Supplement', pp. xxi–xxv; *Mariam*, ed. Weller and Fergusson; *Mariam*, ed. Hodgson-Wright (1996).

[26] Martin (ed.), *Renaissance Women Writers*, pp. 421–30; Salzman (ed.), *Early Modern Women's Writing*, pp. 82–133.

Apart from the fact that full texts were now readily available, there is a single uniting theme in these late twentieth century editions: accessibility. While I have already described how Susan Cerasano and I decided to privilege the 'needs of students' and 'lay readers interested in the fields of Renaissance drama and theatre history, gender studies, woman's history and cultural studies',[27] it is informative to note how often that intention is replicated in the cluster of 1990s playtext editions. In particular, Weller and Ferguson's thoughtful edition notes that they 'wanted to make the play accessible to students' and as such modernized both spelling and punctuation as well as providing 'additional stage directions [when] potentially helpful'.[28] Martin's anthology similarly privileged the needs of a present-day readership, noting that 'spelling and punctuation have been modernized', amplifying stage directions in order to offer the reader a stronger sense of performance, and pointing out that the play 'would probably have been staged in a private house before a small audience'.[29]

The other editors of the single texts have been more emphatic: Straznicky and Rowland highlighted the fact that Cary's 'authorship of *The Tragedy of Mariam* has earned her pride of place as the first known Englishwoman to write an original play',[30] while both Hodgson-Wright and Salzman argued for modernization based on performance. Salzman deduced from textual analysis that '*Love's Victory* is an extremely skilful example of a dramatic form which may, at first, seem highly artificial to a modern reader.'[31] In parallel, Hodgson-Wright pointed out from her knowledge of production:

> In *The Tragedy of Mariam*, the only off-stage actions are the executions; all other action is performed on stage. The presentation of the 'poison' cup to Herod, the sword fight between Constabarus and Silleus, and the physical vacillation of Herod's soldiers, with Mariam as their prisoner, as they respond to Herod's constantly changing orders, are actions which need physical representation in order to achieve their full dramatic potential. To claim that *The Tragedy of Mariam* was not intended for performance, is to reimpose upon the text the material and ideological restraints under which it was produced – those very conditions which *The Tragedy of Mariam* seeks to critique.[32]

This is a long but useful quotation in that it provides solid evidence for where stage action is necessary in order to understand the dramatic import

---

[27] Cerasano and Wynne-Davies (eds.), *Renaissance Drama by Women*, p. x.
[28] *Mariam*, ed. Weller and Ferguson, pp. 48–9.
[29] Martin (ed.), *Renaissance Women Writers*, pp. 11, 402.
[30] Straznicky and Rowland, 'Supplement', p. xxiv.
[31] Salzman (ed.), *Early Modern Women's Writing*, p. xix.
[32] *Mariam*, ed. Hodgson-Wright, pp. 21–2.

of the play; indeed, I intend to return later in this chapter to one of the moments highlighted by Hodgson-Wright – the sword fight between Constabarus and Silleus – in order to test the impact editorial policy has had upon possible performance. Moreover, Hodgson-Wright produced a direct challenge by noting that the prejudices of twentieth-century editors have served to replicate the patriarchal restraints imposed upon women in the seventeenth century. In other words, Cary's focus upon how Mariam's speech is curtailed echoes the ways in which the 'voices' of early modern women dramatists have been muted by the lack of modern editions of their works.

The 1990s heralded, therefore, a change in the editing of plays written by early modern Englishwomen. It was no longer sufficient to prove that they existed, either in early edited versions or later anthologized extracts; instead, it was seen as important to make the works accessible to scholars, students, professionals, and the general reader/audience alike, a shift that would have seemed antithetical to the first editors who universally condemned the texts' dramatic quality. These strategies – to render the material into modernized English, to add well-researched performance histories, and to formulate elucidating stage directions – were the first steps towards a scholarly rebuttal of the assumption that the plays were unperformable. The late twentieth century saw, therefore, the beginning of a real debate about the possibilities of staging that not only changed editorial practice but prompted actual productions. It comes as no surprise that the pioneering editions of the 1990s developed alongside the first stagings of the same plays; for example, the 'Women and Dramatic Production 1570–1670' project ran from 1994 to 2000 and showed *Iphigenia*, *Mariam*, *The Concealed Fancies*, and Margaret Cavendish's *The Convent of Pleasure*, as well as Liz Schafer's 1995 production of *Mariam* at Royal Holloway College, which were primarily conceived as academic projects and staged for university audiences.[33] Yet, the successes achieved by these scholarly performances need to be set alongside the contiguous debate over authenticity and accessibility. At this point, therefore, it is important to do full justice to the alternative editorial practice of remaining faithful to the original text, as was evidenced in Diane Purkiss's exceptional contribution to the field of early modern women's drama.

---

[33] For details of the Women and Dramatic Production project see: http://wp.lancs.ac.uk/performance-ceremony-ritual/women-and-dramatic-production/ and Findlay, Hodgson-Wright, and Williams, *Women and Dramatic*. See Liz Schafer's production of *Mariam* at http://rhul.mediacore.tv/media/mariam. Cavendish is another interesting case of gradual albeit non professional production; see the account of further performances in Alexandra Bennett, 'The Duchess Takes the Stage'.

*Three Tragedies by Renaissance Women* was edited in 1998 by Purkiss for a series, Renaissance Dramatists, published by Penguin Books. In the 'Series Statement' the General Editor, John Pitcher, explained that 'the text of the plays . . . reproduce, wherever possible, the spelling and punctuation of the first printed editions and manuscripts' and went on to address material intended to refer to performance: 'where necessary, the act and scene divisions of the original texts are regularized and expanded, as are stage directions, entrances and exits'.[34] In line with this overall editorial policy, Purkiss added entrances and exits in order to provide a clear sense of whether characters are on- or offstage. For example: at the end of *Iphigenia* the concluding final exit from the stage is signified with '[Exeunt Omnes.]'; at the beginning of Sidney Herbert's work, 'Antonius' is determined to enter '[sola]'; and the Chorus in *The Tragedy of Mariam* is kept resolutely onstage throughout the whole play as designated by the lack of any original stage directions with regard to this group.[35] These are logical and consistent choices made by an editor who, faced with original texts that make no explicit reference to performance, makes sense of an imagined staging. In theatrical terms, therefore, the cast does '[Exeunt]' at the conclusion of the play, an actor giving a soliloquy must be '[sola]' and, in alignment with classical tradition, the Chorus does remain onstage throughout the play to comment upon the moral message of the work. But this leaves a stark contradiction, since the series guidelines demanded both that the text was a close reproduction of the original manuscript or first edition, and that the text be transformed into a work that must conceptualize performance. However, tellingly, Purkiss's edition became embroiled in a wider – and much more public – debate about the publication of 'authentic' editions.

To the regret of those of us working on early modern women dramatists, the series was axed by Penguin in 1999 after the publication of only four books, an action that was reported by the *Guardian* in an article entitled 'Cost-cutting Penguin in flap over "dumbing-down"' in which Andrew Rosenheim, Penguin Press Managing Director, was quoted as saying, '[the] editions are not appropriate for today's market'. The point was backed up by an anonymous Penguin spokeswoman who elaborated: 'the idea was to publish texts in the original spelling. It did not work. We could not get support from the market in the UK or the US. Publishers do sometimes get things wrong.'[36] In turn, the *Oxford Mail* cited Pitcher's counter-argument that this would 'leave a gap in the range'.[37] There are a host of

---

[34]  Pitcher, 'Series Statement', in Purkiss (ed.), *Three Tragedies*, pp. vi–vii.
[35]  Purkiss (ed.), *Three Tragedies*, pp. 35, 41.
[36]  www.theguardian.com/uk/1999/jan/16/johnezard.        [37]  *Oxford Mail*, 27 January 1999.

conflicting interests embedded in Penguin's decision, the press reports, and Pitcher's laconic comment. Primarily, the idea of 'dumbing-down' imagines a world in which the scholarly Oxford don fights for the integrity of the original text against the mercenary materialism of an international publisher only interested in sales. But there is also a suggestion that present-day readers are not as intellectual or accomplished as those of an earlier age; we are, in effect, 'dumber' than our ancestors because we are unable, or unwilling, to read early modern drama presented in its original spelling.

While not questioning the passion with which these different views are expressed, I would like to suggest that there was another reason for the failure of this series, one which lies primarily in the constructed expectations of the genre and one which, therefore, had a significant impact upon the editing of plays by early modern women. Indeed, the anxiety displayed by the early editors as they tried to make sense of the stage directions and plot devices that encoded performance in works that seemed antithetical to their experience of sophisticated public Renaissance drama is particularly apposite here. What they and subsequent editors have to contend with is that any text written consciously as a drama embeds within it the expectation of performance, whether that be dramatized reading, household theatre, or public performance. Moreover, this belief is manifest in Pitcher's direction to his editors to 'expand' the original in order to include 'stage directions' as well as in Purkiss's careful use of those all-important square brackets. Indeed, Purkiss notes with meticulous honesty in the 'Textual Procedure' section of the book that 'stage directions have been greatly expanded' but goes on to pursue the somewhat contradictory argument that, since 'none of these plays was destined for performance' stage directions are needed to 'turn the brain into the stage',[38] thereby allowing the imagination of the reader to envisage an actual production. In this sense, I would argue that Purkiss's job was harder than those of those editors who chose to modernize the text since she had to produce an authentic replication, while at the same time turning three plays by neglected women dramatists into dramas that imagined staging. Yet this, I believe, is the key point, for the words Purkiss used to envisage production derive from Margaret Cavendish. Indeed, Cavendish's phrase, 'my brain, the stage' encapsulates the implacable conundrum for those who have attempted to edit plays written by early modern Englishwomen: yes, performance is imagined, but no, not on the public stage.[39]

---

[38] Purkiss (ed.), *Three Tragedies*, p. xlvi.     [39] See Tomlinson, 'My Brain the Stage'.

As has been described, for nineteenth-century editors the notion of 'performance' had implied the public stage, although by the late twentieth and early twenty-first centuries the term had developed a more nuanced interpretation with regard to actual productions. For textual editors, therefore, the debate over performability became inextricably linked to the battle between authenticity and modernizing for if 'true' to the text, then the drama remained imagined, whereas if changes were made the plays could be performed successfully. Such challenges, of course, face all present-day editors and directors attempting to popularize early modern drama, but for early modern women's plays the expectation of gender roles had militated against performance. A good example of this problem may be evidenced by the prevalent use of closet drama by early modern women dramatists. Although this specific genre was not exclusive to women, the privacy accorded to productions made them more attractive to female dramatists since they protected the writer's reputation. However, this very choice makes the transference from a secluded and intimate reading of the text into a public performance all the more difficult for a present-day director. At first, this confined editorial practice to scholarly endeavour, feminist polemic, and authenticity. However, by the end of the twentieth century, the combination of performance history, modernization, and the addition of imaginative stage directions began to make early modern women's drama accessible and, more intriguingly, the centre for heated debate.

## 2000–12: The Bestseller

It is now just over four hundred years since Elizabeth Cary's *Mariam* was first published and since then it has become, if not a bestseller, then at least the scholarly equivalent to popular fiction. *Mariam* has been continually edited for the last 100 years: from the early editions (Dunstan and Greg's 1914 Malone text), through the feminist anthologies (Mahl and Koon in 1977 and Travitsky in 1981) to an impressive six out of the eleven single editions of the late twentieth century (the Malone reprint of 1992, Weller and Ferguson in 1994, Purkiss twice in both 1994 and 1998, Wynne-Davies and Cerasano in 1996, and Hodgson-Wright in 1996). Nor has its popularity waned. For example, *Mariam* is the only drama by an early modern Englishwoman to achieve 'Norton' status, with Acts 3 to 5 being included in David Bevington's *English Renaissance Drama* (2002) and, as a 'much-requested complete longer work', the full text is available in the *Supplemental Ebook* made freely available to those who purchase the hardcopy, *The Norton Anthology of English Literature*.[40] In addition, *Mariam* was edited in two of the most respected drama series: in 2010 by Karen Britland for Methuen's New Mermaids series and in 2012 by Ramona Wray for the Arden Early Modern Drama series.[41] This does not mean to say that other anthologies and e-resources have not continued to include editions of plays by Renaissance women,[42] but that *Mariam* has so exceeded other works that such success necessitates analysis.

There are a number of possible reasons for *Mariam*'s popularity in the editorial stakes. First, the play is deservedly renowned as the first original tragedy written by an Englishwoman and that single adjective, 'original', raises it above translations (such as, Lumley's *Iphigenia* and Sidney Herbert's *Antonie*) both because of the cultural value awarded to originality as well as, I suspect, because editing translations (especially those that derive from both Latin and Greek) is a much more time-consuming and laborious task. Second, the text upon which editors work is the remarkably clean 1613 printed version which has very few variations across extant copies, making it much simpler to work on than a play like Wroth's *Love's Victory* which exists in two distinct manuscript forms, one of which remains in private hands. Third, the initial editorial work on the play, undertaken by Dunstan and Greg in 1914, has been amply supplemented by the further six editions referred to above and, therefore, provides an excellent basis for any further editorial work. Fourth, in terms of genre, both the play's identification as a tragedy and its identification as a closet drama provide lengthy speeches laden with references and allusion, ensuring that annotation is both interesting and extensive. Fifth, and most importantly, *Mariam* may be compared fruitfully to a number of Shakespeare plays – for example, *Antony and Cleopatra* and *Othello* – making it simultaneously a popular teaching text and a profitable publication. Perhaps, therefore, the question should not be, why is *Mariam* edited so frequently, but how could any other play by an early modern Englishwoman compete? That said, the trends in the *Mariam* editorial practice both align with wider tendencies and suggest ways in which the canon might continue to be expanded.

Whereas Bevington's Norton edition remained conventional – for example with the assertion that the play was 'designed for reading and not for performance'[43] – both Britland and Wray provided detailed scholarly works

---

[40] Bevington et al. (eds.), *English Renaissance Drama: A Norton Anthology*, pp. 1536–42. The Norton E-text is available at: www.wwnorton.com/college/english/nael9/ebook.aspx.

[41] *Mariam*, ed. Britland; *Mariam*, ed. Wray.

[42] For example, Hodgson-Wright (ed.), *Women's Writing*; Ostovich and Sauer (eds.), *Reading Early Modern Women*.

[43] Bevington et al. (eds.), *English Renaissance Drama: A Norton Anthology*, p. 615.

that, at the same time, challenged the ways in which drama by early modern Englishwomen has been edited. Thus, although Britland came to the by-now-expected conclusion that 'Cary's play was not, however, written for the commercial theatre, and may not have been intended for performance at all', her reasons are based on close textual anlysis and thorough historical contextualization. She argued that the reason for the play being 'read and not acted' was because the content was 'hot property', since the play deals explicitly with divorce at a time when both Robert Rich and Robert Devereux were 'involved in the ending their marriages', and as such would have been impossible to perform publicly.[44] Moreover, Britland accepted that *Mariam* was – and is – able to be performed, providing a useful 'Performance History' that extended to the late twentieth century, the modernization of the text, and the amplification of stage directions.

In parallel, Wray's edition provided the scholarly prefatory material that characterizes the Arden series, with detailed work on sources and a range of thematic focal points such as female speech, race, and martyrdom. Moreover, the notion of performance became more nuanced with a direct challenge to the common denigration of closet drama: 'The dominant assumption that closet drama was not performed has resulted in a limited appreciation of the form's richness and depth as dramatic representation.'[45] This is a significant development because, unlike earlier editors who have championed performance by promoting the possibility of producing the play on the stage (for example, by modernizing the language and amplifying stage directions), Wray argues that the line between public and private text is porous. *Mariam*, therefore, may shift from a closeted reading to a staged play because the text allows for such multiple interpretations. Wray expands this argument in considerable detail in her chapter in this volume, arguing that *Mariam* is better seen in relation to its precise historical *and* dramatic context, rather than as a manifestation of Cary's biography. For Wray, *Mariam* is more fruitfully seen in relation to popular early modern theatrical genres than in relation to other plays by women.

In order to explore the possibility of staging along such lines, and to explore how the editorial process can facilitate or illuminate these moments, it is useful to analyse a single moment from the play. But which to choose? There are very few stage directions in the 1613 edition and these overwhelmingly denote entrances and exits. This is perfectly in line with the form of classical tragedy Cary utilizes and the closet drama genre, since in the first action should occur offstage and in the second reading would preclude any excessive movement. A perfect example of how this works effectively is when Mariam's execution is reported to Herod rather than witnessed on either a real or an imagined stage. As such, there is one moment in *Mariam* that stands out as a problem: Act 2 Scene 4, when Constabarus and Silleus fight. It is quite clear from the dialogue that Cary envisages the two men battling, Silleus for Salome and Constabarus, reluctantly, to defend his honour. Indeed, Constabarus comments directly, 'Here gins the fight' and Silleus refers to his own wounds, 'Thy sword hath made some windowes for/ To shew a horred crimson phisnomie'.[46] Not only does the violent action demanded by the text contravene the rules of classical tragedy, but the reference to the 'horred crimson' blood gushing from Silleus suggests devices of the public stage rather than the sedate readings suggested by closet drama. Act 2 Scene 4 provides us, therefore, with evidence that *Mariam* is simultaneously both a classical/closet drama and an action-packed, bloodthirsty public performance. Moreover, this mutability is further underlined by the only stage direction in the play to denote something other than an entrance or an exit: 'they fight'.[47]

## 2013–: Public Performance

The multiple editions of *Mariam* have ensured that Cary's play has been projected into a frame different from those occupied by other plays considered in this chapter, since its status as a 'bestseller' has enabled editors to expand the possibilities of both textual meaning and performance. For *Mariam* the need to prove existence, as with the early editions and feminist anthologies, no longer exists, nor does the play need to become the focus of a debate either between scholarly endeavour versus accessibility or authenticity versus modernization. Instead, the first original drama written by an Englishwoman has become the first play by an Englishwoman to demonstrate what we knew all along: that drama is a genre that metamorphoses easily and effectively. The path-breaking work undertaken by directors such as Alison Findlay, Gweno Williams, and Stephanie Hodgson-Wright (Women and Dramatic Production) and Liz Schafer (*Mariam* at Royal Holloway College) has been followed by a number of current – very small – developments. For example, the Globe Theatre's Read Not Dead Company undertook a production of Wroth's *Love's Victory* in Penshurst Place in the summer of 2013 and at the close of the same year a further production of Wroth's comedy was staged in New York by the On Her

---

[46] Elizabeth Cary, *The Tragedie of Mariam* (1613), p. D3r.     [47] *Ibid.*, p. D3v.

Shoulders Company.[48] Both companies have a self-confessed interest in staging previously neglected works and both court an academic audience, but they are also decidedly public enterprises used to working with material in a way that makes it accessible to the general public. It is essential that we record this incipient stage history, but it is also informative to trace how, in the context of public performance, editorial practice slips inexorably from scholar to practitioner.

In this context, I would like to consider briefly the 2013 production of Lumley's *Iphigenia* by The Rose Company, since I was able to interview both director and cast with regard to their 'editorial' decisions, as dramaturgs and performers, as well as to discuss the performance afterwards with the audience.[49] Like the early editors, we can never know for certain whether this early modern Englishwoman intended her translation of Euripides' *Iphigenia at Aulis* to be staged. However, certain elements suggest an envisaged performance: the loose translation suggests that she reworked the Greek verse into hard-edged English prose all the better to suit spoken dialogue; the cast are certainly expected to move; Lumley's family was conversant with household theatre; and, perhaps most persuasive of all, they possessed a performance space in the Banqueting House at Nonsuch. We may even argue that the use of the St Paul's Boys by Lumley's father, the Earl of Arundel, and the fact that the company had a – now lost – *Iphigenia* in their repertory, suggest that this play, written by a woman, was performed in public on the early modern stage. But we can prove nothing. This is acutely frustrating for academics, but what became apparent during The Rose Company's staging of Lumley's *Iphigenia* was that these scholarly hypotheses are not very relevant when the work of a production begins. As the director, Emma Ruscastle, made clear, 'anything that looks like a script is a script' and, what's more, companies such as The Rose always begin by looking at how a play 'works on its feet'.[50] So, rather than consider how an academic would edit the play, in order to consider performability it is essential to consider how a director reworks the text in order to make it a successful stage production.

The Rose Company is a newly formed all-female theatre company based in Lancaster dedicated to bringing dramatic texts from the past to contemporary life. As they note on their website:

---

[48] For further information see: http://www.shakespearesglobe.com/uploads/files/2014/06/rnd_penshurst_final_format1.pdf http://onhershoulders.weebly.com/index.html.

[49] For further information see: http://therosecompany.posthaven.com.

[50] This and subsequent quotations from the director and cast of The Rose Company are taken from the author's own interview notes.

To that end, our first production will be Lady Jane Lumley's adaptation of Euripides' *Iphigenia At Aulis*, which is the first translation of Euripides into English and the first known dramatic work by a woman in English. It is a dynamic, surprisingly modern-feeling translation of the Greek and will be a challenging and fun text to work with and perform.[51]

Indeed, what was immediately apparent from the performance was how the cast emphasized the contemporary relevance of the play. For example, after Agamemnon agrees to sacrifice his daughter, Iphigenia, he lies to his wife, Clytemnestra, telling her that there will be a marriage, rather than an execution. In the following exchange, the interplay between Agamemnon (Ruth Gregson) and Clytemnestra (Aliki Chapple) sparked with the undercurrents of his guilt and her bewildered resentment that she was not allowed to attend the 'wedding'. While the characters might have had their genesis in Greek drama and an Early Modern translation, Gregson and Chapple ensured that the primary focus was upon the fraught relationship between husband and wife. These emotions were commented upon by both actors in the post-production discussion with Gregson pointing out that Agamemnon was torn between 'doing the right thing for his country and the right thing for his daughter . . . he is not a monster', while Chapple noted, in stark contrast, that Clytemnestra's experiences mirror those of women in abusive relationships, 'you go along with his ego until you reach a point where you don't say yes'. There could be no question from this production that present-day concerns, such as male duty and female repression, were to the fore.

The appeal to the commonality of human emotion was aided by the use of the simple costumes and set. The cast was in basic black and a single emblematic garment, with the exception of Iphigenia, who was dressed in a long red gown, thereby allowing the audience to prefigure the tragedy through the symbolic use of colour. For Madie Howard, who played the part of Iphigenia, however, this sense of inevitability was undercut by the awareness of the character's self-choice; in the post-production discussion she noted that the part seems to be 'written from a feminist perspective' allowing the character to be more than 'a commodity'. Her allusion to the proto-feminist concerns of the play were echoed by other cast members, for example, Chapple's comment on 'the female-angle of the play and its critique of patriarchy'.

The division between male and female characters was underscored by the effective use of the bare set and the in-the-round space. There were

---

[51] http://therosecompany.posthaven.com/.

key moments when Ruscastle's direction focused attention upon how the women – Clytemnestra, Iphigenia, and the Chorus – set themselves against a frustrated Agamemnon. At one point, the Chorus, who were cast as women with the additional prop of the 'baby' Orestes, band together in one corner leaving the king exposed on the middle of an empty stage. Then again, when Iphigenia goes self-knowingly to her death, she turns away from Achilles and towards her mother thereby exposing the limitations of his thwarted chivalric rescue. Indeed, Elle Lund's portrayal of Achilles' increasing lack of understanding at the women's choices turned what could have been a two-dimensional character into one whose role fully echoed that of the king. Finally, at the play's denouement, Chapple laid stress upon the word 'doubt' as she leaves her husband standing centre stage bellowing out his triumph. Indeed, Gregson's played these last lines superbly, provoking 'doubt' from the audience: was Agamemnon right to sacrifice his family for the good of his country, or did he expose the inadequacy of patriarchal rule? This combination of action, speech, blocking, and costume allowed the director and cast to 'edit' the text in order to foreground contemporary relevance and in particular the proto-feminist elements of the play that they hoped would make it relevant to a present-day audience.

Fortuitously, and in many ways unusually, it was here that I was able to ascertain the audience response through a circulation of questionnaires. For Harold H. Child, that first editor of *Iphigenia*, the responses would have been utterly confounding, for rather than find it '[an] exercise . . . of child-hood', the audience praised the production for its maturity and modernity both in terms of language – 'very easy to follow' and 'original text not a barrier' – and theme – 'family schism', 'women as commodities', and 'female self-sacrifice'. An additional welcome outcome for the director was that the whole audience delighted in the addition of haunting Greek pipe music: Seikilos' *Epitaph*. But, above all, 80 per cent of the audience affirmed that the play had been staged successfully. So, whether or not Lumley ever intended her play to be performed became, to a certain extent, irrelevant, since *Iphigenia* has now been successfully staged by The Rose Company. Indeed, as Ruscastle reminded us, 'anything that looks like a script is a script' – a timely reminder to practitioners, scholars, and audiences alike that plays written by early modern Englishwomen may come out of the closet and take their rightful place on the public stage. Therefore, what matters in terms of performance is not scholarly editorial pigeonholing, but the fluidity of interpretation that can only be achieved through a range of processes – speech, movement, costume, set, music, light – that enable a director to edit the play so that it focuses on issues that are relevant to a present-day audience. Indeed, the production strategies that have long been a commonplace for plays written by early modern Englishmen are now finally becoming accessible for their female counterparts.

## Conclusion

The history of editing plays by early modern Englishwomen is hardly the stuff of dry scholarship. Rather, it encompasses the wider changing processes of editing drama, from early editions that prove the existence of the texts, through careful contextualized scholarship, to opening out the possibility of multiple forms of performance. It has become immersed in serious academic debate that has set authenticity against modernizing and research against accessibility both in the classroom and onstage. Along the way, the history has proved to be surprisingly engaging. But what about that café next to Russell Square Tube station? This chapter began by invoking an image, not unlike those used by Margaret Cavendish on her 'the stage my brain', to conjure the room, the furniture, the sights, and the smells of, if you like, the set of a dramatic production. Like the history of the plays and editions considered here, the plot was set in the past, yet, again with reference to the plays and editions, it suggests future performance. The success of Elizabeth Cary's *The Tragedy of Mariam* and Jane Lumley's *Iphigenia at Aulis* allows editors and directors of plays written by early modern Englishwomen to plan and hope for a time when these works will be accorded parallel attention and investment. So, imagine that café and, whether you are there or in any similar space across the globe, invite colleagues to a meeting that will result in further, more detailed, better financed, and, primarily, single-text editions of the plays that may be performed. [She gestures to the right] Oh, and try to sit where you'll get more coffee and cake.

# CHAPTER 10

# Single-Author Manuscripts, Poems (1664), and the Editing of Katherine Philips

## Marie-Louise Coolahan

The publication of *Poems* (1664) has long confounded scholars working on Katherine Philips. The extent to which she may, or may not, have had a hand in this apparently unauthorized print volume has been intensively debated and reached an impasse that cannot be resolved until further evidence of Philips's intentions comes to light. The integrity of the texts in the volume has also been at issue. Philips protested in a letter that was intended for public circulation, that the poems were stolen, and represented false copies, 'abominably transcribed'.[1] Such protestations were common enough among those entering the arena of the single-author print publication, as discussed below. Germaine Greer's challenge to a literal reading of this letter entailed comparison of *Poems* (1664) with authoritative witnesses and its textual integrity has been more or less acknowledged since.[2] This chapter begins with an examination of recent editorial practices in anthologizing Philips's work. It then interrogates the most contemporary manuscript witnesses, arguing that Philips's earliest editors followed her lead in presenting her as a singular author. Using the *Catalogue of English Literary Manuscripts*, it analyses the posthumous miscellany circulation of Philips in order to illuminate two strands of early modern editorial practice and consider how these might be represented in the modern editing of early modern women.

*Poems* (1664) has never been a serious consideration as copytext for modern editions. Editors of anthologies compiling Philips's work have ducked the question, tending to summarize the debate. Their copytexts are those justified (often implicitly) by the concept of 'final intention' – in Philips's case, the posthumous print *Poems* of 1667, or the 'Rosania manuscript', prepared between 1664 and 1667. Philips died in June 1664, five months after Marriott's advertisement of his edition of her *Poems* and

---

[1] Philips, *Collected Works*, ed. Thomas, Greer, and Little, vol. II, Letter XLV, pp. 128–31.

[2] Greer, *Slip-Shod Sibyls*, pp. 147–72; Beal, *In Praise of Scribes*, pp. 147–91; Hageman, 'Treacherous Accidents'; Wright, *Producing Women's Poetry*, p. 127.

her epistolary disavowal of it. An unknown editor (sometimes presumed to have been her friend, Sir Charles Cotterell) then gathered her works, which were published by Henry Herringman as *Poems* in 1667. Twenty-one poems are found only in this collection, which was reprinted in 1669, 1678, and 1710.[3] As the most comprehensive compilation of Philips's work, with the assumed imprimatur of her closest confidant, this volume has taken up a position at the opposite side of the ring to 1664: the legitimate Superman to 1664's rogue Iron Man. The Rosania manuscript, also compiled by an unidentified editor, who signs his dedicatory epistle Polexander, is so-called because it was compiled as a presentation collection of Philips's works for her close friend Mary (née Aubrey) Montagu, the 'Rosania' of her poems. Expressly intended as a memorial volume, and urging a posthumous print edition, this manuscript was compiled between Philips's death and the publication of *Poems* (1667).

The major undergraduate anthologies tend not to foreground their editorial choices. It is not stated which editions were used in the *Norton Anthology of Literature by Women*, 2nd edition (1996). *The Longman Anthology of British Literature* (2010) relegates such information to its supporting website.[4] Both Broadview collections – *The Broadview Anthology of Seventeenth-Century Verse and Prose* (2001) and *The Broadview Anthology of British Literature: The Renaissance and the Early Seventeenth Century* (2010) – clearly imply that *Poems* (1667) is the copytext. Each Philips text is subscribed with that date, regardless of the poem's date as given in the headnote. A special case is made for the juvenile poem that survives as a separate: 'A Married State' is printed in both anthologies and associated with the date 1648. In the *Anthology of Seventeenth-Century Verse and Prose*, an additional note is appended, explaining that the poem is sourced from a unique manuscript copy.[5] Such copytext issues are not entirely ignored in anthologies, however. The editor of the Blackwell anthology of *British Literature 1640–1789* (1996) clearly states a preference for 'first editions' in the introductory material. For the Philips selection, this means *Poems* (1667) – in fact, the earliest of the most comprehensive print editions, but the latest of the standard copytexts.[6] Stephanie Hodgson-Wright's *Women's Writing*

[3] An additional two poems are extant in separate autograph copies; see Wright, *Producing Women's Poetry*, p. 140.

[4] Gilbert and Gubar (eds.), *The Norton Anthology of Literature by Women*, pp. 101–5, 2411; Carroll and Hadfield (eds.), *The Longman Anthology of British Literature*, vol. 1B, pp. 1668–77. www.myliteraturekit.com.

[5] Rudrum et al. (eds.) *The Broadview Seventeenth-Century Verse and Prose*, vol. 1: *Verse*, pp. 422–30; Black et al. (eds.), *The Broadview British Literature*, vol. 11: *The Renaissance and the Early Seventeenth Century*, pp. 783–7.

[6] Demaria, Jr (ed.), *British Literature 1640–1789*, pp. xxxi, 358.

*of the Early Modern Period* (2002) also cites *Poems* (1667) as the source for those by Philips.[7]

This preference for the posthumous print edition can be a pragmatic issue of copyright as much as an editorial valorization of the authority of final intention. It is also understandable from an editorial perspective; these anthologies gather together, by design, a wide range of authors and genres – it is simplest to avoid areas of controversy and plump for the safe bet. This editorial decision in turn reinforces that edition's authority. The politics and consequences of editorial decisions regarding form and modernization are fully explored in this volume by Sarah Ross and Elizabeth Scott-Baumann; the issues at stake in rendering early modern women's writing accessible to non-expert readers are the subject of Pamela Hammons's chapter on Katherine Austen and Mary Ellen Lamb's on Mary Wroth's *Urania*.

Inspired by advances in early modern manuscript studies, a number of anthologies aimed at students as well as scholars have sought to propagate the insights of such scholarship and present modern readers with editions that acknowledge, reflect, and even foreground the manuscript contexts for Philips's work. Ostovich and Sauer's *Reading Early Modern Women* (2004) anthologizes short extracts that emphasize the materiality of the texts' presentation, reproducing originals side by side with short commentaries and modernized transcriptions for manuscript material. The juxtaposition of print and manuscript, paratext and extract, and all the genres of women's writing is important in its insistence on material contexts and the media of dissemination. However, the Philips extracts lean toward print publication: a page from the printed *Pompey* of 1663 and the first page of 'An Epitaph on my Honoured Mother-in-Law Mrs. Phillips of Portheynon in Cardiganshire' from *Poems* (1667).[8]

Stevenson and Davidson's *Early Modern Women Poets* (2001) – highly innovative in its geographical and linguistic distribution as well as attentiveness to scribal publication – navigates the choice of copytexts thus: 'our principle has been to try and identify the text nearest to what the author chose to *circulate* in her lifetime' (their italics). Significantly, Philips herself is the illustrative example that follows: 'Thus, for a poet such as Katherine Philips, who circulated verse in manuscript, fair-copy manuscripts made from her own papers are the obvious choice, rather than the posthumous printed editions.'[9] In the case of the five poems collected here by Philips, two are from the autograph (Tutin) manuscript she compiled in the 1650s,

7  Hodgson-Wright (ed.), *Women's Writing of the Early Modern Period*, p. 448.
8  Ostovich and Sauer (eds.), *Reading Early Modern Women*, pp. 347–9, 395–7.
9  Stevenson and Davidson (eds.), *Early Modern Women Poets*, p. l.

and three from the Rosania manuscript (which is posthumous). These are followed by a reworking by an unidentified author of her juvenile poem, 'A marryd state', in a later miscellany manuscript.[10] Their editorial decisions highlight pertinent issues. As Danielle Clarke has observed, their preference retains the concern with authorial intention: 'the basic categories of copy-text, author, and intentionality... remain intact'.[11] The editors draw attention to the living author's circulation practices. But 60 per cent of the texts edited are derived from a posthumous manuscript source. Proximity to the author, here, is the key consideration. This anthology aims to marry the principles of social editing with those of authorial intention. The agent of circulation, as conceived by Stevenson and Davidson, remains the author but the authority of the Rosania manuscript derives, not from what Philips chose to circulate, but from what was edited in a manuscript prepared for one of her closest friends. As this chapter will attempt to show, her contemporary readers were important agents of circulation – and they almost inevitably presented Philips's writing, when alive, as a collection of works produced by a single, and singular, author.

*Early Modern Women's Manuscript Poetry* (2005), for which I edited the Philips selection, arose from the Perdita project's excavation of manuscripts compiled by early modern women. It expressly sought to present the manuscript contexts for women's poetry. Aiming 'to emphasise the importance of the manuscripts themselves – the material artefacts in which the poetry is present – at least as much as their absent authors', we chose to use the Rosania manuscript as copytext for Philips in order to highlight its role as 'part of the contemporary drive to consolidate her reputation'.[12] Thirteen of the fourteen poets edited for this anthology were represented by a single manuscript in order to show the range of manuscript contexts in which a single poet's work occurred: six presentation manuscripts (Philips, Seager, Cavendish, Roper, Astell, Burghope), six fair-copy manuscripts (Hutchinson, Palmer, Pulter, Sidney, Southwell, Wroth) and three miscellany manuscripts (Southwell, Ley, Walsh).[13] As Gibson and Wright explain, this approach sought to combine a gynocritical, author-centred approach with the more social and material approach taken by manuscript scholars. The gynocritical focus is also reflected in the fact that, of fifteen manuscripts, eleven contain almost entirely the work of a single female poet (Seager, Wroth, Cavendish, Hutchinson, Pulter, Philips, Roper, Palmer,

---

[10] Stevenson and Davidson (eds.), *Early Modern Women Poets*, pp. 1, 327–35, 552–4.
[11] Danielle Clarke, 'Nostalgia', p. 200.
[12] Millman and Wright (eds.), *Early Modern Women's Manuscript Poetry*, pp. 2, 3.
[13] Anne Southwell is the fourteenth poet, represented by two different manuscripts.

Astell, Burghope, Walsh). With regard to Philips, the Rosania manuscript
was selected as copytext because of the anthology's primary concern with
manuscript culture. Many of these authors are represented only by a single
surviving manuscript. In the case of authors like Philips and Sidney, for
whom multiple manuscript witnesses exist, we decided against producing
a critical text that noted variants in order to focus on the representation
of their work in a single manuscript, as being 'consistent with our materialist bibliographical aim of trying to represent the unfamiliar world of
early modern manuscript culture to new readers'.[14] The individual author,
and the single-author manuscript volume, were preferred to manuscript
miscellany culture.

Currently, the only modern critical edition of Philips is that edited by
Patrick Thomas. Now long out of print, this has been the standard edition
to which most critics refer, in part because it is the only scholarly edition
and evinces a clear statement of editorial principles. Thomas's edition was
ground-breaking in its mapping of contemporary manuscripts containing
Philips's work, both derived and not derived from printed editions, and of
her publishing history. His editorial principle was 'to establish a text that is
as close as possible to Orinda's final intention'. To that end, his preference
was for social proximity as the guarantor of authorial intention: 'As a general
rule Orinda's autograph manuscripts and those manuscripts derived from
her close circle of friends have been preferred to the printed editions'.[15] The
two pioneering scholars who have done most to recover and raise awareness
of the manuscript contexts for Philips's work are Elizabeth Hageman and
Andrea Sununu. They are currently working on their scholarly edition of
Philips for Oxford University Press, an edition that is likely to prove a
landmark in the combining of single-author and social editing principles.

*Poems* (1664) occupies a nebulous position in relation to these editorial choices; compiled and issued in the author's lifetime, its relation to the
author as yet indefinable. Despite its established textual integrity, editors of
modern anthologies have tended to seek sanctuary in the authority offered
either by the immediately posthumous editions (the Rosania manuscript
or 1667) or contemporary manuscript circulation. The 1664 volume looms
as an inescapable artefact in Philips scholarship, usefully serving as a light-
ning rod for discussions of private and public, manuscript and print,
female and male authorship. But its single-author presentation is not out
of kilter with the standard manuscript witnesses: the autograph (Tutin)

---

[14]   Gibson and Wright, 'Editing Perdita', pp. 162–4, 167.
[15]   Philips, *Collected Works*, ed. Thomas, vol. I, p. 64.

manuscript of the 1650s, the Dering and Clarke manuscripts compiled in the early 1660s, and the immediately posthumous Rosania manuscript.[16] Tutin, so named after Philips's early twentieth-century editor, is entirely in Philips's hand. Compiled over a number of years, the latest datable piece is 1658.[17] Edward Dering (Philips's 'Silvander') and William Clarke overlapped with Philips in Restoration Dublin, leading Wright to suggest that these manuscripts were 'probably produced between June 1662 and July 1663', a likelihood supported by their close connection with her three poems printed in *Poems, by Several Persons* (Dublin, 1663).[18] Another single-author manuscript, bearing Philips's autograph corrections, is the copy of her play-translation, *Pompey*. The 1663 print edition's incorporation of these authorial revisions identifies this as a pre-print text – possibly one of the number whose circulation was bewailed by Philips in an undated letter from Dublin: 'There are . . . more Copies of it abroad than I could have imagin'd'.[19]

The single-author nature of these manuscript volumes becomes starkly apparent when set against the prevailing traditions of manuscript culture. It is worth contrasting them with another manuscript associated with a woman writer, the miscellany in which much of Anne Southwell's poetry is compiled. Edited by Jean Klene as *The Southwell-Sibthorpe Commonplace Book*, this manuscript represents the kind of 'informal manuscript miscellany' that is compiled at different times and for different reasons, 'better thought of as texts in process than as unified works of art'. Gibson warns against editing such a complicated manuscript 'as if it is a coherent, single printed volume with a single point of origin'.[20] The dominant strain of Philips-related manuscripts, however, did correspond to that atypical, single-author model.

[16] Respectively: NLW MS 775B; University of Texas at Austin, HRC MS 151; Worcester College, Oxford MS 6.13; NLW MS 776B. For descriptions of these manuscripts, see Philips, *Collected Works*, ed. Thomas, vol. I, pp. 41–2, 44–6; *Catalogue of English Literary Manuscripts* (hereafter *CELM*) entries at: www.celm-ms.org.uk/repositories/national-library-of-wales.html; www.celm-ms.org .uk/repositories/university-of-texas-at-austin.html; www.celm-ms.org.uk/repositories/worcester-college-oxford.html.

[17] Scholars have differed over how to read the arrangements of the poems in this manuscript: Coolahan, '"We live by Chance"'; Salzman, *Reading Early Modern Women's Writing*, pp. 183–7; Wright, *Producing Women's Poetry*, pp. 102–20. Hageman has convincingly argued that a number of excised pages may have originally copied five poems in the order currently found in the Clarke manuscript: 'Treacherous Accidents', pp. 91–2. See also Hageman and Sununu, 'New Manuscript Texts'.

[18] Wright, *Producing Women's Poetry*, pp. 99, 120–3. Hageman and Sununu ('"More Copies of it abroad"', p. 151) note that the Clarke manuscript, opening with Cowley's ode to Philips, uses the same title exactly as that in *Poems* (1664).

[19] Philips, *Collected Works*, ed. Thomas, vol. II, Letter XIX, p. 60. NLW MS 21867B; see also Hageman and Sununu, 'New Manuscript Texts', p. 188.

[20] Gibson, 'Synchrony and Process', pp. 86, 90.

The few miscellany manuscripts associated with Philips prior to *Poems* (1664) are of uncertain date. A quarto verse miscellany (the Cardiff manuscript) in several hands includes fourteen poems by Philips, copied by a single hand. These are headed 'Verse of Madam Orindas'; the fact that none date later than 1650–1 means the volume could represent an instance of the miscellany circulation of her poems during her lifetime (although the date 1686 also suggests ongoing compilation).[21] A miscellany compiled by Nicholas Crouch (1640–90), student and later bursar of Balliol College, Oxford, includes two poems by Philips, in which the sobriquet 'Lucasia' has been changed to 'Syndaenia', and a list of her coterie's pseudonyms. It has been argued that Crouch came by this information through his contemporary at Balliol in the 1650s, Francis Finch (Orinda's 'Palaemon'). However, the *Catalogue of English Literary Manuscripts* now ascribes this manuscript to the late seventeenth century.[22]

There is substantial evidence of her verse circulating as separates when Philips was alive. The separate containing three juvenilia, often anthologized, is discussed above.[23] Five autograph copies of verse circulated as separates: her 'Ode upon Retirement, made upon occasion of Mr. Cowley's on that subject'; 'To the Queen's Majesty'; 'Rosania to Lucasia on some letters'; her poem to the Duke of Ormond, dating from 1663; and that to Alice (née Egerton), Countess of Carberry.[24] The 'Ode upon Retirement' illustrates some of the difficulties attendant upon assessing the circulation of Philips's verse while she was alive. Elizabeth Scott-Baumann explores the idea of mutual influence, 'that Philips and Cowley wrote in dialogue with both the ethos and the forms of each other's poems', whereas Penelope Anderson interprets Cowley's commendatory poems on Orinda as 'entirely failing to understand how her poems work'.[25] There are numerous tantalizing references to a vibrant and dynamic system of circulation as manuscript separates. For example, her response to Vavasour Powell's poem (itself known only in a journal compiled after her death, from 1671–3), suggests the exchange of verse in Wales. John Taylor, the Water-Poet, who composed a vitriolic poem against Philips, compiled in a 1650s royalist miscellany, must have gained access to her work – although it likely

[21] Cardiff City Library MS 2 1073. See also Philips, *Collected Works*, ed. Thomas, vol. I, p. 44; *CELM* www.celm-ms.org.uk/repositories/cardiff-central-library.html#cardiff-central-library_id679780.

[22] Balliol College, Oxford, MS 336. For discussions of this manuscript, see *CELM* www.celm-ms .org.uk/repositories/balliol-college-oxford.html; Philips, *Collected Works*, ed. Thomas vol. I, p. 46; Hageman and Sununu, 'Further Manuscript Texts', pp. 132–4.

[23] NLW, Orielton Estate MSS Parcel 24.        [24] *CELM* PsK 218.5, 485.5, 319, 437, 491.

[25] Scott-Baumann, *Forms of Engagement*, p. 112; Anderson, *Friendship's Shadows*, p. 171.

reinforces our sympathies for Philips's careful attitude to dissemination.[26] The poem 'To my Lady Elizabeth Boyle, Singing – Since affairs of the State &c' attests to the circulation of her *Pompey* songs at the Restoration Dublin court, as does her letter to Cotterell on these songs.[27]

The print contexts for Philips's work prior to 1664 also fit this pattern of separate circulation. Her tribute to William Cartwright, printed at the beginning of the 1651 edition of his works, and her two poems printed in Henry Lawes's *Second Book of Ayres and Dialogues* in 1655 have been discussed as examples of royalist coterie publications that were therefore 'safe' venues – as has *Poems, by Several Persons* (Dublin, 1663), which included three poems by Philips attributed to 'a Lady'.[28] *To the Queene on her arrivall at Portsmouth. May. 1662* was printed anonymously as a broadside in 1662.[29]

The evidence suggests that Philips's work circulated either as separates or in single-author manuscripts. *Poems* (1664) may not have been planned by Philips but it accorded fully with the pattern of circulation in the early 1660s and it was textually reliable. It may be that 'single author' is the wrong nomenclature here, as its invocation of authorial intention is inaccurate. Only the Tutin manuscript bears the hallmarks of Philips's own intentions; the others are compilations of work by a single author (Philips) made by her earliest readers/editors. Their intentions, not hers, are represented. In this sense, Anderson is right to read these manuscripts as evidence of how her contemporaries read Philips.[30] As discussed in the first chapter of this volume, modern editorial practice has developed along two poles: that of the Greg-Bowers school, in which the goal is to capture the author's (ideally final) intention, and the approach advocated by McGann, in which the social and material contexts of the text's production and circulation are pursued. However, the dominance of contemporary reader-compiler-editors over the single-author manuscript volumes associated with Philips suggests a third kind of agency. If we are concerned with intentionality, these manuscripts feature a different agent – the reader who compiles and (inevitably) edits Philips's work during her lifetime. Rather than a miscreant print editor, these manuscripts have been accorded priority because of their adjacency in time and place to the author. Social proximity is seen to elucidate authorial intention. Yet one of these manuscripts is posthumous

---

[26] For this discovery, see Beal, *In Praise of Scribes*, p. 150 and Appendix VI.

[27] Philips, *Collected Works*, ed. Thomas, vol. II, Letters XXIII, XXIV, pp. 68–71, 72–3.

[28] Gray, 'Katherine Philips and the Post-Courtly Coterie'; Beal, *In Praise of Scribes*, pp. 155–60.

[29] Hageman, 'The "false printed" Broadside'.

[30] Anderson, *Friendship's Shadows*, pp. 96–7; see also pp. 153–88.

and compiled in the aftermath of 1664's publication. In attending so closely to social proximity, we may have lost sight of the idea that these manuscripts themselves are the earliest editions – that they represent the intentionality of Philips's earliest readers rather than that of the author herself.

What is also evident is that these reader-editors were following Philips's construction of herself as a singular female author. Creativity is gendered in her writing and this feeds into her self-construction as exceptional – a deliberate and careful management of her profile that is thrown into stark relief by the claims to female authorial solidarity made by her Dublin admirer, Philo-Philippa. 'A Friend' takes its lead from theology to insist on friendship's gender neutrality:

> If soules no sexes have, for men t'exclude
> Women from friendship's vast capacity,
> Is a design injurious and rude.[31]

But Philips's poetic practice of friendship was overwhelmingly in favour of women. Of the poems addressed to named living acquaintances, three-quarters are addressed to women.[32] Her poems to women perform friend-ship and chart its ups and downs. Her female friends are extolled as the source of happiness; admonished for their coolness or even dissension; and lamented as they depart.[33] But the female friend's voice is rarely heard; when it is, it is as a construct of the female poet. This point is highlighted by poems in which Orinda ventriloquizes her friends' voices: 'A Dialogue between Lucasia and Orinda', 'A Dialogue betwixt Lucasia & Rosania', and 'Rosania to Lucasia on her Letters'. Is this a fantasy of her female friends engaging creatively with Philips? Or is it an attempt to control their voices; by providing their lines, enacting a fantasy of authoring them, in the realm of poetry if not in real life? Philips's poetry may be dominated by her friendships with women, but her friends' voices are never heard unless Philips herself creates them.[34] Poems to the women of the Restora-tion Dublin court serve as vehicles for her own literary reputation. 'To my Lady Elizabeth Boyle, Singing . . . ' is a case in point. The song for which

---

[31] Although the Thomas edition provides this line as 'If no soules no sexes have', this reading is incorrect; Philips, *Collected Works*, ed. Thomas, vol. I, p. 166. The key manuscripts have 'If souls no sexes have'; see NLW MS 775B (Tutin MS), p. 164; Texas HRC MS 151 (Dering MS), p. 83; NLW MS 776B (Rosania MS), p. 331.

[32] By my count, there are 71 poems to specific living persons (of 130 total in Thomas's edition), of which 53 are to women.

[33] For stimulating discussions of Philips's handling of betrayal and friendship, see Anderson, *Friend-ship's Shadows*, pp. 85–103, and Menges, 'Authorship, Friendship, and Forms of Publication'.

[34] Anderson also notes this, suggesting it is accidental rather than by design, as I argue (*Friendship's Shadows*, pp. 95–6).

she praises Boyle is of Philips's own making: it is the song concluding Act
I of *Pompey*. More senior women of the Dublin and London courts were
approached as patrons for Philips's dramatic writing.[35]

The poems addressed to male friends and acquaintances, on the other
hand, participate in royalist dissemination networks and literary exchange.
They anticipate responses in kind. As Salzman has observed, the 'early
poems addressed to men . . . reveal how rapidly Philips established herself
as a central figure within an active coterie, as the men concerned not only
circulated and promoted Philips's own poems, but also wrote back to her
and took up her themes'.[36] Philips's poems to men – both within and
outside her coterie – inevitably praise them for creative endeavour, and the
singular female poet is inserted into the dynamic of male artistic creativity.
For example, John Berkenhead, editor of the royalist newsbook *Mercurius
Aulicus*, was addressed in verse by Philips specifically on the topic of his
writing. The title – 'To Mr J. B. the noble Cratander, upon a composition
of his, which he was not willing to own publiquely' – signals the writerly
focus of the poem and the author's coterie relationship with her addressee.
She adopts the submissive pose of the inferior writer, praising Berkenhead
but all the while drawing attention to her own writing:

> So from a lower soule I might well feare
> A critique censure, when survey'd too neare;
> But from Cratander, (who, above the best,
> Lives in a height which levells all the rest,)
> I may that royalty of soule expect,
> That can at once both pardon and neglect.
> Thus I approach, and wanting wit and sence,
> Let trepidation be my Reverence.[37]

Disarming any criticism of her own poem by appealing to a chivalric notion
of magnanimity, she nevertheless invites judgment. Ostensibly writing a
poem in praise of Berkenhead's writing, she switches its focus back on
herself.

Her verse approaches to more established male poets follow the same
pattern of literary praise couched in a back-handed, attention-seeking
impulse. In 'To Mr Henry Vaughan, Silurist, on his Poems', Philips again
writes herself into the male poet's artistry. Here adopting the pose of

---

[35] 'To the right honourable the Countess of Cork', 'To her royall highnesse, the Dutchesse of Yorke,
on her command to send her some things I had wrote'; Philips, *Collected Works*, ed. Thomas,
vol. I, pp. 241–2, 80, respectively.

[36] Salzman, *Reading Early Modern Women's Writing*, p. 179.

[37] Philips, *Collected Works*, ed. Thomas, vol. I, p. 101.

apprentice, Philips proposes that closeness to the lauded male poet will improve her own verse:

> Instructing us, thou so secur'st thy fame,
> That nothing can disturb it but my name;
> Nay I have hopes that standing so near thine
> 'Twill loose its drosse, and by degrees refine.[38]

In building her reputation as poet, Philips grafts herself onto male artists of her acquaintance. Female camaraderie is practised in friendship, but writerly community pertains to male friends and acquaintances. One of her most successful artistic connections was with the composer and royalist musician Henry Lawes, who set two of her poems to music in his *Second Book of Ayres and Dialogues* (1655). Flanked by fellow royalist poets, and most particularly by male poets of her circle – Dering, Berkenhead, and Finch – the collection is also a showcase for her coterie.

But this collection also points up some glaring sins of omission with regard to Philips's gendered celebrations of creative endeavour. Mary Harvey, schoolfriend of Philips and married to Dering/Silvander, was an exalted contributor to the volume. She collaborated with her husband, providing musical settings for his three poems. She is the only composer other than Lawes whose music is published in the collection. The volume itself is dedicated to her, 'Not only', says Lawes,

> in regard of that honour and esteem you have for Musick, but because those Songs which fill this Book have receiv'd much lustre by your excellent performance of them; and . . . some which I esteem the best of these Ayres, were of your own Composition, after your Noble Husband was pleased to give the words . . . [you] are your self so good a Composer, that few of any Sex have arriv'd to such perfection.[39]

Publicly lauded by Lawes as both performer and composer, schoolfriend of Philips, and spouse to one of her coterie, Harvey is surprisingly absent from Philips's verse.

A second puzzling evasion arises from a poem written to another of Lawes's distinguished pupils, Lady Alice Egerton, dedicatee of his first book of airs and dialogues (1653). Best known to history as the Lady in Milton's *Comus*, Alice Egerton was an accomplished musician, masque

---

[38] See also 'An Ode upon Retirement, made upon occasion of Mr. Cowley's on that subject', 'Upon the engraving. K: P: on a Tree in the short walke at Barn=Elms', 'To the truly noble Mr Henry Lawes'; Philips, *Collected Works*, ed. Thomas, vol. I, pp. 97, 193–5, 208, 87–8, respectively.

[39] Henry Lawes, *The Second Book of Ayres, and Dialogues* (1655), sig. aʳ.

performer, and allegedly a poet herself in her youth.[40] She had further connections to Philips. She was first cousin to Elizabeth Ker (allegedly Philips's 'Berenice'). In 1652, she married Richard Vaughan, Earl of Carberry. Carberry was patron to Jeremy Taylor, whose prose *Discourse . . . on Friendship* was written at Philips's prompting. Taylor resided with the couple at their Welsh seat, Golden Grove in Carmarthenshire, during the Interregnum. Unlike Harvey, Egerton is the subject of a single poem by Philips, welcoming her to Wales. Yet the female poet makes no mention at all of her addressee's considerable artistic connections, nor of her reputation as poet or performer. Rather, Egerton is praised in terms of a conventional distinction between town and country.[41] There is a distinct lack of female solidarity in Philips's silences on these two women, however historically anachronistic such a formulation may seem. It is an oversight that stands in stark contrast to her persistent lauding of male artistic activities and throws into relief the very different terms in which she praises her female friends. It is an absence that was noticed by her seventeenth-century readers, as is suggested by a poem in Lucasia's voice, 'Friendship. An Elegy, by Lucasia', published in the *Gentleman's Journal* in 1694 – startling in its uniqueness.[42]

A key question underpinning any exploration of the gendering of creativity in Philips's writing is: who writes back? Her male acquaintances inevitably responded: Francis Finch and Jeremy Taylor wrote prose treatises on friendship; Edward Dering engaged creatively to the extent of impersonating her poetic voice. Vaughan and Cowley wrote poems to her. Male writers of the Dublin court – Orrery, Wentworth Dillon, Earl of Roscommon – also responded in kind. The musical settings for the *Pompey* songs were provided by men of the Dublin court. Lawes set three of her poems to music; his fellow royalist composer Charles Coleman set another. The main collaborator of her late career was Charles Cotterell, the king's master of ceremonies and a vital ally not only in her husband's political rehabilitation on the Restoration but also in the furthering of Philips's literary reputation at court. Trolander and Tenger have written insightfully on their correspondence (which testifies to the exchange of texts as

---

[40] She played in Aurelian Townsend's *Tempe Restored* in 1632. Jane Cavendish attributes to her a poem ('I pretty send me back my heart'), attributed to Henry Hughes in Lawes's third book of airs and dialogues (1658). The Cavendish attribution, in two manuscripts compiled during the 1640s, predates that in Lawes. At the very least, it suggests that the song was established in Egerton's singing repertoire. See Beinecke Library, Yale University, MS b. 233, p. 18 [fol. 9v]; Bodleian Library, University of Oxford, MS Rawl. poet. 16, p. 16.

[41] Philips, *Collected Works*, ed. Thomas, vol. 1, pp. 84–5

[42] Hageman and Sununu, 'Further Manuscript Texts', pp. 137–8; see also Anderson, *Friendship's Shadows*, pp. 179–80.

separates) as an arena for critical commentary and a literary economy in which social credit is accrued via the exchange of literary texts.[43] But the literary-critical circle they document is comprised of men – with, of course, the honourable exception of the singular Philips. The women of her circle did write, but they confined themselves to letters. Confirming the success of her self-construction, it is primarily Philips's side of this correspondence that survives. Claudia Limbert has noted that there is 'no evidence . . . except for letters, that they were in any way literary'. She argues that Philips needed writerly role models and that these happened to be men: 'Since it is difficult for any writer to write without the stimulus of other writers, evidence suggests that Philips may have turned to friendships with male writers to fill this void in her creative life.'[44] But such a conservative conclusion elides the fact that the poet's female friendships in themselves provided plentiful stimulus for the composition of verse. Were her female friends recalcitrant, refusing to engage with her poetically? Or is it that Philips had allotted other, less creative roles for them as muses, vehicles, and patrons?

Philips is often contrasted with her more infamous contemporary, Margaret Cavendish. This stems partly from their different approaches to career management: Cavendish pursued literary fame via a very modern attitude to print publication, eschewing the modes of manuscript culture exploited so skilfully by Philips. However, Cavendish was the other female writer who had a single-author print volume printed in 1664: *Poems, and Phancies*, the second edition of *Poems, and Fancies* (1653). Scott-Baumann has shown that, contrary to her own declarations, Cavendish was a serious reviser of her own work. Arguing that, for Cavendish, 'print is malleable; not only in the chaotic way in which she seems to have provided copy to the printer but also, paradoxically, in allowing her to create a more polished and regular style as her career progressed', Scott-Baumann carefully tracks the formal, syntactical, and organizational changes made to this second edition, assessing them as responses to 'early readers' complaints about her prosody'.[45] Like Philips, Cavendish's self-construction as female author is rooted in singularity and a rejection of collective female creativity (ironically pointing to a shared sense of female authorship). But Cavendish, surely, functioned as a barometer of what could go wrong for Philips if she failed to protest Marriott's edition of the same year.

---

[43] Trolander and Tenger, 'Katherine Philips and Coterie Critical Practices'.
[44] Limbert, '"The Unison of Well-Tun'd Hearts"', p. 25.
[45] Scott-Baumann, *Forms of Engagement*, pp. 60, 63.

Philips's complaints against *Poems* (1664) were not without parallel among male contemporaries. Henry King, the royalist Bishop of Chichester, had a second edition of his poems printed by Henry Herringman in 1664. Like Philips, King had retained careful control over the manuscript circulation of his works as single-author collections. His *Poems, Elegies and Paradoxes* was published by Herringman and Richard Marriott, apparently without his permission, in 1657. Their second edition of 1664 is prefaced by an epistle from both publishers to the author. Their justification for this print edition is relatively conventional – 'in your own defence, preventing the present attempts of others, who to their theft would (by their false copies of these Poems) have added violence, and some way have wounded your reputation' – as was that of the printer (Herringman again) to the reader prefacing Edmund Waller's *Poems*, also published in 1664. Here, Herringman narrates a familiar story: the author's instinctive reaction to finding his verses in print was to be 'satisfied to see his lines so ill rendred that he might justly disown them'. But, on the pressings of the publishers, and the sequestration of his estates for his royalism, '[he] has at last given us leave, To assure the Reader, That the Poems which have been so long and so ill set forth under his name, are here to be found as he first writ them'.[46] The motives attributed to Waller – final authorial intention, damage limitation following an unsought entry to print – are similar to those tentatively voiced by Philips in her 1664 letter to Cotterell.

Philips's *Poems* of 1664 was neither inconsistent with her contemporary manuscript manifestations nor with other volumes of collected poems printed by individual authors that year. Marriott's pedigree as a printer was respectable. His father John was a pioneer in the publication of single-author poetic collections, responsible for all editions of Donne's *Poems* up to 1650. As we have seen, he was jointly responsible for Henry King's two print editions. Where Philips was distinct from these analogous cases is in her novelty; unlike the volumes printed by Cavendish, King, or Waller, *Poems* (1664) was a new, original edition.[47] Whether or not it eventuated in a decision by Philips to consider print publication more readily is a moot point – Wright argues for signs of such a move in the early 1660s.[48] But the analogous royalist models are there.

How, then, should we evaluate the modes of dissemination for Philips's work that were employed by her contemporaries? Wright adverts to the

[46]  Henry King, *Poems, Elegies, Paradoxes, And Sonets* (1664), sig. A3ᵛ; Edmund Waller, *Poems, &c. Written Upon Several Occasions, and to Several Persons* (1664).
[47]  See Crabstick, 'Katherine Philips, Richard Marriott'.
[48]  Wright, *Producing Women's Poetry*, pp. 130–5.

relatively late transmission of her writing: 'It is worth stressing that much of the evidence for the manuscript circulation of Philips's poetry dates from the 1660s; this includes the transcription of the Dering and Clarke manuscripts, which were, as far as we know, the first large-scale collections of Philips's poetry to leave her own possession.'[49] Similarly, Salzman divides Philips's career into two: the first, pre-Dublin phase in which Philips controlled her Society and the second, following the performance of *Pompey* in Dublin, in which her 'more public fame' extended to the '1667 folio and numerous imitations and circulations of her writing'.[50] We could configure these valuable insights in a slightly different way: single-author manuscript volumes and separates dominate how Philips's work appears to have circulated during her lifetime. But her widespread penetration of miscellany culture occurred only after her death and the single-author print editions, a view that is confirmed by the *Catalogue of English Literary Manuscripts*.

Of the six manuscript miscellanies that contain more than ten Philips poems, five date from the sixty years following her death in 1664. The manuscript most obviously indebted to Philips's print publications retains the single-author character of those discussed above while replicating the more monumental layout of the folio edition. Folger MS V.b.231, itself a folio, is an exact transcript of the 1669 print edition of Philips's *Poems*, prefaced by an original poem, 'Cassandra preferr'd to Orinda' and dated to 1670. The Trevor manuscript (Beinecke Library Osborn MS b 118) is an octavo miscellany, stamped with the crest of Marcus Trevor's family. He married Anne Owen, Philips's 'Lucasia', in 1662; Hageman and Sununu suggest this manuscript belonged to her son John (1668–87).[51] It contains eighteen Philips poems, transcribed from a print source, and dates from the late seventeenth century. Bodleian Library MS Rawl. poet. 65 is an octavo verse miscellany, in a single hand, containing twenty-one poems by Philips and dated to the late seventeenth century. Bodleian Library MS Rawl. poet. 90 is a quarto verse miscellany ('A Collection of Verses Fancyes and Poems, Morrall and Devine') also transcribed in a single hand, containing fifteen poems by Philips, and dated to the early eighteenth century. Bodleian Library MS Rawl. poet. 173 is a folio verse miscellany ('The Muse's Magazine'), again in a single hand, including eleven poems by Katherine Philips and dating from the early eighteenth century. This manuscript was bought from its compiler Thomas Corbett by the

---

[49] Wright, 'Textuality, Privacy and Politics', p. 175.
[50] Salzman, *Reading Early Modern Women's Writing*, p. 182.
[51] Hageman and Sununu, 'Further Manuscript Texts', p. 139.

bookseller John Dunton and is dated both 1718 and 1724. The only exception, the Cardiff manuscript, could also have been compiled into the second half of the seventeenth century, as discussed above.

Other miscellanies known to compile Philips's work can be divided into two categories: those that transcribe her poems and those that extract from them. Again, almost all of these date from the period after 1664. In the former category falls that associated with John Locke, Bodleian Library MS Locke e.17, which dates from the third quarter of the seventeenth century and contains three Philips poems. Bodleian Library MS Tanner 306 is a two-volume miscellany into which are bound copies of two Restoration poems by Philips, circulated as a single separate and dated to the late seventeenth century. Beinecke Library Osborn MS b 207, dated 1665, compiles Philips's poem on Charles II's restoration. Elizabeth Lyttelton's miscellany, Cambridge University Library MS Add. 8460, dates from 1692 and copies 'The Virgin'.[52] Rosenbach MS 239/16, dating from 1714, copies six poems by Philips as well as some extracts. A volume begun by Sarah Cowper in 1690 contains 'God'.[53] Katherine Butler's verse miscellany, compiled 1693–6, has extracts from two poems, sourced from one of the folio editions.[54] Of miscellanies that compile extracts from Philips, retooling them for their own purposes, arguably the best known are the Parliamentarian Robert Overton's memorial manuscript for his wife, compiled 1671–2, and the Duke of Monmouth's pocket book, taken at his capture following the Battle of Sedgemoor in 1685.[55] Two verse miscellanies compiled by Henry Hall in the early eighteenth century revise and answer poems by Philips.[56] Two miscellanies contain versions of Philips's elegy on Frances Philips, both recycling the first ten lines for an elegy commemorating one Mary Morris, who died in 1695 aged three.[57]

Beyond such examples, we can probe *CELM* for more quantitative information. 571 copies are listed for 135 different poems or songs by Philips. Only nine of these can be securely dated prior to 1664. Five are autograph copies: 'Ode upon Retirement', 'To the Queen's majesty',

[52] See also Hageman and Sununu, 'Further Manuscript Texts', p. 139; Burke, 'Contexts for Women's Manuscript Miscellanies'.

[53] Hertfordshire Record Office, MS DE/P F43. See also Bod. MS Rawl. D 214, an early eighteenth-century miscellany containing one Philips poem.

[54] Hageman and Sununu, 'Further Manuscript Texts', p. 139. Hageman and Sununu cite a similar example, in which couplets from Philips poems are credited to the print edition; 'Further Manuscript Texts', p. 136; and see Burke, 'The Couplet and the Poem'.

[55] Norbrook, '"This blushing tribute"'; Hageman and Sununu, 'New Manuscript Texts', pp. 209–14.

[56] Leeds University Library, Brotherton MSS Lt q 5, 6.        [57] *CELM* PsK 138, 139.

'Rosania to Lucasia on her Letters', the poems to the Duke of Ormond and Alice, Countess of Carberry.[58] Two poems are included in a verse miscellany compiled by royalists and dated to the late 1650s.[59] A copy of the first stanza of her elegy on Hector Philips with musical setting is copied into John Playford's songbook, dated to 1660; and a copy of 'Song, to the tune of, Sommes nous pas trop heureux' is on a separate, with some accounts dating to 1659–60 in William Trumbull's hand.[60] A further eleven poems occur in three manuscripts of indeterminate date. British Library Add. MS 28758 contains six poems by Philips. George Sacheverell began compiling this manuscript in 1651, and there are dated inscriptions from 1662 and 1663; its compilation is dated *c.* 1651–66 by Beal.[61] Another verse miscellany containing two Philips poems is dated broadly mid-to-late seventeenth century. This bears the inscriptions of William Godolphin and Henry Savile – likely the diplomats working in Spain and France in the 1670s.[62] Finally, one poem is reported to have been compiled in a seventeenth-century manuscript connected with the Tixall poets.[63] There is also a collection of French poems, including two royal Restoration poems by Philips, although this is also late, dated either 1662 or 1683.[64]

Ironically, given the depth and breadth of Philips's association with manuscript culture, miscellany compilers grabbed hold of her work only after her death. Prior to this point, and as many have acknowledged, Philips exerted close control over her writing, even to the extent that she worried about its loss in numerous letters to Cotterell. The evidence collated in *CELM* is, of course, subject to the vagaries of manuscript survival. Nevertheless, the dearth of miscellanies compiling her work prior to 1664 as opposed to the wealth and variety of such manuscripts afterwards is striking. It is not that we have no pre-1667 manuscript witnesses – we do; in fact, we have a lot, relative to other (female) writers. But these are all single-author collections, contextualized by the evidence of further circulation in separate form. Philips's circulation during her lifetime occurred via separates or manuscript collections of her work according to the single-author paradigm. Her work was adopted by and incorporated to the melée of miscellany manuscript culture only after this authorial reputation was established through these modes of circulation. The manuscript tradition

---

[58]  *CELM* PsK 218.5, 485.5, 319, 437, 491. This figure does not take account of the additional copies catalogued as sub-items.

[59]  *CELM* PsK 248.5, 318.5.    [60]  *CELM* PsK 249, 335.

[61]  *CELM* PsK 165.2, 3, 5; 266.5; 274.5; 455.5; 481.8; 488.5.

[62]  Cambridge University Library, MS Dd. 6 43; *CELM* PsK 165.8, 280.5.    [63]  *CELM* PsK 224.

[64]  BL, Harley MS 6900; see Hageman and Sununu, 'Further Manuscript Texts', pp. 139–44.

of appropriation and recycling occurs in the later seventeenth century and its texts are usually derived from the single-author print editions – not unlike John Donne and George Herbert.[65]

*Poems* (1664) is neither out of step with Philips's own self-construction nor with that of her manuscript circulation. It does mark the moment at which intentionality leaves the author behind – and that is the key to modern editors' avoidance of the volume as potential copytext. If we locate textual authority in the social contexts of the author's lifetime, we have inherited multiple single-author versions of Katherine Philips. Rather than a stable notion of authorship, this represents refracted versions of authorship that concatenate around the historical figure. From an editorial perspective, each compiler (whether of manuscript or print) contemporary with her shaped a slightly different Katherine Philips. Intentionality, then, is as much a question to be asked of the reader-compiler-editor as of the author. What we have is a series of roughly contemporaneous single-author collections, only one of which is actually authorial. This brings us to a different kind of editorial intentionality, even if informed by and agreeing with the author's self-construction as singular.

What is more, it is clear that, although Philips exerted tight control over the circulation of her work during her lifetime, both print single-author volumes led to the reverse in the years following her death. Print publication facilitated the reader's control over Philips's poetry. Erin McCarthy has recently directed attention to the second print edition of Donne's *Poems* (1635) and its role in framing subsequent biographical and critical interpretations of Donne.[66] Philips's earliest manuscript editors were following her lead, whereas her posthumous print editor was constructing her for later consumption. However, where McCarthy argues that the contours of Donne's reputation as laid out in the 1635 edition enjoyed tremendous longevity, miscellany culture's appropriation of Philips suggests the opposite: that 1667 was the last gasp of such biographical coherence. Philips, in this posthumous phase, not only gained wider prominence as a matchless woman writer, she was opened up for use by later readers. Compilers such as Overton and others remade Philips, and often in ways that dissented from her own points of view – revisions that do not conform with any authorial final intention.

The single-author paradigm goes to the heart of feminist editing practices, raising questions about canon integration and segregation, and about

---

[65] Todd and Wilcox, 'The Challenges of Editing Donne and Herbert', pp. 188–9.
[66] McCarthy, '*Poems, by J. D.* (1635)'.

the field of women's writing. If we accept, first, that Philips was known
to her own contemporaries as an accomplished 'collection' author and to
her later seventeenth- and eighteenth-century readers as an author whose
single-author volume (usually print) could be plundered to create their own
manuscript compilations, that implies two divergent kinds of reception but
also two different forms of editorial practice in the early modern period.
The remarkably modern concern of her earliest editors to compile a comprehensive collection of Philips's work follows her own self-construction.
As we have seen, modern concepts of solidarity were not shared by Philips
herself, whose poetry evinces a clear demarcation between male interlocu-
tors as creative agents and female allies as mediators or the raw material
for forging verse. Their approach to compiling her work chimes nicely
with modern gynocritical aims. Yet Danielle Clarke has warned against
the tendency to focus on 'an identity politics based upon the author
figure... because a singular author figure is a highly effective means of
circumscribing the functions of texts... but it is also true that... agency
is by no means a singular entity'.[67] Indeed, agency was dispersed – to
Philips's contemporaries, who tended to present her as a singular figure,
and to her later readers, who re-made her poetry in the context of a multi-
author miscellany culture. Gibson has argued for an editorial approach to
single-author critical editions that embraces the intentionality and creativity of manuscript compilers: 'Scribes and compilers will have had all sorts
of reasons for rearranging, correcting, adapting, and supplementing their
copy texts. Thus the editorial grouping of variant readings... will have to
take a mass of heterogeneous, manuscript-specific material into account'.[68]
This approach would ensure cognizance of the varieties of dissemination
and reception, but it does retain the pre-eminence of the individual author.
The more radical option would be to shift attention away from the author
and onto the intentions of the early modern compiler-editor.[69]

---

[67] Clarke, 'Nostalgia', p. 204.    [68] Gibson, 'Synchrony and Process', p. 96.

[69] Research for this chapter has received funding from the European Research Council under
the European Union's Seventh Framework Programme (FP/2007–2013)/ERC Grant Agreement
n. 615545.

# PART III

# Out of the Archives, into the Classroom

# CHAPTER 11

# Out of the Archives
## Mary Wroth's Countess of Montgomery's Urania

### Mary Ellen Lamb

Impelled by an urgent concern that Mary Wroth's romance was seldom taught in classrooms, I undertook an abridged edition of *The Countess of Montgomery's Urania*, published in 2011.[1] Because of its sheer size (almost 600,000 words), Wroth's unabridged romance had not received the readership its quality deserves. It is too massive to include in the syllabi of the academic classes that train up the next generation of scholars. Even some specialists have confessed that they found it a challenge to read Wroth's long romance all the way through. At the same time, Wroth's poetry is increasingly included in standard anthologies of Renaissance literature, and her verse and her play *Love's Victory* are easily available in inexpensive editions.[2] But except for Paul Salzman's tantalizing sample of the first of the four books of *The First Part of the Countess of Montgomery's Urania* in his Oxford *Anthology of Seventeenth-Century Fiction*, Wroth's romance was primarily accessible only in the large two-volume set meticulously edited by Josephine Roberts, and completed by Janel Mueller and Suzanne Gossett after Roberts's death. Volume I, *The First Part of the Countess of Montgomery's Urania*, presented the portion of the romance published in 1621; volume II, *The Second Part of the Countess of Montgomery's Urania*, presented Wroth's unpublished continuation, found only in a single

---

[1] Wroth, *The Countess of Montgomery's Urania (Abridged)*, ed. Lamb (Tempe Az: ACMRS, 2011).

[2] See, for example, Payne and Hunter (eds.), *Renaissance Literature*; Fowler (ed.), *The New Oxford Book of Seventeenth-Century Verse*; as well as classroom anthologies suitable for surveys extending beyond the Renaissance such as *The Norton Anthology of English Literature*, vol. 1 (8th edn), ed. Abrams, and Keegan (ed.), *The Penguin Book of English Verse*. Hefty chapters on Wroth are now included in general guides, such as Hattaway (ed.), *Companion*; and Cheney et al. (eds.), *Early Modern English Poetry*. Wroth's writing has even entered the popular domain in such works as the Kaplan reviews for the *SAT Subject Tests: Literature 2004–5* and *2005–6* (Kaplan Publishing, 2005 and 2006); and Timpane (ed.), *Poetry for Dummies*. Accessible anthologies of Wroth's drama and poetry include inexpensive paperbacks Cerasano and Wynne-Davies (eds.), *Renaissance Drama by Women*, and *The Poems of Lady Mary Wroth*, ed. Roberts.

autograph manuscript.[3] The inaccessibility of Wroth's romance to a class-room setting was, to my mind, a great shame because, even aside from its significance as the first extant romance by an early modern woman, the *Urania* is, I believe, a masterpiece of early modern romance. For this reason, my abridgement represents my attempt to bring the *Urania* to students and to general readers, with an ulterior motive of luring them to the complete two-volume set.

Providing a classroom edition of the two parts of Wroth's *Countess of Montgomery's Urania* led to a number of difficult decisions. First, I decided to modernize spelling and punctuation for the following reasons: (1) the two-volume set with original spelling and punctuation is already available for consultation by readers; (2) the spelling and punctuation of the *First Part* was determined primarily by the printer in 1621; (3) especially for undergraduate students, reading all or a substantial portion of the 280-page abridged text in original spelling and punctuation might prove very slow going; and (4) we don't ask our students to read the original spelling of Shakespeare's plays, Donne's poems, or other early modern canonical works. Three other most prominent concerns that I confronted were these, discussed in more detail below:

1. How should I abridge the massive scale of Wroth's romance and, related to this, how much help should I offer to readers? When does intervention become excessive interference, an imposition of my own agendas?

2. How do we choose the materials, especially in our introductions, to provide a context for reading an early modern work by a woman writer? Does the lens of gender distort or more truly reveal Wroth's achievement? What is the place of the biographical, especially in light of new textualism, with its move away from an author's life as a context for interpretation?[4]

3. What is the role of modern feminist ideologies in the interpretation of an early modern woman's text? Critics are radically divided on whether the protagonist Pamphilia's constant love for her serially unfaithful Amphilanthus is admirably heroic or pathologically self-destructive. The *Urania* provides abundant evidence for both positions. What is the role of an edition in promoting or framing this debate?

---

[3] Wroth, *The First Part of Urania*, ed. Roberts; Wroth, *The Second Part of Urania*, ed. Roberts, Gossett, and Mueller. See also Salzman (ed.), *Anthology*, pp. 1–208. *First Part* was also available online through the Brown Women Writers project.

[4] New textualism is ably described by Hurley and Goodblatt in the Preface to *Women Editing/Editing Women*, pp. xi–xviii.

## Abridging the *Urania*: Its Aesthetic of Abundance

No edition, I would submit, can be entirely innocent of designs upon a reader. In this case, the amount of text to be selected was limited by the pressing economic concern of offering a price ($US25) feasible for the class-room or the general reader; and I remain grateful to the Arizona Center for Medieval and Renaissance Studies for pricing this still relatively substantial classroom volume, coming in at 280 pages, this low. Abridging the *Urania* was perhaps the most difficult academic task I have ever encountered. There are so many plots and so many characters competing for inclusion. My first strategy (which didn't work) was to limit the abridgement to the plots of the two main protagonists, the constantly loving Pamphilia and the unfaith-ful Amphilanthus, who repeatedly find each other only to be separated again, perhaps united at the end, although complications prevent any true conclusion. This strategy quickly dissolved. Since the title explicitly names the character Urania, Urania's narrative obviously must be included, with her love of a prince who deserts her, her discovery of her royal parentage (she was raised as a shepherdess), and her happy marriage to another after a magical cure expunged her first feelings of love. Other intriguing characters have taken their place in the burgeoning criticism of this romance: Limena, tortured and nearly killed by her jealous husband Philarchos for her love of Perissus; the princess Nereana, stripped to her petticoat by a madman who believes she is a goddess when she becomes lost in a forest in her fruitless search for her disdainful beloved; the unruly Antissia, whose poetry is so execrable that the wise Melissea subjects her to water immersion to cure her. The *Second Part* is even more complicated, with the additional narratives of offspring, including the mysterious Fair Design, born to the protagonists of the *First Part*. I tended to omit narratives involving characters who do not appear again; I included material on women characters who were also authors of poetry; and I was, regretfully, a bit light on pirates.

The magnificent tangle of Wroth's plots, proliferating beyond even those of other romances such as Montemayor's *Diana* and Ariosto's *Orlando Furioso*, remains an essential feature of the *Urania*; and I struggled with the question of how to present a chaotic plot without conveying a false sense of order. This raised what is for me a difficult question of how much to help. I decided to help a lot. I summarized each of the sixty-four excerpts with a sentence or two, placed at the top of each excerpt. I listed these summaries at the end to help readers to know where a given plot weaves in and out. I compiled an index of characters. The introduction discussed three structuring devices: (1) the relationship between Pamphilia and Amphilanthus, which overarches both the published part and the manuscript continuation; (2) the three enchantments organizing the *First Part* and the complex or unfinished quest-enchantments that fail or, as I prefer, refuse to organize the *Second Part*; (3) the role of the wise woman Melissea, arguably an author figure, who accurately prophesies the futures of the primary characters.

For classroom teachers who have time on their syllabuses only for a section of the romance, I included a selection of suggested episodes on specific topics (love, enchantments, authorship, politics) with questions to consider. Paper topics can come out of these, as can class discussion. Under 'love', for example, I provided numbers of relevant episodes to consider the question:

> Does your response to Amphilanthus change as you read? If so, where and why? Does your response to Pamphilia change? If so, where and why? Are there cues within the text as to how it is designed to encourage you to respond? If so, do you accept or resist them? Why? Responses may vary considerably from reader to reader. Consider episodes etc. (with numbers).

I provided the numbers of other episodes to ask other questions:

> What is the persona of the narrator? What are the narrator's attitudes towards the characters? Some of the narrator's explicit comments occur on the following pages (page numbers listed). Can you detect a pattern that determines when the narrator makes a comment? Does the narrator's attitude affect your reading, or not? Why or why not?

The point of these questions is to encourage personal responses to the romance to get discussion started, and to help students to own the text. But I realize also that no matter how much I attempt to adopt neutrality to the content, in all of these aspects – in my selection of episodes, in my summaries of plot and indexing, in my questions for discussion – I am intervening in the reading process. This is, I believe, the necessary cost of introducing this massive text to an ordinary classroom setting. I hope that this abridgement may lead, down the line, to advanced undergraduate or graduate classes, whether on women's writing, on early modern prose, or on early modern romance, that explore the two-volume set for the greater part of a semester.

Providing study aides to ease difficulties of reading is the easiest and also, to my mind, the most questionable strategy for addressing the difficulties posed by Wroth's plot conducted through myriads of characters. To me, the more central and pressing issue is to account for the presence of the difficulties in the first place, to justify the ways of Wroth to readers, and to make them acceptable and even exciting to readers coming to this text for the first time. A possible parallel here is Paul Salzman's explanation of the obscurity of Wroth's verse in her sonnet sequence as intentional, as a form of 'resistance to interpretation' similar to that used by the speaker for her own protection.[5] Wroth may be doing something of this sort in the *Urania* which, like the sonnet sequence, alludes to some personal details of her life. The many versions of a woman faithful (or, rarely, not faithful) to a wandering beloved decentre any one narrative or any one interpretation. Pamphilia continues to love Amphilanthus; the rejected Antissia takes out a contract on him to have him murdered. Is the sheer massiveness of the plot a means of complicating the central narrative, to discourage a sense of mastery over this text? An explanation I offered in my introduction was that Wroth was heightening already standard romance conventions, such as deferral of narrative closures, linear interweaving of plots, the sudden intervention of the magical or miraculous to evoke a response of wonder, characteristic of romance. She is doing romance, only more so.[6]

These romance techniques become more understandable in terms of an early modern aesthetic, later culminating in the baroque, which finds in abundance a form of delight rather than frustration. I could have said more: coherence, unity, predictability: these are the values of the novel, not of romance. Incoherence, fragmentation, surprise ('where did *that* character come from?' and 'Who knew?'): these are closer to the aesthetic of the early modern romance.[7] This aesthetic of abundance enables Wroth, much like Spenser (only more so), to take up a theme or topic, such as constancy, and to vary it in as many different situations as possible, to evoke as many outcomes as possible, as a way to explore this trait from a myriad of perspectives, never finally reducing it to one. An outcome of the abundance of plots and characters is that the *Urania* also conveys the rich complexity surrounding Wroth in her experience of Jacobean life and the politics of the Jacobean court. There are so many narratives; and, as we will discuss in the next section, a number of them were recognized as factually and biographically 'true' by contemporaries. I am hoping that the material in my introduction will encourage the focus of classroom discussion to move the *what* (the difficulty of keeping track of characters) to a *why* (a more interesting question that gets us deeper into the romance).

---

[5] Salzman, 'Critical Introduction', in *Mary Wroth's Poetry: An Electronic Edition*, p. 39.

[6] Clare Kinney ably argues that in *The Second Part* Wroth 'undoes romance', showing the limitations of this genre in representing authentic experience ('"Beleeve"'). See also Lamb, 'Topicality and the Interrogation of Wonder'.

[7] A few prominent discussions of romance include Cooper, *English Romance*; Fuchs, *Romance*; Jameson, *The Political Unconscious*; Parker, *Inescapable Romance*; Frye, *Secular Scripture*.

Figure 11.1 Frontispiece to Mary Wroth's *Urania* (1621).

The new textualism, with its focus on the materiality of the text and the creativity of non-authorial agents, provided a useful resource in introducing Wroth's abundant aesthetic, so foreign to modern readers accustomed to the tighter plotting of the novel. In line with the new textualism, I opened my edition with a brief discussion of the frontispiece for *The First Part*, engraved by Dutch artist Simon van de Passe which represents – and markets – Wroth's romance to readers (see Figure 11.1). Often printed separately from a work and hung in the bookseller's shop as an advertisement to prospective buyers, frontispieces served as a crucial textual engagement between the bookseller and the consumer.[8] Rahel Orgis has plausibly described this frontispiece as providing directions for reading: two small figures at the bottom left, who are about to enter the landscape before them, would seem to represent prospective readers.[9] Like the plot of the *Urania*, this landscape is filled with wandering paths that promise delight, in the walled formal gardens, in the curving tree-lined avenues, domesticated by the presence of some houses ahead on the left. Like the romance, this landscape invites non-purposive meandering; it raises questions that cannot be resolved. Does the windmill on the right up ahead signify a Sidneian investment in the Protestant Netherlands? Or does it evoke the scepticism towards romance of Cervantes' Don Quixote, as Maureen Quilligan has eloquently argued?[10] The two reader-figures are facing the romance's enchantment of the three towers, which confine lovers under the spell of inferior forms of love governed by Cupid or by Venus rather than by Constancy. Are they reader-versions of Pamphilia and Amphilanthus, with the power to set lovers free?[11] Or are they more likely, in the process of reading Wroth's romance, themselves to become temporarily trapped? These reader-figures invite us, as readers, whatever our actual location in class, to become virtual aristocrats as we enter a distinctly Sidneian landscape announced by the cartouche at the top of the triumphal arch. More specifically, the woman's long veil and the man's buskins invite us to perform as participants in masques. How is reading like masquing? Is this frontispiece inviting us, as masquers, to take on a virtual identity that is not quite ourselves yet not quite someone else? What are the operations of this text – perhaps in some sense of any text – to stretch the boundaries of our readerly identities, to submit to the flow of the text, its meandering plots, its myriad characters?

---

[8] Saenger, *Commodification*, p. 38.          [9] Orgis, 'Structured Proliferation', pp. 5–28, esp. p. 14.

[10] Quilligan, *Incest and Agency*, p. 187. Quilligan's discussion of this frontispiece, pp. 168–91, is classic.

[11] Quilligan interprets these figures as Pamphilia and Amphilanthus, *Incest and Agency*, p. 169.

## Choosing Contexts: The Place of Gender, Biography, Politics

It is a mark of the maturity of its political position that feminism no longer espouses single viewpoints. While united by core values, feminists (among whom I count myself) engage in productive debates over the most effective means to advocate for women's issues. It has become more appropriate to refer to feminist ideologies in the plural. The diversity of feminist approaches has created the context for writings by early modern women as a fraught topic. On the one hand, it is important not to ghettoize women writers. To take their rightful place in the mainstream of the literary canon, their works must be understood in terms of their male contemporaries. On the other hand, to discount the formative role of gender is to ignore the conditions under which women wrote and lived. For example, an understanding of the contemporary perception of romance as gendered reveals the magnificent audacity of Wroth's choice of genre. Women were imagined as its primary market, not because men did not also read romance – there is strong evidence that men did read romance, even including Wroth's *Urania*[12] – but because the category of woman reader signified the relatively low status of romance as a 'woman's' genre. This is because, as the increased numbers of early modern readers diminished reading itself as a form of distinction, the print culture created a hierarchy of reading, placing the conceptual category of the woman reader of romance at a low level and the male humanist reader of Latin at a high level.[13] This imagined readership for romance did not, however, authorize women to write romance. On the contrary, the risks to a woman writer only intensified, for this constructed woman reader of romance was eroticized, to become the target of strictures levelled by moralists.[14] Wroth defied these strictures. Even more, in what can only be construed as a direct challenge to cultural anxieties aroused by the imagined sexuality of women readers, Wroth's romance foregrounds the amorous desires of her female characters (and by implication of her women readers), generally validating rather than condemning them. More remarkably, in what Helen Hackett has described as Wroth's most 'radical intervention' in representations of women in romance,[15] topical allusions identify Wroth in some sense with

---

[12] Edward Lord Denny identified himself as the father-in-law of Sirelius, in Wroth's *Urania*; for other male readers see Orgis, '"[A] Story Very Well Woorth Readinge"'. For male readers of romance more generally see Hackett, *Women and Romance Fiction*, p. 11; Hackel, *Reading Material*.

[13] See Newcomb, *Reading Popular Romance*, pp. 1–19.

[14] Hackett, '"Yet Tell me Some Such Fiction"', pp. 44–5; and Lamb, *Gender and Authorship*, pp. 112–14, and 'Constructions of Early Modern Women Readers'.

[15] Hackett, *Women and Romance Fiction*, p. 163.

Pamphilia, whose love for the inveterately fickle Amphilanthus overarches the *Urania*. Without an understanding of the status of seventeenth-century romance, the audacity of Wroth's validation of women's erotic desires can be downplayed or even critiqued as false consciousness, as a form of interpellation into a patriarchal social structure that reduces women to the primarily domestic domain of emotions, excluding them from the wider social sphere in which men, with their allegedly greater powers of reason, were once thought to be better suited to assume power.

It would be a mistake, however, to perceive the love interest of early modern romance as a primarily female concern. As much as she showed special empathy for the amorous desires of female characters, Wroth was still working in a predominantly male tradition. Wroth drew extensively from romances by authors such as Ariosto, Montemayor, Cervantes, Spenser, and Sidney, all of whom show considerable sympathy to women in love.[16] It is against the context of male authors that Wroth's radical interventions into romance tradition become most visible. Productive scholarship has shown the extent to which Wroth adapted elements of Spenser's *Faerie Queene* and Sidney's *Countess of Pembroke's Arcadia* to critique their treatment of gender.[17] Wroth's referencing of Sidney's romance is especially explicit in an episode taking place in Arcadia, in which a male character rescues his beloved from a lion and a bear (conflating rescues by Sidney's Pyrocles and Musidorus), and also cross-dresses (like Pyrocles) to gain access to her company. The exploration of Wroth's romance against a context of male authors has just begun, and there is more work to be done.

Wroth's use of her uncle's *Arcadia* has raised its own issues within feminist ideologies. In its echo of her uncle's *Countess of Pembroke's Arcadia*, Wroth's title *The Countess of Montgomery's Urania* foregrounds a familial connection that challenges a feminist and a new textual swerve away from the biographical. Wroth was not only writing as a woman; she was openly and emphatically writing as a Sidney. Early Wroth critics used this connection to represent the *Urania* as derivative, as a watered-down version of Sidney's *Arcadia*.[18] The text of the cartouche at the top of its 1621

---

[16] *First Part*, ed. Roberts, pp. xx–xxx.

[17] Shannon Miller, '"Mirrours More Then One"', and Jacqueline Miller, 'Lady Mary Wroth in the House of Busirane', have each analysed Wroth's rewriting of Spenser's House of Busirane (*Faerie Queene*, III, cantos 11–12) in the third enchantment of the *First Part*, the Hell of Deceit in which the evil magician is female rather than male, and Spenser's victim Amoret is split into two figures, Pamphilia and Amphilanthus. Starke, 'Love's True Habit', has demonstrated Wroth's critique of Sidney's *Countess of Pembroke's Arcadia* in her refusal to present a male character's cross-dressing as debasing to his masculinity.

[18] These early representations are surveyed in Kinney, 'Introduction', to Kinney (ed.), *Ashgate Critical Essays*, volume IV: *Mary Wroth*, pp. xv–xvi.

frontispiece similarly trumpets the public importance of Wroth's familial identity as a Sidney to the *Urania*: it was written by the 'lady Mary
Wroath, daughter to the right Noble Robert Earle of Leicester. And Neece
to the ever famous, and renowned Sr Phillips [sic] Sidney knight. And to
the most excellent Lady Mary Countesse of Pembroke late deceased'.[19] In
its stubborn insistence on the biographical/familial identity of the author,
this cartouche, together with the title of Wroth's romance, moves prospective readers towards an author-centred reading of the text dissonant with
a new textual approach and similarly dissonant with a feminist ideology
that would liberate Wroth's writings from a familial identity perceived as
limiting her to a domestic sphere.[20]

Wroth's aristocratic and specifically Sidneian familial network contests
a mindset that would separate the biographical from the larger political
sphere.[21] Wroth's familial identity as a Sidney in fact propelled her into
the powerful faction of Sidney-Herberts consistently advocating Protestant
causes in Europe against James's pro-Spanish policies. Deriving ideological
authority from Sir Philip Sidney's death from wounds incurred defending
the Protestant cause in the Netherlands, Wroth's father Robert, her aunt
Mary Sidney, and her cousin William Herbert, Earl of Pembroke were all
united in a political faction supporting military intervention in Europe
for the Protestant cause, especially in the matter of Bohemia, where the
brief rule of the Protestant King Ferdinand and his wife Elizabeth (James's
daughter) was overturned by Catholic forces. This interventionist faction
directly opposed the pacifist and predominantly pro-Spanish policies of
King James. Josephine Roberts's extensive 'Political Contexts' in the *First
Part* launched this context in a political reading of the *Urania* in which
Amphilanthus's attempts, in his role as Holy Roman Emperor, to unify
the Western world reflected the political crisis of the fractured Europe of
the early seventeenth century.[22] Topical markers identify Amphilanthus as
a version of William Herbert, third Earl of Pembroke, Lord Chamberlain

---

[19] Maureen Quilligan has ably argued the landscape depicted below the cartouche represents an
'idealized family seat', legitimating the authority of the Sidneys in feudal terms in their own right as
aristocratic land-holders (*Incest and Agency*, pp. 181–5, esp. p. 181). For the importance of her family
connection to Wroth's *Urania*, see also Lamb, 'Biopolitics'.

[20] In this volume, Ramona Wray expresses this concern for Elizabeth Cary's work. Wynne-Davies,
*Women Writers and Familial Discourse*, has described the political meanings of Wroth's *Love's Victory*
as a means of breaking out of an authorship based on kinship to one 'newly formed from authorial
commonality' (p. 103).

[21] Salzman, 'The Strang[e] Constructions of Mary Wroth's *Urania*', notes that the personal cannot
be separated from the political at this time (p. 118). Zurcher, 'Ethics', points out that aristocratic
women derived substantial power and political access through their familial identities.

[22] Roberts, 'Critical Introduction', in *First Part*, pp. xxxix–l.

to James. As king of the Romans and later elected Holy Roman Emperor, Amphilanthus was actively engaged in restoring rightful kings to their thrones and uniting Western countries. But it was felt that Pembroke could have been doing more. Roberts observed that Amphilanthus's active role as king of the Romans may veil 'a desire for Pembroke to assume a more public and assertive role as leader of the Puritan faction'.[23] There has been much scholarship done since Roberts's study, and scholarly discussions of the political implications of Wroth's *Urania* remain a strength in Wroth studies.[24]

In her current analysis of Wroth's romance as advocating the cause of international Protestantism, Julie Crawford, like Josephine Roberts, makes significant use of Wroth's topical allusions.[25] This technique of topicality runs directly counter to new textual as well as any feminist approaches that discourage the use of biographical contexts and author-centred meanings. Decoding topical allusions tends to be uncomfortable for modern readers. The full context necessary to decode an allusion is sometimes no longer available; and readings sometimes use allusions to reduce the meanings of a text. Some allusions are deliberately opaque. Yet there is no doubt that topical allusions were part of a sophisticated early modern repertoire. In his *Arcadia* Philip Sidney, for example, clearly meant for readers to understand the stranger-knight Philisides (Phili + Sid) as a version of himself. Rather than shutting down or fixing meanings, however, Philisides's mysterious melancholy raised more questions than it answered. Was it self-parody? Was it an appeal to an unresponsive beloved? Was it an implicit plea for Queen Elizabeth to excuse his unwanted advice against a marriage with the Duke d'Alençon? More important than the referents themselves is their function within Sidney's romance. While deliberately opaque to all but familial insiders, the function of Philisides as a self-referent evokes provocative contexts beyond the romance. To ignore Sidney's allusion to himself, or to shut down its meaning as only a reference to himself, is to miss out on a core operation of the text.

[23]  Roberts, 'Critical Introduction', in *First Part*, p. xlvii, n. 34.
[24]  In addition to the analysis of gendered power dynamics in Danielle Clarke, *The Politics of Early Modern Women's Writing*, there are specific discussions of Jacobean politics: Paul Salzman's essays, including his analysis of the Elizabethan and Jacobean courts in his 'Contextual Biography' to *Mary Wroth's Poetry: An Electronic Edition*; Wynne-Davies, '"For *Worth*, Not Weakness, Makes in Use but One"'; Sanchez, Ch. 5 '"Love, Thou Dost Master Me": Political Masochism in Mary Wroth's Urania', *Erotic Subjects*, pp. 117–44; Bassnett, 'The Politics of Election'.
[25]  I am grateful to Julie Crawford for her paper 'Wroth's Cabinets', delivered at Shakespeare Association in March 2013, and for her subsequent sharing of her chapter 'Wroth's Cabinets' from her current book project (now published as *Mediatrix*).

The topical allusions within the *Urania* also represent an intended operation on its readers. Much of the most obvious topicality of the *Urania* is not only political, but also personal, especially in the unwavering love of Pamphilia (with clear topical referents to Wroth) for the fickle Amphilanthus (with clear topical referents to Pembroke). This personal aspect is indisputable, signalled in various ways. The near-anagram Rosindy for Pamphilia's oldest brother obviously alludes, on some level, to 'Robert Sidney', Wroth's oldest brother. It is surely no accident that the name of Forsandurus for Amphilanthus's former tutor is a near-anagram for Pembroke's former tutor Hugh Sanford, or that Dettareus's odd disclosure that his daughter is exactly twenty-four years younger than himself and born under the same planet corresponds to the exact same time-difference between the ages of Mary Wroth and her father. Pamphilia's slip into a personal pronoun reveals that her narrative of Lindamira is topical to herself, as details in the *Urania* signify that Pamphilia is in some sense topical to Wroth. Contemporaries such as the gossipy John Chamberlain had no doubts about the presence of topicality, nor did Edward Denny, who (injudiciously I might add) made a public display of a purported topical reference to himself as the father who attempted to murder his own daughter for adultery. He addressed Wroth as 'Pamphilia' in the title of his poem disparaging her authorship: 'To Pamphilia from the father-in-law of Seralius'. Yet topical allusions within Wroth's romance often deliberately unsettle interpretation, even as they invite it. An incident may begin by signalling topical referents but then veer off into the fantastic. There are always discrepancies: Pembroke, for example, was never a Holy Roman Emperor, and what he could do as a leader of an interventionist anti-Catholic faction was limited by King James's pacific policies.

We know all this. The explicit topical allusions in the *Urania* have been pointed out many times, and they are convincingly well set out for example in Roberts's 'Personal Contexts'.[26] But a lot of readers don't like it, and for good reason. It runs against the grain of what has been taught to readers for decades, that is, *never* to confuse a narrator with an author, or to try to read an author's life or an author's personal feelings into a literary text. And once critics, or even worse students, start to collapse these categories, the consequent readings are appalling. Some students collapse author and narrator entirely, to perceive Wroth as simply a deserted woman pouring out her unmediated feelings in her writing; this perception is further over-simplified by the sense that women of a previous

---

[26] Roberts, 'Personal Contexts' in 'Critical Introduction', *First Part*, pp. lxix–xcvii.

time (as opposed to freer modern times) were necessarily neurotic and repressed by a patriarchal society that required them to be 'chaste, silent, and obedient'.[27] Such bad or naïve topical readings are embarrassing. The solid biographical material enabling good or sophisticated topical readings of various characters has largely disappeared with time, as have the skills necessary to read a sophisticated topical text. So why should we bring them up? Why shouldn't we discount topicality, along with a focus on the love interest of Pamphilia and Amphilanthus, and move on as though the *Urania* were a more modern text that did not invite such readings? What is the point of acknowledging topical allusions at all?

Perhaps a better question is to ask how we may move out of a naïve reading (i.e. 'Wroth was really upset when Pembroke deserted her') to something we can respect? There is more to be said than the brief point I mention in my introduction, that the answer for me lies in the *function* of the immersion of the plots of Wroth's romance in the real lives not only of herself but of her contemporaries. From Malory through Sidney, representations of the unhappiness of arranged marriages were a staple of romance. For Wroth, however, depictions of the torments of women (there are literally scores of them) suffering in arranged marriages are not hypothetical. Through topical allusions she is insisting that they are real, not to relieve her feelings in some way, not to exhibit or to indulge herself, but to discover ways of dealing with the situation, or if no respite is possible, at least of enduring it. The various ways that women characters respond provide a range of alternatives, a play of possibility. More than managing painful feelings, the *Urania* asserts the need for change. In the metaphor advanced by Jennifer Carrell, 'romance is a magic mirror that produces distorted images of the truth; these fictional images, in turn, have the power to alter – at least temporarily – the reality they partially reflect'.[28] Wroth's numerous female protagonists who continue to love one man even after they are married to another cannot be dismissed as fictional constructs. While it is naïve and even vulgar to interpret too closely, to reduce the play of allusion to correspondences lying on the surface, the sense that referents exist (whether they can now or even could then be reliably identified) creates 'an autobiographical effect',[29] a testing of its fictions for some emotional 'truth'. The large extent to which Wroth's romance plays with this effect represents, as I argue elsewhere, one of her most important contributions to the

---

[27] This is the title of a seminal book by Suzanne Hull, *Chaste, Silent, and Obedient* (1988).
[28] Carrell, 'A Pack of Lies', p. 102.
[29] This phrase was invented in another context by Skura, *Tudor Autobiography*, p. 27.

genre of romance.[30] Still, even so, is it less than academically respectable – perhaps a little embarrassing – to sense that beneath the artificiality of this sophisticated text lies what Helen Hackett has called 'a charge from the sense both of glimpsed confessions, and of . . . griefs and joys strongly felt'?[31] While political readings are undoubtedly central to the *Urania*, is it perhaps *safer* to focus only on political readings while denying or ignoring the personal ones? Do we need to be embarrassed, as feminists, as postmoderns, as committed academics, if we find in Wroth's romance what Hackett has proclaimed to be 'a passionate read'?[32]

## Feminist Ideologies and the Question of Pamphilia

The answer to that question just posed above is, apparently, 'yes'. Perhaps the greatest challenge that Wroth's *Urania* poses to modern readers is its representation of Pamphilia's constancy to the unfaithful Amphilanthus. This section discusses how a number of critics, primarily feminists, have taken positions on this issue with passion and verve. On the one hand, some perceive Pamphilia's insistence on constant love as a narrative of masochistic self-oppression, eliciting the most disappointing potential possible to the category of women writers. Others, on the other hand, perceive Pamphilia's constant love as a mode of independent self-definition, providing autonomy from a beloved's response as well as creating for Pamphilia (and presumably for Wroth) a productive role as poet.

A sympathetic response to Pamphilia's suffering over her lover's infidelities is, from one standpoint, utterly offensive to some current feminist ideologies. At stake is more than merely a reaction to a character in a romance. It reifies a concern, eloquently expressed by Hurley and Goodblatt, that 'too frequently essays focused on women can be too narrowly focused on gender issues and become a little like laments about victimization'.[33] Consequently, in sharply divided responses among reputable and well-published critics, anti-Pamphilia feelings run unusually high. In Christina Luckyj's reading, Wroth's portrayal of Pamphilia's constant passion as 'self-indulgent and self-destructive' casts into question her character's identification as an author figure.[34] Similarly, Danielle Clarke describes Pamphilia's constancy as a 'ludicrous adherence to the uncaring and careless Amphilanthus', which creates of her 'a stock romance figure, with all of the mock-exaggeration

[30] Lamb, 'Topicality in Mary Wroth's *Countess of Montgomery's Urania*'.
[31] Hackett, *Women and Romance Fiction*, p. 182.    [32] *Ibid.*
[33] Hurley and Goodblatt, 'Preface' to *Women Editing/Editing Women*, p. xii.
[34] Luckyj, 'The Politics of Genre', p. 259.

that this suggests'.[35] Finally, most explicitly, Melissa Sanchez characterizes Pamphilia as 'a deluded, self-dramatizing mess, who willfully embraces her own misery'.[36]

Sanchez's larger argument is political. Interpreting James's self-description as a husband to his people as feminizing his subjects, Sanchez uses relationships in the *Urania* to argue that these debasing power dynamics register Wroth's criticism of monarchy. In her words, 'by stressing the masochistic elements of female desire, Wroth insists on the irrationality of the political bonds for which love was one of the period's most common analogues'.[37] This elaborate allegory conflating love relationships with allegiances of subjects to sovereigns does not account for the fact that, from the beginning to the end of the *Urania*, sympathetic characters are engaged in the restoration of rightful kings against usurpers or rebels. While Wroth's romance criticizes weak kings (especially James), it strongly espouses monarchy as an institution. Every major character is either the monarch of a country, or married to one. Underlying the issue of the politics of the *Urania*, which deserves continued discussion beyond what is possible here, is another question. Is an allegorical reading of Pamphilia's love for Amphilanthus as *really* about a political relationship between subject and sovereign more palatable to those modern readers who would not wish their Wroth to be fixated on erotic passion? And even if we would decide that Pamphilia's passion pertains primarily to politics, would we want to base our conclusions on a dismissal of the primary protagonist of the *Urania* as simply a 'mess'? Perhaps the love interests of the *Urania* seem to move a bit too close to those of Harlequin romances for our comfort zone? Here I would like to take the opportunity to voice my concern about what I see as a recent discounting of the personal, of the topical, and especially a discounting of love, particularly of heterosexual love, that would change the *Urania* from a nuanced and complex meditation, a unresolved and unresolvable debate, on the value of the constant love of Pamphilia for an irredeemably inconstant Amphilanthus, to a simple flat dismissal.

There are of course numerous recent critics who line up on the other side of this divide. Positive perceptions of Pamphilia are still mainstream in recent criticism. In one article Amelia Zurcher characterizes Pamphilia's constancy as 'heroic', precisely because of the difficulties she encounters; she defends Pamphilia also as the 'most fully realized figure for Wroth's authorial persona', expressing 'a kind of agency' in her self-awareness and 'expressive

---

[35] Danielle Clarke, *Politics*, p. 216.    [36] Sanchez, *Erotic Subjects*, p. 135.    [37] *Ibid.*, p. 118.

power'.[38] In another, Zurcher states that Pamphilia 'outdoes everyone else in the romance in her single-mindedness, which is clearly meant to be admirable'.[39] Paul Salzman's 'Biographical Introduction' to his online edition describes her as 'the wholly admirable Pamphilia'.[40] Julie Crawford validates Pamphilia's constancy as a political as well as a personal value.[41] There are others. On this side of the argument, one might point out that Pamphilia remains high in the esteem of other characters. In contrast to Antissia, she is consistently commended as a model of discretion in her ability to conceal her feelings. The narrator expresses frequent admiration for her, for example praising her 'infinite and just passions', and her 'hart as great, ore farr excelling anys, soe surpassing all, yet more truly subject to love than thos who made more outward blaze of that power, which ought onely to be secrett' (Second Part, pp. 276–7). Constancy is a clear-cut value, even a mode of liberation, in the first of the three enchantments structuring the First Part, for Pamphilia's constancy frees lovers imprisoned by the inferior ways of loving according to the more traditional codes of Cupid and Venus. (In the second enchantment, however, constancy is not enough, and Pamphilia herself is imprisoned in a magic Theatre.)

All of this being said, the critics dismissive of Pamphilia's passion are not completely wrong. Just as the frontispiece offers various winding paths through the landscape, so Wroth's Urania offers several vistas on the subject of love; and anti-Pamphilia animus is not entirely unfounded in this self-critical romance. As is almost universally cited beginning with Roberts's introduction to the First Part, the sensible Urania herself counsels Pamphilia against constancy, arguing that ''tis pittie . . . that ever that fruitlesse thing Constancy was taught you as a vertue' (p. 470). Urania's own narrative represents an alternative to Pamphilia's constancy; for, magically cured of her love for Parselius, she is happily married to her second love Steriamus. The conversation between Urania and Pamphilia is, however, a dialogue that opens out rather than shutting down the question of Pamphilia's constancy. Pamphilia mounts a thought-provoking defence: 'To leave him for being false, would shew my love was not for his sake, but mine owne, that because he loved me, I therefore loved him . . . O no, deere Cousen I loved him for himselfe, and would have loved him had hee not loved mee, and will love though he despise me' (p. 470). And Urania's motive for arguing against constancy was not entirely disinterested; she spoke out of concern

---

[38] Zurcher, 'Ethics', pp. 93, 96.       [39] Zurcher Sandy, 'Pastoral', p. 107.
[40] Salzman, 'Biographical Introduction', Mary Wroth's Poetry: An Electronic Edition, p. 10.
[41] Crawford, Mediatrix, pp. 160–73. Crawford's political reading does not discount the value of Pamphilia's love for Amphilanthus.

for her friend's health: 'Urania seeing her passion, and the assurance of her end if thus she continued . . . thus spake' (p. 467).

Early in Wroth criticism and continuing in a recent essay, Maureen Quilligan expands on Pamphilia's self defence, asserting that it is precisely because her love is not requited that Pamphilia can express an 'autonomous desire' independent of her lover's response. This insistence on constancy becomes, for her, not a delusion but a chosen act of 'willful self-definition'. It is in the 'gap between husband and beloved' that Pamphilia can create herself, against the 'entirely different set of terms' that would come into play if she succeeded in living as Amphilanthus's wife.[42] As Quilligan observes, it is easy, in a discussion of virtuous-sounding constancy, to lose track of how radical this resolve in fact is. For Pamphilia, as for other women characters such as Limena, emotional loyalty to one's beloved trumps devotion even to one's husband. This is quite shocking for its time and perhaps even for today. The fact that it is characterized as a virtue, both by Urania and even by dismissive critics, suggests that Wroth was at least partially successful in promoting a woman's right freely to choose whom she loves, against the pressures of society and her family.

Yet it is also true that through much of the *Urania* Pamphilia suffers for her love. And she writes about it. Does this make of her a deluded victim or a self-critical author figure? Do we sympathize or do we advise her to 'just get over it'? The respectable academic argument, to which classroom teachers might guide their students, is of course that the *Urania* itself presents a range of alternative ways of loving, and a range of attitudes towards unwavering constant love. What is significant, perhaps, is not which critics are right or wrong, but why this debate is so heated and why the divisions are so sharp. The disagreements between scholars of Wroth's *Urania* are, in my experience, also played out in the classroom; and for this reason Wroth's romance represents an ideal text for a college class. Students take sides, and the opinions that they express really matter to them. Pamphilia's passion becomes a vehicle for the exploration of their own values and cultural assumptions, as well as a way of encountering a sensibility from the past. The openness of this text evokes passionate responses. A parallel may be found in constructions of the character Hamlet. Precisely because the play *Hamlet* offers various self-contradictory cues to his character, readers (and actors) must choose to invest, intellectually and also emotionally, in a version of Hamlet that is 'theirs'. Wroth's *Urania*, and other works by

---

[42] Quilligan, 'Lady Mary Wroth', p. 273; Quilligan, 'The Constant Subject', p. 321; and see Quilligan, 'Allegory and Female Agency'.

early modern women as well, challenge our understandings of ourselves as readers, by providing an opportunity for introspection of our own responses to early modern sensibilities. They also challenge our understanding of ourselves as feminists, opening out feminist ideologies in all their plurality and productive contradictions. The excellent opportunity provided by passionately opposed responses, even by readers who share feminist values, is a circumstance 'devoutly to be wished',[43] as early women's texts emerge from the archives to engage a wider and more diverse readership.

[43]  I am, of course, here quoting Hamlet's famous 'To be or not to be' soliloquy.

CHAPTER 12

# Anthologizing Early Modern Women's Poetry
## Women Poets of the English Civil War

*Sarah C. E. Ross and Elizabeth Scott-Baumann*

Since the first interventions of modern feminist scholars in early modern literary studies, the anthology has been an essential vehicle for the recuperation of women writers, offering a selection of women's voices and getting them into classrooms and bookstores more quickly than is possible with a comprehensive 'complete works' edition.[1] The distillation of early modern women's writing into the exemplary *poetic* anthology is in fact a tradition dating back to the eighteenth century, as we have explored in the Introduction to this volume: George Ballard's *Memoirs of Several Ladies of Great Britain* (1752) is a precursor in its presentation of early modern female authorial accomplishment to anthologies such as Colman and Thornton's *Poems by Eminent Ladies* (1755), or Alexander Dyce's *Specimens of British Poetesses* (1825). But even as feminist editorial scholarship has moved away from a biographical agenda, the centrality of the anthology has hardly diminished, with recent anthologies taking on forms reflective of shifting theoretical concerns. Helen Ostovich and Elizabeth Sauer's *Reading Early Modern Women* (2004) arranges short extracts of women's texts according to the diverse and often non-'literary' genres in which they participate, while Jill Seal Millman and Gillian Wright's *Early Modern Women's Manuscript Poetry* (2005) foregrounds a single, specific manuscript collection for each of the poets it anthologizes, and presents its poems in original spelling, punctuation, and layout.

The ongoing popularity of the anthology in packaging early modern women's writing for student consumption is of course integrally bound up in its cultural and economic pre-eminence in making literary texts widely available and in bestowing canonical status upon those that are chosen. Only a limited number of early modern women's poems have found

---

[1] See, for example, Travitsky (ed.), *The Paradise of Women* (1981); Greer et al. (eds.), *Kissing the Rod* (1988); Stevenson and Davidson (eds.), *Early Modern Women Poets* (2001).

their way into the hegemonic Norton and comparable anthologies,[2] and so a powerful conceptual and economic means of redressing the paucity of women's texts in the mainstream classroom is to meet like with like, presenting a counter-tradition of women's writing in an equally affordable form. But the uncomfortable relationship between the generic, stylistic, and material diversity of early modern women's writing and the normative model of the mainstream anthology has generated a number of productive explorations of the gender politics of anthologizing. Margaret Ezell has drawn attention to the conventional anthology's assumption of 'anachronistic and restrictive' models of literary history.[3] Ramona Wray called in 2000 for 'a new "politics of selection"', a hefty contextual apparatus, and a playful presentational framework' in anthologizing the early modern female voice 'if readers are to gain a complex understanding of the literary output of women in the early modern period' – a challenge that a volume such as *Reading Early Modern Women* could be seen as taking up.[4] Danielle Clarke's equally influential exploration of feminist editorial principles advocates 'editorial strategies which attend as much to *textuality* as to authorship'.[5] Nigel Smith has argued at the other end of the critical spectrum, and not without controversy, for a frankly populist anthology of the women's poetry of the period which offers 'a "good read"'.[6]

These are just some of the explorations of anthologizing early modern women, and related questions of editorial practice, that inform our own forthcoming *Women Poets of the English Civil War*, the focus of this chapter. This is an anthology of poetry by 'the five most accomplished women poets of the mid-seventeenth century', to cite our initial proposal to its publishers, Manchester University Press, and it includes substantial selections of poetry by Hester Pulter, Anne Bradstreet, Katherine Philips, Margaret Cavendish, and Lucy Hutchinson. The anthology is focused exclusively on poetry, at the risk of reinforcing conventional literary hierarchies, but we had one simple, if slightly surprising, starting point. For none of the five poets included in our anthology is (or was) there a single, affordable, clear-text edition in which student readers could encounter the poetic texts, nor were they sufficiently represented in the large mainstream anthologies which we continue to set for our students. The first full edition of Hester

---

[2] This situation is changing to a degree, but not comprehensively enough to remove the need for a parallel anthology. Elizabeth I, Mary Sidney, and Mary Wroth are all well represented in Greenblatt (gen. ed.), *The Norton Anthology*, 9th edn, but it contains only five Katherine Philips poems, and two by Margaret Cavendish (as well as two prose extracts).

[3] Ezell, *Writing Women's Literary History*, pp. 40–1.    [4] Wray, 'Anthologizing', p. 57.

[5] Danielle Clarke, 'Nostalgia', p. 189.    [6] Smith, 'The Rod and the Canon', p. 233.

Pulter's poetry was published in 2014, eighteen years after the discovery of her manuscript.[7] Lucy Hutchinson's exquisite elegies on the loss of her husband, some of the most readily teachable women's poems of the seventeenth century, remain available to students and teachers only in David Norbrook's diplomatic transcriptions of 1997, at least until the forthcoming publication of the Oxford *Works* poetry volumes.[8] Even the poems of Anne Bradstreet, Margaret Cavendish, and Katherine Philips suffer from varying degrees of limited and dated availability. Perhaps to our initial surprise, we found ourselves engaging in part in a programme of making available, the necessity of which had not disappeared in the twenty-first century.

Our potentially retrograde stance in selecting and editing *poems* in *Women Poets of the English Civil War* is not limited to a sole-genre focus: it also extends to thorough modernization of those poems. As teachers of women writers, we wanted students to close read these poems, and we and our colleagues found ourselves thwarted not only by the poems' lack of ready availability, but by the forms in which the limited – and scattered – texts did exist. We found ourselves *in this context* agreeing less with Danielle Clarke's call for a set of specifically gendered editorial practices than with her acknowledgement that 'there are dangers in driving a wedge between the conventions used for men and those for women, including . . . imbalances in presentation'.[9] In this context, we explicitly wanted students to encounter these women's poetry in the editorial form that they regularly encounter the most canonical of early modern male authors: Shakespeare, Marvell, Milton. Our text is, then, frankly populist, and in seeking specifically to bring texts out of the archives and into the classroom we found ourselves, like Pamela Hammons and Mary Ellen Lamb in the projects discussed in their chapters in this section, deliberately and strategically adopting mainstream editorial policies.

At the same time, however, our own textualist and historicist bents as literary-critical researchers – our awareness of scribal and social contexts, of textual variabilities and material manifestations – meant that we did not want entirely to efface the indicators of textual fragmentation, messiness, and contingency of poetry by women. If at all possible, we hoped to be able to introduce a non-specialist audience to these facets of the early modern woman's poem. Most acutely, we hoped to introduce them to

---

[7] *Lady Hester Pulter: Poems, Emblems, and 'The Unfortunate Florinda'*, ed. Eardley.

[8] Norbrook, 'Lucy Hutchinson's "Elegies"'; *The Works of Lucy Hutchinson*, gen. ed. Norbrook; available so far is Volume I: *The Translation of Lucretius*.

[9] Danielle Clarke, 'Nostalgia', p. 208.

the historicity of women's poetry *of the English Civil War*. This titular rubric is more than a convenient temporal shorthand: it points to the way in which all of the poetry gathered in the anthology is *of* the distinct literary environment of the mid seventeenth century, a period in which the revolutions in state politics and personal identities revolutionized literary production. Our primary challenges then, were as follows. How can we produce a self-consciously populist edition that does not altogether elide textual and contextual contingencies? Is it possible to produce a populist, mainstream anthology that does not subscribe to the anachronisms and restrictions characteristic of the genre, or is the populist anthology a truly intransigent beast?

## Flowers Not Weeds? Women and the Poem

The poem occupies a fraught and contested place in the editorial and anthological history of early modern women's writing, as a kind of crucible in which feminist arguments about literary values are tested. Virginia Woolf's evocative lament that no woman wrote a word of 'that extraordinary literature' of Elizabethan England, that no early modern woman 'was capable of song or sonnet', provided a provocation to a generation of feminist literary archaeologists seeking women's poems, including Greer and her co-editors of *Kissing the Rod*.[10] Woolf's search for women writers of 'extraordinary' (viz., poetic) literature, however, can also be held up as an emblem of a high literary focus that is itself problematic for the early modern woman writer. Ezell, Wray, and Danielle Clarke have issued just some of the most compelling calls to look beyond privileged literary forms in exploring women's writerly activity in the early modern period, and one of happiest outcomes of feminist literary scholarship's confluence with the historicism of the late 1980s and 1990s has been a push to discover and to acknowledge the diversity of the a-canonical forms in which women most frequently wrote. Religious texts, diaries, advice pieces, and letters are all modes of writing vital to our expanded sense of early modern women's 'literary' culture, as several chapters in this volume attest (see Felch, Trill, Elizabeth Clarke, Barnes). Suzanne Trill explores precisely the question of the critical categories that we use in retrieving women's texts from the archives; and Elizabeth Clarke highlights the unique generic properties of many women's texts, particularly those penned in a manuscript environment.

[10]   Woolf, *A Room of One's Own*, p. 39; and Greer et al. (eds.), *Kissing the Rod*, p. 31.

All happy critical confluences, however, necessarily effect other exclusions. Women did not write large quantities of 'high' literary poetry or, typically, define themselves as poets in the early modern period, at least before the print-published example of Katherine Philips; some early exceptions include Mary Wroth and perhaps Aemilia Lanyer. Notable new examples have, however, come to light: Hester Pulter's lyrics were uncovered in 1996, and Lucy Hutchinson's elegies and *Order and Disorder* were recuperated at around the same time. The attribution of a large cache of poetry to Elizabeth Melville in recent years reminds us that the process of retrieval out of the archives is far from complete, especially if that process is understood as more than a mere act of identification.[11] The corpus of early modern women's poetry has expanded in volume and character since Greer et al.'s *Kissing the Rod* or even Stevenson and Davidson's *Early Modern Women Poets*, and it is no longer sufficient to construe all seventeenth-century women as '*guerrilleras*' excluded from the 'sacred citadel' of male poetic traditions.[12] Conversely, it is also no longer possible to ignore the particularities of women's education and cultural capital in influencing their relationship to high literary traditions, or to assume that 'poet' in the seventeenth century was an ungendered category. '*[A]ccess* to literary forms . . . has a profoundly gendered history', in Sasha Roberts's words,[13] and as she and others have recognized, that gendered history is more complex and nuanced than a stark narrative of full inclusion or complete isolation.

An expanded corpus of early modern women's poetic writing, then, raises new questions, and invests older ones with a new urgency. Why *did* women write relatively little poetry, and in what intellectual and social exchanges does women's poetry emerge? Is the poetry that women write of the same kind – genre, form, style – as that of men? How does their poetry speak to the 'great' and more minor poetic works and traditions of the sixteenth and seventeenth centuries? And how does their poetry either reinforce or enable us to unpack such critical categories of enquiry and of aesthetic value, and to think about early modern poetry in a new way? Does their poetry in fact enable us to challenge and complicate the hegemonic literary tradition that the anthology has conventionally perpetuated – in relation to male poets as well as to women?

*Women Poets of the English Civil War* provided an opportunity to anthologize poems that would allow students and their tertiary teachers to explore these questions for themselves. We chose poems that would speak to the

---

[11] See *Poems of Elizabeth Melville*, ed. Jamie Reid Baxter.
[12] Greer et al. (eds.), *Kissing the Rod*, p. 1.
[13] Roberts, 'Women's Literary Capital', p. 247 (emphasis hers).

most-taught works of Donne, Herbert, Marvell, and Milton, and also those that would speak among themselves; those that articulate themselves most clearly in relation to canonical poetic traditions, and also those that do not. Specific genres, such as elegy, emerge as particularly important, as well as particularly diverse. Margaret Cavendish's 'Upon the funeral of my dear brother, killed in these unhappy wars', Hester Pulter's 'On the death of my dear and lovely daughter', and Lucy Hutchinson's elegies on the death of her husband are 'personal' as well as 'political', speaking to each other, to Katherine Philips's political poems, and to Anne Bradstreet's late poems of personal loss, as well as to the political-poetic articulations of Herrick, Marvell, and numerous royalist elegists. The retirement and friendship poems of Philips and Pulter are comparable to each other and to those of Cowley and Marvell; each speaks to the poetic 'mainstream', and also illustrates ways in which these tropes are, in some cases, feminized, enabling an expanded exploration of that central, evolving trope in seventeenth-century personal and political poetry. Female complaint and its relationship to the dialogue poem can be explored via Pulter's 'Complaint of Thames 1647' and Bradstreet's extended *A Dialogue Between Old England and New*. Margaret Cavendish's 'A Dialogue between the Body, and the Mind' is in the medieval tradition of dialogues between body and soul rather than in the vein of the contentious dialogue poem that was a popular Civil War genre, and her dialogues between mankind and hare or oak tree place her as a leading voice of environmental consciousness.

What emerges in our selection of poems – approximately twenty lyrics or extracts of longer poems for each author – is a corpus of poetry by mid-seventeenth-century women that is more extensive, more complex, and more formally diverse than scholars have recognized until recently. Lucy Hutchinson's translation of Lucretius' *De rerum natura*, excerpted in the anthology, is the first translation into English of a linguistically difficult, ideologically radical Latin poem; it can be read alongside Cavendish's different, but equally materialist, 'A World Made by Atoms' and 'Nature Calls a Council', and alongside Pulter's philosophically speculative lyrics. Hutchinson's *Order and Disorder*, also excerpted, is of interest as a comparator to Milton's *Paradise Lost* (as well as for its relationships to multiple other poetic modes, such as Philips's paradisal garden poetry); its biblical poetics are also usefully considered in comparison to Anne Bradstreet's Bartasian hexameral poems, *The Four Monarchies*. New critical insights into early modern women and the poem, in our own recent monographs and in important work by Susan Wiseman, Gillian Wright, and others, are based on poems that have not been readily accessible.[14] Anthologizing these poems in a single, affordable volume enables students and teachers to explore the poetic work that is continuing to challenge perceptions of seventeenth-century women poets as anomalies, isolates, or eccentric authors working outside the boundaries of 'high' literary traditions.

The poem is – or has been seen as – a high-status literary artefact in relation to which early modern women stand in a peculiarly tense and intriguing relationship, but one insight that women's poems provide is that the early modern poem is not always as 'high' a literary entity as is often assumed. Our notes direct readers to connections not only to Marvell, Milton, Donne, and Herrick, and to other women within the anthology, but to more 'minor' male poets and genres: the hexameral poems of Du Bartas, the emblems of Francis Quarles, and the anonymous royalist elegies of 1649. The expanded corpus of poetry anthologized in *Women Poets of the English Civil War* both suggests a closer relationship to hegemonic poetic culture than has been assumed and, at the same time, encourages us to expand the category of poetry itself, and not only in relation to women writers. If our anthology was born in part out of a lack of space in the pre-existing structures of the Norton and comparable anthologies, one hope is that a single-genre anthology of women's poetry can both stand close enough to Norton that it can be readily adopted, and provide enough sense of a counter-narrative that it begins to expand and challenge the parameters of a narrow literary tradition on which that sort of anthology is based.

## Poetic Form and Editorial Policy

The questions around women poets' engagement with poetic forms and traditions high and low chime with a renewed interest in poetic formalism in early modern studies more broadly: a return to close reading of the rich linguistic and structural features of a poem, the 'sounds and shapes of the text',[15] and often an analysis of forms as they act within and are shaped by political and social history. Renewed interest in poetic formalism has highlighted the extent to which the reception and reproduction of early modern women's writing in recent decades is characterized not only by a historicist focus on non-'literary' genres, but also by what Danielle

---

[14] Ross, *Women, Poetry, and Politics*; Scott-Baumann, *Forms of Engagement*; Wiseman, *Conspiracy and Virtue*; Wiseman (ed.), *Early Modern Women and the Poem*; Wright, *Producing Women's Poetry*.
[15] Derek Attridge, qtd. in Roberts, 'Women's Literary Capital', p. 247.

Clarke and Marie-Louise Coolahan describe as an 'evasion of discussion of form', and particularly of formal poetic qualities.[16] Clarke and Coolahan suggest that this evasion may be because of a tendency not to take women's 'decisions about form seriously *as choices*'; their call to attend to women's formal choices echo those of Sasha Roberts, and of Elizabeth Scott-Baumann in her engagement of a 'feminist formalism, or a formalist feminism'.[17] Clarke and Coolahan's subtle re-readings of Anne Southwell's lyrics in light of her literary-critical writings reveal just how much close formalist reading remains to be done on women's poems that have been in circulation for (in Southwell's case) almost twenty years, and how new that close reading feels.

Rich formalist readings of poetic texts are very often made possible only through the processes of intensive editorial scholarship. (Clarke and Coolahan's reading of Southwell is an exception here, but illustrates what might be more widely possible if a new, modernized edition of Southwell were available.) Nigel Smith associates the rise of new formalism in mainstream early modern studies with the fulfilment of several major 'complete works' editorial projects after 2000 (the Longman Dryden, Marvell, and Donne; the Oxford Milton; and the Cambridge Jonson), and notes the potential 'stimulus to close textual reading from the digital humanities environment for new texts'.[18] Clarke and Coolahan refer in passing to 'the enumeration of formal matters required by the editing process' in their 'brief account of the (non) history of form' in the field of early modern women's writing,[19] and editorial scholarship need not only promote the bare identification of form or mode (sonnet, dream vision, complaint). As any editor will attest, editorial scholarship is inclined not only to the identification of form in broad terms, but to the intensive engagement with the intricacies of its exposition and development. To pursue the musical analogy: any act of editing is an act of interpretation, a kind of 'performance' of a text; and as any musical performer will attest, the interpretation of a work in order to perform requires an interrogation of a musical – or poetic – line and overall form more intimate and intense than the act of listening (or reading).

---

[16] Clarke and Coolahan, 'Gender, Reception, and Form', p. 151.
[17] Clarke and Coolahan, 'Gender, Reception, and Form', p. 151; Roberts, 'Women's Literary Capital'; Scott-Baumann, *Forms of Engagement*, esp. p. 9.
[18] *Dryden: Selected Poems*, ed. Hammond and Hopkins (2007), *The Poems of Andrew Marvell*, ed. Smith (2003); *The Complete Poems of John Donne*, ed. Robbins (2010); *The Cambridge Ben Jonson*, ed. Bevington, Butler, and Donaldson (2012); *The Complete Works of John Milton*, ed. Cullington et al. (2008–). Nigel Smith, 'Foreword' to Burton and Scott-Baumann (eds.), *The Work of Form*, pp. vii–xv (p. xi).
[19] Clarke and Coolahan, 'Gender, Reception, and Form', pp. 149, 145.

If any act of editing requires formalist interrogation of a text, however, making close formalist readings of women's poetry possible for a wider audience is in our view dependent on a very particular kind of editorial scholarship. Our own experiences as classroom teachers are those of countless colleagues: a student presented with an old-spelling version of a woman's sonnet, for example a Mary Wroth sonnet taken from Josephine Roberts's wonderful old-spelling edition, to read alongside a Shakespeare sonnet from Norton, Oxford, or countless other readily available modernized editions will immediately and falsely believe that early modern women couldn't spell and that men could; that women's punctuation was erratic and men's wasn't; that women were ill-educated and men weren't. Even a reader who of course consciously realizes that there are editorial factors at play will be less consciously affected by the different presentation of male and female writer. As Leah Marcus reflects in her chapter in this volume: 'Whether appropriately or not, the modern-spelling Shakespeares have set a standard for other authors of the period', and 'Modern spelling, or at least the availability of modern-spelling editions, makes an author appear more like Shakespeare, which is to say more canonical' (p. 143).[20] To invite students to read women's poems in genuine conversation and comparison with those of canonical men, we need to meet like with like: to present them with texts that have been afforded mainstream editorial parity, whatever the limitations of mainstream editorial protocol may be.

Editorial parity via modernization is not only an issue of the perception of canonicity, the perception that a poem *deserves* a formalist reading: it also makes that kind of close reading possible, and not only for our students. The process of editing *Women Poets of the English Civil War* has confirmed with striking intensity how difficult – how obscuring – it can be for readers including ourselves to read a poem in only an original material or diplomatic transcription context. Poems that we have worked with for over a decade in manuscript and diplomatic transcription appeared quite differently in our modernized texts, and the need to be able to 'turn down the noise' of the diplomatic transcription for a student as well as a scholarly audience struck us afresh. Pulter's moving elegy on the death of her daughter Jane, for example, has received some critical attention since Peter Davidson's notice of it in the *Times Literary Supplement* in 1999 for its possible debts to or influence on Andrew Marvell's *The Nymph Complaining for the Death of her Fawn*.[21] One of its intriguing features is an

---

[20] See also Marcus in her 'Confessions of a Reformed Uneditor (II)': 'the act of modernisation makes a statement about the canonicity of the author in question' (p. 1076).
[21] Davidson, 'Green Thoughts'.

extended simile, comparing pox on her dying daughter's skin to the blood of a dying stag on fresh snow, that has clearly been added to the poem after its original composition. In critical work on the poem, the intriguing materiality of this politicized simile's insertion has largely taken precedence over formalist discussion of the poem.[22] Our modernization of the lyric for this anthology draws fresh attention to its intricate formal structure: its anaphoric reliance on the phrase 'Twice hath' (the poem is ostensibly written two years after her daughter's death); and a delicately understated double turn in its final line, 'I turned a Niobe as she turned earth'. Through the modernized text in our anthology, readers will be able to explore these formal features, and (via our annotations) to expand upon the substantial literary tradition of the poetic Niobe into which Pulter is stepping, and the lyric's place in the tradition of women's – and men's – elegies on personal and political states, a tradition in which it deserves inclusion.

The feeling that we had not read poems such as this one qua poems until we got to know them as modernizing editors is echoed in Pamela Hammons's chapter in this volume on editing and modernizing Katherine Austen's *Book M* for a student audience. Hammons describes how, despite having worked on Austen for twenty years, the 'arduous process of modernizing *Book M* taught me that I had seriously underestimated Austen as a writer – particularly as a poet' (p. 240). Modernization for Hammons is a crucial act of poetic interpretation – and if we are flat-footed readers, then we would hazard that most of our students are. In the context of the exciting and enormously rewarding material turn in early modern studies and editorial practice there remains a concurrent need to make women's poetry available in ways that make it easy to explore the verbal, imagistic, and formal qualities of a poem, and its participation in the cultural aesthetics of its day. To revisit the musical analogy for the final time, students and scholars need to be able to encounter women's poems in full symphony-orchestra renditions, not just on period instruments, because whatever its distortions and anachronisms, a full symphony-orchestra sound is what our ear is attuned to.

These, then, are the challenges and perceived needs behind our core editorial principles in *Women Poets of the English Civil War*: to modernize spelling and punctuation; to regularize capitalizations, italicizations, and orthographical idiosyncrasies; to annotate at a level that aims to be helpful but uncluttered. We seek, in other words, to produce texts that resemble Norton style in their surface features; however, we *are* committed to a

---

[22] This critical work includes Ross, *Women, Poetry, and Politics*, pp. 148–52.

textual specificity and acknowledged collation that is (in our view) more rigorous than that adopted by Norton and many comparable anthologies.[23] Choice of copytext is identified for every poem, and all variations beyond spelling or punctuation between our copytext and the selected variants are identified in the quite extensive collation notes. Collation notes are relegated to the back of the volume – we recognize the potential for them to generate more white noise for the uninitiated reader – but they are there for the most informed and interested users of the volume, and because they are the connection to textual and historical intricacies in which we, as specialist scholars, retain a deep interest.

These editorial decisions about copytexts and collation were, in the end, the most challenging for us, from an ideological as well as a practical point of view. Spelling and punctuation are (arguably, of course) surface features that are very often already far from authorial or originary, altered by scribes or in printing houses.[24] Collation, however, not only carries the spectre of the ideal, composite text, but also the potential to elide aspects of a copytext that can speak very powerfully to variant contexts and variant iterations. Of particular import in our case, variant copytexts speak to variant political moments, moments in which these are poems *of the English Civil War*. Rendering accurately the poems' political engagements became our greatest editorial challenge.

## Collating Texts and Editing Contexts: *Women Poets of the English Civil War*

Notwithstanding our declared commitment to presenting clean, modernized texts in this anthology, we had no desire to revert to outdated notions of 'ideal', composite texts, or to ignore the insights of the new textualism that has changed the terrain of mainstream editorial theory in the last half of the twentieth century (see the Introduction to this volume). As scholars who are ourselves deeply interested in scribal transmission, we have a keen sense that early modern poems often exist in multiple versions, where no one is definitively more authoritative than any other. Even new formalism in its best scholarly instantiations is not narrow and restrictive, and does not elide the historical context or even the material features of a text in transmission. Formalist approaches in the twenty-first century incorporate 'historically-informed detail', and the pressure to reconcile history and

---

[23] An important influence on our collation practice was Paul Salzman's excellent *Early Modern Women's Writing: An Anthology*.

[24] See Eardley, "'I haue not time to point y$^r$ booke'".

form is something that early modern women's writing can demonstrate to mainstream new formalism, as Mark Rasmussen, Sasha Roberts, and others have recognized.[25]

It is perhaps a relatively new recognition that early modern women's texts often exist in several and competing versions: there can be multiple possible copytexts, and the early modern editorial histories of women's texts are complex, as chapters by Susan Felch, Danielle Clarke, Suzanne Trill, Marie-Louise Coolahan, and others in this volume explore.[26] Hester Pulter is the only one of our five poets whose texts exist in a single, manuscript iteration – and unsurprisingly, her poems were therefore the easiest to deal with from an editorial point of view. Katherine Philips sits at the other end of the spectrum in her notoriously complex textual history, with two printed editions of contested degrees of authorial sanction, an early autograph manuscript (known as Tutin), and several other manuscript volumes, including the important Rosania manuscript compiled after her death.[27] Anne Bradstreet's poetry was printed in two highly variant versions: the poems in the second, *Several Poems* (1678), may or may not have been 'corrected by the author' as its title page declares (and not least because she was long dead at the time of its publication). While much of Lucy Hutchinson's poetry existed only in manuscript until the twentieth century, her major poem *Order and Disorder* was published during her lifetime in a short, anonymous form as well as circulating among relatives at least in a longer manuscript version. And Margaret Cavendish may have sought to monumentalize her own authorship in print, but this did not prevent her from significant alteration of her poems, not least their metre and rhyme.

The textual complexity of our poets' corpora is, in many instances, clearly reflective of several specific political moments. Bradstreet's *A Dialogue between Old England and New*, for example, takes up the Civil War genre of the dialogue poem, popular for political comment and debate, and the poem is starkly political in parts of the first version printed in 1650. It contains a vivid description of the treatment of Nonconformist preachers:

> These prophets' mouths (alas the while) was stopped,
> Unworthily, some backs whipped, and ears cropped;
> Their reverent cheeks did bear the glorious marks
> Of stinking, stigmatizing, Romish clerks.

---

[25]  Smith, 'Foreword', p. xi; Rasmussen (ed.), *Renaissance Literature and its Formal Engagements*, p. 9; Roberts, 'Feminist Criticism'.

[26]  Recent scholarship such as these chapters complicates Ramona Wray's suggestion in 2000 that 'where male-authored texts arrive with an arsenal of manuscript, folio and quarto versions, women's texts are normally confined to a single leaf' ('Anthologizing', p. 56).

[27]  For details, see Marie-Louise Coolahan's chapter in this volume, pp. 179–181.

These lines, however, are softened and shortened in 1678, where the description is limited to: 'Some lost their livings, some in prison pent, / Some fined, from house and friends to exile went' (lines 129–30). Several other revisions to the 1678 version of the poem seem to 'tone down' the political engagements of the 1650 text, and in this case, it seemed vital to us to reproduce the 1650 text, even if the 1678 one might have been 'corrected by the author'. The decision to prioritize the first version of the poem is based not on authorial intention, which is elusive, but on a desire to represent the poem in its most immediate and acutely political iteration. It is also a decision to edit her as a poet *of the English Civil War*, crucially informed by political events in her native England, rather than as the first female American poet, a competing critical and pedagogical narrative, and one that the Boston-printed 1678 edition can be seen as inaugurating.

Considerations such as these led us to use *The Tenth Muse* (1650) as the copytext for all Bradstreet poems contained in it, and to make selections from the 1678 *Several Poems* for poems printed only there. This enabled us to retain the sharpness of the 1640s political moment, but also to include later poems. Our choice of copytext for Philips is complex, but based on a similar set of principles: the autograph Tutin manuscript is our copytext for poems that occur in it; we have used *Poems* (1664) for those that are not in Tutin; and we have used *Poems* (1667) for those that occur in neither of the earlier two copytexts. Poems are arranged in our anthology according to these groups, with interesting effects; for example, the state-political poems that are printed together at the beginning of *Poems* (1664) are also grouped together in our anthology, offering a sense of Philips's presentation in that volume as a state-political poet.[28] Our arrangement of Philips's poems, then, is not chronological (any attempt to impose chronology on Philips's *oeuvre* could only be speculative), but according to their grouping in these important original locations; here, we hope to provide students with some sense of the social contexts, poetic clusters, and material forms in which the early modern woman poet was produced. This can, of course, be only a small taste, but we hope that for the keenest of readers, this arrangement may be a provocation to explore further the complexities of production and publication, in manuscript and in print.

For Margaret Cavendish, the two major editions of *Poems, and Fancies* in 1653 and 1664 (the latter published as *Poems, and Phancies*) each have

---

[28] The sense that we provide of this is, of course, only partial (as we have selected only some poems), as well as only partially representative of the enormous textual complexity of Philips's *oeuvre*. For example, we present the highly political 'Upon the Double Murder of King Charles' and 'To Antenor, on a Paper of Mine' in the group of poems from *Poems* (1664), although Elizabeth Hageman argues convincingly that these poems were almost certainly once in Tutin, and later excised ('Treacherous Accidents', p. 91).

strongly competing claims both to textual authority and to the more resonant political moment. While 1653 is usually prioritized as the first iteration of Cavendish's distinctive poetry in print (Salzman's Oxford anthology is an exception), there is a strong case to be made that she corrected, or arranged correction of, the second edition of 1664 which does indeed represent a more fluid verse style. While there are arguments to be made to value both the earlier, 'rougher' and the later, 'smoother' style, critics' tendency to prioritize the former does present Cavendish as a less skilful writer, ignoring her own evident sense of the improved quality of the poems in 1664. In terms of the political moment, 1653 is of course resonant as Cavendish wrote it in exile on the Continent, having it published in London at a moment where her friends, family, and fellow royalists were in a position of disenfranchisement. But 1664 marks an interesting political moment for the author too, as she had returned to England with her husband and they were attempting to rebuild their lives and careers in relation to the newly Restored monarchy. We opted, then, to use 1664. Lucy Hutchinson's corpus is largely extant in single manuscript witnesses. The exception is *Order and Disorder*, of which a five-canto version was printed anonymously in 1679, and a longer version exists in manuscript only. In this case, we took the print version as our copytext where the poem existed in print, collated with the manuscript, and used the manuscript as copytext for the passage from a later canto which was not published. It was neither possible nor, on reflection, desirable to impose a single editorial policy across the whole volume and indeed we hope that the resulting anthology offers students an interesting glimpse of the varieties of print and manuscript production and circulation through the notes and introduction, while presenting poems with textual integrity rather than as composites.

Inevitably, our solutions to the challenges of copytext and collation felt happier at some points than at others, where the extent of the textual complexities put pressure on the possibilities for reconciliation. This pressure was so great in the case of Bradstreet's 'An Elegy upon that Honourable and Renowned Knight, Sir Philip Sidney' that we felt compelled to present two full versions of the text, to adopt in the case of this poem only the principle of versioning.[29] It is a decision that makes sense for that specific poem: the alterations between the 1650 and 1678 versions of the text are too extensive and complex to handle through collation alone (142 lines become 92, with significant rearrangement within those lines), and the possible reasons for

---

[29] See Reiman, '"Versioning": The Presentation of Multiple Texts', in his *Romantic Texts and Contexts*, pp. 167–80.

the alterations are intriguing enough to warrant extended discussion. The poem in its two versions also stands in the anthology as exemplary of the radical nature of potential poetic revision, even between printed texts, in early modern women's poetry.

Our decision to 'version' is, on a much smaller scale, the same as that of Leah Marcus and her co-editors of *Elizabeth I: Collected Works* outlined in her chapter in this volume, with a subtle but important difference. Their decision to present multiple versions of some of Elizabeth I's most important speeches was based on competing claims for textual 'authority' in a context of multiple manuscript copies made by auditors, whose versions might be more accurate than a speech's printed text (see pp. 143–5). Ours is based not only on equal claims to textual authority (or not), but also on the ways in which variant multiple textual versions speak to varying political moments and material manifestations of the author's work – to different 'publication events'.[30] Beyond this single example of a versioned poem, however, we have relied on our notes and headnotes to the poems to provide access to textual and contextual issues as well as to formal ones, providing multiple leads for further exploration. Our aim in these notes is to focus on the poems' poetic features, their intellectual, cultural, and political contexts, avoiding reductive 'life and works' readings and 'engaging in alternate ways' to read the poems (to recall Ramona Wray).[31] Our anthology is designed to facilitate close, formalist reading in its most open and responsive form, and simultaneously to encourage readers to ask broader, more complex, less enclosed, less hierarchical, sets of cultural and political questions.

## Conclusions

*Women Poets of the English Civil War* is an avowedly mainstream anthology. It aims to present poems that are a 'good read' to students exploring the literary canon for the first time, whose sense of 'the literary' is under construction, and whose attention to women writers will inevitably be constructed by the 'great works' focus that continues to dominate twelve-week undergraduate courses at tertiary level. It provides the undergraduate student of Donne, Herbert, Marvell, and Milton with poetic texts that can be read in conversation with those canonical poets, as well as with the less canonical male poets they may experience on a Civil War course. It offers

---

[30] See Cohen, *The Networked Wilderness*, pp. 1–28, cited in Pender and Smith's chapter in this volume (pp. 266–7).
[31] Wray, 'Anthologizing', p. 57.

to students who will otherwise think that 'men inhabit literature-land; women inhabit history-land', that men write poems and women write paraliterature,[32] a set of poems that indicates otherwise; that demonstrates that there is a narrative of early modern women and poetry within a broader narrative of early modern women and writing; that allows for engagement with poetry as a set of genres; and that stages a more comprehensive act of intervention in the canon of early modern poetry than the Norton anthology and its ilk are able to do. *Women Poets of the English Civil War* offers its contents to be read and taught as its own group of poems, united by the authors' gender and (partly) political motivations, but also offers poems to be taught as part of a Civil War or seventeenth-century course alongside male writers. As such it aims to meet like with like in the presentation of the poems, seeing such modernized, clean-text editing as only one part of a wider feminist literary-critical agenda, but an important part.

This sense of our anthology's aims as delightfully, liberatingly partial can come only with the relatively new state of plurality in which the editing of early modern women finds itself, as the chapters in this volume and the diversity of their concerns attest. Pulter's poems are now also available in Alice Eardley's new edition, and an edition of Margaret Cavendish's poems, edited by Brandie Siegfried, is forthcoming with The Other Voice's Toronto series. Lucy Hutchinson's poetry will be in volumes 3 and 4 of the Oxford *Works*, described in Elizabeth Clarke's chapter in this volume. Images of Pulter's manuscript are available online in the Adam Matthews database of *Perdita Manuscripts*, as are images of Philips's poems in Tutin, as well as the Dering and Rosania manuscripts. Readers can use *Early English Books Online* to compare the variant printed editions of Bradstreet and Cavendish for themselves. If the poets included in this anthology have not until now been widely available in modernized form, we are nonetheless attaining a 'healthy plurality of editions' which has previously been absent in women's writing, and which has freed us to 'edit *for*' our particular audience in a newly liberated way, holding up our anthology as only one of many possible interventions.[33]

For these poets, individually and in concert with each other, an affordable anthology of selected poems, modernized and in print format, is a powerful and useful kind of edition: this is the form in which students (and general

---

[32] Woodbridge, 'Dark Ladies', p. 62; Smith, 'Foreword', p. ix.

[33] Danielle Clarke, 'Nostalgia', p. 189; Paul Eggert argued for editing as 'transactional', always 'leaning outwards to a readership', always an act of 'editing *for*', in a paper at the book:logic conference, Newcastle, Australia, April 2014.

readers) are most accustomed to encountering canonical poets, and one that ensures the widest readership. For all its modernization, cleanness, and lack of white noise, however, *Women Poets of the English Civil War* seeks to pay attention to principles that are often overlooked in large-scale mainstream anthologies. Marie-Louise Coolahan quite rightly points out that 'the major undergraduate anthologies tend not to foreground their editorial choices' (p. 177): we outline our editorial choices fully in our textual notes, and aim to provide, accurately, all the leads that a curious or more specialist reader would need to explore textual and contextual issues further. We hope that in its attitudes to copytext, and in making available in conjunction with each other five women poets from one of the most intriguing phases of early modern English literature (if not one that matches conventional periodization), our anthology participates in the processes of reshaping the anthology as conventionally conceived, even while subscribing to its ongoing value as a pedagogical and canon-making tool.

# CHAPTER 13

# Modernizing Katherine Austen's Book M *(1664) for the Twenty-First-Century, Non-Expert Reader*

## Pamela S. Hammons

What is at stake in modernizing an early modern woman's manuscript to make it easily accessible to today's non-expert reader? This chapter builds upon the discussions in Sarah Ross and Elizabeth Scott-Baumann's chapter on women poets of the Civil War and Mary Ellen Lamb's contribution on Mary Wroth's *Urania* regarding questions of accessibility. If some of the benefits of accessibility include enabling the widest possible range of readers to appreciate and therefore to value a unique early modern woman's intellectual and creative achievements and to learn about her previously lost personal history, what are the costs? Given the significant differences between early modern manuscripts and twenty-first-century printed and electronic texts – differences in material form, genre, vocabulary, spelling, punctuation, mode of textual transmission, reading practices, historical context, gendered cultural assumptions, and so on – an editor must think simultaneously about the past and present, and must attempt to bring them into mutually illuminating contact with each other. In the specific case of modernizing Katherine Austen's *Book M* (1664) for The Other Voice in Early Modern Europe: The Toronto Series, the practices of regularizing spelling, punctuation, and capitalization and extensively glossing her seventeenth-century vocabulary and editorial revisions help the non-expert reader to recognize that her writing, particularly her poetry, is much more complex and sophisticated than one might first assume. On the other hand, twenty-first-century print regrettably erases Austen's visual and material cues regarding how her diverse texts relate – and sometimes even speak directly – to each other on the manuscript page. The modernized print format thus risks limiting *Book M*'s full range of possible meanings and consequently necessitates including representative images of the book's pages to retain a sense of those visual and material cues.

Because the risk of losing meaning in the process of transcription to print is inherent to the material differences between the early modern manuscript and modern print formats, it is certainly not isolated to the case of editing

Austen's *Book M* for the non-expert reader. Attending to this fundamental problem as it arises specifically in relation to editing Austen's manuscript therefore helps to illuminate an array of issues that appear in a wide variety of modern editions, whether the original manuscripts were authored, compiled, or owned by men or women. At the same time, analysing the benefits and limitations of rendering *Book M* accessible for a general reader has the added advantage of putting into relief the asymmetrical – sometimes sexist – ways in which scholars have previously responded to the material and historical differences of textual transmission as they apply to men's and women's texts. As a book series, The Other Voice in Early Modern Europe – a long-standing, multi-lingual, international intellectual project – is defined by its feminist commitment to making women's texts (and male-authored texts about women) available to a general readership and thereby promoting the teaching of and research on women's cultural output and roles.[1] The still-urgent need for such a project stems from the many complex, intertwined forces in play across the centuries that have worked together to result, among other things, in prioritizing and rewarding scholarly efforts to produce authorized, monumentalizing, canonical editions of male-authored works.[2]

Elizabeth Heale's recent volume for The Other Voice, *The Devonshire Manuscript: A Women's Book of Courtly Poetry* by Lady Margaret Douglas and others, serves as an especially instructive control case for understanding the often profoundly unequal, distorting publication histories of early modern men and women's manuscript writings because one of the distinctive features of the Devonshire Manuscript is that it contains examples of male- and female-authored verse alike. As Heale explains in her introduction,

> The Devonshire Manuscript has long been known to scholars of Tudor literature, but its significance as a testimony of the central role women played in the practice of courtly verse has only recently been recognized. Since the nineteenth century, the manuscript has been valued mainly as a source for the work of Sir Thomas Wyatt and for the insights it provides into the social context in which he and Henry Howard, Earl of Surrey, produced their poetry.[3]

---

[1] For more on the almost twenty-year publication history and founding principles of The Other Voice in Early Modern Europe, see www.othervoiceineme.com/index.html. To date, nearly two hundred volumes have been produced between the Chicago and the Toronto lists.

[2] For a landmark analysis of the relationship between the history of women's writing and canonical cultural forces, see Ezell's *Writing Women's Literary History*.

[3] Introduction to *Devonshire*, ed. Heale, p. 2.

This trend towards overlooking women's contributions, as Heale explains further, stretches back centuries to the decades immediately following the production of the Devonshire Manuscript: the development of the Elizabethan lyric tradition,

> as mediated through printed collections of verse throughout the sixteenth century is almost exclusively male. With very rare exceptions, it was the work of male poets that was printed, and the printed volumes were, explicitly or implicitly, most often addressed to male readers. The centrality of women to the genre, as participants, recipients, and contributors, was almost entirely erased. This erasure continued into the nineteenth and twentieth centuries with the predominant modern emphasis on creating definitive editions of the authorial texts of male poets.[4]

Heale's volume admirably returns the women at the heart of Henry VIII's court to their central location in relation to the production of the Devonshire Manuscript. Although composed over one hundred years later, Austen's *Book M* similarly enriches our knowledge of the extent and nature of women's active contributions to early modern manuscript culture. The endeavour of modernizing her writings – her poems, in particular – highlights their importance and value, while simultaneously reminding us to continue questioning unexamined assumptions regarding the authority, textual stability, and original manuscript contexts of modern editions of poetry, whether authored by early modern women or men.[5]

Before turning to *Book M* itself, it will be helpful to consider briefly how Arthur Marotti's research on early modern textual transmission provides a crucial context for understanding the significance of material form in creating meaning and therefore in participating in transmitting the value of early modern verse. As he notes when discussing differences during the early modern era between manuscript and printed poetry, regardless of

---

[4] Introduction to *Devonshire*, ed. Heale, pp. 3–4. Arthur Marotti also critiques the traditional scholarly focus on Wyatt's poems in the Devonshire Manuscript for 'distort[ing] its character' because 'it unjustifiably draws the works of other writers into the Wyatt canon ... prevents an appreciation of the collection as a document illustrating some of the uses of lyric verse within an actual social environment ... [and] has discouraged our seeing Wyatt's poems themselves as typical lyric utterances that could be used by individuals other than their author for their own purposes' (*Manuscript*, p. 40). Although less interested in women's key contributions to the Devonshire Manuscript than Heale, Marotti still usefully calls attention to the fact that the process of transmitting Wyatt's verse in print loses the valuable socio-cultural meanings attached to it in the specific manuscript context.

[5] In their Introduction to Millman and Wright (eds.), *Early Modern Women's Manuscript Poetry*, Elizabeth Clarke and Jonathan Gibson explain that the 'anthology illustrates ways in which the study of well-known women authors can be deepened and made more valuable by consideration of the medium in which they normally wrote'; thus, the collection includes transcriptions of manuscript poems by Mary Sidney, Mary Wroth, and Katherine Philips – now-canonical female poets who are known to today's readers primarily through their printed texts (p. 2).

whether authored or compiled by men or women, 'Generally . . . there is a marked difference between the iconicity of ornamented or unornamented texts in printed editions and the appearance of the same texts in manuscript collections where their physical appearance does not call attention to them as aesthetic objects.'[6] Through his extensive research on John Donne's verse, Marotti has shown how the watershed posthumous publication of his *Poems* in 1633 'had an important place in the history of printed verse – a context that ultimately wrought the transformation of Donne from a literary amateur into a canonical English author, from someone writing for manuscript circulation for coterie readers, sometimes within the framework of social and political patronage, into an "author" in the modern institution of literature'.[7] Importantly, Marotti's scholarship has demonstrated not only how the movement from manuscript to print transmission solidified Donne's respectable reputation and 'identity as Doctor Donne, dean of St. Paul's' through the many editions of his writing published between his death and the early eighteenth century, but it also reveals how his 'install[ation] in literary history as an author in the modern sense of the term' through the printing of his poetry and sermons deeply influenced the practices of twentieth-century editors who produced volumes of Donne's works.[8] Marotti argues, for example, that in her Oxford University Press editions of Donne, Helen Gardner's editorial practices 'distance Donne from the erotic behavior dramatized in the amorous verse' and that this 'continues the process generated not only by Walton's hagiographical model of Donne's life but also by the editorial frame in which the verse was first presented'.[9] Marotti's thorough examination of the intertwining historical, cultural, and material forces at work across centuries in creating the canonical 'John Donne' familiar to us today exposes some of the potent, yet often invisible, shaping effects of editorial practices. Doctor Donne was a particular favourite of Katherine Austen, who refers to the esteemed dean in *Book M*; she certainly read his sermons and probably read his poetry, too. Of course, *Book M* is radically different in many ways from Donne's works. Nevertheless, Austen's verse shares more with Donne's than first meets the eye, and rendering it accessible to today's general reader helps to make its value much more apparent.

[6] Marotti, *Manuscript*, p. 29. In their introduction to *Early Modern Women Poets*, Jane Stevenson and Peter Davidson also comment upon visual differences between early modern manuscript and print: 'We include two poems by Elizabeth Taylor, one from a miscellany manuscript, one from a printed text: the manuscript poem looks semi-literate, while the confidence and elegance of her writing is far more clearly to be seen in print' (p. li).

[7] Marotti, *Manuscript*, p. 252.    [8] *Ibid.*, p. 255.    [9] *Ibid.*, p. 252.

Katherine Austen (1628–83) was an upwardly mobile, relatively young London widow, and her manuscript, *Book M*, serves as a rich resource for understanding early modern women's writing, especially their verse. Austen's book includes her spiritual meditations, sermon notes, financial records, letters, personal essays, and more than thirty occasional and religious lyrics, such as psalms, elegies, and country house verse. Because she interspersed her poems among her other life writings, her manuscript gives us a rare glimpse of the importance poetic composition had to an ambitious seventeenth-century widow whose everyday concerns focused primarily upon managing her finances, educating her children and providing for their future, and avoiding the considerable dangers of her era, including smallpox, the plague, and the Great Fire of London.[10] Given Austen's fascination with various monarchs – especially Queen Elizabeth I – attending to the particularities of editing *Book M* makes for a compelling counterpoint to Leah Marcus's chapter in this volume on editing the works of Elizabeth Tudor. Making the writings of Queen Elizabeth I accessible to a non-expert reader has obvious significance because of her stature as a culturally and politically influential historical figure. When one adds to this reason her personal, charismatic eloquence as a speaker and writer, her powerful example as a successful female political leader, and her importance to women's history, it is even easier to see how valuable it is to make her life's work of writing accessible to a general reader. Austen's social location, historical role, and literary contributions were strikingly different from those of Elizabeth Tudor, but her writings are still significant because they illuminate early modern English history – as analysed by a literate female witness – and because they increase our understanding of life writing, including imaginative writing, in one early modern person's everyday life, and also add to our growing knowledge of early modern women specifically.

*Book M* sharpens our awareness of precise ways in which the materiality of early modern texts shapes readers' perceptions. In many cases, Austen elaborated across several entries in multiple genres upon a similar theme, concern, or specific personal or historical event. The sheer number of related entries gathered closely together across the handwritten pages of

---

[10]   As Clarke and Gibson explain in their Introduction to Millman and Wright (eds.), *Early Modern Women's Manuscript Poetry*, 'Daily occupations – daily work – set the framework for the involvement of both women and men in manuscript writing. While many men's manuscripts were connected with the compilers' professional careers (two particularly important fields being the law and the church) and with political debate, most women's manuscripts formed part of their work as wives and mothers' (p. 3).

*Book M* thus helps to convey how much importance Austen ascribed to the topic at hand. If she squeezed lines of writing into small spaces between paragraphs, around the edges of the page, or into tight corners, it is clear from the size of the words and their positioning that she must have decided at some later point that she had more to say on the given issue and sought a way to keep her thoughts on it in proximity to each other. The layout of her entries in their manuscript form also communicates the widow's organizational principles. Some texts are given more prominence than others. She establishes hierarchies among her entries not only by giving some, but not all, titles or numbers in the case of poems – a practice that can be readily communicated through modern print – but also by allocating generous amounts of space to key texts to make them stand out in contrast to surrounding entries that are tightly clustered together. When valuing Austen as a poet, it is crucial to recognize that she used the visual dynamics of page layout to establish the context for her impulse to write certain poems (e.g. to celebrate divine gifts or to work through her feelings about specific matters, such as economic worries or the plague) and also to call attention to particular poems by giving them extra space.

Editing *Book M* for a twenty-first-century readership taught me, as I discuss in detail below, that Austen was a much more deliberate, skilful poet than I had previously thought; this new knowledge made me realize – to my great surprise and chagrin as a feminist literary scholar – how much my own flawed assumptions had limited my ability to perceive Austen's considerable intelligence and craft before I began to modernize her manuscript. This chapter thus engages with issues similar to those with which Danielle Clarke grapples in her study of the various editions of Mary Sidney Herbert's poetry and the ways in which many of them seriously underplay and misrepresent Sidney's poetic achievements. Although the practice of modernizing risks losing aspects of an early modern manuscript's meaning, rendering a seventeenth-century woman poet's verse into contemporary, regularized English has the great virtue of challenging uninformed assumptions that her writing is simply illiterate or without aesthetic value.

Creating a volume for a general reader for The Other Voice required several kinds of editorial intervention. First, I modernized Austen's spelling and regularized the letters 'i'/ 'j', 'u'/ 'v', the long 's', and 'F' and 'ff' for upper-case 'f'. I also regularized her capitalization, including the capitalization of the first word of each new line of verse, but retained her use of capital letters for personified, allegorized, or generalized figures. Because Austen used punctuation inconsistently and did not always write in complete sentences, I altered or added punctuation (including commas, semicolons,

colons, question marks, dashes, quotation marks, apostrophe marks, and periods) to make her writing conform to twenty-first-century conventions of English. Of course, changes to punctuation can be quite significant. In her 'Textual Introduction' to her excellent scholarly diplomatic edition of *Book M*, Sarah C. E. Ross asserts,

> To modernize Austen's punctuation would be to impose onto the text a large number of substantive judgements about what is and is not a complete sentence; in my view, this would represent too great a level of intervention on the part of myself as an editor. For this reason, her idiosyncratic punctuation is retained in this edition, with one exception: on a few occasions, she follows a phrase with both a comma and a full stop; in these cases, I have silently chosen one over the other.[11]

Ross rightly calls attention to the strong impact on the creation of meaning that the practice of modernizing punctuation can have. Similarly, in their introduction to *Early Modern Women Poets: An Anthology*, Jane Stevenson and Peter Davidson note that 'punctuation has been one of the most difficult editorial questions which have had to be answered' in creating their anthology and raise 'the problem of poems which simply look unfinished to a modern eye'.[12] Because of the necessarily shaping influence of punctuation, in preparing *Book M* for the non-expert reader I attempted to achieve maximum clarity through punctuation while trying to affect Austen's meaning as little as possible. Because of the possibility of multiple or unavoidably ambiguous meanings in parts of *Book M*, however, I have undoubtedly imposed interpretations on the text in places.[13]

In addition to modernizing Austen's punctuation as carefully as possible, I expanded contractions and abbreviations that are no longer used and thus kept 'etc.' but expanded 'y^e' into 'the' and 'w^ch' into 'which'. I retained all contractions that Austen used to make her words fit the meter of her verse: for example, I kept ''tis' and 'th'eternal' instead of changing them to 'it is' and 'the eternal'.[14] I silently corrected transposed letters (for example, 'noen' becomes 'none') and other obviously accidental misspellings (for instance, when Austen wrote 'in' but context indicates she meant 'it').

I could not reproduce Austen's horizontal or vertical spacing between letters, words, or lines; the layout of her writing on the page; or her page

---

[11] Textual Introduction to *Katherine Austen's 'Book M'*, ed. Ross, p. 45.
[12] Stevenson and Davidson, *Early Modern Women Poets*, p. li.
[13] Heale also discusses the problem of addressing ambiguity, especially when punctuating early modern poetry (Introduction to *Devonshire*, pp. 34–5).
[14] On preserving meter in modern transcriptions of poetry, also see Heale, Introduction to *Devonshire*, p. 35.

breaks. These features are thus regularized, with just a few exceptions. This means that Austen's strategic spatial positioning of her various life writings on the page and in relation to each other to enhance their meaning is unfortunately lost in many cases; below I provide examples of how spatial positioning affects the meaning of Austen's verse. To mitigate this problem, the volume includes eight representative images of the original manuscript. Because Austen gave *Book M* front matter – a title page, author page, and table of contents – I followed her breaks for the first few folia to convey a sense of the way in which she formalized and organized her writings; her careful organization of her book at its beginning indicates her deliberation, experience, and skill as author and compiler. She was inconsistent in her placement on the page of the titles she assigns to distinct parts of her manuscript; I centred them all. While I attempted to keep Austen's division of paragraphs when those divisions are clear – which she indicates by left justifying new ones – I formatted them by indenting their first words to make them look familiar to today's readers. Austen numbered many, but not all, poems next to or above each one in the left margin; I consistently placed her numbers next to the title of each poem (or next to the first line, in the absence of a title). I did not add numbers to poems that she did not number. Austen did not give line numbers for her verse, so I added them every five lines, in square brackets.

An important feature of Austen's manuscript is that it shows signs of ongoing revision: she often included marks indicating that particular words or phrases should be inserted, replaced, or deleted. I silently incorporated what appear to be her latest revisions into the main text, but to preserve the strong sense of *Book M* as an ongoing project of life writing, I explained each of her revisions in detail in the footnotes so that anyone wishing to trace her thinking process as a writer may easily do so. Austen not only revised her phrasing and word choices, but she also added material to *Book M* for several years after she started writing it. At the beginning of her book, in particular, she wrote mostly on the recto folios and typically left the versos blank. Thus, she would write on a recto, turn the page, and continue writing the same passage – sometimes midword or midsentence – at the top of the next recto. However, in some cases, she added new material to the versos she originally left blank. This material is usually related to whatever she first wrote on the rectos and serves as marginalia or side commentaries on her previous writing.[15] Because my volume for The Other Voice could not

---

[15] Todd offers the following speculation on Austen's composition techniques: 'Judging from how she numbered her pages in this volume, Austen's practice was to use the first third of her working

reproduce Austen's page breaks, it was impossible to represent the layout of this later material perfectly in relation to the earlier writing. Thus, I italicized the added passages, put them in curly brackets ('{ . . . }'), and placed them as close as possible to the material upon which they comment. For each case of added material, I included detailed explanatory footnotes to help a reader envision Austen's writing practices; however, this technique cannot completely capture all of the potential meanings that may resonate between suggestively juxtaposed passages.

The arduous process of modernizing *Book M* taught me that I had seriously underestimated Austen as a writer – particularly as a poet. To understand this young London widow and mother of three as a skilled poet, one must first know that she was a dedicated reader and an experienced writer who was undoubtedly more prolific than *Book M* alone makes evident. Throughout *Book M*, she includes cross-references to other books.[16] In some cases, those books were authored by other people, but she also refers to books designated by other letters of the alphabet that were probably her own. Thus, *Book M* was almost certainly one of many such books Austen wrote and compiled across her lifetime. According to what we currently know, those other books – *A* to *L* and after *M* – are now tragically lost. If Austen named *Book M* as she did to catalogue it among her other writings, then she had probably been an active writer for many years before she began to pen *Book M* in 1664. Indeed, her inclusion of introductory pages giving her book a title and a table of contents indicates her experience with reading and writing and the deliberate care that went into her creation of *Book M*. In all likelihood, Austen was a much more practised writer and an even more important chronicler of a remarkable century than *Book M* by itself reveals her to be.[17] Thus, although we cannot yet be certain of the existence of other books compiled and authored by Austen, it is probable that *Book M* has much in common with Anne, Lady Halkett's archive, as discussed by Suzanne Trill in this volume.

---

notebooks for study, abstracting her spiritual reading (mainly sermons) on the right-hand page, leaving the facing page blank and unnumbered for later comment and research . . . Meanwhile, in the latter two-thirds of her notebook, Austen followed a different practice, numbering these pages continuously, writing her meditations, poems and prayers on both sides of each sheet' ('Property', pp. 190–1). See also Ross, textual introduction to *Katherine Austen's 'Book M'*, pp. 41–2, on Austen's use of space and numbering of pages.

[16]   Also on Austen's cross-referencing, see Ross, textual introduction to *Katherine Austen's 'Book M'*, pp. 42–3.

[17]   Todd proposes that *Book M* was 'focused on interpreting dreams and apparitions (earlier books may have examined other topics such as honour)' ('Property', p. 190). Raymond A. Anselment speculates that 'Austen intended to combine the surviving folios into a work that presumably included her earlier widowed years' ('Austen and the Widow's Might', p. 6).

The critical reception of *Book M* began in the last decades of the twentieth century. Feminist historians such as Barbara J. Todd, Sara Mendelson, and Patricia Crawford first showed interest in Austen's manuscript because of its rich, detailed first-person account of a widow's daily life.[18] Todd and Mendelson have focused upon Austen's financial records and the crucial information her accounts provide about her economic management. Raymond A. Anselment has examined how Austen shaped her widowhood in relation to her Christian beliefs.[19] While *Book M* certainly gives us important insights into the historical events of Austen's era and a widow's financial and religious life, it also enables us to recognize the importance of creative or imaginative writing in a woman's everyday life. Austen wrote over thirty poems in *Book M*, and it is highly likely that she wrote many more than that – thus suggesting that she was a far more experienced poet than one might first assume.[20] Austen wove her poetic composition into the fabric of her everyday life. Not only did she attempt to shape her experiences, thoughts, and opinions into meter and verse, but she also must have spent a significant amount of time reading other people's writing. While it is unsurprising that a widow so dedicated to propriety and upward mobility read sermons in prose and wrote meditations on them, it is refreshing to realize – as I discuss more thoroughly below – that she must have also read a fairly wide variety of poems, including secular love lyrics, country house verse, psalms, and elegies.

Most of Austen's poems in *Book M* are spiritual meditations or biblical paraphrases – forms of religious reflection that were considered especially appropriate writing activities for women. She often uses verse to praise, to thank, or to express devotion to God; in several cases, her poems are inspired by or reflect upon specific psalms in the Bible.[21] Although she did not systematically attempt to create her own version of the Book of Psalms, her strong general interest in psalms aligns her lyrical composition with a widespread poetic practice of her place and time; Hill notes that '[i]t is difficult to find a notable poet from Wyatt to Milton who did not try his [sic] hand at a version of the Psalms' and lists George Herbert, Henry Vaughn, Thomas Carew, Richard Crashawe, Henry King, Elizabeth I, James I, and

[18]  Todd, 'The Remarrying Widow'; Todd, '"I Do No Injury by Not Loving"'; Todd, 'Property'; Mendelson, 'Stuart Women's Diaries'; Mendelson and Crawford, *Women in Early Modern England*.
[19]  Anselment, 'Austen and the Widow's Might'.
[20]  As Marotti notes, 'Typically, lyrics were inserted in books given over to other sorts of texts' (*Manuscript*, p. 17).
[21]  Also see Ross, '"And Trophes of His Praises Make"', pp. 187–8; Ross, Introduction to *Katherine Austen's 'Book M'*, pp. 28–32; and Anselment, 'Austen and the Widow's Might', pp. 15–16, on Austen's engagement with the Book of Psalms.

Mary and Philip Sidney among the well-known poets who did so.[22] As Ross observes, 'Interaction with and meditation through the Psalms permeate the life-writings of Lady Margaret Hoby, Alice Thornton, Lady Mary Rich, and Lady Anne Halkett, although none identifies herself as closely and explicitly with the Psalmist as does Katherine Austen.'[23] It makes sense that Austen, like so many of her predecessors and contemporaries, would reflect both in prose and verse upon the Book of Psalms, given the great importance ascribed to it during her lifetime. Barbara Lewalski details the forms of knowledge and emotion associated with the Psalms: 'On all sides the Book of Psalms is seen as a compendium of all theological, doctrinal, and moral knowledge; of all the modes of God's revelation – law, prophecy, history, proverbs; of all the emotions and passions of the human soul; and apparently, of all the lyric genres and styles appropriate to divine poetry'.[24]

While some of Austen's poems are biblical meditations, others interpret the events of her life as guided by the protective hand of divine providence.[25] The first half of her poem 'On My Fall off the Tree', for instance, provides an especially vivid, dramatic rendering of an accident in which she fell down from the branches of a tree she had climbed. All of Austen's poems include religious content, but a few simultaneously experiment with secular poetic conventions. This aspect of her verse composition strongly suggests that she avidly read the works of other poets.[26] For example, she is likely to have read poetry by Ben Jonson and, as I note above, John Donne. 'On Valentine's Day, This 14 February 1665/6: My Jewel' borrows from and reshapes ideas typical of secular, male-authored Renaissance love poetry, such as

[22]  Christopher Hill, *English Bible*, pp. 358, 359; on specifically royalist translations of the Psalms, see pp. 360–2.
[23]  Introduction to *Katherine Austen's 'Book M'*, ed. Ross, p. 29.
[24]  Lewalski, *Protestant Poetics*, p. 50.
[25]  Austen displays an ongoing interest in how divine providence shapes her life. Sara Mendelson explains that '[t]he providential interpretation of life's accidents which moulded contemporary spiritual diaries offered a coherent and satisfying explanation of world-historical events. It could also transform an outwardly dull and unhappy life into scenes of high drama, punctuated by hairbreadth escapes from death or damnation' ('Stuart Women's Diaries', p. 186). On Austen's 'providential world view', especially as it pertains to her verse composition, see Ross, '"And Trophes of His Praises Make"', p. 182.
[26]  She was an active reader of several genres of prose, drama, and verse. Todd notes that Austen was familiar with John Donne's sermons and refers to 'Ralegh's *History of England* and Isaak Walton's *Lives*; she found inspiration in Thomas Fuller's account of the life and achievement of Hildegarde of Bingen' ('"I Do No Injury"', p. 212). Ross points out that '[s]he draws on the writings of Daniel Featley, Jeremy Taylor and other Church of England divines' ('Katherine Austen', *Perdita Manuscripts*, www.perditamanuscripts.amdigital.co.uk.). Ross has also discovered that Austen borrows without attribution from William Shakespeare's *Henry IV, Part 2*, Richard Brome's *A Jovial Crew; or, the Merry Beggars*, Samuel Daniel's *The Complaint of Rosamond*, and Henry King's 'The Legacy' (Introduction to *Katherine Austen's 'Book M'*, p. 32). For a thorough discussion of the significance of Austen's reading practices, see Ross, '"Like Penelope"'.

Donne's 'The Funeral' and 'A Jet Ring Sent'.[27] Her country house poem,
'On the Situation of Highbury', reveals her familiarity with the conventions
of that widespread, popular genre, of which Jonson's 'To Penshurst' and
Aemilia Lanyer's 'The Description of Cooke-ham' are particularly famous
examples.[28] Like these other country house poems, Austen's 'On the Situation of Highbury' celebrates a manorial estate – in this case, her own –
by praising its seemingly supernatural Edenic pleasures and beauty and its
limitless, labour-free, spontaneously occurring natural abundance:

### 23. On the Situation of Highbury

So fairly mounted in a fertile soil,
Affords the dweller pleasure, without toil.
Th'adjacent prospects gives so rare a sight
That Nature did resolve to frame delight
On this fair hill, and with a bounteous load,                    [5]
Produce rich burdens, making the abode
As full of joy, as where fat valleys smile,
And greater far, here sickness doth exile.
'Tis an unhappy fate to paint that place
By my unpolished lines, with so bad grace                        [10]
Amidst its beauty; if a stream did rise
To clear my muddy brain and misty eyes
And find a Helicon t'enlarge my Muse,
Then I no better place than this would choose:
In such a laver and on this bright hill,                         [15]
I wish Parnassus to adorn my quill.[29]

While Austen's poem borrows liberally from the conventions of country
house verse, she also avoids employing certain characteristic features
(extensive, direct praise of the landowner, in particular, which would
be tantamount to praising herself). Regardless of what she leaves out,
however, this poem engages so thoroughly with the typical tropes of
the genre that she must have studied other poets' country house verse –
Jonson's almost certainly, but possibly others, too.

---

[27] For a detailed discussion of Austen's Valentine's Day poem, see my *Gender, Sexuality, and Material Objects*, pp. 1–4 and 103–6.

[28] For a comprehensive, detailed analysis of how 'On the Situation of Highbury' borrows specifically from the tradition of country house poetry and a thorough discussion of this poem in context with related verse by Jonson, Lanyer, Robert Herrick, Andrew Marvell, Thomas Carew, Mildmay Fane, King James, Richard Lovelace, Richard Fanshawe, Thomas Randolph, Thomas Stanley, and George Aglionby, see my *Poetic Resistance*, pp. 149–63, and 'Katherine Austen's Country House Innovations'.

[29] Austen, *Book M*, ed. Hammons, p. 181.

Introducing modern punctuation and ample footnotes clarifying Austen's seventeenth-century vocabulary not only makes 'On the Situation of Highbury' more accessible but also helps to highlight Austen's self-consciously literary efforts. When today's reader can consult a footnote, for instance, to see at a glance that in this poetic context 'burdens' means 'What is borne by the soil; produce, crop' (*OED*), the connection between the country house tradition of Edenic abundance is made clearer. Similarly, glosses on 'Helicon' (i.e., 'Name of a mountain in Boeotia, sacred to the Muses, in which rose the fountains of Aganippe and Hippocrene; by 16th and 17th c. writers often confused these. Hence used allusively in reference to poetic inspiration' *OED*) and 'Parnassus' (i.e., 'Mount Parnassus, regarded as the source of literary, esp. poetic, inspiration' *OED*) help the non-specialist reader understand that this country house poem boldly announces Austen's self-positioning in relation to a long-standing tradition in which the poet seeks inspiration from her muse. With 'Helicon' and 'Parnassus' thus explained, Austen's use of the term 'laver' ('The basin of a fountain' *OED*) then becomes a clear link to her sources of poetic inspiration. As is the case for many of Austen's poems, using modern punctuation to signal the rhythm of each line of verse highlights her periodic use of enjambment (e.g. lines 4, 6, 9, 10, 11) and caesura (e.g. lines 5, 6, 7, 8, 10, 11) to vary her phrasing throughout the poem and thus guides today's reader away from overemphasizing her rhyming couplets in a way that flattens out the poem's complex, uneven rhythms into a relentless, monotonous beat of mere end-rhymes. Furthermore, using a colon at the end of line 14 signals to the non-expert audience to pause and give appropriate weight to the final couplet celebrating her estate.

'On the Situation of Highbury' is perhaps Austen's most deliberately literary poem, and modernization brings out that quality. Unfortunately, however, there is also something important lost in modernizing her country house verse: Austen gave 'On the Situation of Highbury' its own prominent page alone, but that recto faces a verso on which she included a meditation and another poem on Highbury (see Figure 13.1). In fact, Ross notes that the poem 'is given a page to itself (fol. 104$^r$), and the verso of the leaf is also left blank (fol. 104$^v$); such profligate use of textual space is rare at this point in *Book M*, and indicates that Austen is affording the poem a kind of special presentation status'.[30] Austen thus clearly meant to position her country house poem in context with related writings but to give it prominence visually in relation to those associated writings.

[30]  Introduction to *Katherine Austen's 'Book M'*, ed. Ross, p. 34.

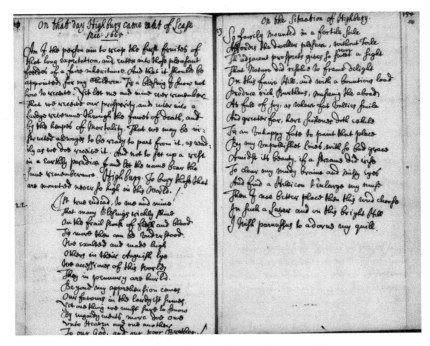

Figure 13.1 *Book M*, British Library, Additional MS 4454, folios 103v–104r.

Here, modernization in contemporary print emphasizes her efforts towards foregrounding the monumental, literary quality of her poem, but at the same time, it loses the additional meaning conveyed by the manuscript format: the specific historical and personal context, and the hierarchical positioning of this poem over juxtaposed, related material. Including an image is necessary to capture this additional visual meaning.

In addition to having read and studied the country house verse of other poets, Austen must have studied the elegy as a form – especially the subgenre of child loss verse. A striking number of seventeenth-century poets composed child loss elegies, including men such as Jonson, John Milton, Thomas Carew, and Robert Herrick and women such as Anne Bradstreet, Katherine Philips, Elizabeth Egerton, Gertrude Aston Thimelby, and Mary Carey. Austen's elegy in this tradition, 'On the Death of My Niece, Grace Ashe, 4 Years Old',[31] which she numbers her third poem, contains the most metrically complex stanzas she composed in *Book M*.

---

[31]   The daughter of Austen's sister, Mary, and brother-in-law, Sir Joseph Ashe (Todd, 'Property', p. 183).

Sweet blooming bud
Cropped from its stud
When growing up
Unto fair hope,
Thy pretty sweetness time hath hid.                    [5]
As soon as shown, we are forbid
To gaze upon that lovely hue
On which Time's shady curtain drew.

Yet, when we know
The best mayn't grow                                   [10]
In this dark vale,
Where ills still ail,
The great disposer sets them free,
Whose better character doth see,
And early in their nonage place,                       [15]
Where their chiefest part will grace.[32]

As is typical of seventeenth-century child loss poems written by non-parental consolers, Austen's lyric for her niece objectifies and aestheticizes the dead girl by figuring her as a beautiful, sweet budding flower cut prematurely from the stalk by God. As in the case of modernizing Austen's 'On the Situation of Highbury', including glosses for key terms such as 'stud' ('A stem, trunk [of a tree]' *OED*); 'vale' (figuratively, 'the world regarded as a place of trouble, sorrow, misery, or weeping' *OED*); and 'disposer' ('One who regulates or governs' *OED*; in Austen's use, God, specifically) should make the dominant imagery of the elegy easily accessible to general readers. As expected in an elegy, Austen attempts to help her audience – certainly family but also possibly members of a more extended coterie of readers – achieve emotional catharsis by working through their grief; she suggests that readers conceptualize her niece's death positively, as a welcome means of escape from the 'dark vale' of earthly life where 'ills still ail'. Given that Austen clearly engages with the conventions particular to child loss verse in two of her lyrics, she must have encountered examples written by other poets that she used as models for her own.[33]

Although glossing key terms and modernizing punctuation make this child loss poem quite simple to grasp in its basic sense, printing it in modern type unfortunately means that one cannot see at a glance the prominence that Austen ascribed to it via its physical placement in *Book M*.

[32] Austen, *Book M*, ed. Hammons, pp. 99–100.
[33] On elegies for children, including detailed analyses of Austen's, see my 'Despised Creatures'; and *Poetic Resistance*, pp. 13–54.

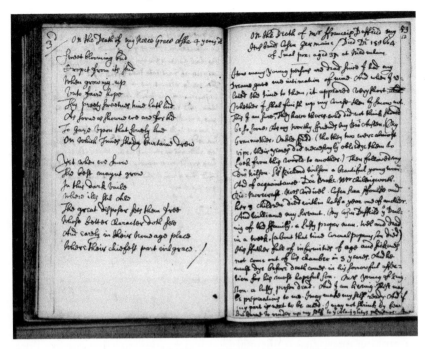

Figure 13.2 *Book M*, British Library, Additional MS 4454, folios 53v–54r.

Austen numbered this elegy to set it apart from other poems and also positioned it visually so that it occupied an entire page by itself, thus setting it in relief in relation to her other life writings on the surrounding pages (see Figure 13.2). Whereas she habitually interspersed her poetry and prose liberally – sometimes crowding them close together against each other on a page – she makes sure that this poignant family elegy does not share space at all with her other writings. Also atypically for Austen, the poem has no corrections or editorial marks and thus announces itself as a complete, final version of the elegy – perhaps a copy of the poem that she might have sent to her sister in shared mourning in a letter or on a single, separate piece of paper. It is not possible in a modernized print edition to convey how the elegy is given this special placement, and thus, to convey this additional meaning in *Book M: A London Widow's Life Writings* for The Other Voice, it was necessary to insert an image into the edition showing the poem in Austen's own handwriting.

As in the cases above, strategic glosses and modernized punctuation highlight the emotional intensity and craft of the poem Austen numbers her fourteenth:

What makes me melancholy? What black cloud
Does intercept my peace, does me enshroud,
And entertains me with the shades of night?
Is all thy splendid favors darkened quite?
Where is the signal smiles did oft display?                    [5]
In great eclipses, joy did reconvey
Those radiant marks, which, when I sat alone
Did seem a heaven so much glory shown.
And am I now enveloped in fear
And former ravishments forget to hear?                         [10]
O God, my sin 'tis my declining soul
Flies from thy altar, to the world's does roll –
A Lethe stupefaction from that snare,
Creating much unnecessary care.
Restore me, Jesu, that live saving balm,                       [15]
As these discordances may ever calm.[34]

Like the first two poems discussed in this chapter, Austen's fourteenth numbered poem has a more literary quality than some others, and modernization helps to bring out that quality by helping the non-expert reader more easily understand the poet's rhythm and phrasing. Uncharacteristically, this poem's opening sequence of five lines uses the striking repetition of probing questions of unequal length (i.e., four questions in five lines, where the first question is three and a half feet, the next is one and a half feet complexly connected to the following two lines, and the next two questions are exactly one line each) and uneven meter (e.g., the spondaic foot – 'black cloud' – at the end of line 1, which is also enjambed) to highlight her dark melancholy and twisting emotional turmoil. A modern gloss explaining that 'entertains' in this context means 'To engage, keep occupied the attention, thoughts, or time of (a person)' helps to prevent the non-expert reader from mistakenly invoking the contemporary commonplace notion of that which 'entertains' as fun and engaging in a positive sense (*OED*). Another gloss helping with the unfamiliar use of 'signal' (i.e. 'That constitutes or serves as a sign or symbol; symbolic' *OED*) keeps such a reader from assuming wrongly that this unfamiliar use of the word means that Austen is uneducated or semi-literate. When punctuated according to contemporary conventions, lines 6–8 – which include two instances of caesura and two enjambments in one three-line sentence – suddenly appear much more complex syntactically and rhythmically than they might appear otherwise. Adding a footnote that indicates how Austen lingered over these

---

[34] Austen, *Book M*, ed. Hammons, pp. 152–3.

lines helps to communicate the care with which she chose her words here. In the footnote, I explain that Austen inserted something above 'marks' – possibly 'signs of' – but crossed out her insertion and kept 'marks', perhaps because she noticed that she had used 'marks' twice in three lines; she seems to have considered changing the second instance of 'marks' (line 7) but ultimately changed the first one (line 5) to 'smiles' instead. On one hand, explaining Austen's editorial revisions to this poem in footnotes in this manner means that a reader who decides to skip the notes will lose the sense of her vital, intense, immediate engagement with her poem. On the other hand, explaining her revisions in notes allows the result of her editorial practice to shine through clearly by presenting a clean copy of the poem to a general reader no doubt used to modernized, printed copies of male seventeenth-century poets' work – like Donne's – that similarly focus upon readerly accessibility and authorial final intentions. Without access to a modernized edition, many non-expert readers might tend to undervalue Austen's efforts and to ascribe to her gender – in an uninformed, automatically negative manner – traits typical of manuscript verse composition itself. Lines 11–14 continue to use a complicated syntax to communicate the sense of painful, contorted difficulty involved in directing her soul's intentions in the right way, and contemporary punctuation, such as the comma indicating the direct address to God and the dash connecting lines 12 and 13, helps to bring alive the drama of the speaker's misguided soul. The dire threat to a soul in jeopardy and Austen's self-conscious literariness in this poem are further called to the general reader's attention with a footnote explaining that the important, possibly unfamiliar term 'Lethe' means 'A river in Hades, the water of which produced, in those who drank it, forgetfulness of the past' (*OED*). That Austen ends this twisting, convoluted exploration of the spiritually dangerous paths of melancholy with a regular couplet with no enjambment provides an effective sense of rest and resolution.

One can make an especially fruitful comparison here between modernizing for a general reader and the parallel need for co-existing scholarly diplomatic transcriptions of early modern women's manuscripts. Ross's transcription of Austen's fourteenth-numbered poem preserves crucial features of the text for the scholarly expert:

> What makes me mellancholy. what black cloud
> Dus intercept my peace, dus me inshroud.
> And entertaines me with the shades of night
> Is all thy splended favours darkened quite
> Where is the signal ~~markes~~^smiles^ did oft display

In great Ecclipses, joy did reconvay
Those radiant ~~markes~~ ^signes^, which when I sat alone
Did seeme a Heaven, so much glory showne.
And am I now inveloped in feare
And former ravishments forget to heare
O God my sin, Tis my diclining Soule
Flies from thy Alter. To the world's dus roule.
A Leethe Stupefaction from that snare
Creating much vnnecessary care
Restore me ~~Iesy~~ Iesu: that live saveing balme
That^as^ these discordancies may ever Calme.[35]

This version usefully foregrounds at a glance – without requiring the reader to consult footnotes – the author's process of crafting her verse through the careful revision of her diction, and it allows the specialist to see Austen's original spellings and sparse punctuation. Importantly, Ross's transcription also enables scholars to wrestle seriously with all of the poem's ambiguities. Since experts should be knowledgeable enough about manuscript culture and early modern literature and history to interpret these material features of Austen's texts for themselves, Ross's scholarly diplomatic edition plays a crucial role in fostering future research on *Book M.*

A poem near the end of *Book M* that Austen originally numbered her twenty-sixth (before marking out the number for unknown reasons) serves as a final brief example of the ways in which modernization not only helps to make an early modern woman's poetry more accessible to the non-expert reader but also highlights her craft. As in her fourteenth poem, she begins here with a question that helps to generate – and possibly to justify – the rest of the poem that follows:

Great God, thy mercies how can I unfold?
They are so numerous not to be told.
Deep are th'impressions of th'Almighty's love,
To wonder and astonishment do move,
Impossible to think, to speak, to write, [5]
And what's innumerable to indite.
Lord, in the mass and of their volumes, I
Can only speak, and they transcend the sky.
But the particulars that my God hath wrought
For soul and body is beyond all thought. [10]
My wonder rises still to such a height
Can only gaze upon that mountain's sight.
'Tis my high joy, when in Heaven's orb refin'd,

---

[35] *Katherine Austen's 'Book M'*, ed. Ross, p. 135.

Shall understand that love with a new mind,
With new capacities, and with a beam                    [15]
Drawn from his glory, clarify my dim,
My purblind soul. Fit me for that abode
To enter in the temple of my God;
Celestial soliloquies inspired shall learn
And to eternity sing notes serene.[36]                  [20]

Austen's long, complex sentence across lines 3–6 puts into relief the one-line question that begins the poem and the sharply end-stopped statement in line 2, which suggests the difficulty, at first, of answering the call to number God's mercies, Austen's self-imposed task in this poem. The editorial decision to connect lines 3 and 4 with a comma helps to communicate the joyful, progressive acceleration – especially after the first two end-stopped lines – of the poetic speaker's increasing ability to pour forth her words detailing divine mercies. Thus, even though the explicit meaning of the first six lines reiterates in different ways the sheer impossibility of numbering God's mercies, the increasingly rapid rhythm across those lines – which, again, can be made more perceptible through contemporary punctuation – provides an upbeat counterpoint of positive momentum. Lines 7–8 are striking not only for the enjambment across them and the caesura in line 8, but also for line 7's two dactylic feet in the first half of the line, followed by a spondee and final iamb. The overall effect of this metrical variation strongly emphasizes 'Lord', 'mass', the first syllable of 'volumes', and 'I' and thus links them together associatively, as if to hint at the idea that the poet might after all be up for the task of praising God's innumerable gifts. Lines 13–20 – two long sentences when punctuated according to contemporary conventions – are among the most complex in Austen's writing. In this case, modernizing is especially helpful in that it calls attention to and heightens the drama of the speaker's pause in the middle of line 17. Although it is an editorial judgment call to decide whether to use a comma or period to mark this particular caesura, using a period helps to highlight to the non-expert reader the speaker's confident switch to the imperative mode (and spondaic foot) when she commands, 'Fit me . . . ' Using a period to mark the pause in the middle of line 17, and thereby clarifying the last three lines and a half as one coherent unit of meaning, also has the effect of showcasing how the poem's triumphantly sibilant concluding couplet answers its own opening question – performatively and provocatively suggesting, in the end, that Austen need not wait until she reaches heaven to 'sing notes serene' after all.

---

[36] Austen, *Book M*, ed. Hammons, pp. 195–6.

The greatest benefit of modernizing *Book M* is that a wider audience can better hear the poet sing across the centuries to us. Ultimately, *Book M: A London Widow's Life Writings* for The Other Voice in Early Modern Europe can work productively in concert with Ross's scholarly diplomatic edition, *Katherine Austen's 'Book M'*, for Medieval and Renaissance Texts and Studies, and the complete digital image available in the *Perdita Manuscripts* online database to convey the fullest possible range of meanings of an important early modern writer's work to twenty-first century scholars, students, and general readers alike.

# PART IV

# Editorial Possibilities

# CHAPTER 14

# Editing Early Modern Women in the Digital Age

## Patricia Pender and Rosalind Smith

Because the recuperation of early modern women's texts has burgeoned at precisely the point that the digital medium started providing new possibilities for editing, early modern women's writing stands in a unique relationship to online editing and knowledge-construction. Scholars of early modern women have been quick to respond to the major editorial opportunities afforded by the digital medium: those of the database, the online edition, and the archive. But how have these opportunities impacted the ways we approach editing early modern women's texts? What lessons have been learnt from early experiments in the field and what current possibilities warrant further exploration? This chapter approaches these questions by asking what possible *solutions* the digital medium might provide to the editorial issues raised in this volume. To what extent does the author remain the determining principle of early modern editing in general, the editing of early modern women in particular, and digital editions of both? How well do editorial practices designed to produce scholarly editions of canonical male writers translate to the editing of women's texts – in both print and digital formats? And what specific opportunities and challenges are involved in reproducing the texts of early modern women in today's digital environment?

In order to address these questions more closely we consider a variety of digital representations of early modern women's writing, from the first encyclopaedic databases produced by the Brown Women Writers project and the Perdita project, to more recent smaller scale online editions and archives such as Paul Salzman's edition of Mary Wroth's poetry, Alison Wiggins's Bess of Hardwick letters project, and our own forthcoming digital archive, *Material Cultures of Early Modern Women's Writing*. The scale and heterogeneity of the current corpora of early modern women's writing has given birth to a range of different approaches to digitization that fosters experimentation with form, content, context, and rationale. While the digital medium might be seen to provide innovative answers to unresolved issues in feminist editing surrounding copytext, author, and the foregrounding of gender as an organizational category, it has also generated new problems of access, legibility, coherence, and longevity that are equally pressing. In what follows we consider how the digital environment has been deployed in disseminating early modern women's writing and how the distinctive material properties of this medium might best be harnessed in future representations of this rapidly expanding field.

Even in its most mainstream configurations, early modern literature has long been an important site for developments in editorial theory and the twenty-first century is proving no exception. As Christopher Burlinson and Ruth Connolly note, new print editions of the poetry of John Wilmot, Earl of Rochester, George Villiers, Duke of Buckingham, and Sir Walter Ralegh employ a spectrum of editing approaches ranging from copytext editing for texts with single print or authorial manuscript sources, through the retention of the author's name as a kind of collective brand under which many texts might be gathered, to the more radical approach of Michael Rudick to the works of Sir Walter Ralegh.[1] Rudick's historical edition self-consciously refuses to work back to authorial originals, shifting its focus from author to reader, and presents a Ralegh canon of 'what comprised Ralegh's poetic work for sixteenth- and seventeenth-century readers'.[2] This shift in editorial focus towards the reader, collaboration, and authorial instability means that different kinds of texts are being edited – particularly manuscripts and verse miscellanies – in new ways that emphasize the text's material properties, modes of transmission, and place in social networks of readership and exchange. However, editions de-privileging authorial intention and focusing on the reader have by no means created a new, widespread orthodoxy. Across the field, author-oriented editions of early modern male writers continue to be produced, including new multi-volume editions of Donne, Jonson, Spenser, Milton, Herbert, and Herrick.[3] In response to new, more experimental editing practice, some editors of single-author editions have argued for the advantages of the old, of using a specific and situated authorial voice as one pathway among many

---

[1] Burlinson and Connolly, 'Editing Stuart Poetry', pp. 1–3.

[2] *The Works of John Wilmot Earl of Rochester*, ed. Love; Wilmot, *Selected Poems*, ed. Davis; *Plays, Poems, and Miscellaneous Writings, associated with George Villiers, Second Duke of Buckingham*, ed. Hume and Love; *The Poems of Sir Walter Ralegh*, ed. Rudick, p. xvi.

[3] See for example *The Variorium John Donne*, gen. ed. Stringer; *The Cambridge Ben Jonson*, ed. Bevington et al.; *Edmund Spenser: Selected Letters and Other Papers*, ed. Burlinson; *The Complete Works of John Milton*, ed. Cullington et al.; *The English Poems of George Herbert*, ed. Wilcox; *The Complete Poetry of Robert Herrick*, ed. Cain and Connolly.

to understanding early modern literature and culture.[4] Unsurprisingly, it nevertheless remains the case that with very few exceptions, early modern women are rarely afforded such major-press 'complete works' treatment.[5]

The competing models of authorship at work in print editions of male-authored early modern texts have significant implications for the field of early modern women's writing, as Sarah Ross and Paul Salzman discuss in the Introduction to this volume. In summarizing the forty-year history of second-wave feminist editing in 2009, for instance, Betty Travitsky argues that socially or materially based editing, which has been applied to better-known parts of the traditional canon, 'may well be appropriate to some early modern women writers whose texts have become well-explored', but that a shift to the wholesale use of such techniques for early modern women writers 'would be better left to a future in which the recovery of the canon of their writings is closer to complete'.[6] While this pronouncement seems to be merely advocating common sense, it effectively erects a hierarchy and chronology of editorial practice: a conventional edition must be produced before its deconstruction can occur. The unspoken premise here is that an objective edition of an early modern woman's text can in fact be established prior to, and untrammelled by, the analysis of material and textual mediation that social text editing entails. This issue taps into a crux in early modern women's studies that needs to be faced directly. Travitsky is by no means alone when she takes umbrage with the fact that the Death of the Author came along at roughly the time that we started to discover early modern *women* authors. But to respond to this ideological collision by resurrecting authorial intention at the expense of important breakthroughs in editorial theory seems counterintuitive to say the least, especially at a point where exciting new models for rethinking editing practice are emerging in the editing of early modern women's writing, and in early modern studies more broadly.

As the chapters in this volume attest, however, these issues are still critically contested. Danielle Clarke has argued trenchantly against the implication that we need women authors to look like canonical male authors in order to be taken seriously.[7] Clarke's charge against editions that mimic rather than challenge the male-authored canon is that they present early modern texts as though 'they are transparent, autonomous,

---

[4] Todd and Wilcox, 'The Challenges of Editing Donne and Herbert'.

[5] See Elizabeth Clarke's chapter in this volume for discussion of the Oxford *Works* of Lucy Hutchinson.

[6] Travitsky and Prescott, 'Studying and Editing Early Modern Englishwomen', p. 14.

[7] Danielle Clarke, 'Nostalgia', p. 208.

and stable vehicles of meaning, as if a female authored or feminist equivalent of "some notional platonic ideal" of a text might be found'.[8] Yet Leah
Marcus, in her provocative self-reflection, 'Confessions of a Reformed
UnEditor (II)', writes persuasively of the need for more 'complete works'
of early modern women writers, in modernized print editions, as a means
of conferring canonicity. Writing in 2003, before the large-scale onset of
digital editorial projects in either mainstream or feminist editing, Clarke
voices a concern that early modern women's texts have been presented
in editions that are too conservative, 'erasing specific linguistic features
that may help us establish the parameters of women's discourse in the
early modern period' and subordinating the materiality of the early modern text to the demands of modern legibility.[9] To an extent, this critique has been embraced and addressed by subsequent anthologies that
foreground the social materiality of women's writing (such as Ostovich-
Sauer's *Reading Early Modern Women* and Millman-Wright's *Early Modern
Women's Manuscript Poetry*) and diplomatic editions of women's writing (such as Jean Klene's Southwell-Sibthorpe commonplace book and
Deborah Aldrich-Watson's Constance Aston Fowler).[10] At the same time,
Marcus's call for canonical editions of early modern women has been
answered not only by the *Elizabeth I: Collected Works* volumes in which
she was involved, but also by Janel Mueller's magisterial *Katherine Parr:
Complete Works* and the new, multi-volume Oxford University Press *Works
of Lucy Hutchinson*.[11]

It is also notable that several chapters in the present volume argue that
some editions of early modern women *do* need to mimic the editorial
presentation of the male-authored canon if they are going to be 'taken
seriously', particularly those targeted at student audiences (see the chapters
by Leah Marcus, and Sarah Ross and Elizabeth Scott-Baumann). Perhaps
at issue here is less the efficacy of the category of authorship *per se* than
an understandable – even necessary – conversation about the methods of
its deployment and its historical relationship with shifting ideologies of
gender. Several contributors to this volume raise important concerns about
the way gender ideologies – both those of the early modern period and of

---

[8] Danielle Clarke, 'Nostalgia', p. 193.     [9] Danielle Clarke, 'Nostalgia', p. 203.
[10] Ostovich and Sauer (eds.), *Reading Early Modern Women*; Millman and Wright (eds.), *Early
Modern Women's Manuscript Poetry*; *The Southwell-Sibthorpe Commonplace Book*, ed. Klene; *The
Verse Miscellany of Constance Aston Fowler*, ed. Aldrich-Watson.
[11] *Elizabeth I: Collected Works*, ed. Marcus, Mueller, and Rose; *Elizabeth I: Autograph Compositions
and Foreign Language Originals*, ed. Mueller and Marcus; *Elizabeth I: Translations, 1544–1589*, ed.
Mueller and Scodel; *Katherine Parr: Complete Works and Correspondence*, ed. Mueller; *The Works
of Lucy Hutchinson*, volume I: *The Translation of Lucretius*, ed. Barbour and Norbrook.

its subsequent scholarship – have circumscribed the editing of early modern women writers. For instance, Ramona Wray critiques certain modern editions of Elizabeth Cary's *Mariam* that she sees as 'ensnared within a specific interpretive design (a prioritizing of biography, gender, or a mixture of the two)' and that consequently 'negated other, more relational avenues of investigation' (p. 66). In discussing her edition of Elizabeth Tyrwhit's *Morning and Evening Prayers*, Susan Felch similarly exhorts editors to pay detailed attention to the multiple historical contexts that surround early modern women's texts, which, in her eloquent summation, are 'gender-inflected' but not 'gender-exclusive'. Meticulous investigation of these contexts, Felch suggests, provides 'a certain self-correcting mechanism that can unclench tightly held ideological assumptions' (p. 25).

Felch's insight provides a valuable reminder of 'the contingency of all our scholarly assumptions' – not least those employed in editing today. As the field of early modern women's writing expands, a broad spectrum of difference is becoming apparent, with some examples of women's writing seeming quite similar to male-authored writing and others noticeably different. As Danielle Clarke, citing Margaret Ezell, notes in the present volume, while there is still no agreed-upon 'feminist cladistics' there is now 'a wide range of editorial practice'. Keeping these differences in mind could help us assess and mediate between apparently competing critical agendas: editions of women's writing shaped by methodologies that expand authorship need not be seen as automatically devalued by their difference to editions of male-authored writing and, conversely, new editions of women's writing following canonical protocols need not be seen as simply reinforcing second-wave or, more problematically, post-feminist editorial ideologies (although in each case critical vigilance – what Susan Felch calls the 'scrupulosity' of the 'backward gaze' (p. 25) – is required). The expanding field of early modern women's writing means that specific and historicized sets of editorial principles are increasingly being developed in response to individual texts and projects. A single set of principles for feminist editing no longer seems adequate to the diversity of texts in the field, nor to the needs of their various readers. What is emerging instead are editions that 'fit to purpose'; that are responsive, historicized, and draw from a range of available editorial options.

The new technologies and resources of digital media are clearly capable of pushing at the boundaries of the ways even comparatively experimental print editions have been conceptualized and produced. So what specific opportunities for editing early modern texts are opened up by the digital medium? In her chapter in *The Renaissance Computer* (2000), Leah Marcus argues that in facilitating the quick access and retrieval of materials, the computer fulfils the same function as the late medieval and early modern book wheel – a cleverly constructed machine that holds from twelve to twenty large folio volumes, 'so that when the books are laid in its lecterns they never fall or move from the place where they are laid even when the wheel is turned and revolved all the way around', making the required volumes almost instantly available for consultation.[12] Marcus suggests that computers can function 'very much like such a scholar's wheel, only ampler and much more compact, allowing modern scholars to locate and correlate passages on similar subjects with great ease and precision'.[13] Moreover, digital technology allows us to create our own versions of Renaissance commonplace books or *florilegia*, using 'both the accuracy of reproduction enabled by print technology and the potential for individual customization associated with the copying of texts in manuscript'.[14] For Marcus, what the digital world promises to replicate 'is the noisy, chattering texture which is the hall-mark of pre-modern encounters between readers and texts. The idealized "silence" of the archive is being replaced by a form of textual reproduction which appears far more alive and mutable.'[15]

Patricia Fumerton, editor of the *English Broadside Ballad Archive*, further suggests that the digital platform can approximate a very early modern sense of the material text as something 'cobbled together'. She suggests that the intensive fragmentation of vision made available by databases such as *Early English Books Online* paradoxically allows us 'a more whole vision of the past' precisely because it offers us multiple, fragmentary 'views'. Fumerton argues that our use of early modern texts in the digital environment approximates the early modern period's own access to printed materials.[16] A sense of the contingency of print, the multiple hands and processes through which it was constructed, remained with the early modern reader because cheap print in particular everywhere bore the marks of its 'rearrangeable bits and pieces, differently assembled and movable parts'.[17] In the case of ballads, the same typefaces, woodcuts, tunes, and even stories reappeared in different contexts, either reproduced exactly or slightly altered, and often renamed as new. These processes have been variously described as an 'aesthetics of vagrancy', or an 'art of collage': all terms point, however, to an early modern view of the material text as something other than stable,

---

[12]  M. T. Gnudi and E. S. Ferguson (trans. and eds.), *The Various and Ingenious Machines of Agostino Rameli (1588)* (Baltimore, MD: Johns Hopkins University Press and Scholar Press, 1976), p. 508, cited in Marcus, 'Silence', p. 18.
[13]  Marcus, 'Silence', p. 18.     [14]  *Ibid.*     [15]  *Ibid.*
[16]  *Fumerton,* 'Remembering by Dismembering', p. 16.     [17]  *Ibid.*, p. 17.

original, and fixed.[18] As Fumerton's own work on the *English Broad-side Ballad Archive* shows, the digital environment can be constructed to approximate this sense of contingency in the twenty-first-century reader: presenting the text in multiple versions, both oral and print.

At play here are a series of binary oppositions that work to construct the digital realm's relationship to the medium of print, especially as these concern early modern editions. The noise and chatter of the web are contrasted with the silence of the physical archive; the fragmentation of texts facilitated by digital technology is compared to the singularity favoured by the print edition; and the contingency foregrounded by contextual comparison is juxtaposed with the ideal of a stable text. The capacity of the digital environment to represent complex textual (and contextual) configurations holds obvious allure for editors of early modern women's writing. At the most basic level, as Suzanne Trill notes in this volume, a comprehensive edition of Anne, Lady Halkett's 'complete works' is one that could only be produced in the online environment, given the hitherto unrecognized scale of this project. Similarly, in its capacity to include a multitude of contextual documents, an electronic edition of *The Tragedy of Mariam* need not prioritize (or downplay) biography and gender over the other illuminating intertexts Ramona Wray has unearthed concerning place, religion, and genre in the play. Finally, Marcus's notion of the digital book wheel and Fumerton's notion of the contingent, cobbled-together digital text provide potential solutions to the challenge Susan Felch faced in making visible (both literally and metaphorically) the many types of private prayerbook to which Tyrwhit's is indebted and might usefully be compared. These opportunities for new, large-scale, historicized, and material editions of early modern women's writing offered by the digital medium have not, however, always been realized in practice. In 2010, Margaret Ezell offered the following warning about editing early modern women's texts in the digital environment:

> What concerns me is that I hear in the narratives told by the current history of the book and in the rhetorics of editorial principles and practices for early modern texts the same types of language which obscured, misrepresented, and 'lost' for generations the writings of early modern women. Because of this easy transference of older critical terms and textual conceptualizations into a new editorial media, I would argue that editors of electronic projects, too, still need to be more aware of the significance of the materiality of texts, of the social conventions of handwritten culture as they may differ

---

[18] *Ibid.*, p. 19; Franklin, 'Illustration in Bodleian Broadside Ballads'. See also Fumerton, *Unsettled*.

from print cultures, and the multiple ways in which these unique, single copy-texts are of interest and value to scholars. Otherwise we will run the risk of continuing to classify, describe, and edit them in ways that 'edit' out the richness and complexity of their ways of communicating.[19]

So how *have* the possibilities of the digital medium been utilized in the representation of early modern women's writing? Have they opened up newly historicized environments approximating the noise, fragmentation, and contingency of early modern textuality, or closed down that richness and complexity in a return to editorial practices that work to exclude women's writing or limit its representation? The answer to this question is complex. With some notable exceptions, the digital representation of early modern women's writing to date has been dominated by the model of the encyclopaedic online database. The most significant of these in the English context have been the Brown Women Writers project and the Perdita project.[20] The Brown Women Writers project began in the 1980s as the first large-scale project to make early women's writing accessible online. After leading experimentation in developing an encoding system, Brown launched *Women Writers Online* in 1999, providing transcriptions of early women's writing, largely circulated in print between 1526 and 1850, in a searchable database.[21] The Perdita project, on the other hand, created a 'comprehensive list of substantial manuscripts written by British women in major and minor libraries', and, in partnership with Adam Matthew Digital, has linked catalogue descriptions with full digital facsimiles of 230 entries.[22] Although this database does not provide transcriptions, it is searchable in terms of its extensive metadata: searches can be made by genre, author, and date, but also by material elements of the manuscript such as layout, binding, and foliation, repository, bibliographic data, and first and last lines. Together, both resources have opened up the field of early modern women's writing by providing access for scholars outside the elite library to not only a broad set of texts, some hitherto unknown, but also to genuinely new ways of looking at those texts through the expanded search functions afforded by the digital archive. The relatively unmediated

---

[19] Ezell, 'Editing Early Modern Women's Manuscripts', p. 108.

[20] Other related encyclopaedic databases include the 'textbase' of secondary materials, *Orlando: Women's Writing in the British Isles from the Beginning to the Present*, documenting women writers' lives and works (orlando.cambridge.org); the women's biographical database *Project Continua* (www.projectcontinua.org); and Marie-Louise Coolahan is leading 'RECIRC: The Reception and Circulation of Early Modern Women's Writing, 1550–1700', a project funded by the European Research Council (www.nuigalway.ie/english/marie_louise_coolahan.html).

[21] *Women Writers Online*, www.wwp.northeastern.edu/wwo/.

[22] *Perdita Manuscripts*, www.Perditamanuscripts.amdigital.co.uk/default.aspx.

presentation of texts in these databases – as visual artefacts or facsimiles in the case of *Perdita Manuscripts* and the conscious refusal to 'create critical or synthetic editions' in the case of *Women Writers Online* – is underpinned by the new possibilities of recreating the material and historical specificity of texts in a digital environment.[23] Alongside the growing number of early modern women's texts that have been edited for print in the last decade, these unedited or minimally edited digital texts currently 'stand in' for scholarly editions of many early modern women's works.

Despite great gains in coverage and dissemination, then, the representation of early modern women's writing in encyclopaedic databases has produced other, more equivocal consequences. Recent criticism has noted that the scale and form of the types of database that have reproduced early modern women's writing to date might, inadvertently, have become a means to obscure women's writing in other ways.[24] Not only can the presentation of these texts as artefacts or transcriptions deprioritize the urgency of editing early modern women's work, but it restricts their legibility to a particular group of specialized readers. As the exhibits editor of the Brown database comments, 'these historical texts can still appear inaccessible to scholars, students, and general audiences who are unfamiliar with the historical period or the traditions, themes and other issues early women's writing often engaged, as the textbase collection currently operates primarily by way of sophisticated, targeted search function features'.[25] This is a problem common to large additive databases of all kinds. As Dan Cohen and Roy Rosenzweig note, digital media allow us to do many things better, including capacity, fluidity, interactivity, and user diversity, but they also provide a platform for doing many things less well, including quality, durability, readability, passivity, and inaccessibility.[26] In response to these problems embedded in the form of the large additive database, Jacqueline Wernimont and Julia Flanders suggest that a different type of online repository might be developed, one which helps users to sort through an abundance of data, and which values particularity rather than volume.[27]

In 2013, the Brown Women Writers project responded to such critiques by proposing to include 'online exhibits' as part of the ongoing development

---

[23] Women Writers project, 'Methodology for Transcription and Editing: Theory of the Text', www.wwp.northeastern.edu/wwo/help/editorial_principles.html.

[24] Wernimont, 'Whence Feminism?', paras. 4–6.

[25] Anna Fisher, 'Curating Digital Research: A Working Paper on the Use of Online Exhibitions in Textbased Scholarly Collections', White Paper, Women Writers project, Brown University, January 2010, p. 6.

[26] Cohen and Rosenzweig, *Digital History*, pp. 3–6.

[27] Wernimont and Flanders, 'Feminism in the Age of the Digital Archive', pp. 433–4.

of the *WWO* website. The online exhibit is not a new concept, but borrows from the digital curation practices of museums and galleries, where artefacts are coupled with other multimedia elements, such as sounds, music, maps, and timelines, and often include interactive elements where other users respond to and create content.[28] *WWO*'s proposed inclusion of online exhibits is framed as a new kind of peer-reviewed publication, combining traditional written forms with digital visualizations and other multimedia, offering both a site of scholarly experimentation and a way to shape readers' interaction with the database through an emphasis on a particular theme, genre, or literary form. This is one way to embed within the encyclopaedic database the kind of new, particularized pathways proposed by Wernimont and Flanders. Although, as yet, no exhibits have been added to the *WWO* database, this model of navigation and non-traditional publication provides a productive supplement to the problem of information overload within the large additive database. It also potentially bridges the gap between current scholarship of early modern women's writing and electronic texts, by modelling specific scholarly approaches to early modern women's writing at the same time as providing readers with ways to approach and understand its material.

Alongside large online databases, over the past decade a number of other digital sites have emerged that present smaller-scale scholarly digital editions of particular early modern women's works. Paul Salzman's award-winning online edition of Lady Mary Wroth's *Pamphilia to Amphilanthus* offers images of these sonnets from the Folger manuscript and the print edition of the *Urania* side by side, with transcriptions in old spelling and in modernized spelling and punctuation.[29] Readers can select which sources they wish to view and use according to purposes that might range from material analysis to the generation of teaching texts for undergraduates, aided by detailed biographical and textual histories. Using a similar model, *Bess of Hardwick's Letters: The Complete Correspondence c. 1550–1608* provides a searchable database of 234 letters as transcripts in a variety of forms (diplomatic, normalized, print-friendly, or xml), with colour images of 185 letters and the option to create user-generated transcripts.[30] These edited texts are supplemented by commentaries, providing biographical information, contextualizing material related to the letters and to the material

---

[28] For a broad range of examples of kinds of online exhibition, see Jennifer Mundy and Jane Burton, 'Online Exhibitions,' mw2013.museumsandtheweb.com/paper/online-exhibitions/.

[29] Paul Salzman (ed.), *Mary Wroth's Poetry: An Electronic Edition*, http://wroth.latrobe.edu.au/all-poems.html.

[30] *Bess of Hardwick's Letters: A Complete Correspondence c. 1550–1608*, www.bessofhardwick.org.

features and language of early modern letters more generally. Approaching in its multimedia components the *WWO* concept of an online exhibit, the site also includes podcasts of performances in which the letters are read.[31] Building on recent critical work highlighting women's extensive participation in epistolary networks, the 'flexible, customisable, extensible, multi media environment' offered digitally means that the letters can be read out of sequence, following themes, correspondents, or dates, in ways that approximate the local textual cultures of exchange from which they emerge.

In both Salzman's and Wiggins's scholarly online editions, emendations and editorial interventions can be hidden or revealed according to user preference, and images allow the complex material cultures of the poems and letters to be foregrounded. This is one of the dazzling advantages of the digital environment for editing: that materiality, the stuff of size, folds, seals, ribbon and floss, paper and handwriting, can be captured through images and considered as part of the text to the user outside the elite library. It is not perfect: some aspects of paper, such as watermarks, chain lines, and thickness, cannot be gauged from an image. But much else can be, and these new kinds of digital edition present a mass of primary and secondary material in new ways that suggest routes towards interpretation while maintaining textual, material, and historical complexity.

In contrast to the encyclopaedic databases of the Perdita project and *WWO*, and to the single-author online editions produced by Salzman and Wiggins, the Material Cultures of Early Modern Women's Writing website will provide something quite different: a digital archive of seven author-based case studies, linked by a thematic focus on material cultures of production, transmission, and circulation. Initially conceived as a series of online editions based on the model of Salzman's *Pamphilia to Amphilanthus*,[32] in execution this project has become something more heterogeneous: a collection of different case studies that range from established scholarly editions to more experimental textual assemblages. This site is an archive rather than a database or an edition because of the diversity of its content and its thematic, rather than authorial, mode of organization.[33] Responding to the specific material conditions of each text, different

---

[31] Alison Wiggins, 'Letters and Lives: Locating Bess of Hardwick's Letters in Early Modern Epistolary Culture', www.bessofhardwick.org/background.jsp?id=186.

[32] Salzman (ed.), *Mary Wroth's Poetry: An Electronic Edition*, http://wroth.latrobe.edu.au/all-poems .html.

[33] Archive is a highly contested term in criticism of digital forms. See Trevor Owens, 'What Do You Mean by Archive? Genres of Usage for Digital Preservers', The Signal Digital Preservation, 27 February 2014, http://blogs.loc.gov/digitalpreservation.

'editorial' strategies were designed that 'fit to purpose', resulting in a customized set of editorial approaches.

On one hand, the archive contains relatively traditional scholarly online editions of *Love's Victory* by Lady Mary Wroth, the poetry of Mary Queen of Scots, and the lesser-known manuscript poems of Elizabeth Melville, all of which follow Salzman's digital model.[34] Images of manuscript or early print text are placed alongside multiple transcriptions in old spelling and new, translations in the case of the Mary Stuart poems, supplemented by light annotation and a scholarly paratext contextualizing the life of the author, the circulation of the texts, and their literary afterlives. Case studies of poetic exchanges involving Lady Mary Jacob and Lucy Harington Russell are also concerned with modes of circulation, but here focus on the transmission of single satirical poems, attributed to their authors in manuscript miscellanies. Using stemmatic principles, these editions reproduce, side by side, the multiple competing versions of these poems as they circulated across the seventeenth century, noting where possible who transcribed and read the poems, where they are positioned in the miscellanies in which they appear, and how they fit within the transmission of other such bawdy verses in the period. All of these digital editions make available lesser-known or previously unedited material, in ways that draw on ideas of 'publication event' to show how material cultures of circulation and transmission shaped the politics, readership, and reception of these texts, in the early modern period and beyond.[35]

Other case studies in the archive depart from conventional models of the scholarly edition in search of ways to better represent the materiality of their production, transmission, and reception. The case study of Elizabeth Delaval's 1677/8 autobiography reproduces the manuscript of her memoir in full-colour, high-quality images alongside selected contextual materials connected to the autobiography: images, letters, and other primary documents. This case study provides a guided pathway through primary materials as a resource for scholars. A second case study pushes this logic several steps further. The Anne Bradstreet case study reproduces the printed paratexts that accompanied the two seventeenth-century editions of this poet in 1650 and 1678. While Bradstreet's poetry has been the subject of several modern editions, the paratexts that accompanied its initial

---

[34] A full edition of the 3,500 lines of Melville's manuscript poetry is currently being undertaken by Jamie Reid Baxter, close collaboration with whom has ensured that Ross's selection for this archive will ultimately inform and complement his scholarly edition of the material.

[35] See Cohen, *The Networked Wilderness*, pp. 1–28.

publication have usually been removed or conflated. Presenting this material in facsimile images, along with annotated transcriptions and contextual material, provides less an edition than a curated assemblage of materials related to Bradstreet's work in transmission.

While the *Material Cultures of Early Modern Women's Writing* archive models some of the new possibilities for disseminating early modern women's writing in the digital age, the role that this digital collection might have in confronting wider questions of feminist editing is more problematic. By including seven case studies and focusing on the material cultures of production and reception surrounding women's writing, the kinds of 'edition' we have produced sometimes look very different from the single-author, multi-volume print editions that continue to confer canonical status upon many early modern male authors. While a variety of digital editions of male authors have begun to experiment with editing the social, rather than the authorial, text, this is not yet the new norm. Further, the archive is itself subject to conditions of production, circulation, and reception imbricated with shifting kinds of social, cultural, and economic capital. It does not come with the imprimatur of a major publisher, nor does it come with their marketing resources. While its editions and textual assemblages might invite readers into the electronic archive and provide pathways through which the texts might be approached, many readers may never find their way to this site. And when they do reach it, the more experimental of these case studies might look too unfamiliar to be legible to some of the very audiences we would like to attract, especially those new to the field of early modern women's writing. We are well aware that the problems Cohen and Rosenzweig identify of status, readability, and access attend our archive as they do any in the digital field, or indeed any edition. The question of durability also haunts our exercise: will the platform supporting our editions exist in twenty years' time? Where will our archive be housed and maintained after its immediate funding has ceased? The very freedom from market-driven constraints that has allowed the level of experimentation on this site might also mean that its impact is limited and its longevity compromised.

On the other hand, the range of digital representations of early modern women's writing that are available today go some way to mediate the gap between the facsimile or transcription editions of large, additive digital databases and the canonical scholarly print editions of selected early modern writers. Indeed, as the Salzman edition of *Pamphilia to Amphilanthus* exemplifies, these online editions can supplement rather than replace existing scholarly editions in print.[36] The complex material histories of dissemination, reception, and attribution that link the texts and authors included in the *Material Cultures of Early Modern Women's Writing* archive mean that these are unlikely to be the subject of commercial editions. Yet here they can be presented in formats that both celebrate the complexity of their textual histories and allow users to generate their own transcripts of these texts according to need. In all of these examples, the material cultures surrounding textual production can be foregrounded through the inclusion of high-quality, zoomable images, producing a kind of hyper-materiality that, although still partial and imperfect, yet goes a long way to show just how broad the material cultures of early modern women's writing might be. These editions do emphasize live, mutable cultures of early modern textuality in the ways that Marcus and Fumerton envisage, and demonstrate that the digital environment can enable the representation of textual materiality in ways that need not deny the specificity particular to individual early modern women's texts. Rather than reinforcing conservative and exclusive principles of editing, they draw upon the possibilities of volume, of organization, and of reinvention offered by the digital world to make new kinds of databases, exhibits, and editions that guide a reader to and through early modern women's texts.

In his contribution to *Scholarly Editing in the Twenty-First Century* (2010), Jerome McGann asserts confidently although perhaps not uncontroversially, that in the twenty-first century, 'Scholarly "editing" no longer confines itself to a focus on textual documents alone, but now pursues investigations into the entire social context that comprises the cultural work.'[37] The digital editions, exhibits, archives, and assemblages that are beginning to supplement large-scale additive databases in the online environment all, to some degree, use the possibilities of the digital world to complicate and re-present what we understand as text and author. They offer a new plurality of edition, as well as a spectrum of editorial approaches, which mean that the new norm in editing early modern women's writing might be the 'bespoke': texts presented in a variety of editorial forms developed with an eye to utility and ultimately determined by the forms and availability of the texts themselves. At the same time as these experiments in the digital environment resolve some of the problems encountered over the last forty years of editing early modern women's texts, they raise new complexities and challenges. Some of these, relating to authorship, textual stability, access,

---

[36] For a print edition of *Pamphilia to Amphilanthus*, see *The Poems of Lady Mary Wroth*, ed. Roberts.
[37] McGann, 'Electronic Archives', p. 37.

and status, rewrite enduring problems through their application within new technologies of dissemination. Other problems, relating to durability, management of volume, and new ways of visually representing early modern texts, are specific to the new processes of feminist editing in the digital environment. It is a platform that offers extraordinary potential for editorial experimentation driven by the agendas of scholars working with these materials rather than those of publishers. Yet in this brave new world of possibility, fresh editorial challenges continue to emerge, forcing us as editors, scholars, and readers to interrogate the theories and practices of editing in both print and digital forms.

# Select Bibliography

## EDITIONS AND ANTHOLOGIES

Astell, Mary and John Norris, *Mary Astell and John Norris, Letters Concerning the Love of God*, ed. Derek E. Taylor and Melvyn New (Aldershot: Ashgate, 2005)

Austen, Katherine, *Book M: A London Widow's Life Writings*, ed. Pamela Hammons (Toronto: Centre for Reformation and Renaissance Studies, 2013)

*Katherine Austen's 'Book M': British Library Additional MS 4454*, ed. Sarah C. E. Ross (Tempe, AZ: ACMRS, 2011)

Behn, Aphra, *Oroonoko*, ed. Joanna Lipking (New York: Norton, 1997)

  *The Rover*, ed. Robyn Bolam (Manchester: New Mermaids, 2014)

  *The Rover*, ed. Stephen Croft and Diana Maybank (Oxford: Oxford Student Texts, 2014)

  *The Rover*, ed. Bill Naismith (London: Methuen Drama Student Editions, 2006)

  *The Works of Aphra Behn*, ed. Janet Todd, 7 vols. (London: Pickering & Chatto, 1992–6)

*Bess of Hardwick's Letters: The Complete Correspondence, c. 1550–1608*, ed. Alison Wiggins, Alan Bryson, Daniel Starza Smith, Anke Timmermann, and Graham Williams, www.bessofhardwick.org

Bevington, David, Lars Engle, Katharine Eisaman Maus, and Eric Rasmussen (eds.), *English Renaissance Drama: A Norton Anthology* (New York and London: W. W. Norton, 2002); and the e-text at www.wwnorton.com/college/english/nael9/ebook.aspx

Black, Joseph et al. (eds.), *The Broadview Anthology of British Literature*, volume II: *The Renaissance and the Early Seventeenth Century*, 2nd edn (Ontario: Broadview, 2010)

Brown, Sylvia, *Women's Writing in Stuart England: The Mothers' Legacies of Dorothy Leigh, Elizabeth Joscelin and Elizabeth Richardson* (Thrupp, Gloucestershire: Sutton Publishing, 1999)

Bullough, Geoffrey (ed.), *Narrative and Dramatic Sources of Shakespeare*, 5 vols. (London: Routledge, 1964)

Carroll, Clare (ed.), *William Shakespeare's 'The Tragedy of Othello, the Moor of Venice' and Elizabeth Cary's 'The Tragedy of Mariam, the Fair Queen of Jewry'* (New York and London: Longman, 2003)

Carroll, Clare and Andrew Hadfield (eds.), *The Longman Anthology of British Literature*, volume IB: *The Early Modern Period*, 4th edn (New York: Longman, 2010)

Cary, Elizabeth, *Elizabeth Cary, Lady Falkland: Life and Letters*, ed. Heather Wolfe (Cambridge: RTM, 2001)

'*The Mirror of the World': A Translation by Elizabeth Tanfield Cary*, ed. Lesley Peterson (Montreal and Kingston: McGill-Queen's University Press, 2012)

*The Tragedy of Mariam*, ed. A. C. Dunstan with W. W. Greg (London: The Malone Society, 1914; repr. ed. Marta Straznicky and Richard Rowland, 1992)

*The Tragedy of Mariam*, ed. Ramona Wray, Arden Early Modern Drama (London: Bloomsbury, 2012)

*The Tragedy of Mariam, The Fair Queen of Jewry*, ed. Karen Britland (London: Methuen Drama, 2010)

*The Tragedy of Mariam The Fair Queen of Jewry*, ed. Stephanie Hodgson-Wright (Keele University Press, 1996; repr. Peterborough, ON: Broadview Press, 2000)

'*The Tragedy of Mariam, The Fair Queen of Jewry*' with '*The Lady Falkland: Her Life*', *by One of Her Daughters*, ed. Barry Weller and Margaret W. Ferguson (Berkeley and London: University of California Press, 1994)

*Works by and Attributed to Elizabeth Cary*, ed. Margaret W. Ferguson, 2 vols., volume II: Part 1: *Printed Writings, 1500–1640*, The Early Modern Englishwoman (Aldershot: Scolar Press, 1996)

*Catalogue of English Literary Manuscripts 1450–1700*, ed. Peter Beal, www.celm-ms .org.uk/

Cavendish, Jane and Elizabeth Brackley, 'The Concealed Fancies: A Play by Lady Jane Cavendish and Lady Elizabeth Brackley', ed. Nathan Comfort Starr, *Proceedings of the Modern Language Association*, 46 (1931), 802–38

Cavendish, Margaret, *Observations Upon Experimental Philosophy*, ed. Eileen O'Neill (Cambridge University Press, 2001)

*Political Writings*, ed. Susan James (Cambridge University Press, 2003)

*Sociable Letters*, ed. James Fitzmaurice (New York: Garland, 1997)

*The Blazing World*, ed. Kate Lilley (London: Penguin, 1994)

*The Convent of Pleasure and Other Plays*, ed. Anne Shaver (Baltimore, MD: Johns Hopkins University Press, 1999)

Cerasano, S. P. and Marion Wynne-Davies (eds.), *Renaissance Drama by Women: Texts and Documents* (London and New York: Routledge, 1996)

Clarke, Danielle (ed.), *Renaissance Women Poets* (Harmondsworth: Penguin, 2000)

Conway, Anne, Viscountess, *The Conway Letters: The Correspondence of Anne, Viscountess Conway, Henry More, and their Friends 1642–1684*, ed. Marjorie Hope Nicolson (1930), rev. ed. Sarah Hutton (Oxford: Clarendon, 1992)

Datini, Margherita, *Letters to Francesco Datini*, trans. and ed. Carolyn James and Antonio Pagliaro (Toronto: Centre for Reformation and Renaissance Studies, 2012)

Demaria, Robert, Jr (ed.), *British Literature 1640–1789: An Anthology* (Oxford: Blackwell, 1996)

*The Devonshire Manuscript (BL Add 17,492): A Social Edition*, ed. Raymond Siemens et al., https://en.wikibooks.org/wiki/The_Devonshire_Manuscript

*The Devonshire Manuscript: A Women's Book of Courtly Poetry*, ed. Elizabeth Heale (Toronto: Centre for Reformation and Renaissance Studies, 2012)

d'Orléans, Anne Marie-Louise, Duchesse de Montpensier, *Against Marriage: The Correspondence of La Grande Mademoiselle*, trans. and ed. Joan De Jean (University of Chicago Press, 2002)

de Scudéry, Madeleine, *Selected Letters, Orations and Rhetorical Dialogues*, trans. and ed. Jane Donawerth and Julie Strongson (University of Chicago Press, 2004)

Donne, John, *Digital Donne: The Online Variorum*, ed. Gary A. Stringer, http://digitaldonne.tamu.edu

   *The Complete Poems of John Donne*, ed. Robin Robbins (Harlow: Longman, 2010)

   *The Variorium Edition of the Poetry of John Donne*, gen. ed. Gary A. Stringer (Vols. II, VI, VII (part I) currently available) (Indiana University Press, 2000, 1995, and 2005)

Douglas, Lady Margaret and others, *The Devonshire Manuscript: A Women's Book of Courtly Poetry*, ed. Elizabeth Heale (Toronto: Centre for Reformation and Renaissance Studies, 2012)

Dryden, John, *Dryden: Selected Poems*, ed. Paul Hammond and David Hopkins (Harlow: Longman, 2007)

Elizabeth I, *Elizabeth I: Autograph Compositions and Foreign Language Originals*, ed. Janel Mueller and Leah Marcus (University of Chicago Press, 2003)

   *Elizabeth I: Collected Works*, ed. Leah S. Marcus, Janel Mueller, and Mary Beth Rose (University of Chicago Press, 2000)

   *Elizabeth I: Translations, 1544–1589*, ed. Janel Mueller and Joshua Scodel (University of Chicago Press, 2009)

Fowler, Alastair (ed.), *The New Oxford Book of Seventeenth-Century Verse* (Oxford University Press, 2008)

Fowler, Constance Aston, *The Verse Miscellany of Constance Aston Fowler: A Diplomatic Edition*, ed. Deborah Aldrich-Watson (Tempe, AZ: MRTS, 2000)

Gilbert, Sandra M. and Susan Gubar (eds.), *The Norton Anthology of Literature by Women*, 2nd edn (New York: Norton, 1996)

Greenblatt, Stephen (gen. ed.), *The Norton Anthology of English Literature*, 9th edn, vol. I (New York: Norton, 2012)

Greer, Germaine, Jeslyn Medoff, Melinda Sansone, and Susan Hastings (eds.), *Kissing the Rod: An Anthology of Seventeenth-Century Women's Verse* (London: Virago, 1988)

Hadfield, Andrew (ed.), *Amazons, Savages, and Machiavels: Travel and Colonial Writing in English, 1550–1630: An Anthology* (Oxford University Press, 2001)

Halkett, Anne, *Lady Anne Halkett: Selected Self-Writings*, ed. Suzanne Trill (Aldershot: Ashgate, 2007)

Herbert, George, *The English Poems of George Herbert*, ed. Helen Wilcox (Cambridge University Press, 2007)

Herrick, Robert, *The Complete Poetry of Robert Herrick*, ed. Tom Cain and Ruth Connolly, 2 vols. (Oxford University Press, 2013)

Hodgson-Wright, Stephanie (ed.), *Women's Writing of the Early Modern Period, 1588–1688: An Anthology* (New York: Columbia University Press, 2002)

Hume, Robert D. and Harold Love (eds.), *Plays, Poems, and Miscellaneous Writings associated with George Villiers, Second Duke of Buckingham* (Oxford University Press, 2007)

Hutchinson, Lucy, *Memoirs of the Life of Colonel Hutchinson*, ed. N. H. Keeble (London: Phoenix Press, 2000)

*The Works of Lucy Hutchinson*, gen. ed. David Norbrook, 4 vols. (Oxford University Press, 2011–)

Jonson, Ben, *The Cambridge Edition of the Works of Ben Jonson*, ed. David Bevington, Martin Butler, and Ian Donaldson, 7 vols. (Cambridge University Press, 2012)

Keegan, Paul (ed.), *The Penguin Book of English Verse* (London and New York: Penguin Classics, 2005)

Lanyer, Aemilia, *The Poems of Aemilia Lanyer*, ed. Susanne Woods (Oxford University Press, 1993)

Loftis, John C. (ed.), *The Memoirs of Anne, Lady Halkett and Ann, Lady Fanshawe* (Oxford: Clarendon Press, 1979)

Mahl, Mary R. and Koon, Helene (eds.), *Female Spectator: English Women Writers Before 1800* (Bloomington: Indiana University Press, 1977)

Marlowe, Christopher, *Doctor Faustus*, ed. David Scott Kastan (New York: Norton, 2005)

*'Doctor Faustus' and Other Plays*, ed. David Bevington and Eric Rasmussen (Oxford University Press, 1995)

Massinger, Philip, *The Selected Plays of Philip Massinger*, ed. Colin Gibson (Cambridge University Press, 1978)

Marvell, Andrew, *The Poems of Andrew Marvell*, ed. Nigel Smith (Harlow: Longman, 2003)

Melville, Elizabeth, *Poems of Elizabeth Melville, Lady Culross*, ed. Jamie Reid Baxter (Edinburgh: Solsequium, 2010)

Millman, Jill Seal and Gillian Wright (eds.), *Early Modern Women's Manuscript Poetry* (Manchester University Press, 2005)

Milton, John, *The Complete Works of John Milton*, ed. J. Donald Cullington, John K. Hale, Estelle Haan, N. H. Keeble, Laura Lunger Knoppers, Barbara Kiefer Lewalski, and Nicholas McDowell (vols. II, III, VI, VIII currently available) (Oxford University Press, 2008, 2013, 2013, 2012)

Montagu, Mary Wortley, *The Complete Letters of Mary Wortley Montagu*, ed. Robert Halsband, 3 vols. (Oxford University Press, 1965–7)

Moore, Dorothy, *The Letters of Dorothy Moore, 1612–64*, ed. Lynette Hunter (Aldershot: Ashgate, 2004)

*Orlando: Women's Writing in the British Isles from the Beginning to the Present* (www
.orlando.cambridge.org)

Ostovich, Helen and Elizabeth Sauer (eds.), *Reading Early Modern Women: An
Anthology of Texts in Manuscript and Print, 1550–1700* (London: Routledge,
2004)

Parr, Katherine, *Katherine Parr: Complete Works and Correspondence*, ed. Janel
Mueller (University of Chicago Press, 2011)

Payne, Michael and John C. Hunter (eds.), *Renaissance Literature: An Anthology*
(Malden, MA: Wiley-Blackwell, 2003)

*Perdita Manuscripts*, www.perditamanuscripts.amdigital.co.uk

Philips, Katherine, *The Collected Works of Katherine Philips: The Matchless Orinda*,
ed. Patrick Thomas, Germaine Greer, and Roger Little, 3 vols. (Stump Cross,
Essex: Stump Cross Books, 1990–3)

*Project Continua* (www.projectcontinua.org)

Pulter, Hester, *Lady Hester Pulter: Poems, Emblems, and The Unfortunate Florinda*,
ed. Alice Eardley (Toronto: Centre for Reformation and Renaissance Studies,
2014)

Purkiss, Diane (ed.), *Renaissance Women: The Plays of Elizabeth Cary, The Poems
of Aemilia Lanyer* (London: Pickering & Chatto, 1994)
 *Three Tragedies by Renaissance Women* (London: Penguin Books, 1998)

Ralegh, Walter, *The Poems of Sir Walter Ralegh: A Historical Edition*, ed. Michael
Rudick (Tempe, AZ: ACMRS, 1999)

Rensselaer, Maria van, *Correspondence of Maria van Rensselaer*, trans. and ed.
A. J. F. van Laer (Albany: Unversity of the State of New York, 1935)

Rich, Mary, *The Occasional Meditations of Mary Rich, Countess of Warwick*, ed.
Raymond A. Anselment (Tempe, AZ: ACMRS, 2009)

Rudrum, Alan, Joseph Black, and Holly Faith Nelson (eds.), *The Broadview
Anthology of Seventeenth-Century Verse and Prose*, volume 1: *Verse* (Ontario:
Broadview Press, 2001)

Salzman, Paul (ed.), *Anthology of Seventeenth-Century Fiction* (Oxford University
Press, 1991)
 *Early Modern Women's Writing: An Anthology, 1560–1700* (Oxford University
Press, 2000)

Shakespeare, William, *Antony and Cleopatra*, ed. John Wilders, New Arden
Shakespeare (London and New York: Methuen, 1995)
 *'Hamlet': The Texts of 1603 and 1623*, ed. Ann Thompson and Neil Taylor
(London: Arden Shakespeare, 2006)
 *The Internet Shakespeare*, http://internetshakespeare.uvic.ca/
 *The Norton Shakespeare, based on the Oxford Edition*, ed. Stephen Greenblatt,
Walter Cohen, Jean E. Howard, and Katharine Eisaman Maus (New York:
Norton, 1997)

Sharp, Jane, *The Midwife's Book: Or, The Whole Art of Midwifry Discovered*, ed.
Elaine Hobby (Oxford University Press, 1999)

Sidney Herbert, Mary, *The Collected Works of Mary Sidney Herbert, Countess of
Pembroke*, ed. Margaret P. Hannay, Noel J. Kinnamon, and Michael G.
Brennan, 2 vols. (Oxford: Clarendon Press, 1998)

Sidney, Mary and Philip, *The Psalms of Sir Philip Sidney and the Countess of Pembroke*, ed. J. C. A. Rathmell (New York: Doubleday, 1963)

The Sidney Psalter: The Psalms of Sir Philip and Mary Sidney, ed. Hannibal Hamlin, Michael G. Brennan, Margaret P. Hannay, and Noel Kinnamon (Oxford University Press, 2009)

Sidney, Philip, *Poems of Sir Philip Sidney*, ed. William A. Ringler (Oxford: Clarendon Press, 1962)

Speght, Rachel, *The Poems and Polemics of Rachel Speght*, ed. Barbara Lewalski (Oxford University Press, 1996)

Spenser, Edmund, *Edmund Spenser: Selected Letters and Other Papers*, ed. Christopher Burlinson (Oxford University Press, 2009)

Southerne, Thomas, *The Works of Thomas Southerne*, ed. Harold Love and Robert Jordan (Oxford University Press, 1987–8)

Southwell, Anne, *The Southwell-Sibthorpe Commonplace Book: Folger MS V.b.198*, ed. Jean Klene (Tempe, AZ: MRTS, 1997)

Stevenson, Jane and Peter Davidson (eds.), *Early Modern Women Poets (1520–1700): An Anthology* (Oxford University Press, 2001)

Stuart, Arbella, *The Letters of Lady Arbella Stuart*, ed. Sara Jayne Steen (Oxford University Press, 1995)

Tarabotti, Arcangela, *Letters Familiar and Formal*, ed. and trans. Meredith K. Ray and Lynn Lara Westwater (Toronto: ITER, Centre for Reformation and Renaissance Studies, 2012)

Thornton, Alice, *My First Booke of My Life: Alice Thornton*, ed. Raymond A. Anselment (Lincoln and London: University of Nebraska Press, 2014)

Travitsky, Betty (ed.), *The Paradise of Women; Writings by Englishwomen of the Renaissance* (Westport, CT: Greenwood Press, 1981)

Tyrwhit, Elizabeth, *Elizabeth Tyrwhit's Morning and Evening Prayers*, ed. Susan M. Felch (Burlington, VT: Ashgate, 2008)

Morning and Evening Prayers, The Early Modern Englishwoman: A Facsimile Library of Essential Works, Series I, Printed Writings, 1500–1640: Part 3, Volume 1: Elizabeth Tyrwhit, ed. Patricia Brace (Aldershot: Ashgate, 2003)

Villiers, George, Duke of Buckingham, *Plays, Poems, and Miscellaneous Writings, associated with George Villiers, Second Duke of Buckingham*, ed. Robert D. Hume and Harold Love (Oxford: Oxford University Press, 2007)

Wilmot, John, *John Wilmot, Earl of Rochester, Selected Poems*, ed. Paul Davis (Oxford University Press, 2013)

The Works of John Wilmot Earl of Rochester, ed. Harold Love (Oxford University Press, 1999)

Wilson, Katharina M. (ed.), *Women Writers of the Renaissance and Reformation* (Athens, GA: University of Georgia Press, 1987)

*Women Writers Project Online*, www.wwp.northeastern.edu/wwo/

Wroth, Mary, *Lady Mary Wroth's Love's Victory: The Penshurst Manuscript*, ed. Michael Brennan (London: The Roxburghe Club, 1988)

Mary Wroth's Poetry: An Electronic Edition, ed. Paul Salzman, http://wroth.latrobe.edu.au/index.html

*The Countess of Montgomery's Urania (Abridged)*, ed. Mary Ellen Lamb (Tempe, AZ: ACMRS, 2011)

*The First Part of the Countess of Montgomery's Urania*, ed. Josephine A. Roberts (Binghamton, NY: Renaissance English Text Society, 1995)

*The Poems of Lady Mary Wroth*, ed. Josephine A. Roberts (Baton Rouge: Louisiana State University Press, 1983; repr. paperback 1992)

*The Second Part of the Countess of Montgomery's Urania*, ed. Josephine A. Roberts, completed by Suzanne Gossett and Janel Mueller (Tempe, AZ: ACMRS, 1999)

## CRITICAL MATERIAL

Alexander, Gavin, *Writing After Sidney: The Literary Response to Sir Philip Sidney, 1586–1640* (Oxford University Press, 2006)

Altman, Janet, 'The Letter Book as a Literary Institution, 1539–1789: Toward a Cultural History of Published Correspondence in France', *Yale French Studies*, 71 (1986), 17–62

Anderson, Penelope, *Friendship's Shadows: Women's Friendship and the Politics of Betrayal in England, 1640–1705* (Edinburgh University Press, 2012)

Anselment, Raymond A., 'Feminine Self-Reflection and the Seventeenth-Century Occasional Meditation', *The Seventeenth Century*, 26.1 (2011), 69–93

'Katherine Austen and the Widow's Might', *Journal for Early Modern Cultural Studies*, 5.1 (2005), 5–25

'Mary Rich, Countess of Warwick, and the Gift of Tears', *The Seventeenth Century*, 22.2 (2007), 336–57

Atherton, Margaret (ed.), *Women Philosophers of the Early Modern Period* (Indianapolis: Hackett, 1994)

Bakhtin, M. M., *Speech Genres and Other Late Essays*, trans. Vern W. McGee, ed. Caryl Emerson and Michael Holquist (Austin: University of Texas Press, 1986)

Bannet, Eve Tabor, *Empire of Letters: Letter Manuals and Transatlantic Correspondence, 1680–1820* (Oxford University Press, 2005)

Barclay, Katie, Tanya Cheadle, and Eleanor Gordon, 'The State of Scottish History: Gender', *Scottish Historical Review*, 234 (2013), 83–107

Barnes, Diana G., *Epistolary Community in Print, 1580–1664* (Farnham: Ashgate, 2013)

Bassnett, Madeline, 'The Politics of Election in Lady Mary Wroth's "Pamphilia to Amphilanthus"', *SEL*, 51.1 (2011), 111–34

Bate, Jonathan, *Shakespeare and Ovid* (Oxford: Clarendon, 1993)

Beal, Peter, *In Praise of Scribes: Manuscripts and their Makers in Seventeenth-Century England* (Oxford: Clarendon, 1998)

Beilin, Elaine V., *Redeeming Eve: Women Writers of the English Renaissance* (Princeton University Press, 1987)

Bennett, Alexandra, 'The Duchess Takes the Stage: An Evening of Margaret Cavendish's Plays in Performance. Margaret Cavendish Performance Project.

Produced by Gweno Williams. Margaret Cavendish Society Conference, Chester College, Saturday, July 19, 2003', *Early Modern Literary Studies*, Special Issue 14 (May, 2004), 15.1–10

Bicks, Caroline and Jennifer Summit (eds.), *The History of British Women's Writing, 1500–1610* (Basingstoke and New York: Palgrave Macmillan, 2010)

Bowers, Fredson, 'Greg's Rationale of Copy-Text Revisited', *Studies in Bibliography*, 31 (1978), 91–162

Brant, Clare, *Eighteenth-Century Letters and British Culture* (Basingstoke: Palgrave Macmillan, 2006)

Brant, Clare and Diane Purkiss (eds.), *Women, Texts & Histories* (London: Routledge, 1992)

Brennan, Michael, Margaret Hannay, Noel J. Kinnamon, and Mary Ellen Lamb (eds.), *The Ashgate Research Companion to the Sidneys 1500–1700*, 2 vols., vol. II (Burlington, VT: Ashgate, 2015)

Broad, Jacqueline, *Women Philosophers of the Seventeenth Century* (Cambridge University Press, 2002)

Broomhall, Susan, '"Burdened with Small Children": Women Defining Poverty in Sixteenth-Century Tours', in Jane Couchman and Ann Crabb (eds.), *Women's Letters Across Europe, 1400–1700: Form and Persuasion* (Aldershot: Ashgate, 2005), pp. 223–40

Brown, Sylvia, 'The Approbation of Elizabeth Jocelin', *EMS*, 9 (2000), 129–64

Buckroyd, Julia, *Church and State in Scotland, 1660–1681* (Edinburgh University Press, 1980)

Burlinson, Christopher and Ruth Connolly, 'Editing Stuart Poetry', *SEL*, 52.1 (2012), 1–12

Burke, Victoria, 'Contexts for Women's Manuscript Miscellanies: The Case of Elizabeth Lyttelton and Sir Thomas Browne', *Yearbook of English Studies*, 33 (2003), 316–28

'The Couplet and the Poem: Late Seventeeth Century Women Reading Katherine Philips', *Women's Writing*, 24 (2017)

'Let's Get Physical: Bibliography, Codicology, and Seventeenth-Century Women's Manuscripts', *Literature Compass*, 4.6 (2007), 1667–82

Burke, Victoria E. and Jonathan Gibson (eds.), *Early Modern Women's Manuscript Writing: Selected Papers from the Trinity/Trent Colloquium* (Aldershot: Ashgate, 2004)

Burton, Ben and Elizabeth Scott-Baumann (eds.), *The Work of Form: Poetics and Materiality in Early Modern Culture* (Oxford University Press, 2014)

Butterworth, Charles C., *The English Primers (1529–1545): Their Publication and Connection with the English Bible and the Reformation in England* (University of Pennsylvania Press, 1953)

Callaghan, Dympna, 'Re-reading Elizabeth Cary's *The Tragedy of Mariam, Faire Queene of Jewry*', in Margo Hendricks and Patricia Parker (eds.), *Women, 'Race', and Writing in the Early Modern Period* (London and New York: Routledge, 1994), pp. 163–77

Callaghan, Dympna (ed.), *The Impact of Feminism in Renaissance Studies* (Basingstoke: Palgrave, 2006)

Campbell, Julie, Anne Larsen, and Gabriella Eschrich (eds.), *Crossing Borders: Early Modern Women and Communities of Letters* (Aldershot: Ashgate, 2009)

Carrell, Jennifer Lee, 'A Pack of Lies in a Looking Glass', *SEL*, 34.1 (1994), 79–107

Cheney, Patrick, Andrew Hadfield, and Garrett Sullivan (eds.), *Early Modern English Poetry: A Critical Companion* (Oxford University Press, 2006)

Cheney, Patrick and Lauren Silberman (eds.), *Worldmaking Spenser* (Lexington: University of Kentucky Press, 2000)

Clarke, Danielle, '"Form'd into Words by your Divided Lips": Women, Rhetoric and the Ovidian Tradition', in Danielle Clarke and Elizabeth Clarke (eds.), *This Double Voice: Gendered Writing in Early Modern England* (Basingstoke: Macmillan, 2000), pp. 61–87

'Nostalgia, Anachronism, and the Editing of Early Modern Women's Texts', *TEXT*, 15 (2003), 187–209

*The Politics of Early Modern Women's Writing* (London: Pearson Education, 2001)

'The Psalms of Mary Sidney Herbert, Countess of Pembroke', in Michael Brennan et al. (eds.), *The Ashgate Research Companion to the Sidneys*, vol. II (Burlington, VT: Ashgate, 2015), ch. 19

Clarke, Danielle and Elizabeth Clarke (eds.), *This Double Voice: Gendered Writing in Early Modern England* (Basingstoke: Macmillan, 2000)

Clarke, Danielle and Marie-Louise Coolahan, 'Gender, Reception and Form: Early Modern Women and the Making of Verse', in Ben Burton and Elizabeth Scott-Baumann (eds.), *The Work of Form: Poetics and Materiality in Early Modern Culture* (Oxford University Press, 2014), pp. 144–61

Clarke, Elizabeth, 'Beyond Microhistory: The Use of Women's Manuscripts in a Widening Political Arena', in James Daybell (ed.), *Women and Politics in Early Modern England, 1450–1700* (Aldershot: Ashgate, 2004), pp. 211–27

*Politics, Religion and the Song of Songs in Seventeenth-Century England* (Basingstoke: Palgrave Macmillan, 2011)

'The Legacy of Mothers and Others: Women's Theological Writing 1640–1660', in Christopher Durston and Judith Maltby (eds.), *Religion in Revolutionary England* (Manchester University Press, 2006), pp. 69–92

Clarke, Elizabeth and Jonathan Gibson, 'Introduction', in Jill Seal Millman and Gillian Wright (eds.), *Early Modern Women's Manuscript Poetry* (Manchester University Press, 2005), pp. 1–10

Clucas, Stephen (ed.), *A Princely Brave Woman: Essays on Margaret Cavendish, Duchess of Newcastle* (Aldershot: Ashgate, 2003)

Cohen, Daniel and Roy Rosenzweig, *Digital History: A Guide to Gathering, Preserving and Presenting the Past on the Web* (Philadelphia: University of Pennsylvania Press, 2006)

Cohen, Matt, *The Networked Wilderness: Communicating in Early New England* (Minneapolis: University of Minnesota Press, 2010)

Comensoli, Viviane and Paul Stevens (eds.), *Discontinuities: New Essays on Renaissance Literature and Criticism* (University of Toronto Press, 1998)

Connolly, Annaliese, 'Peele's *David and Bethsabe*: Reconsidering Biblical Drama of the Long 1590s', *Early Modern Literary Studies*, Special Issue 16 (2007), 9.1–20, http://purl.oclc.org/emls/si-16/connpeel.htm

Coolahan, Marie-Louise, 'Redeeming Parcels of Time: Aesthetics and Practice of Occasional Meditation', *The Seventeenth Century*, 22.1 (2007), 124–43

‘"We live by Chance, and slip into Events": Occasionality and the Manuscript Verse of Katherine Philips', *Eighteenth-Century Ireland*, 18 (2003), 9–23

Cooper, Helen, *The English Romance in Time: Transforming Motifs from Geoffrey of Monmouth to the Death of Shakespeare* (Oxford University Press, 2004)

Couchman, Jane and Ann Crabb (eds.), *Women's Letters Across Europe, 1400–1700: Form and Persuasion* (Aldershot: Ashgate, 2005)

Crabstick, Ben, 'Katherine Philips, Richard Marriot, and the Contemporary Significance of *Poems*', *Women's Writing*, 23 (2016)

Crawford, Julie, *Mediatrix: Women, Politics, and Literary Production in Early Modern England* (Oxford University Press, 2014)

Crowther, Kathleen M., *Adam and Eve in the Protestant Reformation* (Cambridge University Press, 2010)

Dalbello, Marija, 'Digitality, Epistolarity and Reconstituted Letter Archives', *Proceedings of the Eighth International Conference on Conceptions of Information Science, Information Research*, 18.3 (September 2016)

Davidson, Peter, 'Green Thoughts. Marvell's Gardens: Clues to Two Curious Puzzles', *TLS*, 5044 (3 December 1999), 14–15

Daybell, James, 'Women, Politics and Domesticity: The Scribal Publication of Lady Rich's Letter to Elizabeth I', in Anne Lawrence-Mathers and Phillipa Hardman (eds.), *Women and Writing, c. 1340–1650: The Domestication of Print Culture* (Woodbridge: Boydell and Brewer, 2010), pp. 111–30

Daybell, James (ed.), *Early Modern Women's Letter Writing, 1450–1700* (Basingstoke: Palgrave, 2001)

*Women and Politics in Early Modern England, 1450–1700* (Aldershot: Ashgate, 2004)

*Women Letter-Writers in Tudor England* (Oxford University Press, 2006)

Daybell, James and Peter Hinds (eds.), *Material Readings of Early Modern Culture: Texts and Social Practices, 1580–1730* (Basingstoke: Palgrave Macmillan, 2010)

Delany, Paul, *British Autobiography in the Seventeenth Century* (London: Routledge and Kegan Paul, 1969)

Dolan, Frances E., *The Whores of Babylon: Catholicism, Gender and Seventeenth-Century Print Culture* (Ithaca, NY: Cornell University Press, 1999)

Doody, Margaret Anne, 'Response', in Ann M. Hutchinson (ed.), *Editing Women: Papers Given at the Thirty-First Annual Conference on Editorial Problems* (University of Toronto Press, 1998), pp. 125–40

Dowd, Michelle M. and Julie A. Eckerle (eds.), *Genre and Women's Life Writing in Early Modern England* (Aldershot: Ashgate, 2007)

Dragstra, Henk, Sheila Ottway, and Helen Wilcox (eds.), *Betraying Our Selves: Forms of Self-Representation in Early Modern English Texts* (Basingstoke: Macmillan, 2000)

Durston, Christopher and Judith Maltby (eds.), *Religion in Revolutionary England* (Manchester University Press, 2006)

Dutcher, James and Anne Lake Prescott (eds.), *Renaissance Historicisms* (Newark: University of Delaware Press, 2008)

Dzelzainis, Martin, 'Robert Ferguson and Andrew Marvell: An Unnoticed Allusion', *NQ*, 244 (1999), 340–1

Eardley, Alice, 'Hester Pulter's "Indivisibles" and the Challenges of Annotating Early Modern Women's Poetry' *SEL*, 52.1 (2012), 117–41

'"I haue not time to point yr booke . . . which I desire you yourselfe to doe": Editing the Form of Early Modern Manuscript Verse', in Ben Burton and Elizabeth Scott-Baumann (eds.), *The Work of Form: Poetics and Materiality in Early Modern Culture* (Oxford University Press, 2014), pp. 162–78

Eckerle, Julie, *Romancing the Self in Early Modern Englishwomen's Life Writing* (Aldershot: Ashgate, 2013)

Euler, Carrie, *Couriers of the Gospel: England and Zurich, 1531–1558* (Zurich: Theologischer Verlag Zürich, 2006)

Ewan, Elizabeth, 'A New Trumpet? The History of Women in Scotland, 1300–1700', *History Compass*, 7.2 (2009), 431–46

Ezell, Margaret J. M., 'Ann Halkett's Morning Devotions: Posthumous Publication and the Culture of Writing in Late Seventeenth-Century Britain', in Arthur F. Marotti and Michael D. Bristol (eds.), *Print, Manuscript, Performance: The Changing Relations of the Media in Early Modern England* (Columbus: Ohio State University Press, 2000), pp. 215–31

'Editing Early Modern Women's Manuscripts: Theory, Electronic Editions, and the Accidental Copy-Text', *Literature Compass*, 7.2 (2010), 102–9

'Mask of the Feminine in Restoration, Early Eighteenth-Century Print Culture', in Robert Griffin (ed.), *The Faces of Anonymity: Anonymous and Pseudonymous Publication from the Sixteenth to the Twentieth Century* (New York: Palgrave Macmillan, 2003), pp. 63–79

*The Patriarch's Wife: Literary Evidence and the History of the Family* (Chapel Hill: University of North Carolina Press, 1987)

'The Posthumous Publication of Women's Manuscripts and the History of Authorship', in George L. Justice and Nathan Tinker (eds.), *Women's Writing and the Circulation of Ideas: Manuscript Publication in England, 1550–1800* (Cambridge University Press, 2002, repr. 2010), pp. 121–36

*Writing Women's Literary History* (Baltimore and London: Johns Hopkins University Press, 1993)

Felch, Susan M., '"Halff a Scripture Woman": Heteroglossia and Female Authorial Agency in Prayers by Lady Elizabeth Tyrwhit, Anne Lock, and Anne Wheathill', in Micheline White (ed.), *English Women, Religion, and Textual Production, 1500–1625* (Farnham: Ashgate, 2011), pp. 147–66

'Noble Gentlewomen Famous for Their Learning', *American Notes and Queries*, 16.2 (2003), 14–19

'The Exemplary Anne Vaughan Lock', in Johanna Harris and Elizabeth Scott-Baumann (eds.), *The Intellectual Culture of Puritan Women, 1558–1680* (London: Palgrave Macmillan, 2011), pp. 15–27

Fendler, Susanne (ed.), *Feminist Contributions to the Literary Canon: Setting Standards of Taste* (Lewiston, NY: Mellen, 1997)

Findlay, Alison, Stephanie Hodgson-Wright, and Gweno Williams, '"The Play is Ready to be Acted": Women and Dramatic Production, 1570–1670', *Women's Writing*, 6.1 (1999), 129–48

*Women and Dramatic Production, 1550–1700* (Harlow: Longman, 2000)

Fitzmaurice, James, 'Margaret Cavendish on Her Own Writing: Evidence from Revision and Handmade Correction', *Papers of the Bibliographical Society of America*, 85 (1991), 297–307

'Problems with Editing Margaret Cavendish', *Renaissance English Text Society Publications* (1991), 1–17

Foucault, Michel, *The Archaeology of Knowledge*, trans. A. M. Sheridan Smith (London: Routledge, 1989)

'What is an Author?', in Josué V. Harari (ed.), *Textual Strategies: Perspectives in Post-Structuralist Criticism* (Ithaca, NY: Cornell University Press, 1979), pp. 141–60

Franklin, Alexandra, 'The Art of Illustration in Bodleian Broadside Ballads before 1820', *Bodleian Library Record*, 17.5 (2002), 329–31

Frith, Valerie (ed.), *Women and History: Voices of Early Modern England* (Concord: Irwin Publishing, 1997)

Frye, Northrop, *Secular Scripture: A Study of the Structure of Romance* (Cambridge, MA: Harvard University Press, 1976)

Fuchs, Barbara, *Romance* (New York and London: Routledge, 2004)

Fumerton, Patricia, 'Remembering by Dismembering: Databases, Archiving, and the Recollection of Seventeenth-Century Broadside Ballads', in Patricia Fumerton et al. (eds.), *Ballads and Broadsides in Britain, 1500–1800* (Aldershot: Ashgate, 2010), pp. 13–34

*Unsettled: The Culture of Mobility and the Working Poor in Early Modern England* (University of Chicago Press, 2006)

Fumerton, Patricia, Anita Guerrini, and Kris McAbee (eds.), *Ballads and Broadsides in Britain, 1500–1800* (Aldershot: Ashgate, 2010)

Geertz, Clifford, *The Interpretation of Cultures* (New York: Basic Books, 1977)

Gibson, Jonathan, 'Casting Off Blanks: Hidden Structures in Early Modern Paper Books', in James Daybell and Peter Hinds (eds.), *Material Readings of Early Modern Culture: Texts and Social Practices, 1580–1730* (Basingstoke: Palgrave Macmillan, 2010), pp. 208–28

'Synchrony and Process: Editing Manuscript Miscellanies', *SEL*, 52.1 (2012), 85–100

Gibson, Jonathan and Gillian Wright, 'Editing Perdita: Texts, Theories, Readers', in Ann Hollinshead Hurley and Chanita Goodblatt (eds.), *Women Editing/ Editing Women: Early Modern Women Writers and the New Textualism* (Newcastle upon Tyne: Cambridge Scholars Publishing, 2009), pp. 155–73

Gray, Catharine, 'Feeding on the Seed of the Woman: Dorothy Leigh and the Figure of Maternal Dissent', *ELH*, 68 (2001), 563–92

'Katherine Philips and the Post-Courtly Coterie', *ELR*, 32 (2002), 426–51

Green, Ian, *Print and Protestantism in Early Modern England* (Oxford University Press, 2000)

Green, Reina, '"Ears prejudicate" in *Mariam* and *Duchess of Malfi*', *SEL*, 43.2 (2003), 459–74

Greene, Roland, 'Sir Philip Sidney's Psalms, the Sixteenth-century Psalter, and the Nature of Lyric', *SEL*, 30.1 (1990), 19–40

Greer, Germaine, *Slip-Shod Sibyls: Recognition, Rejection and the Woman Poet* (London: Penguin, 1996)

Greg, W. W., 'The Rationale of Copy-Text', *Studies in Bibliography*, 3 (1950), 19–36

Griffin, Robert (ed.), *The Faces of Anonymity: Anonymous and Pseudonymous Publication from the Sixteenth to the Twentieth Century* (New York: Palgrave Macmillan, 2003)

Grundy, Isobel, 'Editing Lady Mary Wortley Montagu', in Ann M. Hutchinson (ed.), *Editing Women: Papers Given at the Thirty-First Annual Conference on Editorial Problems* (University of Toronto Press, 1998), pp. 55–78
*Lady Mary Wortley Montagu: Comet of the Enlightenment* (Oxford University Press, 2001)

Hackel, Heidi Brayman, *Reading Material in Early Modern England* (Cambridge University Press, 2005)

Hackett, Helen, *Women and Romance Fiction in the English Renaissance* (Cambridge University Press, 2000)
'"Yet Tell me Some Such Fiction": Lady Mary Wroth's *Urania* and the "Femininity of Romance"', in Clare Brant and Diane Purkiss (eds.), *Women, Texts & Histories* (London: Routledge, 1992), pp. 39–68

Hadfield, Andrew (ed.), *Oxford Handbook of Early Modern Prose, 1500–1640* (Oxford University Press, 2013)

Hageman, Elizabeth H., 'Making a Good Impression: Early Texts of Poems and Letters by Katherine Philips, the "Matchless Orinda"', *South Central Review*, 11.2 (1994), 39–65
'The "false printed" Broadside of Katherine Philips's "To the Queens Majesty on her Happy Arrival"', *The Library*, 6th Ser. 17 (1995), 321–6
'Treacherous Accidents and the Abominable Printing of Katherine Philips's 1664 Poems', in W. Speed Hill (ed.), *New Ways of Looking at Old Texts, III: Papers of the Renaissance English Text Society, 1997–2001* (Tempe, AZ: ACMRS, 2004), pp. 85–95

Hageman, Elizabeth and Andrea Sununu, '"More Copies of it abroad than I could have imagin'd": Further Manuscript Texts of Katherine Philips, "the Matchless Orinda"', *EMS*, 5 (1994), 127–69
'New Manuscript Texts of Katherine Philips, the "Matchless Orinda"', *EMS*, 4 (1993), 176–80

Hamlin, Hannibal, 'Psalm Culture in the English Renaissance: Readings of Psalm 137 by Shakespeare, Spenser, Milton and Others', *RQ*, 55 (2002), 224–57

Hammons, Pamela S., 'Despised Creatures: The Illusion of Maternal Self-Effacement in Seventeenth-Century Child Loss Poetry', *ELH*, 66 (1999), 25–49

*Gender, Sexuality, and Material Objects in English Renaissance Verse* (Farnham: Ashgate, 2010)

Katherine Austen's Country House Innovations', *SEL*, 40.1 (2000), 123–37

*Poetic Resistance: English Women Writers and the Early Modern Lyric* (Aldershot and Burlington, VT: Ashgate, 2002)

Hannay, Margaret P., 'The Countess of Pembroke's Agency in Print and Scribal Culture', in George L. Justice and Nathan Tinker (eds.), *Women's Writing and the Circulation of Ideas: Manuscript Publiction in England, 1550–1800* (Cambridge University Press, 2002, repr. 2010), pp. 17–49

Harari, Josué V. (ed.), *Textual Strategies: Perspectives in Post-Structuralist Criticism* (Ithaca, NY: Cornell University Press, 1979)

Harris, Johanna and Elizabeth Scott-Baumann (eds.), *The Intellectual Culture of Puritan Women, 1558–1680* (London: Palgrave Macmillan, 2011)

Harvey, Elizabeth and Katherine Eisaman Maus (eds.), *Soliciting Interpretation: Literary Theory and Seventeenth-Century English Poetry* (University of Chicago Press, 1990)

Hattaway, Michael (ed.), *Companion to English Renaissance Literature and Culture* (Oxford: Wiley-Blackwell, 2002)

Heffernan, Teresa, 'Feminism Against the East/West Divide: Lady Mary Wortley Montagu's Turkish Embassy Letters', *Eighteenth-Century Studies*, 33.2 (2000), 201–15

Hegele, Arden, 'Lord Byron, Literary Detective: The Recovery of Lady Mary Wortley Montagu's Long-lost Venetian Letters', *Byron Journal*, 39.1 (2011), 35–44

Hendricks, Margo and Patricia Parker (eds.), *Women, 'Race', and Writing in the Early Modern Period* (London and New York: Routledge, 1994)

Herman, Peter C. (ed.), *Reading Monarchs Writing: The Poetry of Henry VIII, Mary Stuart, Elizabeth I, and James VI/I* (Tempe, AZ: ACMRS, 2002)

Hill, Christopher, *The English Bible and the Seventeenth-Century Revolution* (New York: Penguin, 1993)

Hill, W. Speed, 'Editing Nondramatic Texts of the English Renaissance: A Field Guide with Illustrations', in W. Speed Hill (ed.), *New Ways of Looking at Old Texts: Papers of the Renaissance English Text Society, 1985–1991* (Binghampton, NY: MRTS and RETS, 1993), pp. 1–24

Hill, W. Speed (ed.) *New Ways of Looking at Old Texts: Papers of the Renaissance English Text Society, 1985–1991* (Binghampton, NY: MRTS and RETS, 1993)

*New Ways of Looking at Old Texts, III: Papers of the Renaissance English Text Society, 1997–2001* (Tempe, AZ: ACMRS, 2004)

Hughes, Ann, *Gangraena and the Struggle for The English Revolution* (Oxford University Press, 2004)

Hull, Suzanne, *Chaste, Silent, and Obedient: English Books for Women 1475–1640* (San Marino, CA: Huntington Library Press, rev. 1988)

Hurley, Ann Hollinshead and Chanita Goodblatt (eds.), *Women Editing/Editing Women: Early Modern Women Writers and the New Textualism* (Newcastle upon Tyne: Cambridge Scholars Publishing, 2009)

Hutchinson, Ann M. (ed.), *Editing Women: Papers Given at the Thirty-First Annual Conference on Editorial Problems* (University of Toronto Press, 1998)

Hutton, Sarah, *Anne Conway: A Woman Philosopher* (Cambridge University Press, 2009)

Jackson, Clare, *Restoration Scotland, 1660–1690: Royalist Politics, Religion and Ideas* (Woodbridge: The Boydell Press, 2003)

Jagodzinski, Cecile M., *Privacy and Print: Reading and Writing in Seventeenth-Century England* (Charlottesville: University Press of Virginia, 1999)

Jameson, Frederic, *The Political Unconscious: Narrative as a Socially Symbolic Act* (Ithaca, NY: Cornell University Press, 1981)

Justice, George L. and Nathan Tinker (eds.), *Women's Writing and the Circulation of Ideas: Manuscript Publication in England, 1550–1800* (Cambridge University Press, 2002, repr. 2010)

Kinney, Arthur F. (ed.), *A Companion to Renaissance Drama* (Oxford: Blackwell, 2002)

Kinney, Clare, '"Beleeve This Butt a Fiction": Female Authorship, Narrative Undoing, and the Limits of Romance in *The Second Part of the Countess of Montgomery's Urania*', *Spenser Studies*, 17 (2003), 239–50

Kinney, Clare (ed.), *Ashgate Critical Essays on Women Writers in England, 1550–1700*, volume IV: *Mary Wroth* (Burlington, VT: Ashgate, 2009)

Knight, Jeffrey Todd, '"Furnished" for Action: Renaissance Books as Furniture', *Book History*, 12 (2009), 37–73

Knoppers, Laura Lunger, *Politicizing Domesticity from Henrietta Maria to Milton's Eve* (Cambridge University Press, 2011)

Lamb, Mary Ellen, 'Constructions of Early Modern Women Readers', in Susanne Woods and Margaret Hannay (eds.), *Teaching Tudor and Stuart Women Writers* (New York: MLA, 2000), pp. 23–34

 *Gender and Authorship in the Sidney Circle* (Madison: University of Wisconsin Press, 1990)

 'Merging the Secular and the Spiritual in Lady Anne Halkett's Memoirs', in Michele M. Dowd and Julie A. Eckerle (eds.), *Genre and Women's Life Writing in Early Modern England* (Aldershot: Ashgate, 2007), pp. 81–96

 'The Biopolitics of Romance in Mary Wroth's *Countess of Montgomery's Urania*', *ELR*, 31.1 (2001), 107–30

 'Topicality and the Interrogation of Wonder', in James Dutcher and Anne Lake Prescott (eds.), *Renaissance Historicisms* (Newark: University of Delaware Press, 2008), pp. 247–58

 'Topicality in Mary Wroth's Countess of Montgomery's Urania: Prose Romance, Masque, and Lyric', in Andrew Hadfield (ed.), *Oxford Handbook of Early Modern Prose, 1500–1640* (Oxford University Press, 2013), pp. 235–50

Lawrence-Mathers, Anne and Phillipa Hardman (eds.), *Women and Writing, c. 1340–1650: The Domestication of Print Culture* (Woodbridge: Boydell and Brewer, 2010)

Leod, Randall M [sic] (ed.), *Crisis in Editing: Texts of the English Renaissance* (New York: AMS Press, 1994)

Levy, F. J., 'The Founding of the Camden Society', *Victorian Studies*, 7.3 (1964), 295–305

Lewalski, Barbara Kiefer, *Protestant Poetics and the Seventeenth-Century Religious Lyric* (Princeton University Press, 1979)

    *Writing Women in Jacobean England* (Cambridge, MA: Harvard University Press, 1993)

Lilley, Kate, 'Contracting Readers: "Margaret Newcastle" and the Rhetoric of Conjugality', in Stephen Clucas (ed.), *A Princely Brave Woman: Essays on Margaret Cavendish, Duchess of Newcastle* (Aldershot: Ashgate, 2003), pp. 19–39

    'Fruits of Sodom: The Critical Erotics of Early Modern Women's Writing', *Parergon*, 29.2 (2012), 175–92

Limbert, Claudia, '"The Unison of Well-Tun'd Hearts": Katherine Philips' Friendships with Male Writers', *English Language Notes*, 29 (1991), 25–37

Logan, George M. and Gordon Teskey (eds.), *Unfolded Tales: Essays on Renaissance Romance* (Ithaca, NY: Cornell University Press, 1989)

Longfellow, Erica, 'Public, Private, and the Household in Early Seventeenth-Century England', *Journal of British Studies*, 45 (2006), 313–34

Lopez, Jeremy, *Constructing the Canon of Early Modern Drama* (Cambridge University Press, 2014)

Luckyj, Christina, *'A Moving Rhetoricke': Gender and Silence in Early Modern England* (Manchester University Press, 2002)

    'The Politics of Genre in Early Modern Women's Writing: The Case of Lady Mary Wroth', *English Studies in Canada*, 27 (2001), 253–82

Macdonald, Joyce Green, *Women and Race in Early Modern Texts* (Cambridge University Press, 2002)

Machosky, Brenda (ed.), *Thinking Allegory Otherwise* (Stanford University Press, 2010)

Maddison, R. E., '"The King's Cabinet Opened": A Case Study in Pamphlet History', *NQ*, 13.1 (1966), 2–9

Magnusson, Lynne, 'A Rhetoric of Requests: Genre and Linguistic Scripts in Elizabethan Women's Suitors' Letters', in James Daybell (ed.), *Women and Politics in Early Modern England, 1450–1700* (Aldershot: Ashgate, 2004), pp. 51–66

Mann, Alastair J., *The Scottish Book Trade, 1500–1720: Print Commerce and Print Control in Early Modern Scotland* (East Linton: Tuckwell, 2000)

Manoff, Marlene, 'Theories of the Archive: Across the Disciplines', *Portal: Libraries and the Academy*, 4 (2004), 9–25

Marcus, Leah S., 'Confessions of a Reformed Uneditor (II)', *PMLA*, 115.5 (2000), 1072–7

    'Elizabeth I as Public and Private Poet', in Peter C. Herman (ed.), *Reading Monarchs Writing: The Poetry of Henry VIII, Mary Stuart, Elizabeth I, and James VI/I* (Tempe, AZ: ACMRS, 2002), pp. 135–53

    'Elizabeth on Elizabeth: Underexamined Episodes in an Overexamined Life', in Kevin Sharpe and Steven N. Zwicker (eds.), *Writing Lives: Biography and Textuality, Identity and Representation in Early Modern England* (Oxford University Press, 2008), pp. 209–32

'Elizabeth on Ireland', in Brendan Kane and Valerie McGowan-Doyle (eds.), *Elizabeth I and Ireland* (Cambridge University Press, 2014), pp. 40–59

'From Oral Delivery to Print in the Speeches of Elizabeth I', in Arthur F. Marotti and Michael D. Bristol (eds.), *Print, Manuscript, Performance: The Changing Relations of the Media in Early Modern England* (Columbus: Ohio State University Press, 2000), pp. 33–48

'Textual Scholarship', in David G. Nicholls (ed.), *Introduction to Scholarship in Modern Languages and Literature* (New York: MLA, 2007), pp. 145–9

'The Silence of the Archive and the Noise of Cyberspace', in Neil Rhodes and Jonathan Sawday (eds.), *The Renaissance Computer: Knowledge Technology in the First Age of Print* (London: Routledge, 2000), pp. 18–29

*Unediting the Renaissance: Shakespeare, Marlowe, Milton* (London and New York: Routledge, 1996)

Marotti, Arthur, *Manuscript, Print, and the English Renaissance Lyric* (Ithaca, NY: Cornell University Press, 1995)

Marotti, Arthur F. and Michael D. Bristol (eds.), *Print, Manuscript, Performance: The Changing Relations of the Media in Early Modern England* (Columbus: Ohio State University Press, 2000)

Martin, Randall (ed.), *Renaissance Women Writers in England* (London: Longman, 1997)

Masten, Jeffrey, 'Material Cavendish: Paper, Performance, "Social Virginity"', *MLQ*, 65.1 (2004), 49–68

Mayer, Tamar and Suleiman A. Mourad (eds.), *Jerusalem: Idea and Reality* (London and New York: Routledge, 2008)

McCarthy, Erin A., '*Poems, by J.D.* (1635) and the Creation of John Donne's Literary Biography', *John Donne Journal*, 32 (2013), 57–85

McGann, Jerome, 'Electronic Archives and Digital Editing', in 'Scholarly Editing in the Twenty-First Century', special issue of *Literature Compass*, 7.2 (2010), 37–42

Mendelson, Sara, 'Stuart Women's Diaries and Occasional Memoirs', in Mary Prior (ed.), *Women in English Society, 1500–1800* (London: Methuen, 1985), pp. 181–210

Mendelson, Sara and Patricia Crawford, *Women in Early Modern England* (Oxford University Press, 1999)

Menges, Hilary, 'Authorship, Friendship, and Forms of Publication in Katherine Philips', *SEL*, 52 (2012), 517–41

Miller, Jacqueline, 'Lady Mary Wroth in the House of Busirane', in Patrick Cheney and Lauren Silberman (eds.), *Worldmaking Spenser* (Lexington: University of Kentucky Press, 2000), pp. 115–24

Miller, Shannon, '"Mirrours More Then One": Spenser and Female Authority', in Patrick Cheney and Lauren Silberman (eds.), *Worldmaking Spenser* (Lexington: University of Kentucky Press, 2000), pp. 125–47

Murphy, Andrew, *Shakespeare in Print: A History and Chronology of Shakespeare Publishing* (Cambridge University Press, 2003)

Murphy, Andrew (ed.), *The Renaissance Text: Theory, Editing, Textuality* (Manchester University Press, 2000)

Newbold, W. Webster, 'Letter Writing and Vernacular Literacy in Sixteenth-Century England', in Carol Poster and Linda C. Mitchell (eds.), *Letter-Writing Manuals and Instruction from Antiquity to the Present: Historical and Bibliographic Studies* (Columbia: University of South Carolina Press, 2007), pp. 127–40

Newcomb, Lori Humphrey, *Reading Popular Romance in Early Modern England* (New York: Columbia University Press, 2002)

Nicholls, David G. (ed.), *Introduction to Scholarship in Modern Languages and Literatures* (New York: MLA, 2007)

Norbrook, David, 'Lucy Hutchinson's "Elegies" and the Situation of the Republican Woman Writer (with text)', *ELR*, 27 (1997), 468–521

'"This blushing tribute of a borrowed muse": Robert Overton and his Overturning of the Poetic Canon', *EMS*, 4 (1993), 220–66

Orgel, Stephen, 'What is an Editor?', *Shakespeare Studies*, 24 (1996), 23–9

Orgis, Rahel, '"[A] Story Very Well Woorth Readinge": Why Early Modern Readers Valued Lady Mary Wroth's *Urania*', *Sidney Journal*, 31.1 (2013), 81–100

Owens, W. R. and Lizbeth Goodman (eds.), *Shakespeare, Aphra Behn and the Canon* (Abingdon: Routledge, 1996)

Pal, Carol, *The Republic of Women: Rethinking the Republic of Letters in the Seventeenth Century* (Cambridge University Press, 2012)

Parker, Patricia, *Inescapable Romance: Studies in the Poetics of a Mode* (Princeton University Press, 1979)

Patrick, J. Max, Robert O. Evans, and John W. Wallace (eds.), *'Attic' and Baroque Prose Style: The Anti-Ciceronian Movement, Essays by Morris W. Croll* (Princeton University Press, 1969)

Peikola, Matti, Janne Skaffari, and Sanna-Kaisa Tanskanen (eds.), *Instructional Writing in English: Studies in Honour of Risto Hiltunen* (Amsterdam and Philadelphia, PA: John Benjamins, 2009)

Pender, Patricia, *Early Modern Women's Writing and the Rhetoric of Modesty* (New York: Palgrave Macmillan, 2012)

'The Ghost and the Machine in the Sidney Family Corpus', *SEL*, 51 (2011), 65–85

Pender, Patricia and Rosalind Smith (eds.), *Material Cultures of Early Modern Women's Writing* (Basingstoke: Palgrave Macmillan, 2014)

Poole, Kristen, '"The Fittest Closet for All Goodness": Authorial Strategies of Jacobean Mothers' Manuals', *SEL*, 35 (1995), 69–88

Poster, Carol and Linda C. Mitchell (eds.), *Letter-Writing Manuals and Instruction from Antiquity to the Present: Historical and Bibliographic Studies* (Columbia: University of South Carolina Press, 2007)

Price, Bronwen and Simon Wortham (eds.), *Francis Bacon: New Atlantis* (Manchester University Press, 2003)

Prior, Mary (ed.), *Women in English Society, 1500–1800* (London: Methuen, 1985)

Quilligan, Maureen, 'Allegory and Female Agency', in Brenda Machosky (ed.), *Thinking Allegory Otherwise* (Stanford University Press, 2010), pp. 163–86

  *Incest and Agency in Elizabeth's England* (Philadelphia: University of Pennsylvania Press, 2005)

  'Lady Mary Wroth: Female Authority and the Family Romance', in George M. Logan and Gordon Teskey (eds.), *Unfolded Tales: Essays on Renaissance Romance* (Ithaca, NY: Cornell University Press, 1989), pp. 257–80

  'Staging Gender: William'Shakespeare and Elizabeth Cary', in James Grantham Turner (ed.), *Sexuality and Gender in Early Modern Europe: Institutions, Texts, Images* (Cambridge University Press, 1993), pp. 208–32

  'The Constant Subject: Instability and Authority in Wroth's Urania Poems', in Elizabeth Harvey and Katherine Maus (eds.), *Soliciting Interpretation: Literary Theory and Seventeenth-Century English Poetry* (University of Chicago Press, 1990), pp. 273–306

Raber, Karen, '"Our Wits Joined as in Matrimony": Margaret Cavendish's *Playes* and the Drama of Authority', *ELR*, 28.4 (1998), 464–93

Raber, Karen (ed.), *Ashgate Critical Essays on Women Writers in England, 1550–1700*, volume VI: *Elizabeth Cary* (Aldershot: Ashgate, 2009)

Raffe, Alasdair, *The Culture of Controversy: Religious Arguments in Scotland, 1660–1714* (Woodbridge: Boydell Press, 2012)

Rasmussen, Mark David (ed.), *Renaissance Literature and its Formal Engagements* (Basingstoke: Palgrave, 2003)

Reiman, Donald H., *Romantic Texts and Contexts* (Columbia: University of Missouri Press, 1987)

Reinstra, Debra and Noel Kinnamon, 'Circulating the Sidney-Pembroke Psalter', in George L. Justice and Nathan Tinker (eds.), *Women's Writing and the Circulation of Ideas: Manuscript Publication in England, 1550–1800* (Cambridge University Press, 2002, repr. 2010), pp. 50–72

Rhodes, Neil, *The Power of Eloquence and English Renaissance Literature* (New York: St Martin's Press, 1992)

Rhodes, Neil (ed.), *English Renaissance Prose: History, Language, Politics* (Tempe, AZ: MRTS, 1997)

Rhodes, Neil and Jonathan Sawday (eds.), *The Renaissance Computer: Knowledge Technology in the First Age of Print* (London: Routledge, 2000)

Roberts, Josephine A., 'Editing the Women Writers of Early Modern England', *Shakespeare Studies*, 24 (1996), 63–70

Roberts, Sasha, 'Feminist Criticism and the New Formalism: Early Modern Women and Literary Engagement', in Dympna Callaghan (ed.), *The Impact of Feminism in Renaissance Studies* (Basingstoke: Palgrave, 2006), pp. 67–92

  'Women's Literary Capital in Early Modern England: Formal Composition and Rhetorical Display in Manuscript and Print', *Women's Writing*, 14 (2007), 246–69

Ross, Sarah C. E., '"And Trophes of His Praises Make": Providence and Poetry in Katherine Austen's *Book M, 1664–1668*', in Victoria E. Burke and Jonathan Gibson (eds.), *Early Modern Women's Manuscript Writing: Selected Papers from the Trinity/Trent Colloquium* (Aldershot: Ashgate, 2004), pp. 181–204

'"Like Penelope, Always Employed": Reading, Life-Writing, and the Early Modern Female Self in Katherine Austen's Book M', *Literature Compass*, 9.4 (2012), 306–16

*Women, Poetry, and Politics in Seventeenth-Century Britain* (Oxford University Press, 2015)

Rubenstein, Jill, 'Women's Biography as a Family Affair: Lady Louisa Stuart's Biographical Anecdotes of Lady Mary Wortley Montagu', *Prose Studies*, 9 (1986), 3–21

Rubin, Rehav, 'Sacred Space and Mythic Time in the Early Printed Maps of Jerusalem', in Tamar Mayer and Suleiman Mourad (eds.), *Jerusalem: Idea and Reality* (London and New York: Routledge, 2008), pp. 123–39

Saenger, Michael, *The Commodification of Textual Engagements in the English Renaissance* (Aldershot: Ashgate, 2006)

Samuel, Raphael, 'British Dimensions: "Four Nations History"', *History Workshop Journal*, 40 (1995), iii–xix

Salzman, Paul, 'Narrative Contexts for Francis Bacon's New Atlantis', in Bronwen Price and Simon Wortham (eds.), *Francis Bacon: New Atlantis* (Manchester University Press, 2003), pp. 28–48

*Reading Early Modern Women's Writing* (Oxford University Press, 2006)

'The Strang[e] Constructions of Mary Wroth's *Urania*: Arcadian Romance and the Public Realm', in Neil Rhodes (ed.), *English Renaissance Prose: History, Language, Politics* (Tempe, AZ: MRTS, 1997), pp. 109–24

Sanchez, Melissa, *Erotic Subjects: The Sexuality of Politics in Early Modern English Literature* (Oxford University Press, 2011)

Schneider, Deborah Lucas, 'Anne Hutchinson and Covenant Theology', *Harvard Theological Review*, 103 (2010), 485–500

Scott-Baumann, Elizabeth, *Forms of Engagement: Women, Poetry, and Culture, 1640–1680* (Oxford University Press, 2013)

Seelig, Sharon Cadman, *Autobiography and Gender in Early Modern Literature: Reading Women's Lives, 1600–1800* (Cambridge University Press, 2006)

Sharpe, Kevin and Steven N. Zwicker (eds.), *Writing Lives: Biography and Textuality, Identity and Representation in Early Modern England* (Oxford University Press, 2008)

Shelvin, Eleanor F., '"To Reconcile Book and Title, and Make 'em Kin to One Another": The Evolution of the Title's Contractual Functions', *Book History*, 2 (1999), 42–77

Sherman, William H., *Used Books: Marking Readers in Renaissance England* (University of Pennsylvania Press, 2007)

Skura, Meredith, *Tudor Autobiography: Listening for Inwardness* (University of Chicago Press, 2008)

Smith, Nigel, 'Foreword', in Ben Burton and Elizabeth Scott-Baumann (eds.), *The Work of Form: Poetics and Materiality in Early Modern Culture* (Oxford University Press, 2014), pp. vii–xv

'The Rod and the Canon', *Women's Writing*, 14.2 (2007), 232–45

Stanley, Liz, *The Auto/biographical I: The Theory and Practice of Feminist Auto/biography* (Manchester University Press, 1992)

Starke, Sue, 'Love's True Habit: Cross-Dressing and Pastoral Courtship in Wroth's *Urania* and Sidney's *New Arcadia*', *Sidney Journal*, 24.2 (2006), pp. 15–36

Steen, Sara Jayne, 'Behind the Arras: Editing Renaissance Women's Letters', in W. Speed Hill (ed.), *New Ways of Looking at Old Texts: Papers of the Renaissance English Text Society, 1985–1991* (Binghampton, NY: MRTS and RETS, 1993), pp. 229–39

Straznicky, Marta, 'Closet Drama', in Arthur F. Kinney (ed.), *A Companion to Renaissance Drama* (Oxford: Blackwell, 2002), pp. 416–30

Straznicky, Marta and Richard Rowland, 'A Supplement to the Introduction', in A. C. Dunstan and W. W. Greg (eds.), *The Tragedy of Mariam*, by Elizabeth Cary (London: The Malone Society, 1914), reprinted edition ed. Marta Straznicky and Richard Rowland (1992), pp. xxi–xxv

Summit, Jennifer, '"The Arte of a Ladies Penne": Elizabeth I and the Poetics of Queenship', in Peter C. Herman (ed.), *Reading Monarchs Writing: The Poetry of Henry VIII, Mary Stuart, Elizabeth I and James VI/I* (Tempe, AZ: ACMRS, 2002), pp. 79–108

Tanskanen, Sanna-Kaisa, '"Proper to their Sex": Letter-writing Instruction and Epistolary Model Dialogues in Henry Care's *The Female Secretary*', in Matti Peikola et al. (eds.), *Instructional Writing in English: Studies in Honour of Risto Hiltunen* (Amsterdam and Philadelphia, PA: John Benjamins, 2009), pp. 125–40

Timpane, John (ed.), *Poetry for Dummies* (New York: Hungry Minds, 2001)

Todd, Barbara J., '"I Do No Injury by Not Loving": Katherine Austen, A Young Widow of London', in Valerie Frith (ed.), *Women and History: Voices of Early Modern England* (Concord: Irwin Publishing, 1997), pp. 202–37

'Property and a Woman's Place in Restoration London', *Women's History Review*, 19.2 (2010), 181–200

'The Remarrying Widow: A Stereotype Reconsidered', in Mary Prior (ed.), *Women in English Society, 1500–1800* (London: Methuen, 1985), pp. 54–92

Todd, Richard and Helen Wilcox, 'The Challenges of Editing Donne and Herbert', *SEL*, 52.1 (2012), 187–206

Tomlinson, Sophie, 'My Brain the Stage', in Clare Brant and Diane Purkiss (eds.), *Women, Texts and Histories* (London: Routledge, 1992), pp. 134–63

Travitsky, Betty and Anne Lake Prescott, 'Studying and Editing Early Modern Englishwomen: Then and Now', in Ann Hollinshead Hurley and Chanita Goodblatt (eds.), *Women Editing/Editing Women: Early Modern Women Writers and the New Textualism* (Newcastle upon Tyne: Cambridge Scholars Publishing, 2009), pp. 1–15

Trill, Suzanne, 'A Feminist Critic in the Archives: Reading Anna Walker's *A Sweete Savor for Woman* (*c.* 1606)', *Women's Writing*, 9.2 (2002), 199–214

'Beyond Romance? Re-Reading the "Lives" of Anne, Lady Halkett (1621/2?–1699)', *Literature Compass*, 6.2 (2009), 446–59

'"We thy Sydnean Psalmes Shall Celebrate": Collaborative Authorship, Sidney's Sister and the English Devotional Lyric', in Susan Wiseman (ed.), *Early Modern Women and the Poem* (Manchester University Press, 2013), pp. 97–116

Trolander, Paul and Zeynep Tenger, 'Katherine Philips and Coterie Critical Practices', *Eighteenth-Century Studies*, 37 (2004), 367–87

Turner, James Grantham (ed.), *Sexuality and Gender in Early Modern Europe: Institutions, Texts, Images* (Cambridge University Press, 1993)

Voss, Paul J. and Marta L. Werner, 'Toward a Poetics of the Archive', *Studies in the Literary Imagination*, 32.1 (1999), i–viii

Wabuda, Susan, 'Henry Bull, Miles Coverdale, and the Making of Foxe's *Book of Martyrs*', in Diana Wood (ed.), *Martyrs and Martyrology*, Studies in Church History, 30 (Cambridge: D. S. Brewer, 1993), pp. 245–58

Walker, Kim, '"Divine Chymistry" and Dramatic Character: The Lives of Lady Anne Halkett', in Jo Wallwork and Paul Salzman (eds.), *Women Writing, 1550–1750* (Bundoora, Australia: Meridian, 2001), pp. 133–49

*Women Writers of the English Renaissance* (New York: Twayne Publishers, 1996)

Wall, Wendy, *The Imprint of Gender: Authorship and Publication in the English Renaissance* (Ithaca, NY: Cornell University Press, 1993)

Wallwork, Jo and Paul Salzman (eds.), *Women Writing, 1550–1750* (Bundoora, Australia: Meridian, 2001)

Weintraub, Karl J., 'Autobiography and Historical Consciousness', *Critical Inquiry*, 1.4 (1975), 821–48

Wernimont, Jacqueline, 'Whence Feminism? Assessing Feminist Interventions in Digital Literary Archives', *Digital Humanities Quarterly*, 7.1 (2013), www.digitalhumanities.org/dhq/vol/7/1/000156/000156.html

Wernimont, Jacqueline and Julia Flanders, 'Feminism in the Age of the Digital Archive', *Tulsa Studies in Women's Literature*, 29.2 (2010), 425–35

White, Helen C., *The Tudor Books of Private Devotion* (Madison: University of Wisconsin Press, 1951)

White, Micheline, 'Protestant Women's Writing and Congregational Psalm Singing: From the Song of the Exiled "Handmaid" (1555) to the Countess of Pembroke's Psalmes (1599)', *Sidney Journal*, 23 (2005), 61–82

White, Micheline (ed.), *English Women, Religion, and Textual Production, 1500–1625* (Farnham: Ashgate, 2011)

Williamson, George, *The Senecan Amble: Prose Form from Bacon to Collier* (University of Chicago Press, 1951, repr. 1966)

Winship, Michael, *Seers of God: Puritan Providentialism in the Restoration and Early Enlightenment* (Baltimore: Johns Hopkins University Press, 1996)

Wiseman, Susan, *Conspiracy and Virtue: Women, Writing, and Politics in Seventeenth-Century England* (Oxford University Press, 2006)

'"The Most Considerable of My Troubles": Anne Halkett and the Writing of Civil War Conspiracy', in Jo Wallwork and Paul Salzman (eds.), *Women Writing, 1550–1750* (Bundoora, Australia: Meridian, 2001), pp. 24–45

Wiseman, Susan (ed.), *Early Modern Women and the Poem* (Manchester University Press, 2013)

Wood, Diana (ed.), *Martyrs and Martyrology*, Studies in Church History, 30 (Cambridge: D. S. Brewer, 1993)

Woodbridge, Linda, 'Dark Ladies: Women, Social History, and English Renaissance Literature', in Viviane Comensoli and Paul Stevens (eds.), *Discontinuities: New Essays on Renaissance Literature and Criticism* (University of Toronto Press, 1998), pp. 52–71

Woods, Susanne and Margaret Hannay (eds.), *Teaching Tudor and Stuart Women Writers* (New York: MLA, 2000)

Woolf, Virginia, *A Room of One's Own and Three Guineas*, ed. Hermione Lee (London: Vintage, 1996)

Woudhuysen, Henry, *Sir Philip Sidney and the Circulation of Manuscripts, 1559–1640* (Oxford University Press, 1996, repr. 2003)

Wray, Ramona, 'Anthologizing the Early Modern Female Voice', in Andrew Murphy (ed.), *The Renaissance Text: Theory, Editing, Textuality* (Manchester University Press, 2000), pp. 55–72

Wright, Gillian, *Producing Women's Poetry, 1600–1730: Text and Paratext, Manuscript and Print* (Cambridge University Press, 2013)

'Textuality, Privacy and Politics: Katherine Philips's Poems in Manuscript and Print', in James Daybell and Peter Hinds (eds.), *Material Readings of Early Modern Culture* (Basingstoke: Macmillan, 2010), pp. 163–82

Wynne-Davies, Marion, '"For Worth, Not Weakness, Makes in Use but One": Literary Dialogues in an English Renaissance Family', in Danielle Clarke and Elizabeth Clarke (eds.), *This Double Voice: Gendered Writing in Early Modern England* (Basingstoke: Macmillan, 2000), pp. 164–84

'The Theatre', in Caroline Bicks and Jennifer Summit (eds.), *The History of British Women's Writing, 1500–1610* (Basingstoke: Palgrave Macmillan, 2010), pp. 175–95

*Women Writers and Familial Discourse in the English Renaissance* (Basingstoke: Palgrave Macmillan, 2007)

Zook, Melinda S., *Radical Whigs and Conspiratorial Politics in Late Stuart England* (University Park, PA: Pennsylvania State University Press, 1999)

Zurcher Sandy, Amelia A., 'Ethics and the Political Agent of Early Seventeenth-Century Prose Romance', *ELR*, 35 (2005), 73–101

'Pastoral, Temperance, and the Unitary Self in Wroth's *Urania*', *SEL*, 42.1 (2002), 103–19

## UNPUBLISHED DOCTORAL THESES

Eales, Marion Faith Lanum, 'Anne Halkett: Life and Manuscript', unpublished PhD thesis, University of Cambridge (2005)

Murphy, Sara A., '"A Stranger in a Strange Land": Cultural Alienation in Lady Anne Halkett's Meditations', unpublished MPhil thesis, University of Edinburgh (2005)

Orgis, Rahel, 'Structured Proliferation: Readers and the Narrative Art of Lady Mary Wroth's *Urania*', unpublished PhD thesis, Université de Neuchâtel (2013)

# Index